2/15
2/15

THE PLEASURE'S ALL MINE

The Pleasure's All Mine

A History of Perverse Sex

Julie Peakman

REAKTION BOOKS

For Jad

Published by Reaktion Books Ltd
33 Great Sutton Street
London EC1V 0DX, UK
www.reaktionbooks.co.uk

First published 2013

Copyright © Julie Peakman 2013

Printed and bound in China by Toppan Printing Co. Ltd.

A catalogue record for this book is available from the British Library

ISBN 978 1 78023 185 3

CONTENTS

Introduction 7

ONE

Taking it Straight 13

TWO

From Onanism to Spending 45

THREE

From Ganymedes to Gays 75

FOUR

From Female Friendships to Lipstick Lesbians 109

FIVE

From Transvestites to Transsexuals 145

SIX

A Man's Best Friend: Bestiality 179

SEVEN

The Ties that Bind: Sadomasochism 209

EIGHT

Loving the Dead 239

NINE

Too Close for Comfort: Incest 271

TEN

Child Love or Paedophilia? 295

ELEVEN

The Games People Play 329

TWELVE

On Body Parts: Fellatio, Fetishism,
Infibulations and Fisting 365

Epilogue: A Limit to Tolerance? 397

References 403

Bibliography 439

Acknowledgements 455

Photo Acknowledgements 457

Index 460

Introduction

One person's perversion is another's normality. If we strip sex back to basics, we will find that most sexual acts have been deemed abnormal by someone at one time or another, while conversely, at different times those same sexual behaviours have been deemed acceptable by other groups of people. Previously unacceptable acts (what were thought of as the worst sexual behaviour imaginable) – such 'perversions' as incest, pederasty, sadomasochism and homosexuality – are now acceptable to many people. Nearly every sexual activity that we are aware of today can be traced historically, although there are some decidedly modern types of sexual activity which have arisen as a result of new technology – phone sex, cyber sex and video porn, to name a few.

The Pleasure's All Mine examines the gamut of sexual activity that has been considered strange, abnormal or deviant over the last 2,000 years, and puts it into its cultural context, culminating with the modern-day understanding of sex. It shows how different sexual behaviours were constructed as perverse – by religion and society, in law and medicine – and argues that sexual behaviour is not in itself perverse, but only becomes so when perceived as such by certain groups in society, and that this perception changes over time.

People from different periods – ancient Greece, ancient Rome, medieval, Renaissance and Enlightenment Europe through to Victorian and twentieth-century England – all had different attitudes to sex. People from each time period had different ways of discussing, defining and codifying sex. Heterosexuality, homosexuality, lesbianism, bestiality, necrophilia and paedophilia had different meanings (or sometimes no meaning at all) for people in other times. That said – and although many historians have argued that people from the past had a completely different viewpoint or world view – many of the ideas around sex were also remarkably similar to those current today. It is the continuity, as well as the differences, which make human experiences so compelling in history. After all, sex is the one act we all share, even in its absence (for example, choosing chastity, being identified as a nun or a monk). Sex and sexuality are at the core of all human existence, and have been part of all human institutions and conventions – religious, medical, political, societal and artistic.

My intention here then is to find sexual 'perversion' before it was 'discovered' by sexologists, before its labelling and phraseology, and to trace its development. I use the word 'perversions' here in quotes because not all people agree on which acts are perverted, or have ever been perversions at all. When we look at terminology we step into a quagmire of phrases. Sexual perversions have been termed 'deviant acts', 'abnormal behaviour', 'acts against nature', 'unnatural acts', 'abominable vices' and so on. There have been countless expressions for sexual acts that certain groups find unpalatable. At any one time, a particular phrase or word might be more commonly used to describe these various acts. As far as possible, in order to try to contextualize sexual behaviour within its own time, I use the specific words as they would then have been used – the reason being that certain phrases carry historically specific nuances which need to be explained – differences which may be difficult for us always to grasp. But I will also be using the term 'perversion' as we use it now, and propose that the time has come for a change – perhaps even an end to applying the word to any sexual behaviours (except in its historical context of nineteenth-century sexology, that is), since many of our past sexual perversions have become our present sexual normality.

Sexual perversions began to be categorized in depth by the sexologists only in the second half of the nineteenth century. Among them were Richard von Krafft-Ebing, Havelock Ellis, Albert Moll, Alfred Binet, Iwan Bloch, Magnus Hirschfeld, Sigmund Freud and many others. All contributed to the making of modern sexual perversity and realigned the division between the normal and the abnormal. This involved the labelling of the acts of 'sexual perversion' – and it was sexologists who were responsible for giving us our current-day identification of the acts (although attitudes about them have since shifted). However, many of these sexual behaviours existed long before their nametags. Each century had its own peculiarities, but sexual deviation is rooted in its historical climate.

Within the book, I look backwards to examine each so-called perversion from when it was first visible in history, through to its interpretation by sexologists, to see how it is viewed today. I have focused on Europe and the West, as there is simply too much information to include in a worldwide examination of sexual perversion. In any case, sexual perversions of the East bring in an entirely new dimension worthy of another book. Even with this restriction, there is a limited amount of information that can be included, and inevitably some topics have had to be covered broadly or simply not at all. I have attempted to include a wide enough range of examples to make my case. Through the examination of court records, personal letters, travelogues, medical advice literature, medical and criminal reportage, newspaper accounts, novels, erotica and films, I will reveal exactly how complicated our sexual behaviour is.

Sexual behaviour is difficult enough to trace in any circumstances. Much of it is carried out in private and therefore hidden from view. Where acts were deemed perverse, people were even more keen that their activities should not be known. Their activities were also often also deemed criminal – and people did not want to suffer the consequences, particularly if being caught meant ostracization, flogging or death. Each source comes with its own limitations: court records only show us cases which came to trial; for every one of those, there may have been countless incidents which went unheeded or unexposed. They are also not recorded verbatim but reported through a third party, placing a further barrier between us and the witness or victim. Some deviant acts, such as lesbianism in medieval England, were not considered important enough to bring before the authorities so leave hardly any traces behind, although the ones we have are invaluable. Personal accounts, while offering more depth of feeling and opinion than court records, might not give us the popular viewpoint. Also, people don't tend to record all their sexual activities in journals. When they do, such as in the diaries of Anne Lister and Samuel Pepys, they are golden nuggets for historians. Even then, the parts of diaries that record sexual experiences were often written in code and have taken years of patient cryptography to decipher.

Because the source material is patchy, we know more about some periods than others. On ancient Greece and Rome, remnants have to be pinned together from written or visual forms such as stelae, plays, poems and ceramics. Sometimes we are lucky enough to find whole cities under lava, such as Pompeii and Herculaneum. Some of the texts are coloured with satire or political invective. Unpopular rulers were accused of all sorts of unseemly behaviour – incest with mothers, sisters or daughters, as well as prostitution and buggery – but exactly how true these rumours were is not always obvious. Similarly, much of our knowledge about sex in the early medieval period is also limited and mainly comes from religious works – penitentials, church records, reports of the meetings of religious councils – which gives a skewed viewpoint. These books made delineations between 'good' or 'bad' sex. But this does not necessarily tell us about what people were actually doing in practice. What was *really* happening was simply not written about by a mostly illiterate population. The Renaissance provides us with a little more information from court and inquisition records. The eighteenth and nineteenth centuries began to fill in the gaps with personal diaries, newspaper reports and pamphlets. By the time we get to the twentieth century, we are awash with information about sexual behaviour.

Nowadays, the difference between 'normal' and 'abnormal' behaviour is classified by the *Diagnostic and Statistical Manual of Mental Disorders* (DSM) published by the American Psychiatric Association (APA). This book is considered the medical bible of classification of sexual disorders and other psychological problems. Many so-called 'perversions' were classed as paraphilias and people committing them were classified as mentally ill. The book redefined sexual deviance as 'a symptom of a dysfunction in the individual'. The medical reference bible of Europe is the *International Statistical Classification of Diseases and Related Health Problems* (most commonly known by the abbreviation ICD). The responsibility for the publication of the ICD was first undertaken by the World Health Organization in 1948; it was intended as a world classification of diseases – including their symptoms, complaints, social influences and other external causes. The chapters on mental disorders are essentially the parts which cover 'perversions', and were added to the ICD-6 in 1949. According to the most recent version, ICD-10, sexual deviation is called 'Disorders of Sexual Preference' (DSP) and given the code F65, which covers 'paraphilias'. Paraphilia is a sexual arousal in relation to a certain object, situation or individual which is not regarded as part of normative stimuli. Any one so-called 'perversion' or 'paraphilia' is not necessarily to be found alone, and these behaviours may be found in multiplicities in any one person (or indeed, in groups). The ICD-10 states, 'Sometimes more than one abnormal sexual preference occurs in one person and there is none of first rank. The most common combination is fetishism, transvestism and sadomasochism.' Every situational case of a particular predilection has gradations of other variants: for instance, bestiality might include sadistic behaviour, paedophilia might include incest, homosexuality might include gerontophilia, sadomasochistic behaviour might include a whole host of different fetishisms and so on. Both reference books have had various versions over the years. They have been updated, with some paraphilias (or 'deviations') added and others erased. But there are problems with relying so heavily on these books, and such 'authorities' on sexual perversion are open to question.

In the 1990s, according to the APA, paraphilias were confirmed when they were described as recurrent, intense, sexually arousing fantasies, sexual urges or behaviour generally involving, first, non-human objects; second, the suffering or humiliation of oneself or one's partner; or third, children or other non-consenting persons. They must occur over a period of at least six months, and the 'behavior, sexual urges, or fantasies cause clinically significant distress or impairment in social, occupational, or other important areas of functioning'.[1] There has been much criticism of the DSM in terms of both its diagnostic criteria and its vagueness; for instance, the requirement that there be observable practice of the paraphilia for a period of six months has no obvious basis. In cases where the patient is having fantasies (for example, regarding paedophilia) but is not in distress, nor has acted on his or her urges, he or she would avoid diagnosis.

Furthermore, these reference books are written by a group of people who claim to be experts in their field. In the case of the DSM, it means that the American Psychiatric Association decide which sexual behaviours are 'abnormal' (through working committees and a vote by its membership) and to be considered mental illnesses.

But it is *not* merely a scientific diagnosis – personal, political and non-scientific judgements are part of these definitions. This means that some diagnoses can be subject to challenge. In fact, even within the Association there are continual changes being made to their assessment. There have been many revisions of the DSM since the original was first published in 1952, gradually including more mental disorders, although some have been removed and are no longer considered as such, most notably homosexuality. Here, we see one relatively small section of the community acting as 'experts' deciding what perversion is, while other sections of society think quite differently. After much campaigning by lobbying groups, the decision was made by the APA to remove homosexuality as a psychiatric disorder from the DSM, although it was replaced by 'ego-dystonic homosexuality' for the DSM-3, and removed altogether only in 1987. Pressure groups from the outside had finally managed to obtain a change in the definition of perversion. The DSM-5 was brought out in May 2013. It had been suggested that a new category of 'hypersexual disorder' be inserted but this was ultimately rejected. Each time a new 'disorder' is added or omitted, it brings with it yet another set of questions about what to include or omit, and why. Thus there are obviously shortfalls when relying on particular books or elite groups for definitions of what is sexual perversion and what is not. However, DSM-5 states, there is now 'a subtle but crucial difference that makes it possible for an individual to engage in consenual atypical sexual behaviour without being labelled with a mental disorder'. This new approach destigmatizes unusual sexual practices and behaviours.

My final questions on perversion are connected to intolerance, and why people were – and remain – intolerant of other people's sexual preferences. I also want to look at why individuals committed certain types of acts thought to be abnormal. More importantly, I want to examine the reason for societies' reactions to these acts (from considering them grave transgressions to not finding them serious at all) and the reasons for the changes in these reactions throughout the ages. I want to look at the perceived 'problems' to understand them in their social and cultural contexts; to ascertain why certain behaviour is seen as a problem.

ONE

Taking it Straight

Males [and females] do not represent two discrete populations,
heterosexual and homosexual. The world is not to be divided
into sheep and goats. It is a fundamental of taxonomy that
nature rarely deals with discrete categories . . . The living world
is a continuum in each and every one of its aspects.
Alfred Kinsey et al., *Sexual Behavior in the Human Male* (1948)

Most people believe they have an understanding of what heterosexual sex is – it is usually taken to mean sex between a man and a woman. Generally, this means vaginal penetrative intercourse. The term 'straight' is a substitute for 'heterosexual', and is taken to mean non-gay or non-lesbian. More conservatively, it might be described as the 'missionary' position or 'vanilla' sex – sex with no frills. More worryingly, the concept of heterosexuality has become synonymous with that which society considers 'normal' as contrasted with its opposite, 'abnormal'. In other words, heterosexuality as been held aloft as the ideal, set against all other sexual practices, which are regarded as perverted. However, throughout history, the understanding of what was normal or usual in a society has shifted, and what was regarded as normal in the past was not necessarily heterosexuality.[1]

For the ancient Greeks and Romans, a 'normal' sex life, if it was considered at all, would have included a wide variety of experiences. It was a man's world; men had different women for every aspect of their lives. They kept prostitutes for sex, mistresses for intellectual conversation (as well as sex and affection) and wives in order to legitimize their children and carry on the family line. As Apollodorus is famously supposed to have said, 'We have courtesans for pleasure, concubines to attend to our daily bodily needs, and wives to bear our children.'[2] The world was divided between men and women, and each had their respective role in life. A list of determinate and opposing characteristics ensured these roles: men were strong, women were weak; men were intelligent, women were cunning; men were

13

Face-to-face sex. Detail from a red-figure cup by Triptolemos Painter,
c. 470 BC.

sturdy, reliable and masters of self-control, while women were fickle,
inconstant and unreliable; men stood for culture, women for nature.
All these aspects of a person dominated how other people saw them.
This world view was handed down from classical Greece and Rome
where men were the leaders of wars and women were stalwarts of
the hearth and home. Men might seek sexual pleasures outside the
home while respectable women were expected to marry, be faithful,
keep house and bear children. Women were allowed no freedom
for sexual relationships outside their marriage. Such stereotypes
lasted in the West through the ages, the roles only properly shifting
within the last few decades.

Because of these views, women were economically dependent,
legally disabled and politically disenfranchised, which inevitably had
a knock-on effect on their sexual status; as one nineteenth-century
historian put it, 'women were regarded as a lower order of beings, neg-
lected by nature in comparison with man, both in point of intellect
and heart; incapable of taking part in public life, naturally prone to

evil, and fitted only for propagating the species and gratifying the sensual appetites of the men.'[3] To put it bluntly, women were thought of as 'secondary' and inferior beings – at least in law – and therefore had less say in their own sex lives, be they wives, mothers, daughters, prostitutes or slaves. Women were expected to remain virgins until they married, while men might have sex with as many women as they wanted. Marriage did not entail faithfulness except on behalf of the wife. Virgins were prized, and no self-respecting woman would consent to sex before her wedding day. But not everyone prized virgins. The first-century geographer and historian Strabo revealed his dislike: 'A virgin has no control of her sphincter, lacks erotic technique, has no natural scent to her skin. She has no gently rousing talk and lacks the ingenuous look. Novices are even worse, they are all frigid at the rear, and that is not, at this stage, the place where the hand should wander.'[4]

In ancient Greece a man could have anal intercourse with citizen youths if he wanted without losing his reputation. However, a man must not allow himself to be anally penetrated. Since these

Sex sitting in a lap. Detail from a red-figure jug by Shuvalov Painter,
5th century BC.

relationships were usually between older male mentors and their younger lovers, the youth was expected to bow to the experience of his elders and be the passive partner. This was considered within the range of a normal sexual experience and often part of both a married and a single man's life. Most men were expected to marry and had only one wife in ancient Greece and Rome, but for some richer men in parts of the Mediterranean world, polygamy was possible.[5] Penetrative vaginal sex was not commonly depicted with the partners facing each other lying down – although it *was* undertaken, this position was rare. Sex was more usually depicted as rear-entry (the man entering the woman's vagina from behind) or the woman sitting in the lap of the man. Natural penetration therefore included entrance into a woman's vagina, a man's anus or between a youth's thighs).[6]

Sex from behind depicted in a fresco at Pompeii, 1st century AD.

Sex sitting in a lap; painting from the House of the Centenary at Pompeii, 1st century AD.

Part of the Greek mythology, however, included sexual activities that crossed boundaries and created an uncertain world full of lustful and fickle gods and goddesses. These heavenly beings copulated with cows and bulls; they changed their form and might appear as animals (swans, bulls, cows, snakes) or elements (sea, rain, air, earth, fire). The gods frequently interfered with ordinary mortals and disrupted their lives, impregnated them, conjured up storms and shipwrecked their boats. They created monsters that turned men into stone at a glance. This was a time when a gifted physician might make magical potions to use on an admired young man, and instil passion where there had previously been none. Flaccid penises

François Boucher, *Hercules and Omphale*, 1735.

might become erect, a women's blood be brought to flow and a pregnancy terminated, all undertaken with special herbs and magical spells.

It is therefore impossible to talk about 'straight' or heterosexual sex in the ancient Grecian or Roman world – there was simply a concept of sex for pleasure (with slaves, courtesans or youths) and sex for reproduction (with a wife). Examining its opposite, however, there was a concept from the classical period until the end of the nineteenth century of 'unnatural acts', the closest we can get to 'sexual perversions'. What was meant by these terms was sometimes quite different from our current understanding.

Sex, Health and the Body in the Ancient World

Hippocrates (*c.* 460–*c.* 370 BC), Aristotle (384–322 BC) and Galen (*c.* AD 129–*c.* 210) were the main arbitrators of what was 'good' or 'bad' sex in the ancient world. In essence, good sex meant healthy and reproductive sex. Hippocrates' treatises aimed to achieve a woman's pregnancy, for 'if they become pregnant, they will be healthy'.[7] Marriage, sex and conception were the way to this achievement. If not, a woman may suffer physical problems. In *On the Diseases of Women* he declared, 'I say that a woman who has not had a child suffers more severely and more quickly from menstruation than one who has given birth.'[8] Advice was therefore focused on procreation, a process physicians called 'generation'. In his book *Generation of Animals*, Aristotle declared: 'the male contributes to the principle of the move-ment, the female, the material.'[9] In other words, the woman was responsible for providing the raw materials for creating a foetus, but the man was responsible for sparking them into life. Within this process, man's role was thereby seen as the primary one, the woman's subsidiary. Women were seen as inside-out versions of men and Galen believed that 'women had all those parts belonging to Generation which men have'.[10]

Reproduction was an important aim in a person's sexual life, and ancient sex manuals were full of directions on how to conceive. Aristotle's views, along with other ancient philosophies and sug-gestions, were rehashed and reprinted right into the eighteenth and nineteenth centuries. They advised on all manner of things from what position a couple should use, to what time of month was best time for conception. It was thought that disorders of the body might arise if a regular sex life was not maintained. The four humours of the body – black bile (melancholic), yellow bile (choleric), phlegm (phlegmatic) and blood (sanguine) – were related to the elements – earth, fire, water, and air – which, in turn, related to the different body parts of the spleen, gall bladder, brain, lungs and liver. If they were not kept balanced and regulated, the body would be thrown into disorder. Paul of Aegina (AD 625–690) in his *Seven Books of Medicine* advised partaking in 'sexual enjoyments', which would relieve blood, promote growth and generally make the body more masculine, as it was believed that the male body was the one closest to perfection. He assured the reader that 'the best possible remedy for melancholia is coition'. Luckily for women, many people believed that female orgasm was thought necessary for conception, therefore a woman's pleasure was of importance. The regular evacuation of 'seed', which both men and women were thought to possess (men in their sperm, women in their vaginal juices), was equally essential for a healthy body. For those living in the ancient world, this was normal sexuality.

Even when a person tried to maintain a healthy sex life, events or circumstances could overtake them. Unexpected disorders could flare up, such as love sickness, which physicians described as a sort of melancholia associated with a build-up of black bile. Manic depression would set in where the patient oscillated between fits of excitement and terrible grief. The sight of a loved one would create violent palpations and raise pulses and love songs would cause those smitten to weep uncontrollably. If the disease remained untreated, symptoms would develop and overtake the personality of its owner.

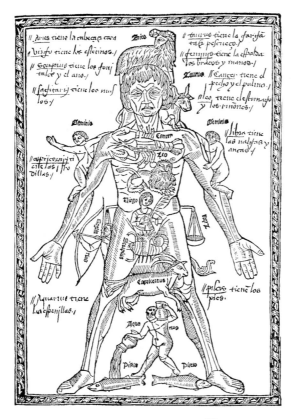

Zodiac man, illustration from Paracelsus, *Astronomia magna* (1537).

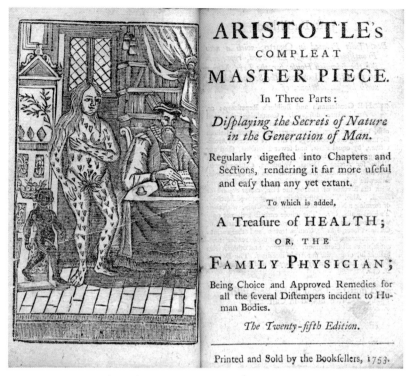

Frontispiece from the 1753 edition of *Aristotle's Masterpiece* (1684).

They would suffer from dramatic rages, sleeplessness, irritability and a pallid complexion. In *Canon of Medicine* (1025), Avicenna advised that if a patient could not get hold of a lover or wife, a physician should obtain a female slave and force her to have sex to cure his lovesickness. According to the Persian physician Al-Razi (865–925), love sickness changed the appearance of the sufferer, who might have weakened eyesight, hollow eyes, a dry tongue and skin pustules. Dog-like bites may appear on the skin of the face, neck and back. An afflicted man might even turn into a werewolf at night and roam through cemeteries. Madness or death could overtake a person. In *Lily of Medicine* (1305), Christian physician Bernard of Gordon, Professor of Medicine in Montpellier, wrote that an authority figure must counsel the victim of lovesickness as it left the soul in danger of eternal torment. If that did not work, the patient should be beaten 'until he begins to rot'.[11] Most physicians did not take such a tough line and advised the rebalancing of the humours through regulation of diet and exercise – nothing more than lots of fresh air, walking, rest and sleep. However, sexual intercourse seems to have been the favoured method of ridding people of lovesickness.

Since 'normal' sex was seen to involved penetrative intercourse with a woman, if a man was impotent, remedies were recommended to ensure his speedy recovery. Herbal medicines such as thyme, pepper, pine, iris root, oil of violets, juices of sage, wormwood and others were all thought to assist, as were baths, listening to music, talking with friends, reciting poetry or going for walks.[12] More serious cases of impotence might need flagellation with a stiff birch, stinging nettles applied to the penis or a red-hot pepper stuffed into the anus. It was hoped that all would restore a man's virility and point him back on course to a healthy sex life.

Sex and the Church

By the time of the first century of the first millennium, the old views were being superseded with the new religion of Christianity. Adam and Eve were seen as the father and mother of humans, and as the quintessential original couple (complete with all their failings). People's perception of the world at large was based around their comprehension of the natural order of the things. The structure of the world around them was ordained by God and any act which upset this order was deemed 'unnatural' – deviant acts were seen to be against God's will and regarded with suspicion. As the word of Christianity spread, so did new ideas on what was considered 'correct' sex and what was forbidden. Monogamy and sexual fidelity became important, while sex outside marriage was deemed fornication.

The Bible became the law of the Christian people, with Leviticus and Deuteronomy acting as the two main books to decree which sexual acts were permitted and which prohibited, though other parts of the Bible reinforced other rules. The Jews knew the first five books of the Bible as the Torah, the 'Teaching'. The Fathers of the new Christian Church added what they deemed appropriate, but the main focus was to establish a code on licit sex. Chastity was the ideal state. In First Corinthians (7:1) Saint Paul the Apostle advised, 'It is good for a man not to touch a woman', implying that if a person could abstain from sex altogether, all the better. Martyrs to chastity were hailed as exemplars for all good Christians: St Juliana of Nicomedia (*d.* 304) was a prime example of a woman who achieved sainthood

Lucas Cranach the Elder, *Adam and Eve*, 1526.

because of her successful attempts to thwart potential suitors. For her efforts, she was hanged by her hair, covered in molten lead and then taken out to be set alight on a bonfire. As the flames began to flicker, they were miraculously doused by an angel from Heaven. If this were not enough, a vat of boiling tar awaited her, but when she was placed inside, it miraculously cooled to the temperature of a bath. She was finally beheaded. Such resilience proved beyond doubt that it was better to remain a virgin than to marry; in the service of this ideal, female saints had their own masochistic hagiography, with holy women suffering all manner of atrocities in the battle to retain their virginity.[13]

Marriage was an acceptable compromise. Sexual connection should only take place with the opposite sex and then only for the purpose of procreation. For single people, St Paul said, 'If they cannot exercise self-control, they should marry. For it is better to marry than to burn.' If a person must go through with it, sexual interaction should be penetrative intercourse between a man and a woman, with the woman on her back and the man on top (now known as the 'missionary position'). Men should no longer keep mistresses or visit prostitutes, but remain faithful to their wives. Men were encouraged to curtail their sexual appetites and bear the burden of bringing up children rather than squandering their appetites on a few moments of pleasure. The Church saw anything outside the realms of marital reproductive sex as sinful and therefore abnormal, though 'aberrations' did take place and were graded according to their closeness or distance from their potential for reproduction. St Augustine (354–430) railed against men's infidelities and believed that reasons for marriage should 'not merely to be on account of the begetting of children, but also on account of the natural association between the two sexes'.[14] He thought friendship and companionship between a man and a woman were also important, his ideas perhaps based on his experience of living with a concubine for thirteen years prior to his conversion. For St Jerome (347–420), women were depicted as insatiable creatures, always on the prowl for sex, always tempting men into evil. He warned, 'It is not the harlot, or the adulteress who is spoke of, but woman's love in general is accused of being insatiable; put it out, it bursts into flames.'[15] Women thereby removed men from the rational world of the mind.

From around the sixth century, penitentials were produced as advice books and provided a lengthy list of rules and regulations regarding sins and suitable penances for unruly flock. Originally, these books were intended as guidance for monastic authorities but soon spread to be used by local priests (although use in the confessional would not become a regular practice until the thirteenth century). The best-known penitential was that of the Bishop of Worms (*d.* 1025) who divided his list into natural and unnatural sins. But it was Thomas Aquinas (1225–1274) who is responsible for many of the ideas on morality and immorality in Christian sex, seen in his summations on what made for 'good' and 'bad' sex. He believed that everything that was 'good' revolved around nature and reason. The 'natural' laws of God were those which involved a hierarchy with man at the apex, women only secondary creatures, and where sex resulted in children. All other sexual activities were either against reason (adultery, rape, seduction, fornication) or worse still, against 'nature' (masturbation, sodomy, bestiality).[16] In Aquinas's categorization, sex between a married man and his wife was not necessarily licit. Oral and anal sex, for example, even when they took place between a married couple, were considered worse than rape as they were not penile–vaginal penetration and would not result in conception. Using a hand, an anus or a mouth – 'using the wrong vessels', as he put it – was worse than using the 'correct' vessel of the vagina, even if the act was consenting and between a married couple. How far these restrictions imposed by the Church actually impeded sexual bliss is impossible to tell, but what we do know is that the Church was responsible for laying down the laws of what was permissible sex and what was not. This was to influence attitudes about sex for centuries to come.

Medieval Marriage

Marriage was the key to a good Christian sex life; all sex outside marriage (adultery or pre-marital sex) was classed as fornication. It was therefore marriage that was the 'normalizing' barometer of sex in the Middle Ages, rather than heterosexuality. This was ratified when in 1215 at the Fourth Lateran Council marriage was declared a sacrament of the Church. However, while the Church warned of the dangers of pre-marital sex, poets contrarily extolled the virtues of romantic love. Romance literature, it seems, met the needs and desires of the reading public and was a repository for Western ideas on masculinity and femininity. It depicted men and women in situations that displayed their 'proper' roles, an ideal based around courtly romance – most conspicuously, it showed men and women how to 'do' heterosexuality. These masculine and feminine roles were associated with dominance and resistance, men displaying their affection and urging their attention on women, women withholding and resisting. However, because of women's perceived insatiability, they were unable to resist for long.[17]

One prime example of romantic love is to be found in the story of Héloïse d'Argenteuil (1101–1164) and Pierre Abélard (1079– 1142). Abélard was a French philosopher who was engaged as Héloïse's teacher. Her uncle, Canon Fulbert, with whom she lived, was foolish enough to allow the daily teaching to be undertaken unchaperoned, leaving them alone together for long periods of time. Unfortunately her education far exceeded what her uncle had planned for her, as the couple fell in love and consummated their relationship. Abélard later wrote about the situation to his friend Philintus: 'As I was with her one day, alone, Charming Héloïse, said I, blushing, if you know yourself, you will not be surprised with what passion you have inspired me with. Uncommon as it is, I can express it but with the common terms; I love you, adorable Héloïse!'[18] After the seduction, Héloïse became pregnant and absconded from her uncle's house to live with Abélard's sister. When Fulbert became aware of the couple's relationship, he was outraged. Abélard wrote: 'Oh, how great was the uncle's grief when he learned the truth, and how bitter was the sorrow of the lovers when we were forced to part!'

After giving birth to her son Astrolabe, at first Héloïse refused to marry Abélard, but he insisted they do so to legitimize the relationship and rescue the honour of her uncle. The marriage was conducted in secret to save Abélard's academic reputation, after which he forced the reluctant Héloïse to retire to the privacy of a nunnery at Argenteuil. Meanwhile, Fulbert plotted his revenge, incensed by what he regarded as Abélard deception, hiring two thugs to undertake the task. After bribing Abélard's servants, the thugs hid in his room awaiting his return; here they castrated him, thus ensuring his total humiliation. Sometime later Abélard lamented, 'they had vengeance on me with a most cruel and most shameful punishment, such as astounded the whole world; for they cut off those parts of my body with which I had done that which was the cause of their sorrow.' In response,

Héloïse wrote to him, 'You know, beloved, as the whole world knows, how much I have lost in you, how at one wretched stroke of fortune that supreme act of flagrant treachery robbed me of my very self in robbing me of you; and how my sorrow for my loss is nothing compared with what I feel for the manner in which I lost you.' The only way for the lovers to redeem themselves was to revert to chastity and join separate encloistered communities. Héloïse eventually succeeded to the position of abbess in a nunnery, but her success

Héloïse and Abélard in the *Roman de la rose*, 14th century.

was gained as a result of her education rather than from any true devotion to her vocation.

For the medieval reader, Abélard's castration would have been recognized not only as the destruction of his future ability to have children but also as the eradication of Héloïse's happiness. By emasculating Abélard, Fulbert had essentially effeminized him, forcing him to live outside the 'normal' life of a 'proper' man. All eunuchs were regarded as lesser men, and Abélard would have been no exception. This tale is not perhaps the love story it initially seems to be – although it is often explained as a tale of passion, it can also be seen as a tale of exploitation of a teacher over his pupil. Abélard abused not only his position of power of his pupil, but also his position of trust in Fulbert's household. After ruining her reputation, Abélard was quite willing to forswear Héloïse and leave her to her fate in the nunnery.

Literature provides an alterative eye-opening account of love, fornication and marriage in the Middle Ages. Giovanni Boccaccio's fourteenth-century allegorical tales, the *Decameron*, are replete with cuckolded men and cunning, lascivious women. One tale tells of a gullible husband who allows a priest to have sex with his wife; and another depicts a hermit monk whose spiritual resolve collapses after spending too long in the close proximity of a beautiful maiden. The book's satire of the Church, and its mockery of its priests and monks in general, conveys Boccaccio's contempt for the ideas emanating from religious quarters. Furthermore, his portrayal of promiscuous and adulterous women reflects the contemporary views of women as highly sexed and continually on the look out for lovers. Similarly, in England at the end of the century, Geoffrey Chaucer's *Canterbury Tales* epitomized the lusty wench in the gap-toothed Wife of Bath, with her 'five churched husbands bringing joy and strife', and conveyed the avarice of the Church in the Monk with his fur-lined sleeves, 'the finest in the land', and his hood fastened with a pin of 'good wrought gold'. The *religieux* are lampooned as hypocrites, the depictions an assumed shared opinion of the reader. This suggests that not everyone agreed with the Church's supposed strict sexual morality. Indeed, the popularity of such literature illustrates just how far people identified with the authors' feelings about religion and sex.

The labouring poor often accepted pre-marital sex despite its condemnation by the Church. A promise of marriage was often enough for a woman to give up her virginity. Matilda Catte of Ingoldmells,

Margaret of Flanders's marriage to Philip 1, Duke of Burgundy. Miniature from the manuscript Chroniques de France ou de St Denis, 14th century.

Lincolnshire, was quite happy to have sex with her suitor Ralph Lamb as they planned to marry in March 1319. But even though the wedding ceremony took place, a type of fine called 'leyrwite' was demanded of Matilda as an unmarried bondwoman (a sort of slave). Leyrwite literally meant a 'fine for lying down' and was aimed mainly at poor women. It began in the mid-thirteenth century and became increasingly common towards the end of the century, all but disappearing after the Black Death of 1348–50. These fines were commonly sixpence. In manorial courts, only *women* seem to have been penalized for succumbing to declarations of love and marriage. For many plebeians though, pre-marital sex was not seen as problematic. Leaders of the Church complained in the 1540s, 'among many, it is counted no sin at all, but rather a pastime, a dalliance, and but a touch of youth: not rebuked, but winked at: not punished, but laughed at.'[19] This shows how great a disjunction there sometimes was between what the Church held aloft as an ideal and what was really happening.

While chastity had been the focus of early Christianity and dominated views about marriage, after the Reformation marriage was considered a preferable way to spend one's life. Martin Luther (1483– 1546), Protestant leader of the Reformation, spearheaded the campaign against celibacy and advocated marriage as the Christian ideal. Luther himself had originally followed a monastic life of fasting, pilgrimage and confession so he was well positioned to understand the temptations such a life had to offer. He had tried his best to avoid sin, but had failed continually, suffering much in the process. He finally decided on a new approach. Since he could not hold to the Church's rules, he decided it was better to invent a new set: he declared that chastity was not important and began to vigorously promote the virtues of marriage, in effect shifting his entire theological viewpoint. He proclaimed, 'priests, monks, and nuns are duty-bound to forsake their vows whenever they find that God's ordinance to produce seed and to multiply is powerful and strong within them.'[20] His declarations were to change people's lives after the Reformation, as a godly life within marriage became possible. Luther practised what he preached and forsook the celibate life, eventually marrying former nun Katherine von Bora, whom he had helped to escape from a convent in Saxony.

Enlightened Sex

By the seventeenth century, attitudes about sex, love and marriage were beginning to change. While marriage was still the recognized harbour within which a 'normal' sexual relationship should take place (in other words, between a man and a woman), men and women were now more prone to marry for love than by arrangement. More specifically, between 1660 and 1800 children were increasingly making their own choice of marriage partners.[21] Marriage, however, was not always the harmonious union it purported to be. James Gillray's prints show us the deterioration from happy married bridal pair to bickering adulterous couple.

If a couple made the wrong choice, it was virtually impossible to divorce until 1857, when the Matrimonial Causes Act was introduced. Until this time, only the very rich could afford the Act of Parliament it took to obtain a divorce and even afterwards divorce was not cheap. Instead, people took to separating and living apart, living with another partner if they so chose. An unofficial 'divorce' or separation was sometimes made, though 'wife sales' were widely practised – a man might put a halter on his wife, take her to market and sell her to the highest bidder, but this did not always mean the wife was unwilling. Sometimes a couple had already agreed to separate and that the 'wife' would be sold to her new lover, using the transaction as a

James Gillray, *Harmony Before Matrimony*, 1805.

method of transferring from one partner to another. However, this was unlikely to have been the case in Carlisle, when in 1832 a farmer sold his wife to a pensioner for 20 shillings and a large Newfoundland dog. He transferred the straw halter from his wife on to his new acquisition, and took off to the nearest tavern.[22] Another way of getting round the divorce law was simply to commit bigamy, though this was taken more seriously than wife sales; at Worcestershire Lent Assizes in 1805, John Enoch Murphy was condemned to be transported for seven years. Yet a Mr Hadley in the same assizes received only twelve months. The discrepancy in sentencing presumably depended on the nature and extent of the deception.

Certain depictions of plebeian sex, such as *Love in a Tub* and *The Happy Huntsman* by Thomas Rowlandson, reflected popular feeling about desire. How people really felt about sex can also be seen in their personal recollections. The diaries of libertine men during the same period – among them Samuel Pepys, James Boswell and William Hickey – indicate that most of them had a preference for vaginal penetrative sex. Pepys might well have enjoyed a grope with his maid, but he still needed to ejaculate inside a woman for complete satisfaction. Though Boswell was frightened to death of catching venereal disease (he thought he had caught it at least fourteen times but he probably never really got rid of it as there was no effective cure), he could not resist finding a prostitute for release. Hickey was more fun, and liked nothing more than to hang out with poor, pock-marked prostitutes, then take them for a pie and a pint. While some unusual activities might well have been practised and accepted, a man like Hickey would only be content if the night ended with 'the last grand one', as he put it. Even in erotic books where fantasies were explored, men's main pleasures seem to have been obtained through straight sexual intercourse resulting in ejaculation.[23] Unfortunately, few women wrote about their own desires and practices so we have less knowledge of how they felt about sex, but those who did write on the subject tended to be employed in the courtesan business. For them, the focus was on love, relationships and security rather than sex, at least in their writings. While men gave gritty details of ejaculations and the actual act of sexual intercourse, women shied away from the lurid and concentrated on their flirtations and courtships.[24] Although it would take more than another century before a distinction was made between 'heterosexual' and all other sorts of sex, there seems to have been a concentration on straight sex as opposed to alternative methods for those who wrote about it.

James Gillray, *Matrimonial Harmonics*, 1805.

The Making of the Heterosexual

In the second half of the nineteenth century, sexologists invented the idea of the 'heterosexual'. Both the terms 'heterosexuality' and 'homosexuality' were first used by Austro-Hungarian poet and translator Karl Maria Kertbeny in 1869, and although in current-day usage we take the term 'heterosexual' to mean 'normal' sex between a man and a woman, originally it meant something quite different. The term was used in the United States by Dr James G. Kierman in 1892 and was linked to 'abnormal manifestations of the sexual appetite'; this included desire for both sexes.[25] A year later, sexologist Richard von Krafft-Ebing viewed sex between a man and a woman as heterosexual sex, with an implicit leaning towards procreative sexual desire. Yet by the time Dorland's *Medical Dictionary* was published in 1901, 'heterosexual' sex was still seen as an 'abnormal or perverted appetite towards the opposite sex'.[26] The meaning of 'heterosexuality', however, would settle down into an understanding as Krafft-Ebing described it – essentially as desire between members of the opposite sex.

Our understanding of the term 'heterosexual' (and indeed our current understanding of sexual perversion) carries its own biases inherited from these men. Since these sexologists were white, Western men, they offered their own particular version of normal and abnormal sex based on the sexual ideology of their time. They lived in a society in which men were seen as the dominant and aggressive force, and in which women were ascribed a passive and subdued sexuality. This is summed up in Krafft-Ebing's remark: 'Woman, if physically and mentally normal, and properly educated, has but little sensual desire.'[27] This was a marked departure from popular understanding in the Enlightenment about women's natural sexual rapaciousness.

Any sexual behaviour apart from straight procreative sex was now described as a perversion. All kinds of behaviours were labelled perverted – oral sex, masturbation, homosexuality, lesbianism, transvestism, bestiality, sadomasochism, incest, paedophilia, necrophilia, fetishism, flagellation, exhibitionism, voyeurism. Nothing was left off their lists. These specialists – psychologists, psychiatrists and psychoanalysts – were largely responsible for the development of our current-day thinking about both heterosexuality and what was seen as its opposite, sexual perversion. These men (for they were all men) consisted of a group of researchers who sought out all the types of sexual acts they could find through interviews with their patients. They sorted and classified people into those with 'normal' sex lives and those with 'abnormal' ones and incorporated medicine, biology, sociology, anthropology and criminology into their research.

During this period, perspectives shifted and certain acts considered deviant or abnormal (in the past distinguished as natural and unnatural) were no longer seen as sinful or criminal, but were regarded as illnesses, a revolutionary idea at the time. These 'conditions' were now medicalized. Furthermore, people committing these perceived deviant acts were no longer seen as sinners but as perverts and labelled as psychopaths, necrophiles, sadists, masochists and so on. As men and women began to approach sexologists for help, or were referred to them from a criminal board, the sexologists took up their cases in an attempt to 'cure' those whose sexual preferences they thought were aberrations. They claimed that sexology was a 'scientific' study of human sexuality; however, it was by no means objective, but rather set in its time and place. To a large extent, these same categories of 'perverse' behaviours continue but now need unpicking if we are to understand sexual behaviour in the past and the present.

Krafft-Ebing was a leading figure in creating our concepts of modern sexuality and its perversities. His influential book *Psychopathia Sexualis*, first published in Germany in 1886, was aimed not at the reading public but at fellow physicians and lawyers taking up cases in court.[28] It underwent several new and expanded editions, seventeen in German between 1886 and 1924, and translations in several languages.[29] As a result, it was ultimately he who was responsible for the creation of modern sexual pathology; as Iwan Bloch stated, 'Krafft-Ebing is, and remains, the true founder of modern sexual pathology.'[30] Krafft-Ebing worked in Vienna as a neuropath and physician at an asylum, then went on to open his own practice where he took on patients with sexual problems. In a series of remarkable case notes on his patients, he developed his theories and expanded understanding of the behaviours considered too perverse for society to accept. Among his patients were those who had committed serious crimes – lust murderers, rapists, paedophiles and necrophiles. Other conditions, such as voyeurism, exhibitionism, urolagnia, coprophilia, uranism (male homosexuality) and fetishism, he considered less criminal but nonetheless problematic.

The cause of perverted behaviour was seen to lie both in a person's mental instability and the increasing pressures of society. Krafft-Ebing promoted the idea that degeneration was caused by the twin evils of bad heredity and modernity. The circulation of a degenerational theory had become common currency from the middle of the nineteenth century, a sort of inversion of Darwin's evolution theory. Instead of an ever-adapting stronger and better population developing, as Darwin had suggested was necessary for evolution, sexologists, scientists and philosophers were promoting the idea that an increasingly depraved society was emerging, with a population declining in physical strength and moral fibre. This was a direct adverse effect of modern 'progress'. The eugenics movement sprang from these anxieties, advocating that only the best-looking, richest and strongest men and women should reproduce and thereby create a new race. The Nazis would take this doctrine to the extreme during the Second World War with the extermination of Jews, gypsies and homosexuals and the promotion of the 'pure' Aryan race.

The emergence of the civilized state or sophistication of society was to be blamed for the rise in 'perverse' forms of sexual behaviour. Krafft-Ebing thought that such behaviour was inherited from an increasing nervous susceptibility of previous generations; in turn, this susceptibility was fostered by the cultured life of modern society, caused excessive sexual excitation and led to abuse. Its culmination was expressed in perverse acts.[31] However, he was careful to point out the difference between perverse *acts* and perverse *instincts*, since the 'most monstrous and most perverse sexual acts have been committed by persons of sound mind'. Cases were divided in two: the individuals who suffered from perversity (a disease of the *moral will*); and those who suffered from perversion (a disease of the *body*). In other words, for an act to be pathological or seen as an illness, 'the perversion of feeling must be shown'. The importance of this division could not be understated, since one apportions culpability and the other does not; this needed to be understood, suggested Krafft-Ebing, 'in order to avoid the danger of covering simple immorality with the cloak of disease'.[32]

Debates arose among the sexologists as to whether such 'depravities' were caused by an increase in the refinement of civilization, or whether sexual aberrations also took place in primitive cultures. Was sexual perversion more prevalent in the cities or in the country?

Were strange sexual behaviours inherited or acquired, biological or psychological? Because of these dilemmas, there was a need to understand these types of behaviour in terms of science, psychology, medicine, instinct, nervous state and civilization. Karl Heinrich Ulrichs had opened up the debate on perversion (or specifically on 'uranism' – the term he used for same-sex desire) in 1864 when he declared homosexuality to be congenital. Havelock Ellis added to the debate on the subject of homosexuality in his book *Sexual Inversion in Men* (the original German version was published in 1896, translated into English the following year), which he co-authored with John Addington Symonds. He discovered a distinct lack of repugnance to 'inversion' or homosexuality 'amongst the lower classes', who found sexual anomalies quite normal. Although the authors were never prosecuted, in 1897 the bookseller Thomas Bedborough was brought to trial for selling obscene material.[33] Others, such as young philosopher Otto Weininger in his book *Sex and Character* (1903), believed that all people had a mixture of both man and woman as part of their characteristics: the male part was the active aspect, the female the passive. Whereas Alfred Binet explained all perversions to be a result of associations of ideas formed in one's youth.

Along with other like-minded physicians and lawyers, these men contributed to the sexology debate and forged new theories about sexuality, many providing individual case studies in order to explain anomalies in sexual behaviour. Yet quite a few sexologists had oddities themselves, which may explain the lure of the new 'science' for them. Freud, the founder of psychoanalysis, was a cocaine user, and Otto Weininger shot himself at the age of only 23. Ellis was married twice, and failed to consummate either marriage until he was 59, then with his second wife. Ellis had a lifelong interest in urolagnia and enjoyed watching women urinate. Olive Shriener, who had a non-consummated but loving relationship with Ellis, wrote to Edward Carpenter saying of Ellis: 'He has a strange reserved spirit. The tragedy of his life is that the outer side of him gives no expression of the wonderful, beautiful soul in him which now and then flashes out on you when you come near him.'[34]

The full blossoming of Ellis's work was collected in *Studies in the Psychology of Sex* (1897), a major contribution to the sexologists' exploration of sexual behaviour, but it is worth looking in some detail at the unusual and sometimes troubled sexual aspects of

Ellis's personal life. Ellis wrote to Olive Schreiner after reading her book *The Story of an African Farm* (1883), and although they met up soon afterwards in 1884 and were taken with each other, he was impotent and unwilling to marry. Three years later he met Edith Lees, a stocky bisexual with thick lips and a man's haircut. They appeared an unlikely couple but were drawn to each other for their intellectual similarities. Unusual for the time, Lees and Ellis agreed to maintain separate households and have no children. Lees was to remain independent financially, making her living through lecturing and writing. However, Lees took up with an old schoolfriend and had a lesbian affair, hardly surprising since Ellis was unable to provide what she needed physically in her relationship with him. In his autobiography, Ellis admitted, 'I had not been the faintest degree jealous of Claire [as he called Edith's lover] but, rightly or wrongly, as I have said, I had felt that Edith's love for Claire involved a diminished tenderness for me.'[35] Meanwhile, Ellis accepted the affections of another young woman. When Lees found out, she was hurt but gradually came to be understanding. She wrote to Ellis, 'I've arrived at this conclusion after *intense* suffering about Amy, but I shall never suffer again. Do what you will – be what you will and don't feel you must ever *make* me understand.'[36] This attitude to free love was part of a rebellion by a small group of middle-class intellectuals but was usually confined to sex before marriage between a man and a woman. Havelock and Edith had taken the concept much further in their open marriage. Ellis later took up with Margaret Sanger, a robust campaigner in favour of contraception, who had fled to England to escape arrest in the U.S. She remained a devoted friend to Ellis after she returned to America to continue her work, setting up clinics and writing about birth control. The claim for free love in heterosexual relationships had now shifted to take in demands for birth control. Ellis eventually found a sexually fulfilling relationship with his second wife, Françoise Laffite-Cyon, after Lees died, a relationship in which he was truly happy.

The push for 'free love' had begun at the end of the nineteenth century with campaigners sending out illegal pamphlets informing people about birth control and abortion. Prosecution was possible in America under the Anti-Obscenity Act of 1873 (later known as the Comstock Law) under which it became a crime to mail 'obscene, lewd, lascivious, indecent, filthy or vile article, matters, thing, device, or substance'; including 'every article or thing designed, adapted, or intended

Cartoon from John B. Ellis, *Free Love and Its Votaries* (c. 1870).

for producing abortion, for any indecent or immoral use'. Nonetheless, the idea that sex should have to involve procreation and production of children was weakening. Rather, sex between consenting adults was coming to be seen as a form of healthy fun. In Britain, Annie Besant and Charles Bradlaugh became household names in 1877 after publishing *The Fruits of Philosophy* (1876), a book on birth control written by the American campaigner Charles Knowlton. Although the couple were arrested and Annie lost the custody of her children because of their campaigning activities, the liberal press supported them and their conviction was overturned on a technicality. During the trial, Besant founded the Malthusian League, a society that promoted contraception and abortion. In 1922 the League published Sanger and Haire's *Hygienic Methods of Family Limitations* advocating birth control. Other self-help manuals came out, such as Marie Stopes's *Married Love* (1918) and Dr Robert Latou Dickenson and Miss Lura Ella Beam's *One Thousand Marriages* (1931). However, most of the campaigners aimed to provide education for married couples rather than single people. Heterosexual sex, it seems, was still supposed to take place within the confines of marriage. However, in America one of the biggest sex surveys ever was about to smash many previous preconceived ideas about human sexual behaviour.

The Sex Surveys

The American biologist Alfred C. Kinsey was the man responsible for making one of the biggest leaps in the understanding of the relationships of men and women in one of the most intricate sexual surveys ever undertaken. Supported by the National Research Council's Committee for Research on Problems of Sex, his results were published in two books, *Sexual Behavior in the Human Male* (1948) and *Sexual Behavior in the Human Female* (1953). In all, his team interviewed around 20,000 men and women between 1938 and 1956,

Caricature of Victoria Woodhull by Thomas Nast, 1872.

aiming to uncover their sexual practices and orientation.[37] Examining the results, Kinsey realized that there was much more overlap in orientation than he had imagined, and less distinction between the sexes than he had previously thought. Men and women's sexual behaviours were not shaped merely by biological influences but formed by cultural and social forces. He also found that people could not be fitted into the three existing categories of heterosexual, bisexual and homosexual. Instead, Kinsey invented the Kinsey Scale, which provided a sliding scale of sexual orientation from completely heterosexual to definitely homosexual. Most people fitted somewhere in between, and some changed their sexual orientation throughout their lives. Although Kinsey received his fair share of critics, his study undoubtedly created one of the grandest shake-ups in beliefs about sexual behaviour that had ever been seen.

Meanwhile, in 1949 Britain revealed the results of a much smaller sex survey of its own when Mass Observation (MO) started collecting records. The Mass Observation Unit was a social organization established in 1937 by Tom Harrisson, Charles Madge and Humphrey Jennings, an anthropologist, poet and film-maker respectively. Their aim was to collect research from everyday life from a group of around 500 volunteers who had been promised anonymity. This was undertaken via open-ended questionnaires and diaries kept to record daily events and opinions. The unit had begun collecting information ten years earlier from 1939, but now they wanted information on sex for their own 'Little Kinsey' report.[38] The method of the British Sex Survey was to take a cross section of 400 people in the British Isles from the 2,000 people written to. The target group was mainly middle-class citizens, with clergymen, schoolmasters and doctors among them. All were given a questionnaire about their attitudes towards sex. The MO provided them with diaries and invited them to keep track of events in their lives and send in day-to-day accounts. Although the survey was considerably less ambitious than Kinsey's and involved fewer people, the synopsis of the MO survey criticized the fact that Kinsey accepted or even condoned what people did; and also criticized the objective stance in Kinsey's Report towards various forms of sexual intercourse. However, the intention of MO was to collect 'not merely what the mass or the people *do* about sex but also what they *say* about it'.[39] Some of the results of the Survey's findings were published in the *Sunday Pictorial* and later in a separate book.

When asked where they had gleaned their sexual knowledge, 25 out of every 100 respondents said that they had picked up information on street corners, at work, 'or even in the marriage bed'. Most people interviewed (76 per cent) were in favour of sex education and over half (54 per cent) thought it should start when a young person was between eleven and fourteen years old. Women thought that sex education should start before puberty because of fears of illegitimate pregnancy and the stigma still attached to it. Lack of knowledge about birth control clearly deterred women from extra-marital affairs: one said her boyfriend told her he used a 'sort of rubber glove' to prevent pregnancy but she did not believe him and afterwards would have nothing to do with him. One in six mentioned fear of pregnancy as their reason for avoiding pre-marital or extra-marital sex. One woman told a teacher who was working in the hospital, 'My husband is awkward like, He do put me in the [family] way every year and he do kick me in the stomach to get rid of it.'[40]

Birth control was becoming an essential part of a heterosexual couple's sex life. Yet answers about birth control showed that there was some confusion about its meaning. Fifteen per cent of people had some implied knowledge, 8 per cent did not know what it was, and 4 per cent got it wrong (which must have left for some future unwanted consequences). Some even thought birth control to be either an analgesic or a new form of government control. The richer a person was, the more in favour they were of birth control. Even Roman Catholics were in favour of some form of birth control, with over one-third expressing approval for it, against the official teachings of their religion. Methods of contraception for those who did use it included the sheath (79 per cent); chemicals (56 per cent); the cap (40 per cent); withdrawal (36 per cent); the 'safe period' (17 per cent) and douching (13 per cent). There was general feeling in favour of marriage and many respondents were against prostitution. Unsurprisingly, men were less so: a quarter of men admitted to having visited a prostitute, 8 per cent admitted to having homosexual relationships and a further 12 per cent confessed to homosexual leanings. One-fifth of women admitted to extra-marital affairs. Heterosexual sex was still incorporating adultery and prostitution but prevention of reproduction was now a main issue.

Although statistics may provide us with an idea of sexual practice, many shared the feelings of one particular young man. His story provides us with an emotional example of how people felt about heterosexual sex during Second World War. A journalist in the forces with the Royal Engineers in Chelmsford, Essex, he kept a diary, writing about the difficulties of his courtship. He lived in lodgings and cycled to see his girl in Tunbridge Wells.

> Now my worry is this: I've known the girl and her family all my life. We've been in love for 2 or 3 years. But although we've indulged in pretty extensive 'necking' or 'petting' (there seems to be no other words!) we haven't yet had intercourse (another horrible word!). What I am wondering is whether if, in view of the situation, I shall broach the subject and suggest that we shall this weekend, and to that end, whether I shall buy contraceptives.[41]

After having given it some thought, he obviously went through with making preparations, 'In Gravesend, I brought my first contraceptive; a sheath for 1s. Embarrassment lessened by fact that I was served by a young male assistant.'[42]

Awkwardness about sex was still prevalent among many couples, especially young courting ones. This was mainly due to ignorance and lack of sex education. There were huge gaps in the sexual knowledge of the general population, which meant they experienced more sexual problems. The shame about talking about sex only hindered the process. Many people did not know what was 'normal' sexual behaviour, let alone what might be considered abnormal. For all the elevation of heterosexuality and its 'normative' status, there seems to be a lot of issues causing its disruption. This was to be rectified when throughout the 1960 and '70s, Masters and Johnson set the new framework for reference about heterosexual behaviour, telling us all how it should be done. In *Human Sexual Response* and *Human Sexual Inadequacy*, published in 1966 and 1970, they outlined heterosexual behaviour, writing about such topics as love, intimacy and 'patterns of sexual responses'.

However, there can be little doubt that one of the biggest changes to sex in human history was the introduction of the pill – its impact was so great that it would radically change the way heterosexual people approached sex. Although contraception had been part of family planning from ancient times, it had remained unreliable right until the pill's introduction in the 1960s – and it was only with this release from the perpetual burden of childbirth that women could start to enjoy an unlicensed freedom in their sex lives. Over the last few decades, with the lifting of the worry of unwanted pregnancy, people have been more inclined to experiment. More sexual behaviours previously construed as perversion have now become mainstream and inserted themselves into the overall understanding of heterosexual behaviour.

A woman masturbates a man (background), from Nicolas Chorier, *L'Académie des dames* (1680).

TWO

From Onanism to Spending

How it crushes nature, stints virility, nips manhood in its bud, and initiates
youth in wickedness.

Anon, *Eronania* (1724)

Judging from the slang terms for masturbation that are currently
circulating, it is viewed today as a fairly innocuous activity. Phrases
such as 'jerking the gherkin', 'polishing your bayonet', 'spanking the
monkey' and 'jackin' the beanstalk' suggest that the activity should
not be taken too seriously. Female masturbation has since acquired
countless jocular names of its own – 'beating the bush', 'petting the
pussy', 'jilling off' and so on. Nowadays, women are quite happy to
shop in Ann Summers and purchase a wide variety of sex toys offered
in all colours and sizes with names such as 'The Vibrating Hand-
Maiden', 'The Pulsating Rabbit' and 'The Pink Love Bullet' with which
to give themselves pleasure. Indeed, masturbation is celebrated as
both a solitary and mutually enjoyable practice, although this was
not always the case. In the past such practices were considered a
perversion against nature, a heinous sin and a habit that had the
potential to bring about serious physical and mental debilities.
While masturbation was thought to be essentially a male preserve,
women no doubt undertook the activity, but wrote about it less. It
was simply more hidden, and fewer people knew about women's
secret pleasures. However, the Sanofix vibrating machine would
surely have done for the Edwardian lady what the Pulsating Rabbit
does today.[1]

The *Oxford English Dictionary* refers to masturbation as 'the
stimulation, usually by the hand, of one's genitals for sexual pleasure; the action or practice of masturbating oneself (or less commonly)
another person'. The earliest English usage of the term 'masturbation' is around 1503, taken from Middle French, although there have
been a variety of names given to the activity throughout history. The
medieval authorities spoke of onanism. By the eighteenth century,

Sanofix hand vibrator, 1913.

the term 'to frig' was used; the verb was taken from the French verb *frotter* meaning 'to rub', but became synonymous with masturbation.[2] The Victorians spoke of 'spending'; nowadays 'wanking' is more commonly used. Although seemingly a non-disruptive act, it is surprising what furore masturbation has caused. Many people in various parts of the world today think it is either harmful or irreligious. Yet we know that the practice was familiar in the ancient world, as it was depicted in paintings and drawings. Through the centuries it has gone from being seen as a health cure to a sin, a medical disorder, a disease of nations, and back to a suggested healthy alternative to sexual intercourse. How this happened depended on the most prominent vocal authority at the time, whether political, religious, medical or legal.

Ancient Spilling of Seed

In ancient Greece, masturbatory images were commonly painted on vases and columns, usually of satyrs such as Pan. During the fourth century BC, the philosopher Diogenes the Cynic blamed the god Hermes for introducing masturbation to the world when he taught his son Pan to masturbate. Diogenes was known for his more provocative behaviour; when he went to Athens, his purpose was to upbraid the false morals of the citizens in what he saw essentially as a corrupt society. As a protest, to demonstrate his displeasure, he ate in the marketplace (which was at that time regarded as improper), after which he proceeded to masturbate in full view of passers-by. He declared, 'If only one could satisfy one's hunger by rubbing one's stomach.'[3] Allegedly, he urinated in public, defecated in the theatre and rejected any normal values of decency. The stories of how he died varied – some say he died holding his breath, others that the cause was an infected dog bite or eating raw octopus.

Although when undertaken in public, masturbation may well have caused consternation, in private it was another matter. Physicians suggested it as a method to relieve tension or sexual frustration, the idea emanating from the medical supposition that the body needed to rid itself of excess seminal fluid. Around 200 BC, Demetrius of Apamea in his book *On the Signs of Diseases* told of an old man who suffered from priapism. He tried, without any success, to obtain relief by masturbation. His erection was so powerful that his organ 'might have been made of horn'.[4] Hippocrates (fifth century BC) and Galen (second century AD) both thought it necessary for men and women to orgasm regularly to release their 'seed' (both men and women were thought to have seed). The most natural way to undertake this was through sexual intercourse with a member of the opposite sex. However, when this was not possible, physicians advocated masturbation as beneficial to health. This was particularly

A Rabbit-type vibrator.

applicable to single women and widows since, without a man, there would be no orgasm and seed would build up inside them – hence unmarried women were thought susceptible to blockages. In order to remedy the situation, in his treatise *Diseases of Women*, Hippocrates suggests rubbing fragrant ointments on the vulva or inserting dildo-like objects to simulate the penis.[5] Galen compared masturbation to the evacuation of a person's bowels and the need to urinate – releasing sperm or female 'seed' was necessary to prevent its unhealthy build-up. By way of an example, Galen related the story of a woman who had been a widow for a long time and suffered from the retention of her female seed. When she explained the problem, the local midwife informed her that her womb had been 'drawn up', and that she needed to apply her usual remedy. As certain substances were rubbed in, the woman experienced 'pain and at the same time the pleasure' associated with sexual intercourse, and passed a large amount of thick 'seed'.[6] However, although masturbation might be enough to alleviate a woman's tension or blockages, ideally she needed to 'lie with a man' as she would also benefit from the restorative qualities of his sperm.

The Sin of Onan

By the medieval period, a new repression of masturbation had emerged. This was not a result of public debate but originated in discussions among the early Church authorities. The Church Fathers took a decidedly dim view of masturbation, and thought the subject was better left unmentioned, mainly for fear that people might try it out for themselves. When the subject of masturbation *was* discussed, there was much debate as to why and when it was a sin. St Augustine (354–430) of Hippo in North Africa thought that onanism was sinful because it was unnatural – he suggested that it was better for a man to visit a prostitute than to masturbate. How far his pronouncement filtered down through the ranks to ordinary men and women is debatable, but nonetheless it became the ruling of the Christian Church on the subject.

Masturbation was regarded as 'unnatural' and against God's natural ordering of the world (a perversion in the eyes of the Church) – reason enough to leave it alone. But another reason behind the thinking of the Church authorities was that masturbation rendered the sperm intended for procreation useless. The Church's stance on sex was that it was meant for reproduction within marriage – in essence, sperm was intended for making babies. The Church Fathers frequently pointed to the story of Onan as an example of the sin; according to Genesis 38:4–11, he 'spilled his seed on the ground' in order to avoid impregnating his brother's wife. In fact this is a mis-interpretation: the sin of Onan was not masturbation but *coitus interruptus*. Nonetheless, Onan was referred to in cases of mastur-bation for centuries to come, his name being used to describe the activity in 'onanism'.

Punishments for the sin of onanism varied according to a per-son's age. One penitential of the year 520 suggested a year's penance for adult men who had masturbated, but only 40 days for a twelve-year-old boy – it was felt that an adult should have better control over himself than a mere youth. The Irish penitential of St Columban (559–615) went further and differentiated between masturbators who were married and those who were not. A penance of a year was given for the former but only six months for the latter, an indication of the Church's feelings about marriage. A married man's job was to impregnate his wife and he should be using his appendage for the proper purpose of procreation. Because of this neglect of duty, mas-turbation was a more serious sin for a married man than for a single one. For an unmarried man with no convenient woman around, it was perhaps more understandable.

Involuntary emissions were another matter altogether. When a man ejaculated in his sleep, or accidentally while awake, could these be considered sins? And if so, how serious were they? Members of religious orders were supposed to refrain from onanism, so the ques-tion of involuntary emissions naturally surfaced within the upper ranks of the Church. Generally, it seems to have been agreed that if masturbation was undertaken while awake, it was a sin. This view was ratified when Pope Leo IX officially condemned masturbation as a sin in 1054. Other leaders of the Church, such as Peter Damian (*c.* 1007–1072), thought masturbation so bad that it was akin to sod-omy and believed that similarly harsh penances should apply to it (usually capital punishment). However, some clerics argued that nocturnal emissions could *not* be the fault of a sleeping person, who could not be held responsible for his ejaculations. Thomas Aquinas (1225–1274), for one, could not bring himself to condemn nocturnal emissions in his discussion on the subject. In his *Summa Theologiae*, although he deemed self-pollution a sin against nature in the same category of importance as sodomy, he considered the *cause* of the emission to be relevant. Indeed, he believed that the Devil might be involved in nocturnal emissions, in which case it could not entirely be a man's own fault.[7] However, if a man had indulged in lascivious thoughts *before* he went to sleep, it was generally surmised that this was a sin in itself. Induced orgasms were therefore considered more serious than accidental ejaculation.[8] Aquinas further believed that fornication was a lesser sin than masturbation, as with the former there was at least a chance of procreation. He believed that masturbation was a form of murder, since it destroyed the semen meant for making a potential human being.[9]

Debates over the issue of sin and masturbation continued to rage right through into the Renaissance. At the end of the sixteenth century, the Franciscan Benedicti declared, 'Whoever engages in voluntary pollution outside of marriage, which is termed *mollities* by the theologians, sins against the natural order.'[10] It does not mention whether it was considered acceptable *inside* marriage, suggesting that it was believed to be a bachelor's problem. The type of sin, whether mortal or venial, was important (mortal sin condemns a person to Hell after death; a venial sin is a lesser sin and forgivable). While purposeful masturbation was deemed to be a mortal sin, nocturnal ejaculation was more acceptable. These night-time emissions were not a mortal sin if, for example, a man had eaten lust-inducing meats, since his ejaculation was considered a result of 'pleasures of the palate'. Since spicy foods might induce involuntary ejaculation in a man's sleep, it was therefore deemed only a venial sin. St Antonius disagreed and believed nocturnal emission through gluttony *was* a mortal sin, presumably because it added the deadly sin of greed and was self-inflicted. Such arguments over details pervaded discussions for years to come.

As we have seen in these arguments, frequently sodomy and masturbation were considered to be the same type of sin, therefore warranting the same sort of punishments. In 1532, Holy Roman Emperor Charles v ratified the Carolina laws, which included the establishment of the death penalty for 'fornication that goes against nature', taken by judicial authorities to include masturbation. Even the Lutheran jurist Benedict Carpoz agreed that capital punishment was a suitable response for people performing such activities. But not everyone agreed. The Scottish legal advocate Sir George Mackenzie, although he accepted the authority of Carpoz in principle, refused to abide with his sentencing policy. He declared that sodomy and bestiality 'are crimes extraordinary and rarely committed in this Kingdom'. His judgement was based on the surmise that no one in Scotland would commit such abominable crimes. Notably, Mackenzie wrote in English when he was discussing the crime of sodomy and bestiality, but resorted to Latin when commenting on masturbation, an indication of just how bad he thought masturbation was. (Knowledgeable professionals such as physicians and legal men frequently used Latin to write about sexual terms thought too obscene to mention in public.) Despite these promulgations, the death penalty was never actually used for masturbation in Europe. Flemish and French lawyers usually accepted banishment as an alternative penalty. The Protestant reproof was to hamstring the perpetrators – crippling them by slicing through their hamstrings.[11]

A 'Fatal' Practice

Although the extent of the practice of masturbation is difficult to estimate, some records survive that give us an idea of how people thought about it. While few women left behind any mention of it, or indeed of sex at all, some seventeenth- and eighteenth-century gentlemen left behind diaries and journals which mention masturbation. A handful of them thought it a fairly normal preoccupation of youth, but others believed it to be a perverted path to follow. William Drummond, the son of a Scottish poet, recorded details of his handiwork between 1657 and 1659.[12] After his mother died, he inherited a huge estate at Hawthorndon in 1649, a small hamlet a few miles from Edinburgh. By the time he wrote his diary, he was leading an isolated life alone in the castle but for a handful of servants. His diary entry for 20 February 1657 admitted to engaging in debauched behaviour and cavorting with fellow delinquents – 'dranke till twelfe a cloke in the night at which time we ranted thorrowe all the little towens with a great bagge pipe, to the admiration [astonishment] of all the countrie people'. Not only did he indulge in competitive drinking and libertine ways, but he lazed about in bed all day and failed to attend church on Sundays. With time on his hands, his thoughts turned to sex. Writing in semi-code, he recorded his masturbatory habits, referring to them as 'fatal' – 'all night fattall' and 'fattall most grivously'. His favourite book was Ovid's *Ars Amandi* (The Art of Love), which at one reading apparently aroused him so much that he masturbated twice. His activities apparently did him no harm (despite what the medics of the day would have said) and he eventually married. He must have had some concerns about his habit or he would not have called it 'fatal', but he does not appear to have felt considerable guilt.[13]

While some men were happy to indulge themselves without feeling guilty, others were not. Unlike Drummond, the Puritan George Trosse felt ashamed of his inclinations. He lamented his past secret activities, recording how he had practised 'a sin too many young men are guilty of and look upon as harmless'.[14] Despite his earlier life of idleness and debauchery, Trosse obtained a knighthood in the 1680s, so masturbation obviously did him no harm. Most people, Samuel Pepys among them, preferred to keep their habits a secret, often assisted by pornographic images and texts as found in *L'Ecole des filles* (Michel Millot and Jean L'Ange, attrib., known as *The School of Venus*, 1655) and *L'Académie des dames* (Nicolas Chorier, 1660). Pepys recorded his masturbatory activities after becoming excited over *L'Ecole des filles*. His diary entry for 9 February 1655 reads: 'it did hazer my prick stand all the while, and una vez to decharger'. He promptly burned the arousing book before his wife could discover it. Just over a century later, James Boswell was more concerned about the adverse physical effects of masturbation when he mentioned it in his diary, also referring to it as a 'fatal practice'. He promised himself that he would stop masturbating and from then on would pleasure himself only with women.

The warnings about masturbation went unheeded by some libertine men, who went so far as to form secret societies in order to celebrate their masturbatory activities. At their initiation ceremonies the Beggar's Benison regularly used masturbation as a bonding mechanism between 'brothers'. The society had been formed by a group of prominent Scottish professionals in 1732 to promote shared business interests, and it continued to operate until 1836. During the initiation ceremony of a new member, a 'test platter' was brought forward, on to which all the members had to masturbate as a sign of their virility. Women were also part of their pleasure; the society's minutes reveal that they hired local girls to strip naked and pose for inspection by members of the group. 'Sylphs' or prostitutes were also taken by coach up to Scotland from London to entertain the men. Meanwhile, in France, the libertine Jean-Jacques Rousseau caused disruption with the publication of his new novel *Emile* (1762), in which he wrote about the 'most deadly habit to which a young man can be subject'. The book caused such an affront that it was publicly burned. Some years later he related in his *Confessions* (1782) that he had masturbated while fantasizing about his nanny. He confessed, 'I learned this dangerous supplement which deceives nature and leads young men of my disposition to many excesses at the expense of their health, their vigour and sometimes their lives.' He claimed he had picked up the habit from a Moorish bandit in Turin.[15]

Authors of sexual advice manuals, such as Nicolas Venette, believed masturbation caused asthma, liver problems, fever, gout and sterility, but was only a habit that affected men. In his *Tableau de l'amour conjugal* (1686), which made its first appearance in English in 1703 as *The Mysteries of Conjugal Love Reveal'd*, he suggested that women could not masturbate, revealing,

> Woman does not have the ability to pollute herself, as does man, nor to expel the superfluous seed. She sometimes retains it lengthily in her testicles or in the horns of her uterus, where it becomes tainted, and turns yellow and murky, or foul smelling, instead of clear and white as it was formerly.[16]

The book was thought decent enough to act as information for young married couples, although such sex manuals were also liable to inflame the passions of young boys. One bunch of apprentices were caught masturbating over another sexual manual, *Aristotle's Master-Piece*, a book which was one of the most popular of its kind running throughout the seventeenth and eighteenth centuries.[17] As the new science of medicine took hold, new theories began to emerge connecting masturbation to physical disability. This accounts for the increasing anxieties surrounding it that began to take hold during the eighteenth century.

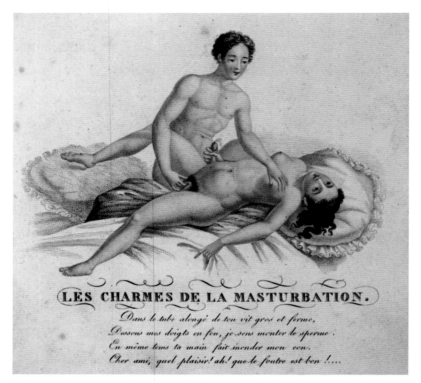

'Les Charmes de la masturbation', from *Invocation à l'amour: Chant philosophique* (c. 1825).

Medicine, Maladies and Masturbation

Although Galen's theories were still popular right up to the eighteenth century, physicians began to question his ideas about masturbation as contributing to health. Enlightenment medics entered the debate with a survey of the dangers of masturbation with physicians, surgeons and anatomists laying out their own campaign against 'self-pollution'. Although religious factions continued their vilification of onanism as sinful, masturbation was now seen not only to be harmful to a person's soul but to threaten to destroy him or her physically. As early as 1587 the French doctor Jean Liébault advised that masturbation and its ensuing seminal loss could cause paralysis and convulsions. In his *Anatomy of Melancholy* (1621) the physician Robert Burton blamed celibacy for causing 'masturbation, satyriasis, priapism, melancholy madness, fornication, adultery, buggery, sodomy, theft, murder, and all manner of mischiefs'.[18] He avowed,

Homunculi in human semen,
engraving, 1699.

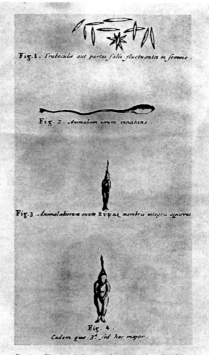

Fig. 12. Figures of the crystals of spermine phosphate
and of homunculi in the male human semen, after Dalen-
patius

'Idleness leads to lust, lust to disease, and disease to untimely death.'
Meanwhile, Puritans such as Richard Capel roundly condemned
masturbation; in his treatise of 1640, he listed an abundance of
sins, of which onanism was by far the worst, more so than adultery
or fornication.[19] The rise of Puritanism in England ran parallel to
the emergence of new medical theories about masturbation and
the making of the new bourgeoisie in France; all three fed into the
creation of a new moral strictness.

These three factions – medics, Puritans and the bourgeoisie –
brought about radical new ideas about masturbation. Up until the
discovery of the microscope by Anton van Leeuwenhoek (1632–
1723), the aversion to masturbation and wasting seed was partly
due to ignorance of the process of procreation. It was believed that
tiny, fully formed humans were carried in the sperm. These cells in
the form of humans were called homunculi. Any waste of the pre-
cious fluid was therefore tantamount to homicide. With greater
medical understanding of procreation, new ideas sprang forth as

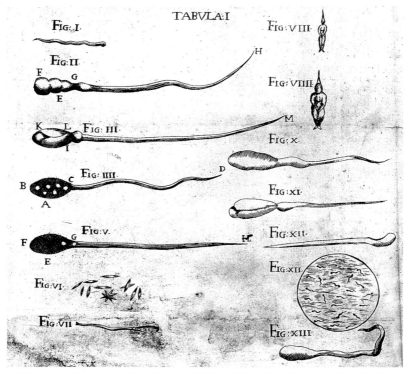

Homunculi in semen, from Antonio Vallisneri, *Istoria della generazione* (1721).

to why masturbation was dangerous, with medics now acting as the moral authorities.

A watershed came with the publication of a new book on masturbation, *Onania; or, The Heinous Sin of Self-pollution, and All Its Frightful Consequences in Both Sexes* (*c.* 1710). The author explained the cause of onanism, its consequences and its cure, and claimed that onanism could cause debilitating diseases, blindness and insanity. Written under anonymous authorship by 'a clergyman', it revolutionized people's perceptions about pleasuring themselves. Although it has been suggested that the author was one Dr Bekker, no one has ever identified such a person, although he was evidently well-read.[20] Nor was he either 'a clergyman' or a medic; instead he was more than likely to have been a quack, given the amount of advertisements for cures placed prominently in the book. John Marten has also been suggested as the author and this may well be the case, as Marten was not only a quack but had also written other books similar in style and content.[21] Two medications in particular were proffered as cures, 'a strengthening tincture' sold at ten shillings a bottle and a 'Prolific powder' for twelve shillings a bag, an extraordinary amount of money given that most labourers' weekly wages were only a few shillings. These medicines promised to cure symptoms of gonorrhoea – gleets, oozings, sores, emissions – and all other manner of problems associated with the venereal disease, including 'nocturnal effusions'.[22] The popularity of the book is shown by the demand. By 1737, it had reached its sixteenth edition, the previously modest 60-page pamphlet extended to 194 pages. Readers had written in outlining their afflictions and hailing the cures (although these may well have been written by the author himself, fabricated for promotional purposes).[23]

For the first time, women were seen to be avid practitioners of onanism alongside men. The author warned his readers that 'to imagine women are much more modest than men is a mistake' as they were just as likely to commit the act. While men might suffer 'stranguaries, priapisms and gonorrheas, thin and waterish seed, fainting fits and epilepsies, consumption, loss of erection and premature ejaculation, and infertility', women might suffer imbecility, *fluor albus* (leucorrhoea), hysteric fits, barrenness and be rendered unfit for the act of generation. Cure involved true repentance along with cold baths and a milk diet.[24]

Onania spawned a flurry of other similar pamphlets used to scare gullible masturbators into parting with their money. One response was *Onanism Display'd* (1719) in which the author agreed that self-pollution was 'a crime in itself, monstrous and unnatural; its practice filthy and odious', and asserted chastity and early marriage as the best cure.[25] Most of the books, such as *Of the Crime of Onan* (1723), *Onanism Examined and Detected* (1724) and *Eronania* (1724), carried adverts for so-called 'cures' in the form of various liquors, potions and powders. Purging lotions could be bought for seven shillings and sixpence to revive one's constitution; an elixir cost a mere guinea. Anodyne necklaces purported to cure everything from exhaustion through over-masturbation to the effects of the pox (not to mention teething in children). The front page of *Eronania* directed the afflicted reader to a place next to the Rose Tavern in Temple Bar where 'the scheme of the secret disease and broken constitutions' might be treated gratis. 'Nothing could be of greater service than to show the guilty how to get rid of so vile a habit and keep the unwary from falling into it', it claimed. Although the consultation may well have been free, the hapless patient was a few shillings lighter by the time he left the shop with his useless bottle of medicine.

But it was not just quacks who were condemning masturbation; respected physicians were coming out in droves to attack the practice. The English physician Robert James in his *Medical Dictionary* (1743–5) deemed it 'a vice not decent to name, but productive of the most deplorable and generally incurable disorders'.[26] Other respectable medical texts condemned the act as dangerous, stating that it could even lead to psychological problems and induce physical changes. A woman could grow an elongated clitoris as a result of over-stimulation, turning her into a 'tribade' (another name for a lesbian). She could become hysterical and uncontrollable (a fate, incidentally, more often applied to rebellious women than the quiet submissive sort). Deranged imaginings filled the mind of the female onanist, and encouraged sexual rapaciousness in her. Masturbation was even blamed for nymphomania in women and satyrism in men. In 1760, the *Critical Review* advised that 'furor uterinus', or raging female nymphomania, could result from women masturbating.[27] Women were vulnerable because they lacked the wherewithal to command or reason, which left their imaginations riskily open.[28] When women masturbated, therefore, they might go mad. Pictures of onanists were reproduced in medical texts depicting delirious women swooning on the verge of insanity and men crippled with fatigue. But why did this panic occur now,[29] and why was it so important for medics to take up the baton condemning masturbation?

Over the preceding century, there had been a gradual decline of belief in magic and witchcraft. By the time of the Enlightenment, rationality and reason were being promoted as the correct path to follow. It was generally thought that a more 'scientific' approach to life was needed. This rationality extended to a need for control over the workings of the body, both publicly and privately. While previously religion had been responsible for matters of moral control, science was gaining an increasing voice of authority on the issue – medicine rather than religion was becoming the arbiter of what was good and bad sex. In turn, this meant that medics were now the new overseers of repression and they therefore felt compelled to write about the topic so as to establish themselves as the new moral authorities.

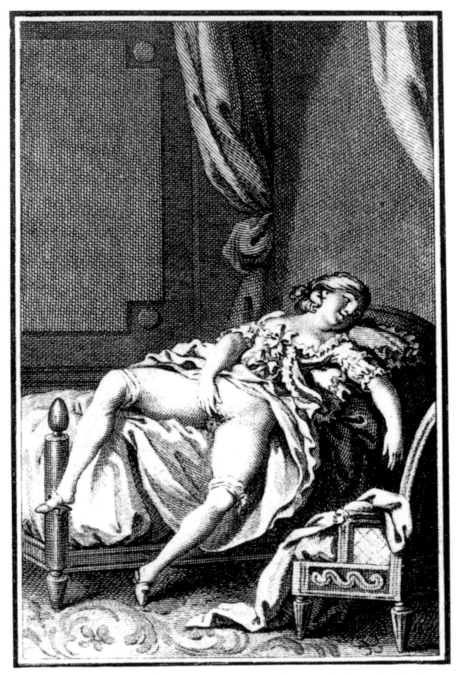

'A Woman Masturbates', drawing by Antoine Borel, engraved by François-Roland Elluin for Jean-Baptiste de Boyer (attrib.), *Thérèse philosophe* (1785 edition).

Frontispiece from an Italian edition of Samuel Tissot's *L'Onanisme* (*L'Onanismo, ovvero dissertazioni sopra le malattie cagionate dalle polluzioni voluntarie*, 1785).

Samuel Tissot's treatise *L'Onanisme, où, dissertation sur les maladies produites par la masturbation* (1760) was to become one of the biggest influences on the understanding of onanism throughout Europe. Tissot described the debilitating effects of masturbation in women who were 'more particularly exposed to hysterical fits, or shocking vapours; to incurable jaundices; to violent cramps in the stomach and back; to acute pains in the nose'.[30] In 1777, M.D.T. Bienville took the matter further when he published a tract on the subject translated into English as *Nymphomania, or Treatise on Uterine Fury* four years later.[31] Less is known about Bienville except that he lived in Holland and he wrote several other scientific works, including two treatises defending smallpox inoculation. However, he described how the female onanist might fall into a dreadful state of passionate insanity, 'the expressions of which even ears not uncommonly chaste cannot listen without horror and astonishment'. Nymphomania, he believed, started with 'a melancholy *delirium*', a sort of brain disorder that resulted from a woman's wild imagination.[32] These women then abandon themselves, throwing themselves at the first available man to 'gratify their insatiable desires'.[33]

By the turn of the century, masturbation was firmly linked to depravity, disabilities and insanity. As physicians became more interested in the way the mind worked, a new area of medicine

Son corps est couvert de Pustules.

'The Female Onanist', from Tissot, *L'Onanisme* (1836).

developed in pathological anatomy. In his book *Medical Inquiries and Observations Upon the Diseases of the Mind* (1812), the famous Philadelphian psychiatrist Benjamin Rush declared that 'chronic aberrations frequently have been found in the cerebellum of the onanist'.[34] He not only associated 'onanism' with insanity, but also 'seminal weakness, impotence, dysury, tabes dorsalis, pulmonary consumption, dyspepsia, dimness of sight, vertigo, epilepsy, hypochondriasis, loss of memory, manalgia, fatuity, and death'.[35] France was just as clogged with strange beliefs about the traumatic effects of masturbation. In 1819, the *Dictionnaire des sciences médicales* advised about the terrible effects of the 'deadly habit of masturbation'.

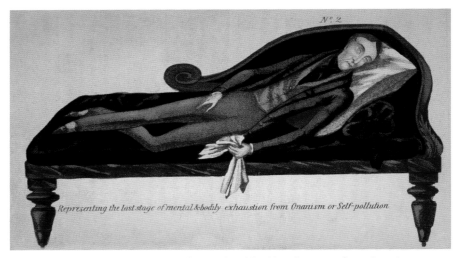

'Representing the last stage of mental and bodily exhaustion from Onanism or Self-pollution', R. J. Brodie, *The Secret Companion* (1845).

The subject was the topic of hot debate between prominent physicians, one who asserted that 'the continual excitement of the genital organs is liable to give rise to almost all the acute or chronic illness which can disturb the harmony of our functions.'[36] Everything and anything was blamed on masturbation. Onanism might affect the brain, the spinal column or the mind; create imbeciles; lead to loss of sight or hearing, paralysis, palpitations, heart lesions or scrofula. With the establishment of lunatic asylums and incarceration of the insane, eighteenth-century physicians could observe 'the sick' at close quarters. What became apparent was that insane in-patients masturbated. Yet, rather than believe patients masturbated from boredom, doctors preferred to believe it was masturbation that caused insanity. The proof was in their hospitals – of 272 mentally ill patients placed in care in Bicêtre and Saltpêtrière hospitals in Paris, 41 were men, and of those eighteen were masturbators.[37]

This concern over masturbation was to last through the reign of Queen Victoria, although again, the reactions were shifting. Having seen the attacks come first from religious quarters and then medical ones, now concerns over masturbation were connected to eugenics, hereditary disease and effects on race.

Keeping the Nation Pure

Masturbation began to affect the body politic, and was now seen as the scourge of nations. One doctor even described it as worse than the plague, war or pox. In France, Reveillé-Parise in his *Revue Medicale française et etrangère* (1828) called it 'the destroyer of civilization'.[38] Many other doctors followed suit and believed Dr Fonssagrives' explanation – that deterioration started in childhood and progressed to adolescence, taking with it 'the shared patrimony of a country's forces.'[39] The problem was seen to affect not just the individual but society as a whole. Masturbators were blamed for causing the degeneration of entire nations, denying king and country the possibility of a strong manpower by enfeebling the bodies of young men and making them unfit to be fathers. Moralists, historians and educators all came together to reinforce the creational myth of the ills of masturbation.[40] The trappist monk Pierre Jean Corneille Debreyne (1786–1867), as moralist, theologian and physician, drew together all the potential negative attributes of the act – a failed physical body, a deranged mental capacity and a blemished soul. He attested that masturbators 'end up falling into a hideous marasmus and a disgusting decrepitude'.[41] Meanwhile, Professor Claude François Lallemand, a physician practising in Montpellier, expressed his concern over masturbation as it caused spermatorrhea, excessive discharge of sperm or involuntary ejaculations. In *A Practical Treatise on the Causes, Symptoms and Treatment of Spermatorrhoea* (1835), he recorded 150 cases he had investigated in his fourteen years of practice. He concluded that masturbation degraded a man, 'poisons the happiness of his best days, and ravages society'.[42]

Meanwhile, Victorian Britain was carrying out its own war against the 'solitary vice'.[43] There was a wave of new-fangled inventions to keep the nation's children free from vice and to act as a deterrent against masturbation. Early detection was imperative if Britain was to avoid spawning a country of defective children. They were therefore warned to keep their hands above the bedclothes to avoid touching their genitals. Parents were advised to put gloves with spikes on their offspring if they wanted them to grow up 'normally'. Even straitjackets were suggested. Erection detectors awoke parents with bells ringing if their son had an erection in his sleep. Other preventative devices included the sleeping ring, the cup with padlock, the truss, the sheath, the hand-jive, the penis plate, the locking pockets, the live wire and the body suit.[44] All these devices inflicted pain as a method of cure. For perpetual offenders, surgical methods were implemented – in extreme measures, clitorodectomies and castrations were suggested, but these were rare. Cauterization was also used, the doctor burning the offending organ to cause the patient pain in order to prevent them touching themselves. Every drug was tried, from potassium bromide to opium, sulphur, hot pepper and strychnine. Even leeches were applied to patients' skin. Thin blankets and cold bathing were less aggressive methods suggested to help relieve the need to masturbate, since heat was thought to agitate the genitals. But according to Samuel Bayard Woodward, writing in the *Boston Medical and Surgical Journal* in 1835, 'Nothing short of total abstinence from the practice can save those who have become the victim of it.'[45]

Both puberty and bachelorhood were seen as particularly problematic periods in a young man's life. In 1854, Sir George Drysdale in his *Elements of Social Science* was revolutionary in that he urged early marriages and the use of contraception as methods against the 'injurious habits of self-pollution', although his detractors criticized him for advocating 'conjugal onanism'. Meanwhile, William Acton was busy scaring the male population with *The Functions and Disorders of the Reproductive Organs in Youth, Adult Age, and Advanced Life* (1857), which induced at least as much panic as *Onania* had done on its publication in the early 1700s. He reiterated the now entrenched opinion that the waste of sperm could lead to debilitating

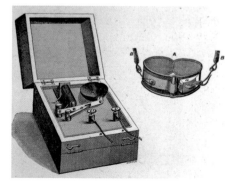

Four-pointed urethral ring, in J. L. Milton, *On the Pathology and Treatment of Gonorrhoea and Spermatorrhoea* (1887).

The Electric Alarm, in Milton, *On the Pathology and Treatment of Gonorrhoea and Spermatorrhoea* (1887).

A woman masturbates. Illustration by Achilles Devéria for Alfred de Musset's novel *Gamiani; or, Two Nights of Excess* (1833).

diseases. So why was there a resurgence of anxiety about the activity in the nineteenth century? Indeed, had it ever gone away? It has been suggested that the renewed anxiety was a result of a confused reaction of parents and medics to the early onset of puberty in Western Europe.[46] Yet if this was the case, surely parents would have been worried about their offspring attempting sexual intercourse earlier, and masturbation should have been seen as a way to avert pre-marital pregnancies? Since marriage was delayed until young people reached their early twenties, parents may well have considered that masturbation for boys was an acceptable way for them to relieve themselves, especially since this might help prevent their sons' seduction of young girls. But this was not the case. Masturbation continued to be seen as a threat to youths' physical and mental abilities and became a particular concern of the middle classes.

One reason for anxieties around masturbation was that the Victorians considered that the reckless 'spending' of sperm threatened to bankrupt the perpetrator both morally and physically. In the economic culture of the mid-nineteenth century onwards, saving and accumulation were vital parts of the creation of a sound future and a morally restrained life. Samuel Smiles had already outlined the need for restraint in his popular books *Self-Help* (1859) and *Thrift* (1875). Discipline was everything to the upstanding Victorian citizen, including self-discipline and the disciplining of one's own children. In order to instil this in youngsters, Acton advised complete 'sexual acquiescence' of the child and infant to the wishes of his or her parents.

Added to the newly enforced Victorian discipline and suggestions for a stricter morality were the fears stirred by the new field of psychology and psychiatry. Old evidence in a new guise provided reasons for the malaised child as the problem of insanity came back to haunt the habitual masturbator. In 1867, Henry Maudsley, the recognized British expert psychiatrist, revealed that masturbation was 'characterized by . . . extreme perversion of feeling and corresponding derangement of thought, in earlier stages, and later by failure of intelligence, nocturnal hallucinations, and suicidal and homicidal propensities'. He particularly identified masturbation as a 'mania of pubescence', a sort of mental disease of egoism whereby the young patient fails to listen to others. This developed into a paranoia whereby the youth feels his entire family is against him. Easily recognizable was the youth who was entirely irreverent to his parents, who 'spent most of the day leaning against a door post, or wandering about in a vacant or abstracted way'.[47] Any parent might have spotted this description in their own children and leapt to the conclusion that their offspring was a masturbator. Another psychiatrist, Edward Charles Spitzka, author of *Insanity: Its Classification, Diagnosis* and *Treatment* (1883), also thought that youths were especially afflicted, particularly those who lay in bed all day. For one particular patient who was impertinent to his mother, he proposed that the youth spend two months in a straitjacket in an asylum. He also saw unwillingness to work as a form of insanity, with hard work as its cure. Masturbators were no longer harmless self-obsessives cured by cooling of temperature or a healthy diet, but potential psychological deviants.

The campaigning of the social purity movements and the publication of new child rearing tracts also had their effect on the social climate – medical anxieties were no longer the only issue as the

Youth in an anti-
masturbation
corset, after
Johann Christoph
Fleck, *Die
Verwirrungen des
Geschlechtstriebes*
(1830).

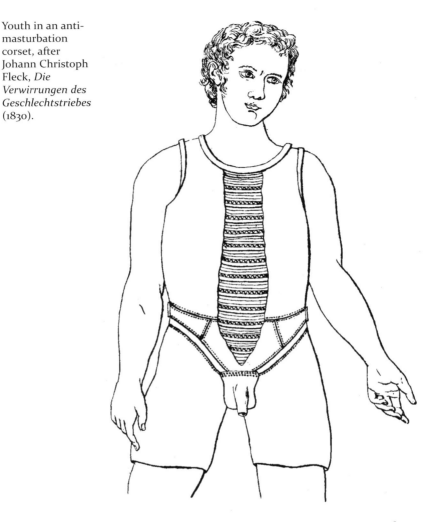

question of salvation gained prominence. Campaigning groups such
as the Social Purity Alliance (founded in 1873), the Moral Reform
Union (1881) and the National Vigilance Association (1885) moved
to combat the double standard of morality, which allowed for men's
infidelity and sexual philandering, and instead pushed for male
sexual purity. These movements emerged from the campaigns against
the Contagious Diseases Acts (1864–9), which introduced legally
enforceable medical inspection of prostitutes for venereal disease.
The Acts were introduced as a method of trying to contain venereal
disease in the armed forces, and police were particularly vigilant in
ports and garrison towns.

Books directed at youths suggested preventative measures against self-pollution. In his *Scouting for Boys* (1908), Robert Baden-Powell, founder of the scout movement, suggested that self-abuse led to degeneracy and that the best way to prevent it was to wash the organ in cold water every morning, then do as much exercise as possible to tire oneself out. He never actually mentions masturbation, but his main advice was on how boys should keep themselves healthy and clean with self-discipline, good temper and cheer. Priscilla Barker was more explicit in *The Secret Book: Containing Information and Instruction for Young Women and Girls* (1888) when she briskly advised 'plenty of cold water on the private parts'.[48] However, she warned that those who ignored her advice might become pale, their eyes grow dull, and their hands become soft and clammy from indulging in the vice.[49] Others suggested the oft-used cures of vigorous exercise, hard beds, a bland diet and prayer.

The amount of anti-masturbatory literature available at this time peaked in 1900 and continued until 1914.[50] Most of the moralists in the second half of the nineteenth and the early twentieth centuries targeted upper- and middle-class boys in the public school system, and little concern was given to the working-class boy. It was the bourgeois boy, surrounded by nannies, domestic servants and personal tutors, who was seen to be the future of the country. Alarmist Joseph Howe blamed servants for inducing a child's later bad habits by playing with its genitals; 'It is an authenticated fact . . . that children at the breast are often excited by their nurses. In order to keep them quiet, the titillation of the child's genitals produces sensations of pleasure which allays its cries.'[51] As they grew older, boys would masturbate for themselves, and suffered from clammy hands, stooped shoulders, flabby muscles and spots as a result. Edward Kirk in his *Talk with Boys about Themselves* (1905) declared dramatically that self-abuse 'will stunt your growth, soften your tissues . . . and wreck your health prematurely'.[52] Annoyed with youngsters' continued self-fondling, one female nurse, Ellen E. Perkins, went a step further and invented a piece of equipment in 1908 for 'keeping the male pure'. This encased the crotch in metal with leather reinforcements along the sides of the thighs and a centre flap on a hinge to allow for urination. It could be locked from behind so the wearer could not get out of it. But this could not help at public schools – potentially hazardous places with dormitories full of boys and no

Ellen Perkins's anti-masturbation device, 1908.

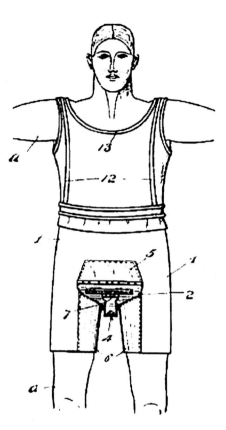

parental control. Addressing a purity rally in 1910, Irish Christian Sir Robert Anderson of the Criminal Investigation Department related 'a harrowing story of an Eton boy, son of a colonel in the army, a brilliant lad, "always ahead of his class" . . . who had been reduced to a drivelling imbecile as the result of a secret sin, induced by the sight of an obscene photograph exhibited by a scoundrel whom he met in a railway train.'[53]

With increasing experiments on the senses, a new set of doctors began to concentrate on how masturbation created mental problems. A new phrase, 'masturbatory neurosis', was promoted by doctors such as George M. Beard, Pierre Janet and Jean-Martin Charcot. In his *Clinical Lectures of Mental Diseases* (1904), Thomas Smith Couston claimed, 'Habit of masturbation [is] very injurious to boys of neurotic temperament'. Krafft-Ebing and Freud were among those who believed masturbation could cause neurosis, even psychosis, while Havelock Ellis thought it was a symptom of a neurotic disorder.

Woman masturbates with a bottle, etching by André Vollot, from the series
Le Voyeur, 1930.

Seventh-day Adventist John Harvey Kellog, MD, now famous for his breakfast cereal, ran a sanatorium based on holistic treatment of nutrition, enemas and exercise; his cornflakes were an invention for a healthy breakfast in keeping with his regime. He connected masturbation to insanity, believing it to cause personality changes, insomnia, indecision, confusion, acne, fear, pimples, shifty eyes, fits and the use of obscenities. Female masturbators suffered all of these, but had some additional symptoms: underdeveloped breasts, hysteria, jaundice, rickets, stomach cramps, womb ulcers, hermaphroditism and even sterility. His favoured preventative technique was to place electrodes in the rectums and urethras of his patients and subject them to mild electric shocks.[54]

Adding to society's anxiety, various surveys were undertaken in the twentieth century that revealed that masturbation was actually more prevalent than previously thought. Max Exner surveyed 700 college students in 1915 and found that it was a regular activity among them, although he continued to try and educate the youths in the error of their ways. Meanwhile, the social worker Dr Katherine Davis revealed that the reality of the situation as regards women was somewhat different from what doctors and moralists were saying. Employed by the Bureau of Social Hygiene to interview 2,200 women, she found that it was not only boys or men who liked to masturbate frequently, but women as well. Although the subject of female masturbation had already been mooted, it was never at the forefront of concerns and not thought to be so widespread as in men. Half of the interviewees were married, half not, and the results were published in *Factors in the Sex Life of Twenty-two Hundred Women* (1929). The number of women who admitted they had masturbated 'frequently' since marriage was nearly as large as that of men. Nearly 65 per cent of unmarried women and 40 per cent of married ones admitted to masturbating. Two out of three of them thought the practice was degrading, an opinion which reflected the repressed morality of the day. Unlike men, the women usually found out about the practice by themselves rather than being taught. Davis concluded that the result showed women's dissatisfaction within marriage.

Kinsey's surveys in the 1950s were to further shock the public when he revealed that masturbation in America was common among both men and women, including married ones. According to his research, 92 per cent of men and 62 per cent of women masturbated. Youths were found to have a particular inclination for masturbation, with the practice slackening off in middle age – yet the opposite was true for women, who grew more adept with age.[55]

Although Kinsey's surveys were the first to take an objective attitude to all things sexual, and to expose masturbation as a prevalent activity, he was not the first to digress from society's generally negative attitude towards masturbation. Throughout the centuries, many medics had disagreed with the ideas being promulgated. At the end of the eighteenth century, reputable surgeons such as John Hunter were beginning to question the alleged ill effects of masturbation on an individual's health. Hunter wondered if impotency was 'by far too rare for it to have originated from a practise so general'.[56] From this, it seems he presumed that masturbation was rife, and that books on the subject had done more harm than good. However, despite rumblings of dissent in the British medical fraternity, the idea that masturbation was a dangerous vice stretched way into the nineteenth century and beyond. Nearly a century after Hunter had questioned the veracity of such claims against masturbation, Sir James Paget came forth to question the reality of spermatorrhea. He denied that masturbation caused harm or could lead to the lunatic asylum, even though he was disgusted by it, calling it, 'An unclean-liness, a filthiness forbidden by God, an unmanliness despised by men'.[57] In 1896 a German doctor, Emil Kraepelin, was the first to prove that masturbation did not cause insanity, as a result of sex research conducted in lunatic asylums. In 1929 the author Ralcy Husted Bell declared that masturbation, 'according to clinical data, according to the plainest commonsense . . . is no more harmful than the co-operative act between mates'.[58] But it was Kinsey's contemporary, the German psychologist Wilhelm Stekel, who took a solid stance against the detractors of masturbation. He condemned traditional beliefs about masturbation, opposing the notion that it induced anxiety and depression or in any way promoted suicide. Instead, he called for the alleviation of religious and societal pres-sures, and encouraged the belief that masturbation was good for personal health and happiness. Although this might have been an end to the matter, the old theories clung fast. Through the centuries, none of these opponents of oddball theories on masturbation were properly heeded.

In 2007, a British national probability survey found that among people aged between sixteen and 44 years old, 95 per cent of men and 71 per cent of women had masturbated at some point in their lives; and 73 per cent of the men and 37 per cent of the women reported masturbating in the four weeks before their interview.[59] During the twenty-first century, there has been a distinct change in approach to the topic, at least among the medical fraternity and educators. In 2009, a leaflet entitled *Pleasure* was published on behalf of the Sheffield National Health Service, aimed at teenagers. It advocated regular masturbation for teens as an alternative to the risk of sexual diseases and teenage pregnancies and carried the slogan 'an orgasm a day keeps the doctor away'. The authors of the guidance say that for too long experts have concentrated on the need for 'safe sex' and committed relationships while ignoring the principal reason why many people have sex (for pleasure). The medical fraternity finally declared that masturbation is healthy. Despite these assertions, the overhang of Christian guilt remains. The Internet demonstrates that there are still religious leaders talking about the 'disordered tendency' and how to stop it.

Ideas about masturbation have therefore undergone a radical change throughout the last 2,000–3,000 years: an activity thought valuable and necessary by physicians in the ancient world became a sin, then a physical and mental disorder, until, finally, it has again become a healthy and necessary alternative to vaginal penetrative sex. Such is the life cycle of a sexual perversion.

Eustache Le Sueur, *The Abduction of Ganymede*, c. 1650, oil on canvas.

THREE

From Ganymedes to Gays

If [the sodomite] truly is a scoundrel or a monster . . . then why has Nature
created him partial to this pleasure?

Marquis de Sade, *La Philosophie dans le boudoir* (1795)

Male homosexuals have been called everything from Ganymedes –
after the beautiful Trojan youth of ancient Greek myth carried
away by Zeus to become his lover and cupbearer to the gods – to
catamites, sodomites and gays. More recently, homosexual men
have moved to reclaim previously disparaging words – queer, poof,
fairy, queen – for themselves. But these derogatory words indicate
a history of negativity towards men who prefer sex with other men.
Antipathy to homosexuality is still prevalent in many parts of the
Western world, and the death penalty for homosexual relationships
is still in place in some Eastern countries. Historically however, sex
between men did not always raise hostility.

Attitudes towards male homosexuality have shifted over the
years from an acceptance of love between men in ancient Greece,
to flogging, hanging and burning of homosexuals in the medieval
period, to permissible unions, legalized 'civil partnerships' and
marriages between men. The study of homosexuality in history
emerged during the 1980s. Since then, arguments have raged among
sociologists and historians about whether such a person as the
'homosexual' existed before Karl-Maria Kertbeny invented the term
in 1869. Was the homosexual a mere social construction?[1] Or did
he exist all along, meaning that he can be traced in history? Given
the wealth of evidence, most historians recognize that whether the
term existed or not at different times in the past, men had sex with
each other, loved each other and lived together. They also had shared
sexual identities and formed subcultures through which they could
share practices.

Before the modern era, people distinguished between themselves
differently from how we do now. They did not 'see' the heterosexual,

the bisexual or the homosexual. Instead they saw people who married or did not, and people who committed deviant sex acts (and they could be married or not) or did not. Although the term 'homosexual' did not exist, there were words with similar or related meanings, such as 'catamite', 'pederast' and 'sodomite' – a man who committed the act known as buggery, sodomy, the 'abominable vice' or a 'crime against nature'. Some of these men might have enjoyed sex with women and they might even have been married. The most important distinction made when assessing men who engaged in sex together was the difference between who was the active or penetrative partner and who was the passive or receiving partner. Those who took the passive role were viewed with disdain and seen to be unmanly, while those taking the active role were considered more manly and therefore were more acceptable. Where the passive partner was a youth, treatment was more lenient. Once a man grew older, he was expected to take the active role in sex. He should also marry and have children, even if he continued to desire other men. This way of thinking prevailed until the nineteenth century, when the 'birth of the homosexual' supposedly came about. Even then, many homosexuals were married and had children. At a time when homosexuality was considered so disreputable a vice, it was easier for a man to take refuge in marriage and continue his activities in secret. There were, of course, many variants on this way of thinking throughout different centuries.

Erastēs and Erōmenos

For the ancient Greeks, there was no division of human sexuality into heterosexuality and homosexuality. Sex for men was a fluid affair with few boundaries. A man might have sex with women other than his wife, as well as with other men, without adverse consequences. He might be married (and indeed was expected to take a wife and produce children) but might also enjoy penetrating a male youth in his spare time without any slight on his reputation. We have evidence of this type of behaviour between adult men in ancient Greece in contemporaneous artwork. Archaeologists have uncovered numerous vases that depict men having sex with each other, but there are also various literary references to such activities. However, there is some question about exactly how much anal intercourse went on, as many of the depictions of male-on-male sex show intercrural (between the thighs) sex.

In 1978, Kenneth Dover examined the subject of homosexuality in the ancient world in his book *Greek Homosexuality*. He found that the relationships of Greek men appear to have taken the form of love between an older man (known as *erastēs*) and a young beardless youth of between about twelve and eighteen (known as *erōmenos*). The youth in question would be expected to proffer his virtue (although not to give in too easily) to his mentor, and take the passive role. Generally the older man would take the active role of penetrator, a role perceived as more masculine. The older man would woo the youth with gifts – perhaps a pack of hunting dogs or a new outfit – and provide the youth with an education. The youth would be expected to temporarily resist his admirer's advances while being wooed, but eventually succumb. While the affair continued, the youth was expected to have a degree of self-control and self-assertion – he would not allow too much penetrative sex to take place and would not have too many suitors at once, nor would he take money for the act (which would make him a prostitute). Both the suitor and the youth came from elite backgrounds. When the youth grew up, he would be

Pederasty depicted on a black-figure amphora by the Painter of Berlin, *c.* 540 BC.

expected to marry and have children and perhaps pursue his own young men. However, there was probably a wider variety of relationships between men than originally thought, not just those between elite men and youths.[2]

In the *Iliad*, Homer described the close relationship between Trojan War hero Achilles and his comrade Patroclus. They shared the life of soldiers, fought side by side in battle and had a strong emotional bond. According to Aeschylus, writing in the fifth century BC, they also had a sexual relationship, with Achilles assigned the role of *erastēs* and Patroclus that of *erōmenos*. In a surviving fragment of his tragedy *Myrmidons*, Achilles speaks of a 'devout union

Bearded man with a youth. Black-figure vase, mid-6th century BC.

78

of the thighs', perhaps referring to intercrural sex.[3] Similarly, in his *Symposium*, written around 385 BC, Plato presents Achilles and Patroclus as lovers. However, the speaker Phaedrus argues that Aeschylus erred in saying that Achilles was the *erastēs*, 'for he excelled in beauty not Patroclus alone but assuredly all the other heroes, being still beardless and, moreover, much the younger, by Homer's account'. Others argued that they were merely close war comrades: a contemporary of Plato, Xenophon, claimed that the pair were devoted to each other, yet chaste. But it seems that in ancient Greece, there was also an understanding of love between adult men; it was recognized that some men shared their lives together and held deep affection for each other. Philolaus the law-giver lived with Dioclese, an Olympic athlete, and requested that they be buried next to each other.[4]

Adult men who had sex with men of their own age were more often viewed with contempt. These *kinaidoi*, as they were known, were older men who allowed themselves to be penetrated and were therefore dismissed by citizens in their community as effeminate. Taking a passive role meant that they had voluntarily lowered their position, and they were seen as wilfully degrading themselves. Athenian citizen men found it difficult to understand how a man could choose another older man above a male youth, prostitute, wife or slave. Aristotle summed up the antagonism against *kinaidoi* in a derogatory description:

> He has drooping eyelids. He is knock-kneed. He inclines his head to the right side. He makes effete gestures with open hands. He has two varieties of gait, one in which he wiggles his bottom, and one in which he keeps it still. He rolls his eyes around a great deal, like Dionysius the sophist.[5]

The world of ancient Rome saw the manly man penetrating anything he could find – other men, women, boys, male prostitutes and slaves. Male prostitution existed but was banned by Emperor Philip the Arab in the third century. However, so long as a man did not succumb to the advances of other men, he could have sex with whomsoever he chose (with the exception of freeborn men and citizens). However, he was expected to retain a degree of self-control. Nonetheless, some Roman rulers gained a bad reputation because of their preference for men well past their youth. It was rumoured that the emperor Galba, who briefly ruled for a few months in AD 68, eschewed youths for 'men, adult and strong' after his wife died. Suetonius says of him, 'In sexual matters, he was more inclined to males, and then none other than the hard bodied and those past their prime.'[6] The problem for Suetonius was not Galba's preference for males but for *adult* men. His predecessor, Emperor Nero, made an even greater negative impact because of his debauchery. He not only raped freeborn youths but also allowed his freedman Doryphorus to penetrate him. These incidents were problematic on three counts: first, defilement of freeborn youths; second, having sex with an adult man; and third, allowing himself to be penetrated.

Sins of Sodom

Christianity brought with it an incendiary hatred of any acts of desire between men. According to the Bible, there were three types of sodomy – anal sex between men and women; anal sex between men and men; and sex between humans and animals – and the Bible was responsible for making these sexual acts prohibited for Christians. Before the term 'homosexuality' was in use, men having sex with each other was therefore understood within the concept of sodomy. Such an act was considered a sin, a perversion of nature's laws and an act against God. Leviticus 18:22 states, 'Thou shalt not lie with mankind as with womankind: it is abomination.' Death was suggested as the suitable punishment (20:13). Despite these instructions and the potential severe punishment, men were still willing to seek out other men in pursuit of sexual pleasure.

Religious leaders of cloistered all-male communities saw the potential for problems where men lived in such close proximity with each other. One example was the reforming monk Peter Damian, prior of a monastery, who was later to become a cardinal. In his *Liber Gomorrhianus* (*Book of Gomorrah*, c. 1048), he voiced his concerns about sodomitical activities in the monasteries and noted that some monks even fondled and kissed young boys. For such indiscretions, he suggested a self-inflicted punishment of flagellation. His followers took their punishment all too willingly, and were so keen to follow his instructions that they injured themselves in their self-inflicted mortifications.[7] His concerns were not isolated and,

Medieval monastic
flagellation.

with the rulings of the Third Lateran Council in 1179, the Church
authorities stepped up their attacks on sodomitical behaviour both
among their own leaders and their flock. Clerics who engaged in
'unnatural' practices were ostracized to monasteries (where they
might actually practice them all the more), whereas lay people were
excommunicated. Church Father Thomas Aquinas reinforced the
need to take a strict line against sodomy, deeming it the most horrendous sin. As a result of the Church's stance, some of the worst ensuing
persecutions were of sodomites.[8] Because of its negative connotations,
sodomy was often used by the leaders of the Church and the State
in accusations against their enemies as a means of political attack.
Both the Cathars and the Knights Templar became targets for the
Catholic Church, and were accused of buggery. In reality, there was
no evidence that either group did anything other than upset the
Pope and the king.

The Cathars had flourished in the twelfth century. After travelling from Bulgaria, they settled in Albi in Languedoc (from where
they gained their alternative name, Albigensians). Known for their

purity of faith (*cathar* means 'pure'), they were to become a thorn in the side of the corrupt Catholic Church. They refused to have children, believing that this would link them to the material world they rejected. They therefore had no doctrinal objection to contraception or suicide, nor did they believe in the need for priests or churches – all issues that upset the Catholic Church. In order to wipe them out, Pope Innocent III called for a crusade and had them hunted down and massacred. In this attack, which became known as the Albigensian Crusade, an estimated 500,000 men, women and children (converts from the Catholic faith) were slaughtered. A similar fate, following similar accusations, befell the Templars, but this time the attack was motivated by greed as well as resentment. With the royal coffers empty after continuous wars, Philip IV of France was simply after the great wealth the Templars had amassed as a result of their plunders during various Crusades. In 1307, on being accused of unnatural sexual activities, as many Templars as could be found were arrested, tortured and murdered. In 1314, Jacques de Molay, Grand Master of the Knights Templar, was sentenced to be burned at the stake. Charges ranged from spitting on the Cross to kissing the initiated man on his mouth, navel and posterior during ceremonies.

Rank had its obligations and even kings were expected to conform sexually. Edward II of England placed himself in jeopardy when he made no secret of his sexual preference for men. Surrounding himself with men at court, his homosexual tendencies led him to grant his favourites outrageous liberties and allowed them to dominate him. Seizing her opportunity, his wife Isabella and her followers accused the king of incompetence and of being unfit to govern. Perhaps outright accusations of sodomy in a king were too much for a country to take, especially as God supposedly appointed the monarch. Such declarations had the potential to undermine the monarchy as an institution. In any case, as a result of the queen's manoeuvrings, Edward was forced to abdicate in 1327 in favour of his fourteen-year-old son. But with Edward still alive, the Crown was still in jeopardy and his death was inevitable. It came in a manner that expressed his opponents' contempt for his sexual habits. One contemporary described the killing:

On 22 September, having suddenly seized him lying in bed and having pressed him down and suffocated him with great

Jacques de Molay, Grand Master of the Knights Templar, sentenced to the stake. From the Chroniques de France ou de St Denis, 14th-century manuscript.

pillows and a weight heavier than fifteen robust men, with a plumber's iron heated red hot, through a horn applied leading to the privy parts of the bowel, they burned out the respiratory organs past the intestines.[9]

Edward's murder was thereby a violent comment on his sex life. A hundred years later, Eriksson, king of Norway and Sweden, was forced to abdicate when he was accused of performing unnatural acts with a knight.[10] As leaders of men, kings were supposed to abide by the rules laid down for them, rules that included having a sexual preference for women, or at least showing no obvious leanings towards men. The rules of sexual behaviour were so powerful that even monarchs had to obey them.

Buggery in Europe

The establishment of the Inquisition in 1233 under the rule of Pope Gregory IX fuelled public anxieties over sodomites and the situation took a more aggressive turn. In Europe over the next three centuries, the persecution of sodomites entailed torture, maiming and death for any man unfortunate enough to be caught. The cities of Siena, Bologna, Florence, Venice, Paris, Ghent and Bruges all brought out new laws to encourage the detection of sodomites, while the public were encouraged to come forward and expose them. The accused men came from all classes but were mainly tradesmen of the middling sort – shoemakers, butchers, carpenters, tailors and grocers. Apprentices or lower-class servants or labourers were among them, while aristocrats accounted for about one-third of the total. As ever, those with money found it easier to evade detection. When caught, the perpetrators might suffer any range of punishments from castration, blinding and amputation of limbs to the death penalty (usually reserved for repeat offenders). Usually they were burned at the stake. In cases where the accused was an older man, he was often married with children. It seems that the notion of single adult homosexual men was not part of the medieval picture.

In Florence the authorities became increasingly concerned about a network of sodomites that flourished in their city. They discovered that certain older adult men, who were often married, were actively pursuing younger men. In 1325, in an attempt to discourage such behaviour, a statute was introduced that prescribed castration for men who sodomized boys. Because remuneration was offered to informers, it provided the opportunity for anyone to extort money from sodomites unlucky enough to attract attention, and blackmail flourished. At this stage, it also became noticed that although some youths were submitting to older men, this was by no means the most usual kind of encounter. More frequently sodomy was occurring between young men of a similar age, who were engaging in mutually consensual acts. Subsequently, penalties were put in place for youths who allowed themselves to be sodomized. Younger offenders were usually lucky enough to escape with fines of anything between 50 and 100 lire, together with a public flogging. Sometimes the authorities thought it prescient to make an example of a youth. Such was the case with the unfortunate fifteen-year-old Giovanni di Giovanni, who admitted to being sodomized by many men over a period of time. First he was paraded on an ass to a place outside the city walls to ensure his plight was fully publicized; in full view of the crowd, he was then castrated and mutilated with a red-hot iron 'in the part of his body where he allowed himself to be known in sodomitical practices'.[11]

In reaction to the amount of illicit sex taking place between men, the appalled authorities embarked on an extended persecution. Between 1432 and 1502, town officials in Florence established the 'Officers of the Night', a police force designated to root out and destroy all sodomites. Even the clergy were attacked: in Bologna in 1475, one captured priest was enclosed in a hut, oil poured over it and set on fire. Male prostitution was particularly rife in fourteenth-century Venice. One man, who called himself Rolandina and sold

Donatello, *David*, 1430, marble; the statue was controversial due to its unusually sexualized, perhaps homoerotic, nature.

85

Caravaggio, *Amor Vincit Omnia* ('Love Conquers All', known as *Victorious Cupid*), 1601–2, oil on canvas.

himself from around the area of the Rialto Bridge, was convicted and burned at the stake. Before his death, in his statement given in 1354, he also bore witness that he believed he was doing nothing wrong. Although he was married, he admitted that he had never felt sexual desire for women.[12] This persecution therefore did not go unchallenged. Some men denied there was anything wrong with the activity and were not afraid of speaking out. During the fifteenth century, persecutions were also taking place in Augsburg, Regensburg, Basel, Ghent and Bruges, with increasing numbers of sodomites placed on trial. In Basel, after being caught attempting to seduce the youth Johannes Müller, the cleric Johannes Stocker used the defence that everyone was committing sodomy. He retorted, 'If everybody who committed this were burnt at the stake, not even fifty men would survive in Basel.'[13]

While this wholesale onslaught was taking place in towns in Italy and the Low Countries, the rest of Europe seems to have been comparatively lax in their punishment of sodomites. Medieval Russia appears to have been quite uninterested in sodomy. Although it was a treated as a sin under the Orthodox Church, there were no

Caravaggio, *Boy with a Basket of Fruit*, *c.* 1593, oil on canvas.

legal sanctions against it. London seems to have been equally detached, with only one man charged between 1420 and 1518. With new laws against sodomy issued by the Holy Roman Empire in 1532, Spain seems to have stepped up its action against homosexuals, burning 65 men between 1578 and 1616.

An alternative attitude to persecution ran concurrently even in Renaissance Italy. Close male friendships were cultivated, and notably captured in visual art. When Donatello encapsulated his Ganymede in his statue of David, he combined both the fighting manly spirit with desire of youth. In Baroque art Caravaggio, with an eye for a beautiful boy, created pictures of idealized, fey youth. Despite the persecution of sodomites, friendships between men and pubescent boys were considered acceptable and mentorship between noble families all over Europe was considered necessary for social integration and elevation. Meanwhile in England, attitudes towards sodomites were slower to shift.

Home-grown Vice

Unlike other parts of Europe, sodomy in England seems to have been fairly well tolerated as a vice up to end of the seventeenth century, so long as the sodomite fulfilled his social functions of marriage and spawning children. The poet John Wilmot, Earl of Rochester, was one of the most notorious libertines of the seventeenth century. He openly declared his love of boys: 'There's a sweet, soft page of mine / Does the trick worth forty wenches.' However, the authorities took offence to his play *Sodom; or, The Quintessence of Debauchery*, published in 1684, which they censored, mostly because of its overt references to sodomy. Restrictions were creeping in to prevent sodomy becoming more widespread. Broadsides decrying sodomites were becoming popular reading material, and most could be brought for a few pennies. John Dunton published a poem entitled 'The He-Strumpets: A Satyr on the Sodomite-Club' in 1707, declaring that men were seeking out sodomites because so many prostitutes had the clap.

> All Cracks are found so full of Ails,
> A *New Society* prevails,
> Call'd *S[o]d[om]ites*; Men worse than Goats,

Who dress themselves in Petticoats,
To Whore as *O[s]born* did with *O[a]tes*.[14]

Sodomy was made a crime in common law for the first time in England in 1533, and remained a capital offence until 1861, with the last execution taking place in 1835.[15] Because private incidents were increasingly being made public through the courts, buggery was now

Woodcut illustration from the broadside ballad *The Women Hater's Lamentation* (1707).

perceived as being on the rise. In 1663, Samuel Pepys reported, 'Sir J Jemmes and Mr Batten both say that buggery is now almost grown as common among our gallants as in Italy.'[16] Certainly there was the opportunity. This was a time when men shared beds, particularly if travelling and staying at inns, and masters shared beds with their apprentices who lived within the same household. These bounds were sometimes overstepped, as in the case of Meredith Davy in Somerset in 1630. According to evidence heard in court, Davy shared a bed with his twelve-year-old apprentice, John Vicary, and after a hard night's drinking Davy would often have sex with the boy. Once, after the boy cried out, Davy ended up in court.[17] Few young boys had the courage, knowledge or money to bring a case to court – most probably simply moved on as soon as they could. Cases that reached the courts were more often brought by other adults as a result of overhearing or seeing the activities.

By the eighteenth century, the death penalty was used less, but the very least a sodomite could expect was a stint in the pillory, a hefty fine and a prison sentence of a couple of years. The pillory in itself could often be a death sentence – people rarely came out unscathed. Regarded by the mob as an occasion of spectacle and entertainment, most of the crowd came armed with rotting food, stinking fish bones, putrid eggs and dead rats and cats to throw at the culprits. The overwhelming avalanche of missiles frequently took out a prisoner's eye or left him otherwise maimed. The extent of alienation felt by victims is made evident in one broadside ballad, or broadsheet, *The Women Hater's Lamentation*, which described in verse the raids taking place in 1707. As a result of the persecution, several men cut their own throats or hanged themselves while awaiting trial.[18]

Even the most religious men were seen to be indulging in the 'the worst of crimes'. On 9 October 1721, George Duffus was indicted for sodomy on Nicholas Leader after they had met at a religious meeting-house in Old Gravel Lane in London. Duffus had first approached Leader to discuss the merits of the sermon and was 'seeming very religious'. According to Leader, Duffus had spoken to him and inveigled his way into his good opinion. At the next visit, Duffus left it too late to go home and asked if he could stay the night with Leader. At the trial, it was reported that

After they had been in Bed a little while, the Prisoner [Duffus] began to kiss and embrace the Prosecutor [Leader], thrust his Tongue in his Mouth, called him his dear Friend, and got on his Back; but the Prosecutor resisting, threw him off 3 or 4 times, telling him if he would not be still, he'd turn him out of Bed. The prisoner then seizing the Prosecutor by the Throat almost strangled him, turned him on his Face, and forcibly entered his Body about an Inch . . .

Leader was able to throw him off, forcing him to withdraw, and 'prevented the prisoner from making an Emission Seminis in his Body; but having thus forced the prisoner to withdraw, he (the prisoner) emitted in his own Hand, clapping it on the tail of the Prosecutor's Shirt. Saying, Now you have it!'[19] Duffus was found guilty of sodomy, fined 20 marks and sentenced to a month's imprisonment and to stand upon the pillory near Old Gravel Lane – still not a very heavy fine for what amounts to attempted sodomitical rape.

Young apprentices still seem to have been fair game for those on the prowl. When Henry Wolf met John Holloway in 1735 on an errand for his master, a brandy merchant, he took him to several pubs where he fondled him, and on to Bishop's Gate Church Yard, where he bought him a nosegay and a penny custard. Eventually he approached Bethlem Royal Hospital, which ran along the south side of the Moorfields. Giving evidence, Holloway announced, 'Coming to Bedlam, he perfectly pull'd and haul'd me in to see the Mad-folks. There he took me into the House of Office, and pull'd down his own Breeches and mine, and – in his Mouth.'[20] Oral sex seems to have been a common sexual approach. When in 1802 the young James Reader applied for a job to the Revd George Donnisthorpe, the vicar offered him liquor and money and said, 'if he were a Lady and had ten thousand a year he would bestow it all on him'. Thereupon Donnisthorpe took the boy's 'private Member in his hand, knelt down on one knee and put it into his Mouth'.[21] Reader went on to see Donnisthorpe four more times before warning him off, so, despite bringing the incident to court, he does not seem to have been entirely unwilling.

While it would seem that some apprentices were targets for older men, the youths themselves sometimes received benefits in the encounter, as sexual enjoyment and/or monetary gain. Others would

Depiction of sodomy in the monastery, engraving for *Histoire de Dom Bougre, portier de Chartreux*, attributed to Jean-Charles Gervaise de Latouche (1741).

shout out for help and adults might intervene. Although attempts on youths were common, some adult men preferred to look for groups of like-minded men rather than individuals, finding the sociability and shared enjoyments more convivial.

Sodomitical Subcultures

Subcultures of sodomites emerged throughout Europe during the eighteenth century, where consensual sexual activities were practised.[22] In France, Police Lieutenant Lenoir estimated that there were around 20,000 sodomites in Paris in 1725. The type of man engaging in this activity appears to have been changing. Previously sodomy had been known as the *beau vice*, as it seemingly affected mainly the nobility; now it was becoming a fashion among everyone 'from dukes down to footmen'. It was no longer the predilection of a few, but crossed class barriers, with merchants, artisans and domestic servants all being caught up in raids and brought to trial. The banks of the Seine were a favourite pick-up place, with some men putting handkerchiefs on their heads and, as one observer commented, 'imitating women, mincing like them . . . They choose each other in these gatherings for mutual fondling and to commit infamies.'[23] In order to keep some sort of control over the situation, police kept a list of pederasts and paid a series of informants – *mouches* (flies), as they were called – to entrap sodomites. However, this method seems to have been ineffective, as by 1780, Lieutenant Lenoir claimed that the number of sodomites in the city had doubled to around 40,000. According to him, there were now as many sodomites as there were prostitutes.[24] Those caught were sent to the dungeon of the general hospital in Bicêtre, south of Paris, a place known for its extremely high mortality rate. Once incarcerated, there was every chance an inmate would not survive. Although legal battles continued against these men, some contemporaries voiced their concerns about how shabbily sodomites were being treated. The forward-thinking French philosopher Nicolas de Condorçet wrote: 'Sodomy when there is no violence involved, cannot be part of the criminal law. It does not violate the rights of anyone.'[25] As public attitudes gradually shifted, the violence of the punishments abated. The hanging of sodomites was no longer considered appropriate and was partially supplanted with their deportation to the French colonies in the West Indies such as Martinique.

In the Netherlands persecutions erupted in the 1730s for the first time. Twenty-two boys and men from one village alone were executed after the confession of a soldier revealed a network of sodomites throughout major cities in the Dutch Republic. It became apparent that there existed a sophisticated subculture in which members knew about each other, often even in other cities. Similar to elsewhere in Europe, pubs, brothels, parks and toilets were used as meeting places in The Hague. In Amsterdam, sodomites picked each other up on the ground floor of the City Hall. Kicking each other's feet, patting one hand with another and looking each other in the eye with hand on hip were all signs and gestures indicating their inclinations. Although anal intercourse took place, so did mutual masturbation, known as 'milking out' or 'throwing the seed with the hand'. Oral sex seemed less popular, at least in the cases that were brought to trial. An edict against sodomy came out when the persecutions started in 1730, which was revised in 1764 and held until 1811 when the country came under the French penal law.[26] However, up to this time, no laws against sodomy had existed in the Netherlands.

Other countries throughout Europe stayed quieter. Most were increasingly reluctant to inflict the death penalty for sodomy. Even those subject to the Inquisition eased up – Portugal, which had 278 arrests under the Inquisition between 1547 and 1768, saw only 23 men arrested in the eighteenth century, and no burnings took place. In Denmark, although the death penalty existed for sodomy from 1683 until 1866, it was never applied. Private acts of sodomy were decriminalized in many places (those under the Napoleonic Laws) but were gradually recriminalized later in the nineteenth century. Publicly, there was a decreasing acceptance of older men conducting such practices, particularly if they were seen to be effeminate or 'mollies'. Meanwhile, in Britain, persecution against sodomites rose after the Society for the Reformation of Manners was founded in 1691 and members actively began pursuing and prosecuting sodomites and prostitutes. As a result, more cases of buggery came to court than ever before.

Raids took place on various bawdy houses thought to harbour sodomites, the places often identified by secret informers. One of the most notorious groups was found in the infamous Mother Clap's Molly House, a private residence where Mother Clap brought in liquor for her customers. Here, men were caught drinking, carousing and having sex with each other; their practice was to dress as women and perform mock marriages, giving 'birth' to wooden dolls and Cheshire cheeses.[27] After her conviction, Mother Clap was sentenced to stand in the pillory in Smithfield, to pay a fine of 20 marks and suffer two years' imprisonment, but she was so badly pilloried that she died of her injuries a couple of days later. Although Mother Clap's case was high-profile for London, other subcultures existed in southern England, such as in Bath and Somerset.[28]

An unprecedented number of prosecutions for sodomy took place at the beginning of the nineteenth century as antagonism towards homosexual subcultures continued unabated.[29] After raids on the White Swan tavern in Vere Street, London in 1810, 27 men were arrested, two of whom hanged and six pilloried. Once again, the anti-vice societies were zealous in their persecution of all-male sexual activity. Perhaps one of the biggest scandals erupted in 1889 after a police raid on an all-male brothel in Cleveland Street, Fitzrovia. The place had been discovered after fifteen-year-old Charles Thomas Swinscow was found with the large sum of fourteen shillings on him. He admitted that he had been working as a male prostitute at the Cleveland Street brothel, and was just one of a handful of telegraph messenger boys employed as prostitutes by the brothel owner Charles Hammond. The prosecution was made more difficult when, to the horror of the police, most of the clients were found to be aristocrats; one was rumoured to be the eldest son of the Prince of Wales; another was Lord Arthur Somerset, equerry to the prince, who quietly fled abroad. Somerset paid for the defence of the boys involved and, as a result, they received light sentences. However, the police were later accused of covering up the arrests in order to protect the wealthy clientele.

While the authorities continued to swoop down on brothels, they also picked off individuals – transvestites made particularly easy targets. In one of the most notorious cases of the century, Ernest Boulton and Frederick William Park, known to their friends as 'Stella and Fanny', were apprehended on the Strand on 28 April 1870 while on a trip to the theatre. At the time, Boulton was wearing a cherry-coloured evening dress, trimmed with white lace and a wig styled in a braided chignon, and he was adorned with bracelets; Park was clad in a plunging, dark-green silk dress, a black lace shawl

Oscar Wilde and Lord Alfred Douglas, 1894.

and white kid gloves, his look completed by a blond curling wig. In this case, the prosecution failed to prove that they had had anal sex, or that it was a crime in Britain for men to dress in women's clothes.[30] While the Offences Against the Persons Act 1861 had finally abolished hanging for the crime of buggery, a person could still be subject to life imprisonment, with penal servitude. The Criminal Law Amendment Act of 1885 further aggravated the situation when it introduced a prohibition on all male-on-male sexual acts. Now not only sodomy was illegal, but 'any act of gross indecency with another male person' was deemed a misdemeanour attracting two years' imprisonment.

For the most part, the authorities had tended to keep quiet about the topic of male-on-male sex as they were worried about possible copycat behaviour, but by the turn of the century, homosexuality was to become more prominent in the public's knowledge. It was ultimately one particular trial – that of the playwright and poet Oscar Wilde – which led to homosexuality being discussed more widely. In 1895, Wilde had unwisely brought a case of libel against the Marquess of Queensberry, father of his lover Sir Alfred Douglas, after Queensberry had accused Wilde of posing as a sodomite. The case backfired and Wilde was arrested for gross indecency. As a result, he was to spend two years in prison serving hard labour. He was in such poor health by the time he was released that he lived only another three years. He and 'Bosie', as he affectionately called Douglas, met up and lived together for a while in Naples, but it did not work out and Bosie returned to England. Bosie was later to repudiate both homosexuality and Wilde, but meanwhile braver men were working behind the scenes to try and decriminalize homosexuality. Now the question being asked was: 'Are these people votaries of vice, or are they insane?'[31]

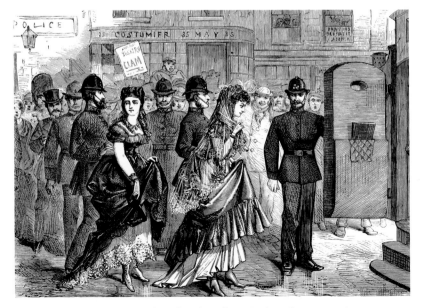

Ernest Boulton and Frederick William Park under arrest, 1870.

The Birth of the Homosexual

With the development of sexology at the end of the nineteenth century, there was a shift in the ideas surrounding homosexuality. Sexologists declared that homosexuality should be seen as an illness rather than as a criminal deviance, and that instead of punishing homosexuals, attempts should be made to 'cure' them. In order to steer the homosexual on a course to 'normal' heterosexual feelings, patients were advised to stop masturbating, and encouraged to fantasize about women – if necessary, they should make regular trips to a brothel. In addition, new medical therapies were introduced to assist their normalization with potential 'remedies' being tried out such as hypnotism, hydrotherapy and faradization (which involved small electrical shocks being passed through the body). At the time, these ideas of the sexologists were considered a revolution in compassionate thinking.

Initially, most of the sexologists concurred with the belief that 'sexual inverts', as they called homosexuals, were born, not made. They argued that because these feelings were innate, homosexuals could not be blamed for their sexual preferences. The onset of the investigation began when Karl Heinrich Ulrichs wrote about an alternative sexuality in which he classified homosexual men as 'urnings' and lesbians as 'urninds'. He had had first-hand knowledge of the experiences of those suffering punishment as a result of their sexual inclinations while working as a legal advisor in Hanover, and his aim was to change the law. However, because of his public persona, when his homosexuality was discovered he lost his job. In a series of books published between 1864 and 1879, beginning with *The Riddle of Male-Male Love*, he urged people to consider urning not as sinful or criminal but as natural. German psychiatrists took up the debate when Carl Westphal published *Die Konträre Sexualempfindung* (1869) on 'contrary sexual feelings'. He was joined by Fabian and philosopher Edward Carpenter, whose publication *The Intermediate Sex* (1908) considered men's right to love each other. For the first time, sexologists were bringing the topic of homosexuality into the medical realm and exposing the injustices of legal punishments.

Within this forum, sexologists began to explore who might become homosexual, and why. In his *Principles of Psychology* (1890), William James favoured the congenital consensus and believed the

Nude male youths photographed by Wilhelm von Gloeden, from his *Taormina*
series, *c.* 1893.

essence of the feeling to be in all men; he saw inversion as 'a kind of
sexual appetite of which very likely most men possess the germinal
possibility'.[32] Albert Moll extended this theory; he believed that there
were feminine and masculine feelings in both sexes from childhood,
'that a homosexual tendency is very frequent in normal children'.[33]
Freud concurred with this idea, stating that most boys and girls display homosexual tendencies when they reached puberty. Indeed,
in Freud's evolvement of psychoanalysis, he placed most anomalies

Male bathers, 1970s.

Thomas Eakins, *Swimming*, 1885, oil on canvas.

of sexual aberration within the frame of childhood experience. Since he believed that these tendencies remained in neurotic people, Freud never carried out any psychoanalysis of men or women 'without discovering a significant homosexual tendency'. Krafft-Ebing, along with these other sexologists, also encouraged a more accepting stance on homosexuality, referring to homosexuals as 'step-children of nature'. Although Krafft-Ebing had initially seen homosexuality as a congenital disease or degeneration, he later modified his view after seeing the mental superiority of some of his homosexual patients, recognizing them to be educated, intelligent men devoid of mental illness or incapacities. Part of this modification of his ideas was a result of patients who, inspired by his non-judgemental stance, had written to him to explain their own feelings and experiences.

Unlike Krafft-Ebing, fellow sexologist Havelock Ellis believed that homosexuality might also be acquired or learned behaviour, and considered the effects of childhood influences. In his book *Sexual Inversion*, published in Britain in 1897, he pondered on the onset of homosexuality while investigating the topic of schoolboys and concluded that most homosexuality begins in school. To illustrate his point, he provided an example letter from one of his correspondents which highlighted this man's own experience of schoolboy sexual inverts. The correspondent suggested there were three types: those who were 'radically inverted', who targeted the corruption of younger boys; those who had been introduced to homosexuality as passive victims in youth, then gone on to practise active and passive acts with other known homosexuals, but would not contemplate 'corrupting fresh victims'; and young boys who found pleasure through masturbation or intercrural sex, but were probably ignorant of any sort of sexual morality. The correspondent thought that the appropriate punishments for the worst offenders should be the birch for their first offence and expulsion for the second; for the third category of offenders – those too young to know better – it was better to leave them to grow out of it. 'After all', he commented, 'there is no reason to ruin a boy's prospects because he is a little beast at sixteen.'[34]

By the time he wrote his treatise, Ellis believed that Krafft-Ebing's definition was no longer acceptable. He believed that the old categories of 'acquired' or 'congenital' inversion were not enough, suggesting rather that both a predisposition to homosexuality and an acquired taste for it were necessary for homosexuality to develop. Even when homosexuality became apparent only in later life, Ellis sees it as a 'retarded' or latent congenital inversion. He refers to Iwan Bloch, who gave the example of pseudo-homosexuality or, as he termed it, 'secondary homosexuality', something which we would now call 'situational homosexuality'. This occurs when members of the same sex are confined together for long periods of time, say in prison, on board ship or in barracks, where there is no alternative sex to choose. Some people in this situation are merely making the best of a bad situation for their particular tastes and revert back to their preferred heterosexuality when out of their institution.

Indeed, most sexologists were keen to differentiate between the 'true' invert and the pseudo-homosexual; to separate those who possessed the sexual impulse or inclination from those involved in homosexual acts for other reasons. Magnus Hirschfeld revealed three types of men whom he called 'spurious inverts', who involved themselves in homosexual acts but could not really to be considered true homosexuals. First, there were those who indulged in acts for money – male prostitutes and blackmailers; second, those who allowed homosexuality for the reasons of friendship, good nature or pity of their homosexual admirers; and finally, those who were in 'situational' homosexuality. The sexual act itself was seen as no proof of sexual impulse or inclination. However, Ellis questioned whether Hirschfeld's categories were worthwhile. There was no proof that people in these categories were bisexual or had true homosexual inclinations.

It may seem obvious now that different people have different leanings to varying degrees. In the past (and to a large extent still, particularly outside the West), social conditioning and laws making homosexuality illegal have pushed many people into heterosexuality who might not have been naturally inclined to the opposite sex. Sexologists helped to bring the topic into the open, at least airing it within medical discussions, and pushed for changes to the law concerning the treatment of homosexuals.

Camping Out

At the beginning of the twentieth century, as men were finding new ways to entertain themselves, the police were finding new ways to prosecute them. Out and out 'queens' were more susceptible to being picked up by police, as they were more obvious by their 'campness' – dressed in frocks, with painted lips and powder, they were hard to miss. Police blotted their faces for traces of make-up to use as evidence. Homosexual men responded to police harassment by forging their own hidden areas where they might pick up like-minded men and have sex – in urinals at the Black Lion pub on Kilburn High Road and in Fair Street, Bermondsey, in London, for example. In the face of these persecutions, men in drag showed considerable personal courage in declaring themselves so openly. The trial of Oscar Wilde was not far behind them and men were well aware of the dangers in being declared a homosexual. Unfortunately, police knew where to find their prey and made visits to the most popular urinals as part of their regular beat. Searching under cubicle doors for more than one pair of feet, they bashed down doors in order to catch men in the act. Parks remained popular cruising grounds. In London, Clapham Common, Hampstead Heath and Hyde Park were old favourites, as were the main throughways of Oxford Street, Leicester Square and Trafalgar Square. A Reverend Peel complained in 1922, 'One only has to walk through Hyde Park . . . to see couples . . . lying on top of each other . . . the sights to be seen near Marble Arch are disgusting.'[35]

Meanwhile, soldiers hung out below the National Gallery, known as the 'meat rack', while queens preferred Piccadilly Circus and the surrounding, less obvious, streets. New clubs emerged where men met to dance and drink together – at the Caravan in Endell Street at the corner of Shaftesbury Avenue, the Criterion bar in Piccadilly Circus and Billie's Club in Little Denmark Street. It was ironic that bathhouses, such as Bermondsey Turkish Baths, built for the working poor as a result of the upright Victorian obsession with cleanliness, emerged as one of the most notorious and favourite places to find homosexual sex. Even the rich and famous found their enjoyment in bathhouses – film star Rock Hudson was a frequent visitor to the Savoy Turkish Baths and the writer Christopher Isherwood took composer Benjamin Britten there for his first 'outing'. For six shillings for an overnight stay, it offered a 'safe' place for men to have sex together, but often little sleep. One man complained, 'I slept for a week in a Turkish bath, which meant virtually, that I did not sleep at all.'[36] A camp language known as Polari allowed men to communicate in code without other people under-standing them. This method of speech could be traced back at least to the seventeenth century and was a mixture of Italian, Greek, German, French and London cockney rhyming slang with a smat-tering of Yiddish and Romany, commonly used by workers in fairgrounds and circuses.

A self-imposed difference existed between men who had sex with other men. Some men who recognized themselves as homosexual during the 1920s and '30s called themselves 'queer'. Others who were also having sex with men did not see themselves as anything other than 'normal' (what we would now call 'straight' or heterosex-ual), and did not see themselves as 'queer'. Working-class men who sold themselves in order to make extra cash were among those who saw themselves as 'normal' and became known as 'rough trade'; some of them were married or had girlfriends. They saw their actions as part of a tough masculine life. Because women were seen as 'hard to get', men had to look for sex where it was offered. This made diffi-culties for some queers who accidentally misjudged them. As one self-confessed queer admitted in a letter to another man after trying to pick him up in the Caravan, 'Just a note to say that I was very dis-appointed of you . . . I honestly thought you were queer, but different from the others'.[37]

A different attitude towards homosexuality developed among many British working-class families and a relationship between a man and a youth might be accepted. It was even welcomed in some families where extra income might be earned from the friendship. When a fourteen-year-old boy, John, delivered groceries to one Charles R every week in 1922, a sexual relationship developed, as the boy explained, 'I used to help clean up. He used to be with me in the bedroom and play about with my privates. He used to undress me and used to undress himself . . . He used to put his privates up my back passage.'[38] Charles used to give him a £10 note every time he visited him and this became an integral part of John's family income. His mother and father knew about their relationship but seemed to have accepted it, even forming their own relationships with Charles. The boy's mother borrowed money from him and in turn gave him coal and chickens during the general strike of 1926. However, gen-eral anti-homosexual sentiment existed at least until the 1960s in Britain and America.

After Stonewall, the first Gay Pride march, New York, 1970.

A seismic shift occurred in public opinion when the Stonewall riots erupted after a raid on a bar in Christopher Street, New York, on 27 June 1969. Gays flooded the streets in protest at the treatment they received from the authorities, resulting in violent demonstrations. Others joined in and the protests continued the following evening, and again some weeks later. Activists gathered and established openly gay and lesbian bars where people could mingle instead of gathering at furtive meetings in oft-raided secret clubs. Gay Pride marches began to take place throughout the world on a yearly basis to commemorate the riots. More exclusive gay and lesbian bars emerged with the arrival of the discos of the 1970s and '80s, where specialized drugs were introduced to enhance sensation – poppers, amphetamines and cocaine became the accessories to a good night out. The gay man as queen gave way to the moustached macho-man in tight denims, white T-shirt and with muscles to die for. Cruising in toilets, bathhouses and parks continued unabated and a new gay culture was born.

Gradually attitudes were changing and laws were introduced to catch up. Activists in both Norway and Denmark had already set up their first homosexual organizations in 1948 and had long been campaigning for gay and lesbian rights – homosexuality was legal from 1933 in Norway and 1944 in Sweden (but was already legal from the 1790s in some countries such as France, Monaco, Luxembourg and

Belgium). For most Western countries changes in the laws around homosexuality came later, from around the 1960s: 1967 in the UK, state by state in America but legal nationwide only in 2003. The Netherlands and Denmark had already begun the new wave of openness to gay living in the 1960s; North America, Britain and Germany did so later, in the 1970s; and Spain not until the 1980s. However, the arrival of Aids in the 1980s saw a speedy halt drawn to the freedom of gays as health officials demanded the closing of all bathhouses, bars and backrooms. Although this period suffocated easily attainable sex, a better understanding emerged about preventing sexually transmitted diseases. A realignment of gay culture in the 1990s saw gay men heading for holiday destinations such as Mykonos, Ibiza, Fire Island, Miami's South Beach and Palm Springs to meet other gay men. Nowadays with Internet culture and sites such as Gaydar, no gay man need be alone.

A complete turn around in attitudes towards gays has occurred in areas of medicine as well as law. In 1973, homosexuality was first removed from the *Diagnostic and Statistical Manual of Mental Disorders* list by the American Psychiatric Association. Before then, medically speaking it was still considered a 'perversion'. Most European countries did not allow same-sex marriage until the end of the first decade of the second millennium. Today 'civil partnerships' or gay marriages are accepted in Norway, Denmark and Britain and many other European countries. Again, Scandinavian countries led the way against homophobic discrimination with Norway becoming the first country to impose laws in 1981; Denmark made the first same-sex unions legal as early as 1989; and gender neutral marriages have been legal in Norway and Sweden since 2009. Slowly, other European countries have followed suit. As a result of the new anti-homophobic laws, at the beginning of 2012, one psychotherapist faced being stripped of her accreditation to the British Association for Counselling and Psychotherapy after treating a patient who said he wanted to be 'cured' of his homosexuality, an illustration as to how far attitudes have changed in the perception of homosexuality. It is not only forbidden in law to discriminate against homosexuals but homosexuality can no longer be seen as an 'illness' to be cured. Although most countries in the West consider homosexuality to be acceptable, there is still much discrimination. In May 2012, St Petersburg's Governor Georgy Poltavchenko approved a law penalizing 'the propaganda of homosexuality and paedophilia among minors'. The law effectively outlawed any Gay Pride events as well as linking homosexuality with paedophilia.

For years there have been discussions about whether homo-sexual feelings are natural or nurtured, determined by biology or constructed by society. The old debate reurfaces in new arguments about whether a 'gay gene' exists, but what should really matter is why people think it is so important to differentiate between different types of sexualities or predilections and why homosexuals were (and still are) not always accorded equal rights with heterosexuals.

Symposium scene, two prostitutes. Red-figure cup, *c.* 5th century.

FOUR

From Female Friendships to Lipstick Lesbians

Homosexuality may nearly always be suspected in females who wear their
hair short, who dress in the fashion of men.

Richard von Krafft-Ebing, *Psychopathia Sexualis* (1886)

Although lesbianism has been considered a perversion at times
in the past, overall it has created less furore than male homosexuality. Close female relationships were of small significance to society at large, probably because women were considered less important
than men. Women could carry out the most intimate of relationships
without raising undue concern from observers. Indeed, passionate
female friendships were considered normal right up until the twentieth century. Although occasionally queries hung over certain women
with more 'masculine' qualities, little attention was paid to them
apart from the odd derogatory remark. Famous women were an
exception and gossip surrounded queens such as Marie Antoinette
of France and Christina of Sweden; both were accused of being lesbians. Such attacks were often used as part of political invective and
a way of denigrating the subject rather than having any basis in fact.

Uncovering the lesbian has proved more difficult than finding
her male homosexual counterpart as she was often hidden from
view. Certainly there were lots of names for her – Sapphist, Tommy,
butch, femme, dyke – and she does occasionally become noticed in
pamphlets, trial reports, medical records and newspapers. But as
long as she was domesticated and modest and deferred to men,
she would be ignored. She might conduct lesbian affairs without
causing suspicion if she resigned herself to an outward appearance
of decorum. Women were rarely arrested or hanged for the crime of
being sexually attracted to their own sex, as men were, and lesbianism was never made illegal, although lesbians were persecuted
under different laws (fraud, indecency, sodomy). It was only when
women were seen to be wayward or stepping out of their allotted
domestic role that they were considered trouble. Then it was often

their rebelliousness that created antagonism rather than their desires. Was this to do with people's ideas of what form lesbian sex might take? Indeed, was there any understanding about it at all?

Over the last few decades, historic cases have emerged which show women who sought each other for sex, companionship and love.[1] In this search, historians have divided lesbians into certain identifiable categories: female hermaphrodites; 'female husbands' who 'married' other women and took them as their wives; women who conducted lifelong 'female friendships' and sometimes shared a home; women who lived with other women in shared communities; and transvestite women who 'passed' as men (although some women who dressed as men did so for work opportunities, for adventure and the sense of freedom it gave them).

Sapphist Beginnings

The earliest well-known lesbian was Sappho, who lived on the island of Lesbos in ancient Greece and was thought to have been born around 612 BC. Her poems were highly regarded, according to an epigram in *Anthologia Palatina* (9.506) ascribed to Plato: 'Some say the Muses are nine: how careless! / Look, there's Sappho too, from Lesbos, the tenth.' Her name came to be associated not only with her poetry but also with the term 'Sapphist', which describes women's desire for their own sex; the term 'lesbian' derives from inhabitants of her island, Lesbos. There, she seems to have run a type of girls' boarding school, where she prepared young women for marriage and taught them singing and music. Although it is not known for sure, she may have led a thiasos (θιασος), a group of women who worshipped Aphrodite and celebrated the Muses. Both these were seen as perfectly acceptable pursuits, and feelings for other women were not considered exceptional. But whether Sappho was a lesbian at all is debatable. Certainly, in her writings she speaks of her desire for certain women and the yearning to fall asleep on the soft bosom of her female companion. She addresses female lovers, lovers of lovers, ex-lovers and other women by name – Anactoria, Atthis, Andromeda, Mnasidika, Eranna (although they may be fictional). But there is nothing more explicit, and since only short fragments of her poems remain, it is hard to infer anything more definite. Her orientation can only be guessed at, although it is thought that she had sex with men too; she

Engraving of
Sappho from Mary
Cowden Clarke,
*World-noted
Women* (1883).

had a daughter, Cleis, 'like a golden flower'.[2] However, none of the details about Sappho's biography are reliable.

Ancient Sparta was another place where women's desire for each other supposedly flourished. Women and girls lived apart from men and boys, and at seven years old boys were taken to live under the *agoge* system in communal barracks, where they were disciplined and trained for war. They could not leave active service until they were 30, but they were encouraged to marry. Girls were brought up together, educated in writing and practised athletics together naked; close affinities existed between girls and women and sometimes developed into sexual relationships. Plutarch informs us that Spartan women often had special relationships, unlike others in Greece, in which older and younger women had erotic feelings for each other.[3] Since men were often at war, women were left to their own devices, and it seems natural they should turn to each other for companionship and sex.

Under the Roman Empire, some prostitutes were alleged to have inclinations for other women. In his *Dialogues of the Courtesans*, written in the late second century AD, the satirist Lucian wrote about

Megilla from Lesbos, who employed the services of a courtesan, Leaina. Her male friend Clonarion tells Leaina, 'People say Megilla, the wealthy lady from Lesbos, is in love with you, as if she were a man, and that she . . . I can't explain . . . but . . . I have heard it said that the two of you couple up just like . . .'. Clonarion is unable to put into words exactly what he means. When Leaina blushes and admits this to be true, more excitedly, he exclaims, 'By the great Adrasteia! You must tell me about it! What does that woman require of you? Exactly what do you do when you get in bed together?' Even then it seems, men wanted to know what two women could do together sexually. Leaina herself was initially curious and asked Megilla, 'Do you have a penis? Do you do to Demonassa what men do?' Megilla replied that she did

Bronze figure of a running girl, *c.* 520–500 BC, found at Prizren, Serbia, and possibly made in or near Sparta, Greece.

not have a penis but something far more pleasant – she had a penis substitute. According to Leaina, Megilla looked like a male athlete, with her head shaven under her wig, and asked to be called under the male name Megillus. Although Megilla believed herself to be a man in the body of a woman, she had no trouble satisfying her lovers sexually. If Lucian's attitude was common among Romans, it would seem that they showed little concern about lesbianism, merely curiosity. They saw their society and sex as essentially phallic and had difficulty construing life in any other way.[4] By the medieval period, this laissez-faire attitude would change to some extent. Although most women's close relationships would be ignored and the subject of sex left unmentioned, when cases did come to light, the women involved were heavily condemned by the authorities.

Medieval 'Sex Without Men'

In the Christian era, the Bible defined its opinion about same-sex relationships. Referring to the unrighteous, it explained,

> For this reason God gave them up to dishonourable passions. For their women exchanged natural relations for those that are contrary to nature; and the men likewise gave up natural relations with women and were consumed with passion for one another (Romans 1:26–7).

There was therefore an understanding that such behaviour existed but it was considered against the natural laws of God. However, surprisingly Leviticus makes no prohibitions about sex between women, as it does about sex between men. Nonetheless, the Church authorities seem to have been aware of the possibilities and gave out subtle warnings. For example, St Augustine expressed his concerns about intimacy between holy women, suggesting that love for a fellow Sister 'ought not to be earthly but spiritual'.[5] Nunneries, in particular, were thought to be places that encouraged lascivious thoughts between women. We know this as the early medieval punishments for women who had 'sex without men' were aimed solely at nuns. The penalties, though, were surprisingly light. Nuns would be given a penance of 38 days on bread and water if they had mutually masturbated each other, 40 days if they had slept together, and two years if such sins took place when either woman was menstruating.[6]

Although lesbianism was not criminalized under civil law, Church authorities treated some sexual acts between women as sodomy. These were acts which involved penetration, with dildo-like devices or homemade strap-on penis substitutes. Hincmar, Archbishop of Reims (d. 882), warned about women who used such 'instruments of diabolical operations' to excite desire. Burchard, Bishop of Worms, recommended three years' penance for women who had used artificial penises.[7] How far these crimes and punishments filtered down into lay people's awareness is hard to detect, but the public would have been aware of certain behaviour when scandals emerged. One such scandal in Speyer, Germany in 1477 involved Katherina Hertzeldorfer, who was arrested after various women reported that she had had sex with them 'like a man'. Hertzeldorfer admitted that she 'made an instrument with a red piece of leather, at the front filled with cotton, and a wooden stick stuck into it, and made a hole through the wooden stick, put a string through, and tied it round'.[8] She informed the prosecution that she had first penetrated her lover with one finger, then with two, then after trying a third, she entered them with the dildo strapped to her. In such cases where a penis substitute had been used for penetration, the Church authorities took a harsh line – they applied capital punishment, just as they did to men who were found guilty of sodomy. Hertzeldorfer was sentenced to be drowned. When similar crimes took place in Treviso, Italy, female sodomites were stripped naked, then staked out for a day and a night. Criminal prosecutions, however, were still rare and when Church authorities did come across sexual incidents between women, they often preferred to deal with the case themselves within the confines of the Church. This was the situation in the case of two lesbian nuns, Benedetta Carlini and Bartolomea Crivelli; their affair was uncovered in 1619 but after a lengthy investigation by the all-male church authorities, the nuns were simply separated and sent to live in different convents.[9]

By the time the authorities of Basel had uncovered the activities of Elisabeth Hertner in 1647, the witchcraft craze had hit Europe and accusations of sodomy were associated with sorcery. Indeed, witches were accused of all sorts of debauchery as well as making pacts with the devil. Part of the pre-trial method of inquiry was to torture the

Etching showing dildo making, from Nicolas Chorier, *L'Académie des dames* (1680).

A nun masturbates a young woman, from Chorier, *L'Académie des dames* (1680).

Hans Baldung
Grien, *The Three
Witches*, 1514.

accused witch and force a confession. Hertner admitted under torture
to having bewitched the wife of the carpenter who happened to be
a cousin of hers, and that the pair had committed 'shameful acts'
together. As was the case with many cases of sodomy, the authorities were unwilling to advertise the crime too broadly for fear of a
public outcry and preferred to keep the case quiet. Instead, they put
Hertner under protective custody.[10]

In America, prior to independence, British law applied (or at
least was enacted with amendments). Since there was no civil law
against lesbians, Puritan leader John Cotton thought it prudent to
try to introduce one. To this end, in 1636 he proposed that sex
between two women (or two men) should be made a capital offence
in Massachusetts Bay. His proposed law reiterated the sentiments of
Romans; 'Unnatural filthiness, to be punished with death, whether
sodomy, which is carnal fellowship of man with man, or woman

with woman, or buggery, which is carnal fellowship of man or woman with beasts or fowls.'[11] However, this law was never enacted.

The Female Hermaphrodite

When hermaphrodites were described in the ancient world, they were identified as having both male and female sex organs. In Greek myth, hermaphrodites were legion: Dyalos, the androgyne; Arsenothelys, the man-woman; Gynnis, the effeminate; Agdistis, with two sexes; Tiresias, who was successively a man and a woman. Medics have known about such bodily forms since ancient times. The most famous was Aphroditus, sometimes known as the later god Hermaphroditus, whose name means 'Aphroditus in the form of a herm'.[12] Aphroditus was portrayed as having a female shapely form and clothing like Aphrodite's but also as having a penis.[13] Hermaphrodites became increasingly discussed during the sixteenth century, with authors such as Ambroise Paré and Jacques Duval writing on the subject. Both medical author and jurist were attempting to impose an identification of a single sex on a person's body, be it male, female or hermaphrodite. From France, the topic spread to the Reformation countries of Germany and Switzerland, but only became popular a century or more later in Britain.[14]

By the seventeenth century, with increasing interest in science and the emergence of the new field of medicine, religious attacks on lesbians – few that they were – were gradually being superseded by investigations by physicians. These doctors were less interested in the state of the women's soul than that of her body. In order to explain a lesbian's condition, they therefore devised theories about a woman's physiology to explain her sexual leanings. Increasingly, the term 'hermaphrodite' came to be applied to women, particularly those who showed masculine tendencies, their bodies seemingly betraying them. The female hermaphrodite was judged to be a woman who desired other women because of her over-large clitoris, and was sometimes labelled a Sapphist or a tribade. A woman may have been born like that, or her clitoris may have grown in later life. In some cases, over-masturbation was blamed for this elongation. When this practice turned into a habit, it could lead to nymphomania or same-sex passions called 'tribadism'.

The clitoris was known to have been the seat of a woman's pleasure. The English midwife Jane Sharpe in *The Midwives Book* (1671)

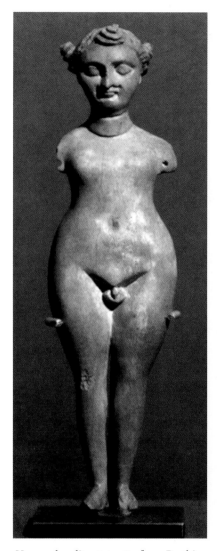

Hermaphrodite statuette from Parthian period Babylonia, 1st century BC–1st century AD

Statue of Hermaphroditus.

pointed out, 'At the bottom of the woman's belly is a little bank called a mountain of pleasure near the well-spring . . .'.[15] The bigger the clitoris, it was thought, the lewder the woman, and the more inclined to tribadism. Sharpe knew of some women in which 'sometimes it grows so long that it stands forth at the slit like a Yard [penis], and will swell and stand stiff if it be provoked, and some lewd women have

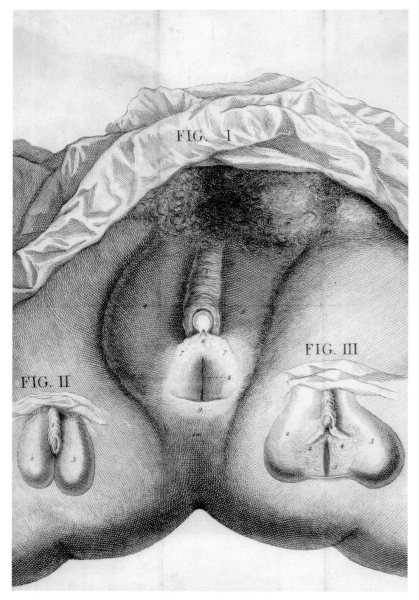

From James Parsons, *A Mechanical and Critical Enquiry into the Nature of Hermaphrodites* (1741).

endeavoured to use it as men do theirs.'[16] Similarly, James Parsons, Fellow of the Royal Society, investigated the nature of hermaphrodites in his book *A Mechanical and Critical Enquiry into the Nature of Hermaphrodites* (1741). When he wrote of hermaphrodites he was in fact writing about women with extremely large clitorises. He declared, 'There are many authors who have given Histories of Women that have been detected in the Abuse of such large Clitorides calling themselves *Tribasi*' (lesbians). He cited another Fellow, Thomas Allen, who had also presented a paper to the Royal Society and had found, 'These Tribades were no more than Women with clitorides larger than ordinary.' But these women were thought to have abnormal reactions. On examination of one such hermaphrodite he found 'That at the Sight of a Woman her Penis was erected, and became flaccid at the Sight of a Man'. From this he concluded, 'I can conceive of no other than that she has more desire to the Woman than the Man.'[17]

Women who dressed as men to live with other women were also sometimes labelled hermaphrodites. These women have been called 'Female Husbands', a stereotypical title that alludes to a woman who played the part of a husband, dressing as a man and going through with a marriage ceremony with another woman. They were more likely to be condemned than the non-masculinized lesbian. They were thought to indulge in sex by committing 'frotterism' (rubbing their genitalia up and down against each other). One such case came to light in London in 1682 after it was found that one Amy Poulter had married Arabella Hunt in Marylebone Church two years previously while disguised as 'James Howard'. At the time, Poulter was still married to her (male) husband Arthur, who only died a year after the case came to light. Poulter suggested that her marriage to Hunt had been undertaken, 'not seriously, but rashly and unduly and in a frollick jocular and facetious manner'.[18] According to a female servant who was called as a witness at the trial, it would seem that Poulter was dressed as a woman when she courted Hunt. This would indicate that Hunt therefore knew Poulter's true sexual identity, particularly since they had lived together 'as Man and Wife at bed and Board' for six months prior to the wedding. Nonetheless, Hunt claimed that she left her (female) husband as soon as she found that Poulter was a 'hermaphrodite'. Yet midwives denied that there was any physical abnormality and attested to the fact that Poulter was 'a perfect woman in all her parts'. The case was strewn with complexities and it would seem that Hunt and her mother were gold-diggers trying to tie themselves to Poulter's wealth, rather than the pursuit coming from the other direction. In this case, the wedding was annulled.

Usually, the authorities reacted more vehemently when women married other women. In his narrative *The Female Husband* (1746), Henry Fielding told of how Mary, aka George Hamilton, was punished for dressing as a man and marrying on numerous occasions: 'The prisoner having been convicted of this base and scandalous crime, was by the court sentenced to be publicly severely whipt for several times, in four market towns within Somerset to wit, once in each market town, and to be imprisoned.'[19] The pamphlet could be brought from booksellers and hawkers for sixpence, so the public was well informed about such behaviour. John Cleland reported another case of tribadism in *Historical and Physical Dissertation on the Case of Catherine Vizzani* (1751), in which the surgeon suspected Catherine might have an elongated clitoris because of her proclivities but was surprised on examination of her body after her death to find her normal. Cleland called her inclinations 'Perversion in the Imagination'.[20]

By the Enlightenment period, although men were persecuted for sodomy, no explanations were sought for their actions. Yet in the case of women, attempts were being made to find the cause of their same-sex desire – men simply did not understand why they might prefer other women rather than men. During the 1600s and 1700s, tribades had been seen as either physiologically different, as hermaphrodites; or as rebellious, purposefully upsetting the natural order of things by aping men; or as witches, and therefore corrupted. Yet explanations that the woman was corrupted physically, morally or spiritually were found wanting, and new medical explanations were sought. This resulted in blame being placed on their hermaphroditism. In cases where there were no outward signs of masculinity or masculine dress, women could carry on with their relationships more easily.

Enlightened Tribades

Female friendships existed between intelligent women, but were sometimes more intimate than at first glance. During the early eighteenth century in the court of Queen Anne, gossip flourished about the intimate relationship the queen had formed with some of her ladies-in-waiting. She was accused of running a court full of tribades, headed by her long-standing lady-in-waiting Sarah Churchill, the

Duchess of Marlborough. Although Sarah was married to a man of political influence and was to bear him seven children, she had become the subject of malicious rumour because of her position. As the main confidante of the queen, she wielded great power and the attacks were no doubt politically motivated. When the queen's affections drifted towards Abigail Marsham (to whom Sarah had introduced her), Sarah became jealous and increasingly belligerent towards the queen, causing a permanent breakdown in their friendship. As a result, Sarah lost her influence at court.[21]

Lesbian coteries existed in country houses where 'female friends' openly loved each other. Anne Lister, who wrote a diary about her relationships, led one such group of women. Her lovers in her community knew each other and shared her desires. Confident enough to walk the lanes picking up the local young women, Lister was obviously successful in her courting. As the prospective owner of Shibden Hall in Halifax, she may have thought her class would offer her some immunity against attack, but this was not to be. With her short hair and masculinized clothes (although she still wore petticoats), she became a target for the local youths, proving that it was still impossible to be overt about being attracted to other women without risk of insult. She took solace in visiting others like herself, travelling to meet the 'Ladies of Llangollen', Sarah Ponsonby and her older partner Eleanor Butler. The pair had fallen in love when young and had been together for 42 years, 31 of them spent in a cottage in Wales. Mrs Davis, their housekeeper, told Anne they were 'so attached, so amiable together'.[22] The couple had become notorious, with socialites from all over the country dropping in to see them. Even where female friendships were seen to be what they really were – lesbian affairs – they often passed without too much adverse comment.

Other all-female communities, such as convents, were seen to be potentially vice-ridden. The image of the lesbian nun was rife in Enlightenment anti-clerical pornographic books. The French philosopher Diderot had already been imprisoned for writing pornography eleven years earlier, when his novel *La Religieuse* (The Nun) was published in 1760. The book was based on the real-life story of Marguerite Delamarre, a woman who had been placed in a convent against her will and had been subjected to cruel treatment by her debauched superiors. Essentially, the memoirs are pornographic fiction seen in the actions of the character of the Mother Superior: 'Let down

Joshua Horner,
Anne Lister
(1791–1840).

your underclothing! I am a woman and your Superior. What a splendid bosom! How firm it is! Am I to allow it to be torn by the nails of that whip?'[23] While Diderot's intention was to expose the hypocrisy of the Church – and the book certainly caused a stir at the time – in fact his attacks were nothing new and Diderot was merely building on a genre which other writers of Enlightenment erotica had already explored. The theme of lesbian nuns had been evident as early as *Venus in the Cloister* (1683), which tells of the seduction of a novice by an older (and therefore more corrupt) nun.

Where most countries in Europe were happy to pretend sex acts between women did not exist, the Netherlands stands out as one of the few that followed a path of focused persecution. During the 1790s, a flurry of cases was brought to court in which women were prosecuted. At least one incident had seemingly taken place in a brothel or 'lewd' house in which Anna Schreuder and Maria Smit were caught after an interfering neighbour had witnessed them when peeping through the wall into the house. Not willing to let it pass, she pulled in another neighbour to watch – which they did for the next two hours. Finally, unable to contain herself, she shouted out, 'you foul whores, we can see you . . . didn't you foul long enough?' and went off to raise a hue and cry. Such a crowd developed that a constable had to rescue Schreuder, who was found cowering naked under her bed, along with four other women who were also in the house. At the trial, the neighbours gave evidence that they had seen the women 'lain with their lower bodies nude and had kissed and caressed one another, like a man is used to do to a women'. They had also conducted oral sex – one 'had licked the womanliness of the other with her tongue'.[24] Although Schreuder and Smit had been involved in prostitution, sex with women was their preferred enjoyment. In other

The Ladies of Llangollen, Eleanor Butler and Sarah Ponsonby, lithograph by
J. H. Lynch, *c.* 1880.

A woman shows off the delights of her friend's posterior in a drawing by Antoine Borel, from Jean-Baptiste de Boyer (attrib.), *Thérèse philosophe* (1785 edition).

parts of Europe, tribadism was invisible. However, a new wave of feminism was to create more focused attacks on women who thrust themselves into public view.

The New Woman

With the emergence of the 'New Woman' in the 1890s, women began to carve out new opportunities for themselves. This 'New Woman' was a modern woman with independent views on work, marriage and dress. She abandoned the traditional 'feminine' aspirations of staying at home and raising children in preference for a career.

As new professions opened up for them, middle-class women flooded to work in areas previously unavailable such as medicine, university teaching, administration and accountancy. The streets filled with female workers travelling to and from jobs outside the home, the women now public in a way they had never been before. Meanwhile, middle-class men were growing increasingly concerned about so many women vying for employment, and about their demands for independence and the vote. In order to try and halt this progressive force, men began to deride these women for their 'masculine' activities, for dressing in 'rational' dress (with its split skirt akin to trousers), smoking cigars and riding bicycles. Male commentators began to connect these new female roles and women's masculine characteristics to nymphomania and lesbianism. They accused the New Woman who espoused free love (sex outside of marital relationships) as being 'vicious' – literally full of vice. Indeed, the idea of women wanting sex at all was considered a breach in normality. To Victorian onlookers, therefore, the New Woman's lifestyle suggested a wholesale sexual aberration. This New Woman was muscular, with a deep voice; her rooms were decorated with sporting scenes and pistols and smelled of smoke.[25]

Some of the women had literary aspirations and made their living through writing, the poet Charlotte Mew being a typical example.[26] One of her stories was published in the *Yellow Book*, a leading quarterly journal of the 1890s associated with aestheticism and decadence, edited by Henry Harland and sometimes illustrated by Aubrey Beardsley. Some of Beardsley's drawings hinted at lesbianism, such as his illustrations for a new edition of *Lysistrata*. Following the fashion of many a New Woman, Mew dressed in masculine costume and wore her hair short. She also happened to be a lesbian, although not all New Women were – in reality, fewer than the British public imagined, although many were characterized as such.

Mew herself has been considered a 'chastely lesbian',[27] in other words, one who never consummated her relationships. However, this seems debateable since Ella D'Arcy accused Mew of chasing her round a bed. Another friend of Mew's, Mrs Dawson Scott, was nicknamed 'Sappho' by Mew after Scott's poem of that name. In response to Mew's sexuality and literary talent, Mrs Dawson Scott wrote in her diary, 'Charlotte is evidently a pervert. Aren't all geniuses perverts?'[28] However, life was not without its problems for Mew. It was difficult enough to pursue a literary career as a woman, and to be a lesbian, but tainted family genes were also to disrupt Mew's life. Mental illness

Charlotte Mew
(1869–1927).

wracked her family so badly that two of her siblings had to be placed
in asylums. As a result, Charlotte and her sister vowed they would
never marry or have children to prevent passing on the insanity.
Worse was to come when her sister Anne died, and Mew became
severely depressed. Unable to overcome her grief, she eventually committed suicide by drinking a bottle of Lysol, a household disinfectant.

The antagonisms and threats New Women had to face were in
addition to their problems of trying to eke out a living on the small
incomes they could make. Their vilification was common; a typical
example was a *Punch* cartoon in which a journalist described the
New Women as Amazonians destroying marriages and families. In
reality, many New Women were simply moving towards a fuller
understanding of heterosexual relations and personal freedom,
although obviously lesbians were attracted to the movement as much
as any other woman.

Meanwhile, in nineteenth-century America, lesbianism was
taking a different form and African American women were finding

Aubrey Beardsley, *Lysistrata Haranguing the Athenian Women*, 1896.

their own ways to forge their identities. Snippets of lesbian relationships emerge through the passionate letters of two African American women, freeborn domestic servant Addie Brown and schoolteacher Rebecca Primus. Their declarations of love to each other while they were separated reflected how much they missed each other. Addie confessed, 'Rebecca, when I bid you good by it's seem to me that my very heart broke . . .', adding, 'No *kisses* is like youres'. She also mentions fondling her lover's breasts, so the relationship was evidently sexual.[29]

Such relationships could not have been easily undertaken, and family members often stepped in to separate women. One passionate affair ended in murder when attempts were made to thwart it. The incident took place in Memphis in 1892 when nineteen-year-old Alice Mitchell met seventeen-year-old Freda Ward and became besotted with her. Their fathers were well known in business circles: Mitchell's was a rich furniture dealer and Ward's a planter and wealthy merchant. Both the young women were, according to the *New York Times*, 'familiar figures in society'. They had become increasingly close, so much so that Mitchell had planned to 'marry' Ward, but, sensing disaster, Ward's sister tried to prevent the relationship going further. Although Ward had stayed with Mitchell on occasions, the relationship had gradually cooled. Mitchell, however, was unwilling to let go and continued to pursue her erstwhile lover. When Ward made some derogatory remarks about Mitchell, no doubt in an attempt to get rid of her, this merely exacerbated Mitchell's feelings of rejection. One night, in a rage, she followed Ward and set upon her, cutting her lover's throat. The *New York Times* reported the incident in lurid detail: 'Grasping Miss Ward by the neck, she drew a bright razor from out of the folds of her dress and without a word, drew it across the throat of her victim.' Ward sank to the floor, her neck pouring with blood, the razor having severed her jugular. Although taken to the nearest hospital by her sister and members of the crowd, she was dead on arrival. Mitchell stated in court that she loved Freda desperately, 'better than anyone in the world', that she could not live without her. She told how they had made a pact that if they should ever be separated they should kill each other.[30] She was judged insane and committed to an asylum. Assessing the case some years later in his book *Sexual Inversion*, Havelock Ellis described Mitchell as a 'congenital invert', stating, 'her face was obviously unsymmetrical and she had an appearance of youthfulness below her age' – proof positive in Ellis's eyes that she had inherited her lesbianism and her 'problem'. He already believed that congenital defects ran in families and, in support of his theory, pointed to the fact that Mitchell's mother had been insane.[31]

The Female Sexual Invert

As with male homosexuality, sexologists saw lesbianism as sexual 'inversion', and classed it as a sort of mental illness. While some believed that lesbianism was congenital (the women were born lesbians), others believed these desires were acquired (as learned behaviour). Most concurred that once female inverts were in bed together, they split into the 'assertive' male and the 'passive' female roles. Most agreed that lesbianism should be repressed.

Again sexologists went on to discuss why and when women might become lesbians. Kraft-Ebbing pronounced that prostitution might turn a woman to lesbianism, a point he picked up from Alexandre Parent-Duchâtelet. The latter had written about prostitution in 1857, asserting that many prostitutes turn to their own sex because they were disgusted by the acts they were expected to perform with their male clients – coitus in the armpit, between the breasts and in the mouth. In fact, contemporary commentators blamed a host of activities that were supposed to turn women into lesbians – reading novels, female servants sleeping in the same bed, even some domestic activities. Contemporary lesbians might have been surprised at the proposal of hack writer Ali Coffignon, who suggested that excessive work on sewing machines enticed a woman into the vice.[32] However, Havelock Ellis disagreed with the idea that the lure of sewing was a means of developing lesbianism, but rather thought the opposite. In *Sexual Inversion* he stated: 'There is a dislike and sometimes incapacity for needlework and other domestic occupations, while there is often some capacity for athletics.'

The signs of lesbianism were all too apparent, and could be seen in a woman's brusqueness, masculine mannerisms and blunt speech. Even the most liberated sexologists associated female homosexuality with masculinity. Edward Carpenter attested to the fact that in 'the extreme type of the homogenic female, we have a rather mark-edly aggressive person, of strong passion, masculine manners and movements, practical in the conduct of life, sensuous rather than sentimental in love, often untidy, and outré in her attire'. The lurking lesbian could also be spotted for her oral appetites: 'In the habits not only is there frequently a pronounced taste for smoking cigarettes, often found in quite feminine women, but also a decided taste and tolerance for cigars.'[33] Physiology was also blamed for a lesbian's inclinations; Hirschfeld found that two-thirds of inverted women were more muscular than 'normal' women. Sometimes these 'defects' might offer hidden advantages: on examination, Flateau found lesbian women to have decidedly masculine larynxes and Ellis deduced as a result that 'inverted women are very good whistlers'.[34] Indeed, Hirschfeld knew of two who were so good they performed in public.

This allusion to masculine traits in some lesbian women was part of a broader understanding among sexologists that when women had sex together, one would automatically take the 'male' role. This, however, was denied by the women themselves in a study undertaken by Beam and Dickinson in America published in 1934, where the majority of women responded that neither of them assumed a male role.[35] Self-identified characteristics did not therefore necessarily mesh with (male) medical ones about how lesbians behave.

The Wild Girls

Paris was evidently more liberated in its attitudes towards lesbians, since it became a major attraction for like-minded women in the early twentieth century. Many American women crossed the ocean to set up home there and join in with the newly emerging creative atmosphere. Wild girls Natalie Clifford Barney and Romaine Brooks moved to the city, opening up a literary salon that became a hub of lesbianism between the 1890s and 1930s. Thirty-nine-year-old Barney had met 41-year-old Romaine Brooks, another rich American and a gifted artist, in 1915, and their relationship was to last more than 50 years. An extravagant poet, Barney insisted that 'living was the first of all the arts', celebrating the work and love of women in her salon at which men were permitted, but were not allowed to dominate. The American Alice B. Toklas described Barney as 'the one bright spot in a fairly cheerless world'.[36]

Lesbian prostitutes, illustration from Léo Taxil, *La Prostitution contemporaine* (1884).

On her father's death Barney inherited his millions, allowing her to fulfil her passion for literature and the arts. She was spoiled and utterly self-centred, and poured her energies into seduction, flirting and wooing her lovers, sometimes pursing women as far as the toilets of Parisian department stores. If they were too mentally well balanced, she would cast them off, preferring her lovers to be more quirky and stimulating. She conducted Sapphic rituals in her garden, which entailed women dancing naked or dressed as wood nymphs, shepherdesses or court pages, much to the disgust of her neighbours. Brooks came from a line of flamboyant insanity – her brother was even madder than her mother. She recalled her vile childhood of abandonment and cruelty in her unpublished autobiography *No Pleasant Memories*, using as her hallmark a wing held down by a chain, an indication of her feelings. While Barney enjoyed a gregarious social life, Brooks disparaged the salons as full of drunkards and society women, not really a fair description of such guests as Gertrude Stein, Colette, Edith Sitwell, Pierre Louÿs and André Gide. Although Barney was devoted to Brooks – she called her 'my angel and cruel love' – this did not stop her from indulging in other long-term relationships, such as a fourteen-year affair with Dolly Wilde, Oscar's drug-addicted niece. Even in 1956, when Barney travelled to see Brooks, she stayed at a hotel so as not to encroach on the artist's sealed world. Left to her own devices, when she was 80 years old, she picked up a new lover on a park bench – unfazed, Brooks simply accused her of showing off.

Alice B. Toklas and Gertrude Stein also recognized Paris as a liberated city where they might set up house together unharassed. In 1903 Stein wrote *Q.E.D.* (published posthumously in 1950 as *Things As They Are*), a lesbian coming-out story. In Paris she wrote her novels and poetry while Alice acted as her partner, maid and lover, and cooked her famous hash brownies.

Germany had its own vibrant lesbian community, symbolized by Marlene Dietrich in the film *The Blue Angel*. Dietrich herself was bisexual and flourished as a singer in the nightclubs of Berlin, enjoying the drag balls and performing at cabarets. The German lesbian scene had its own magazine, *Die Freundin* (The Girlfriend), which ran between 1924 and 1933 and carried stories of 'same-sex loving'. Meanwhile, in New York in 1920s Greenwich and Harlem, certain gay jazz clubs or speakeasies catered for lesbian women. White women attended clubs such as the Clam House and the Ubangi Club, where black singers such as Bessie Smith and Gladys Bentley sang about their female lovers. In these establishments, lesbians carved out swinging, autonomous lives for themselves.

Men were not so happy with the increasingly public roles for women, nor with the new work opportunities afforded to women during the First World War. They quickly tried to encourage their

Romaine Brooks
photographed in
1908.

wives and sisters back into the domestic space of home and children.
As one women's magazine, *Women's Life*, put it in their January issue
for 1920, 'Miss Fluffy femininity carried off all the prizes'.[37] However,
generally among working-class culture, there was an easier acceptance of lesbian couples. British newspaper reports in the *News of
the World* and the *People* exposed various wedding stories of two
women marrying, one taking the role as the groom, the other the
bride. The couples seem to have been accepted by their families and
gained respect as tricksters, with practising lesbians seen to be 'getting
away with it'.[38]

Marlene Dietrich, famous for her androgyny, *c*. 1930.

In 1921, after centuries of having no legislation against lesbianism, a Bill was introduced in Britain to try and make it illegal. During the House of Commons debate, Lieutenant Moore-Brabazon expressed his thoughts on the subject, stating that there were three ways of sorting out perverts. One was to give them the death sentence; the second was to lock them up in insane asylums; and the third – by far the best in his opinion – was to leave them alone. He opined: 'To adopt a Clause of this kind would do harm by introducing into the minds of perfectly innocent people the most revolting thoughts.'[39] In other words, he thought that drawing attention to lesbian activities was a greater threat than the need to prosecute lesbians. In this case, at least, lesbians were let off the hook. The act was never passed, mainly due to the British tradition of keeping quiet about anything considered too unsavoury.

Harassment of lesbians nonetheless existed, and women tended to prefer to keep their relationships private. Vita Sackville-West kept quiet about her lesbian relationships, although as the daughter of a baron she presumably had more freedom than most. When her husband gave her a venereal disease, she took up with Violet Keppel, daughter of the mistress of the Prince of Wales, who seduced her. Sackville-West admitted, 'I hadn't dreamt of such an art of love . . . She appealed to my awakened senses.'[40] Since her husband was also homosexual, it is unsurprising that the two did not find gratification in each other's arms. West went on to have a passionate affair with Virginia Woolf, who wrote *Orlando* in 1928 as a tribute to West, by then her past lover.

It was Radclyffe Hall's book *The Well of Loneliness* (1928) that truly put lesbianism on the map. Her story of female invert Stephen Gordon showed how lesbians lived in a sea of hostility, particularly if they were 'mannish lesbians', as the character was portrayed – and as was Hall herself. Her own perception of both herself and her character echoed the sexologists' understanding of female inverts – 'a man trapped inside a woman's body'. She recognized the isolation suffered by many lesbians, which was her reason for writing the book: she wanted to inspire 'the inverted in general to declare themselves', and at the same time she was well aware of the dangers that might befall her, declaring in a letter to another literary scholar,

> I knew I was running the risk of injuring my career as a writer by rousing up a storm of antagonism; but I was prepared to face this possibility because, being myself a congenital invert, I understood the subject from the inside as well as from the medical and psychological text-books.[41]

In the event, the book was banned in an attempt to suppress knowledge about lesbianism, but as usual with censored books, public demand for it soared. Unsurprisingly, considering the media's view on lesbianism, various newspapers, including the *Daily Express* and the *Daily Telegraph*, exploded in a vitriolic attack on it. James Douglas, editor of the *Sunday Express*, declared, 'I would rather give a healthy boy or a healthy girl a phial of prussic acid than this novel.'[42]

While female emancipation from domesticity was seen as a contributing factor to lesbianism, the medical fraternity continued to see lesbians as suffering from mental illness. During the 1950s, Dr Frank Caprio declared, 'Female homosexuality is becoming an increasingly important problem. It is believed by some that women are becoming rapidly de-feminized by their over desire for emancipation, and the "psychic masculization" of modern woman contributes to frigidity.' In his introduction to his study *Female Homosexuality* (1954), Caprio wrote: 'Many of the naïve and ill-informed are initiated into lesbian practices because of their complete ignorance, which enhances their susceptibility to the advances of the older and experienced invert.'[43] His patients appear to have suffered all sorts of ailments – headaches, fainting, fatigues, insomnia and dizziness. Extreme jealousy was repeatedly stressed as a factor common to all of the women. Caprio decided that lesbians were 'sick individuals' in need of treatment; according to him, many lesbians were sadists, psychopaths, kleptomaniacs or obsessive-compulsive neurotics. Mutual masturbation was, he declared, a symptom of a neurotic personality, a regression to narcissism, a disturbance in childhood development and maladjustment in identification.

The most obvious fact that medics failed to grasp about their female patients was that these women were not frigid; they simply were not attracted to men. Even at this stage, there was a slim understanding of what lesbian feelings entailed. Caprio's main conclusions after personally interviewing many patients over an eighteen-year period was that many prostitutes were lesbians, and 'victims of bisexual conflicts'; that many artists, dancers, musicians, writers and actresses, because of their bohemian lifestyles, tended towards bisexuality; and that the behaviour of these women was environmentally induced rather than congenital, possibly a result of the influence of their unstable parents. Alternatively, he thought lesbian tendencies may result from unpleasant sexual experiences when young, fear of marriage or personality deficiencies. With diagnoses like these, it is unsurprising that women suffered anxiety and guilt. However, he was merely a man of his time trying to help people who had presented themselves to him as suffering from depression.

One female patient who was obviously in love recognized the normality of her feelings, although this seems to have bypassed the doctor who saw them as abnormal. She stated: 'I still feel incensed and outraged that a woman's sex life must be dictated and directed by the public while a man is allowed perfect and complete freedom in this respect.'[44] She had read Radclyffe Hall's *The Well of Loneliness* but felt it gave people the wrong impression of lesbians and that the main character of Stephen cut 'a ridiculous figure'. She had been sexually assaulted by a man when she was nine years old, but her humiliations continued in her adult life when people in the streets who saw her as 'different', spat and snarled at her and called her names. 'Feelings go hang. But it's a terrible physical strain to be struggling against the whole world every waking minute.' Hardly surprisingly, she developed various psychosomatic illnesses, such as tensions, depression, inability to concentrate and feelings of hopelessness. Small wonder, too, that so many people suffered mental breakdowns when they were under the care of medics who had little understanding of the true nature of lesbianism. As late as the 1960s, men with psychology degrees and editors of health magazines were still making such comments as 'Countless Lesbians end their days in lunatic asylums, as the practice of their perversions gets too much for them to bear.'[45] However, while some lesbians felt isolated during the twentieth century, others began to find their own ways to support each other and express their feelings.

Sexual Sororities

Certain institutions were thought to harbour 'unnatural' vices among women – girls' boarding schools, medieval nunneries, women's prisons and female branches of the armed services were all seen as places where female sexual desire ran rampant. Krafft-Ebing believed that although lesbianism was not as common as male homosexuality, it similarly flourished in penal institutions, which he referred to as 'hotbeds of lesbian love'. Lesbian inmates recognized each other through their dress and exchanged glances. Jealousies and passions often broke out as a result of these 'forbidden friendships' and some female inmates would think nothing of beating up a woman who so much as looked at her lover. In her examination of reform schools published in the *Journal of American Psychology* in 1913, Margaret Otis brought racial interactions into the equation and lent a broader understanding of lesbian relationships. Her essay 'A Perversion Not Commonly Noted' was based on her observations of relationships between women in reformatories and it was radical in its sympathy for lesbian relationships: 'sometimes the love [of one young woman for another] is very real and seems almost ennobling'.[46] The process of interaction occurred when one of the white girls received a note

s&M lesbians, postcard, *c.* 1920s.

and a lock of hair from a coloured girl (for so she called her) on arrival at the reformatory. If the white girl was interested, she would make the appropriate responses and an affair would begin. Mostly these girls were working-class, and rarely would they interact with coloured girls once they were no longer incarcerated. However, she noted that these girls found it difficult to reveal themselves as lesbians in the outside world.

The public belief in the flourishing of same-sex inclinations in all-female institutions was reinforced when exposés of lesbian affairs hit the news. Bernard Hollander, who had studied under Krafft-Ebing, revealed in 1922: 'I have known a fashionable girls' school in London to be closed in consequence of the discovery and criminal habits of the head-mistress who for years had seduced one girl after another.' In her autobiography, one history graduate, Ester Hodge, explained her affair with other women in her school in the 1920s. Her junior Latin mistress chased after her, 'I soon responded ardently, going frequently to her flat'. Her mother suspected the relationship and tried to break it up.[47]

Both world wars gave women a new dimension to freedom allowing them to travel away from home, often for the first time. Far from the prying eyes of family and neighbours, they were provided with a chance to indulge in sexual relationships – both hetero- and homosexual. The auxiliary services provided women with the opportunity to meet other women. Jean Mormont recalled meeting up with lesbians in her wartime work in the auxiliary service during the 1940s: 'I never knew what a lesbian was, and I met some girls in there and it used to puzzle me . . . they used to lay on the bed there cuddling one another . . .'. Other women were more savvy and grabbed the opportunity to be together as often as possible. Two nurses in Hastings Hospital, Monica Still and Marya McLean, made secret trips to each other's rooms; they had to creep about in dark cold corridors to avoid the matron. They made vows to each other in church by way of commitment to each other, but they eventually split up after a friend of Marya told her to choose between them. Several decades later, Marya spotted Monica, by then a well-known dog breeder, on television in an advert for Pedigree Chum. The couple met up again and lived together until Marya's death.[48]

Meanwhile, the u.s. Women's Army Corps caused a stir when a handful of women were brought up on charges and placed under barracks arrest. The *Washington Post* for 29 July 1955 reported that around 100 female members of the WAC were under investigation for moral misconduct. One of them had attempted suicide after a series of solicitations by fellow WACs and had left a note indicating what had happened.

Despite continued bad press, lesbians were creating their own strategies for dealing with their lives. Magazines came out in their support, such as the *Ladder*, published 1956–72, a U.S. magazine designed to help the 'variant'. By the twenty-first century, lesbianism was no longer vilified in the press, but used as a form of titillation. It was also seen as a form of free publicity for music industry celebrities and film stars. When Madonna and Britney Spears French-kissed at the MTV Video Awards in 2003, faux lipstick lesbianism made front-page news. Public attitudes had evidently changed enough for them to think that a display of female eroticism might enhance their careers. Other celebrities followed suit. Sandra Bullock and Scarlett Johansson similarly made headlines when they French-kissed at the MTV Movie Awards in 2010. It was a tiny bit edgy, rebellious, and just the way to frighten parents of adolescent daughters by setting a trend among teenage girls.

This type of pretend lesbianism for the sake of fashion irritated some of the stalwarts. Beth Ditto, lead singer of the band The Gossip, attacked popstar Katy Perry for 'playing gay' in order to turn men on, declaring her lyrics 'I Kissed a Girl' to be 'offensive to gay culture'. Others were more frank about their real relationships; comedienne and actress Ellen DeGeneres came out in 1997 on the *Oprah Winfrey Show*, and stars such as Lindsay Lohan helped change attitudes towards lesbianism. Even so, uptight conservatives continue to hold on to their homophobic views; in 2012, heterosexual mothers attacked family mall JC Penney when it hired DeGeneres to head an advertising campaign. Despite the vitriol, the firm held to its decision and the mothers had to drop their protest. DeGeneres declared, 'haters are my motivators'.[49]

Certainly there has been a shift in attitudes over the centuries, as seen from the differences in the acceptance of Sappho in ancient Greece and the antagonism towards the author Radclyffe Hall in the twentieth century. While in the past lesbians may have been seen as perverted, there seems to have been only minor interest in them. As women have gained a more equal stake in political and economic life, they have become more visible – hence so have lesbians. The focus on them has become sharper from the twentieth century onwards, as women have become more prominent in the public sphere and any sexual difference is more obvious (and possibly, to some, more threatening).

Hercules dressed in a pink gown, serving Omphale. Bartholomeus Spranger,
Hercules and Omphale, 1585.

FIVE

From Transvestites to Transsexuals

For the simple man in the street, there are only two sexes. A person is either
male or female, Adam or Eve . . . The more sophisticated realize that every
Adam contains elements of Eve and every Eve harbors traces of Adam,
physically as well as psychologically.

Dr Harry Benjamin, *The Transsexual Phenomenon* (1966)

Throughout history there has been a loose acceptability of cross-dressing for the purposes of work or play, but not for sex. When it was undertaken by someone pretending to be a member of the opposite sex for personal feelings, for a sexual thrill or as a result of confused gender identity, it was roundly condemned. Transsexuality, if anything, has attracted even more animosity. Individuals crossing the boundaries in this way were seen as threatening; they were open to harassment and were generally stigmatized. But in what circumstances would overstepping these boundaries cause offence, and why?

In ancient Greece, men disguised themselves as women to obtain an advantage over their enemies in war: beardless men dressed as women at Thebes to kill the Persian embassy, and later to slaughter the soldiers of the Spartan garrison.[1] In Ovid's *Metamorphoses*, Achilles was dressed as a girl and kept among the daughters of King Lycomedes in Skyros to escape induction into Agamemnon's army.[2] Men also dressed in women's clothes at celebrations: every autumn in Athens, a Dionysian wine festival called the Oschophoria was held, during which two youths dressed up as women and carried grapes from the sanctuary of Dionysus to that of Athena Skirus at Phalerum.

However, in certain cases, men dressed as women because of their feelings about their own sexual persona or cross-dressed for sexual purposes, and these were the areas that caused most concern. One of the most infamous cross-dressers was the Roman emperor Elagabalus, who liked both sexes and married at least three women, but surrounded himself with male lovers. He was only fourteen when he succeeded Marcus Aurelius in AD 218, and managed to pack a range of debaucheries into his short but eventful life. He dressed in women's clothes, plucked out hairs from his body and shocked onlookers by wearing full make-up in public. The historian Cassius Dio told how 'he worked with wool, sometimes wore a hairnet, and painted his eyes, daubing them with lead and alkanet. Once, indeed, he shaved his chin and held a festival to mark the event; but after that he had the hairs plucked out, so as to look more like a woman'.[3] The emperor lived the life of a woman, and spent his days in the company of his concubines, spinning purple garments from the softest wool. In violation of all sorts of Roman taboos, he raped a vestal virgin and was accused of working in the brothels of Rome and offering his sexual services to passers-by.

It has been suggested that Elagabalus was bisexual but he was evidently ambivalent about his own body. It was said that he had attempted to castrate himself and declared he wanted a vagina implanted in his body; this would make him a pioneer of one of the first transsexual surgical operations, although it is more likely that he merely circumcised himself. Praetorian soldiers eventually murdered Elagabalus when he was only eighteen years old; his head was cut off and his body was dragged through the streets before being tossed into the River Tiber.[4] Another, more famous emperor, Nero, tried to turn the boy Sporus into a girl through castration. Suetonius tells us that 'he went though a wedding ceremony with him – dowry, bridal veil and all – which the whole Court attended.'[5] Nero took Sporus home and treated him as a wife, dressing him in fine women's clothes and kissing him in public. Such effeminacy was regarded with disdain in the ancient world as it was believed that an overtly masculine 'manly' man should display authority. For rulers such as emperors, this was even more important.

Many cases of transgression in dress and gender were less dramatic and it is evident that there has been a wide variety of types of cross-dresser. In the medieval West, cross-dressing was allowed at carnivals. While celebrating holidays such as May Day, men commonly dressed as women and ran through the streets. Molly dancing took place in East Anglia on Plough Monday (the Monday after Epiphany), when unemployed ploughboys cross-dressed – they decorated a plough and pushed it round the village, calling at the houses of well-off villagers to beg for money.[6]

Opposition to cross-dressing in the medieval West was empha-
sized in the Bible, which indicated that donning the attire of the
opposite sex was a sin. Deuteronomy states: 'The woman shall not
wear that which pertaineth unto a man, neither shall a man put on
a woman's garment: for all that do so are abominations unto the
Lord thy God' (22:5). Whether authorities or communities were
antagonistic towards cross-dressers, however, depended primarily
on where and why an individual was perceived to be cross-dressing
and on a clear set of guidelines that varied at different times. Most
societies identified specific colours, styles, textures or types of
clothing with one or other of the sexes: in the Victorian period, for
example, it was considered appropriate for women to wear dresses,
and men to wear trousers. This was not always the case, however, and
the notion of what was proper for a man or a woman to wear has
changed throughout the ages. Men might well have worn tights in
the medieval period, but they were part of a woman's attire by the

Medieval men and
women in similar,
but different,
loose clothing,
14th century.

twentieth century. If a man wore tights in the twentieth century, he would have been considered effeminate or a transvestite. The rules also change according to the country. In some places, skirt-like outfits might be allowed – kilts in Scotland, for example, or the *lunghi* (a sort of wraparound skirt for men) in India – but there has always been an appropriate dress code for each sex at any one time. Any swapping of this clothing arrangement was seen as against the norm.

Cross-dressing also had a different meaning depending on the sex of the person doing it. A woman might dress as a man in order to gain status in a patriarchal world or to obtain employment and independence and, although still seen as a transgressive act, her purpose was at least understood. During the medieval and early modern periods through to the Victorian era, single women had fewer work opportunities and while they might find work sewing, spinning, selling wares or in agriculture, these jobs were usually seen as auxiliary to men's work and usually paid at a fraction of a men's pay. It was less acceptable for a man to dress as a woman as he already held the 'superior' position in life; in assuming the role of a woman, he turned the world upside down. A cross-dressing man who was not attempting to be comical or festive would be seen as effeminate – and equated with a sodomite. In these instances, the reaction of society was more antagonistic. Gender rules were therefore defined by dress and overturning the order led to confusion and an aggressive response.

Cross-dressers in Religion

Some cross-dressers created a greater stir because they had cross-dressed for the purposes of entering religious orders, as in two cases that emerged during the medieval period. In his account of the rebellion at the monastery of Poitiers in AD 590, Gregory of Tours recorded that a man had entered a convent and lived there undetected for some years, dressed as a nun. The truth was only revealed when a fellow nun by the name of Clotild accused her abbess of sharing a bed with him. A meeting was hastily called, attended by the nuns and a handful of senior male clergy. Gregory reported:

> Clotild was called before us. She showered abuse on her
> Abbess and made a number of accusations against her. She

maintained that the Abbess kept a man in the nunnery, dressed in woman's clothing and looking like a woman, although in effect there was no doubt that he was a man. His job was to sleep with the Abbess whenever she wanted it. 'Why! There's the fellow!' cried Clotild, pointing with her finger. Thereupon a man stepped forward, dressed in woman's clothing as I have told you.[7]

During the meeting, the man in question told the onlookers, who included six startled bishops and various interested strangers, that he was impotent. It was thought that he had forsaken the outside world, put on the habit of a nun and taken refuge in the nunnery.

The passionate revolt of the nuns at Poitiers began some years after the death of the founder of the convent, St Radegund. Although she had chosen Agnes as her successor, when Agnes died in 589, a rebellion broke out when a women named Leubovera was chosen to succeed her to the title of abbess. This appointment was particular irksome to Clotild, who believed that she herself should have been elected, since she was the daughter of King Charibert I. Relying on her close connection to royalty, she persuaded 40 of her fellow nuns to take an oath that they would help her to remove the hated Leubovera as abbess and appoint herself to the position in her stead. Despite Clotild's assertions that the abbess Leubovera had kept a castrated man as a eunuch for her own sexual pleasures, the man was found innocent of all charges. His physician came forward in his defence, explaining how the circumstances had arisen.

> When this servant was a young lad, he had terrible pains in the groin. Nobody could do anything for him. His mother went to St Radegund and asked her to have the case looked into. I was called in and she told me to do what I could. I cut out the lad's testicles, an operation I had once seen performed by a surgeon in the town of Constantinople.[8]

This case first throws up the question of how a man dressed as a nun – and a man who apparently looked like a man despite his disguise, otherwise Clotild would have been unable to identify him – could go so long unchallenged in a nunnery. He himself said that he lived locally and denied knowing the abbess or living in the convent, but a man dressed as a nun in secular life outside the convent would surely have raised eyebrows. In the end, he was deemed innocent of the accusation and surprisingly little was mentioned about the question of his dress. Second, and more fundamental, is the apparent acceptance by the medieval onlookers of the idea that either an impotent or castrated man was still able to service a woman sexually without penetrative sex. It would seem that medieval cross-dressing men were not always seen as either totally unacceptable or as effeminate.

Although the above case is authenticated, the story of Pope Joan is less certain and brings with it its own set of ambiguities. Her tale became popular in the thirteenth century but it is uncertain whether Joan actually lived, or if she was merely a figment of the imagination of the Dominican monk Jean de Mailly of Metz, who wrote about her around 1250. He tells how the twelve-year-old Joan had absconded from her family in Mainz after being seduced by a monk or a servant. In order to follow her lover, she dressed as a man so that they could either enter into religious orders or a university to be educated together, depending on which version of the story is followed. After a stint of learning in Athens, when her lover died, Joan made her way to Rome in search of employment, finding herself a job as a reader of the scriptures in church. Her astounding learning and piety impressed her colleagues so much that she was eventually elected Pope. Unfortunately, one of her fellow cardinals or possibly a clerk

Pope Joan giving birth. Woodcut from Giovanni Boccaccio, *De mulieribus claris* (*c.* 1539).

The *sede stercoraria*, which became entwined with the Pope Joan legend.

saw through her disguise, with the result that she was seduced, coerced or raped by him. Her downfall came when she suddenly went into labour while out on a religious procession. Having witnessed their pope give birth, shocked and outraged, the crowd stoned her to death – or then again, she may have died of natural causes. Such were the mutations of the story.

Pope Joan allegedly reigned in the ninth century, although there is no mention of her in the Vatican lists of popes; nor are there any unaccountable gaps into which Joan might fit. The story was so popular that other writers added to it; her tale was used by Protestants as a means of challenging the validity of the Papacy. As late as 1675, a book appeared in English entitled *A Present for a Papist; or, The Life and Death of Pope Joan, Plainly Proving Out of the Printed Copies, and Manuscripts of Popish Writers and Others, That a Woman called JOAN, Was Really POPE of ROME, and Was There Deliver'd of a Bastard Son in the Open Street as She Went in Solemn Procession.* But writers such as the sixteenth-century magistrate Florimond de Raemond also reclaimed Joan as defender of the faith in the Catholic Counter-Reformation.[9] It has popularly been argued that the question of her sexual identity would have been uncovered when she was made Pope after the use of the *sede stercoraria*, the throne with a hole in the seat, was introduced; according to rumour, this facilitated the inspection of the testicles of the elected Pope in order to establish his manhood. It has also been argued that the chair was introduced after the papacy of Joan, in order to prevent the likelihood of a similar mistake being made again. Although this toilet-like chair was used in the consecration of Pope Pascal II in 1099, the idea that it was used to check the sex of the Pope is probably a myth. It has alternatively been suggested that the chair was either a birthing stool for the aristocracy or used to check for castration. In any case, most historians agree that the story of Pope Joan is fictional.

These tales reveal remarkably different reasons as to why men and women might disguise themselves as a person of the cloth and enter a religious house. In the first case, it would seem that the man either dressed as a nun as a means of coping with ostracization in the outside world, or to enable himself to live with the abbess as her lover undetected. An impotent man (if he spoke the truth) was no good to a godly wife who needed to produce children. However, he might have been a welcome distraction for an encloistered abbess. In the story, Pope Joan's determination to strive for recognition in a man's world drove her to attain her position. It was the fear of such female fortitude and usurpation that kept the tale leaping along with such vigour. With such efforts, a woman might enter into any area of a man's world undetected.

Joan of Arc was another woman who cross-dressed because of her religious conviction – this time to do battle as a soldier, although unlike Pope Joan, she never denied her true sexual identity. Nonetheless, her cross-dressing would result in her death. She first came to the attention of the authorities as a thirteen-year-old girl, after she had informed them that she had heard voices calling her to battle. Until then she had lived the life of a normal young peasant girl with her parents in Domrémy. Initially she was considered with suspicion, but her mind was set on a higher authority than the local priest. She followed the instructions of her voices and in May 1428, travelled to Chinon to meet with Charles VII. Joan revealed to him the story of the voices instructing her to lead the king's army in battle. After listening to Joan and considering her story with some incredulity, he agreed to support her and gave her an army to lead.

The sheer tenacity of Joan's belief was enough to stir up willingness among even the most dubious of soldiers. Now, backed by sovereignty, the Church authorities were reticent to condemn her. Support grew among her followers as she managed to rouse weary men into battle when all seemed lost – a feat she achieved on successive occasions. With each victory, others watched astounded, and the belief grew that she was unbeatable in battle, with the soldiers heralding her as a saviour. Regardless of whether her religious experience was a case of schizophrenia, or a way to gain recognition in taking leadership of an army, she nonetheless became a cause célèbre.

Joan of Arc on horseback and dressed for battle.

Joan was eventually betrayed by factions among the French and handed over to their enemy, the English. Although her accusers eventually deemed her a heretic, it was her cross-dressing that was at the basis of their arguments. The fact that she had dressed as a man when she took up armour in order to fight was used to discredit her; her actions were deemed as perverse and against God. Bishop Pierre Cauchon, who presided over her trial, was assisted by Jean Delafontaine, Commissary Nicholas Midi and Gerard Feuillet, and witnesses Thomas Fiefvet, Pasquier de Vaux and Nicolas de Houbent were brought forward to give evidence. Although some of the evidence was damning, it was Joan's own responses that finally let her down.

During her cross-examination on 12 March 1431, the interrogators attempted to establish why Joan had cross-dressed and to portray her actions as essentially perverse. They asked her if her military captain had encouraged her. If not the captain, was she told what to do by the voices that spoke to her? Joan defended herself by asserting: 'All that I have done of good, I have done by the command of my Voices . . . even now if I were with those of my own side and in this man's dress, it seems to me it would be a great good for France to do as I did before I was taken.' Her interrogators pursued her cross-dressing through constant questioning on the matter, but Joan was more interested in obtaining permission to attend Mass. She asked them to allow her access to a confessor: 'Send me a dress like a daughter of your citizens that is to say, a long "houppeland". I will wear it to go and hear Mass.' Whatever Joan did, it was not to save her. Her accusers proclaimed against her using her dress as an excuse, in that she had acted:

> against the modesty of the sex, and which are prohibited by the Divine Law, things abominable to God and man . . . dressing herself in the garments of a man, short, tight, dissolute, those underneath as well as above . . . she had attired herself in sumptuous and stately raiment, cloth-of-gold and furs; and not only did she wear short tunics, but she dressed herself in tabards, and garments open at both sides . . . She was always seen with a cap on her head, her hair cut short and a-round in the style of a man. In one word, putting aside the modesty of her sex, she acted not only against all feminine

decency, but even against the reserve which men of good morals, wearing ornaments and garments which only profligate men are accustomed to use, and going so far as to carry arms of offence.[10]

The religious laws she had transgressed were clearly spelled out – she had broken the laws of God in dressing as a man and had broken the hierarchical laws of nature that allotted her an inferior place. Furthermore, she had acted immodestly and avariciously: her male dress was deemed short and tight, with 'garments open on both sides' (yet this was presumably seen as suitable clothing for men), and she was profligate in her wearing of ornaments, decorations and furs. She was burned at the stake as a witch and a heretic in 1431. Both Joans serve as examples of how women used the dress of man to further their own agendas. However, other employment opportunities in which men and women could cross-dress were considered less threatening to the authorities.

Dressing for Work

The public were more accepting of the cross-dressing of both sexes in theatrical plays and actors and actresses have long since taken up the role of the opposite sex in order to entertain audiences. Cross-dressing in the theatre goes back to ancient Greece, where men played all the female roles. This tradition continued into the Renaissance; Shakespeare's plays often depict confused cross-gendered lovers. Julia in *Two Gentlemen of Verona*, Portia in *The Merchant of Venice*, Viola in *Twelfth Night* and Rosalind in *As You Like It* are all female characters dressed as men. These disguises allow the female protagonists to show off their so-called 'masculine' qualities of courage, intelligence and prowess, while keeping more medievally perceived 'feminine' qualities of chastity, tenderness and fragility under wraps. Portia, while dressed as a man, explains to her maid, 'in such a habit . . . they shall think we are accomplished with that we lack'. Dressed in men's clothes, Shakespeare's heroines can move freely about in a masculine world, striding confidently about the streets or in the woods. They shed their passive mantles to take the initiative, make decisions and address men as their equals.

The fact that adolescent boys played the female roles in Eliza-
bethan plays further confused the illusion on stage, with audiences
complicit in the knowledge that they were watching boys acting as
women dressed as men. The situation changed after the Restoration
in 1660, when women were allowed on stage. Actresses began to
incorporate the strategy of cross-dressing in their repertoire, with
women such as Peg Woffington made famous for their 'breeches'
roles. These roles provided the opportunity for actresses to cast off
their own long dresses and don men's tights and a sculptured tunic
in order to show off their shapely figures to appreciative audiences.

Women also cross-dressed in order to join the army or the navy.
Although not encouraged to do so (and a woman could be dismissed
from the forces if discovered), this was not condemned to the same
extent as more sexually overt types of transvestism. An example of
the cordial fellow feeling operating towards such women can be
seen in a report given in a Norwich newspaper. Upon arriving in
town at the beginning of May 1741, one young girl brought herself a
frock coat, shoes, stockings and breeches and entered herself at the
barracks as a drummer boy in Colonel Bland's regiment. Giving her
name as George, she served in the army until she was exposed by an
old acquaintance. As a result, she was dismissed from her position,
but her fellow officers had grown so fond of her that they advanced
her some money 'for her honest and good'.[11] Other eighteenth-
century female soldiers, such as Hannah Snell, fought alongside
male comrades. Some, such as Anne Bonny and Mary Read, became
'seamen' in order to explore the world. Bonny and Read were accepted by their shipmates as men, sharing the same work and the same
pay, and even did a stint as pirates. Such women who had disguised
themselves for purposes of work and adventure were feted in jolly
pamphlets about their exploits dodging musket fire or aboard rolling
ships on the high seas.[12] However, when a lover of the same sex was
involved, the cross-dressing was more problematic.

One celebrated case that was treated severely came to light in the
seventeenth century after a physician examined a soldier in the army
of Prince Frederic Henry of Nassau. Discovering that she had a
'clitoris the size of a child's penis and thickness of half a little finger
and with that had carnal conversation with several women', she was
reprimanded and her case investigated. The woman in question was
Hendrikje Verschuur, who had fought in the battle of Breda in 1637.

Female cross-
dressers in
Shakespeare: an
engraving of
Rosalind in *As
You Like It*, 1870s.

She was in love with another woman, Trijntje Barends, and 'they had been so besotted with one another that they would have liked to marry if it had been possible'.[13] Verschuur was whipped and exiled for 25 years.

Strikingly, from extant cases it appears that although women dressed as men in order to live with another woman, men rarely took on a female persona in order to live with another man (although they may have sometimes dressed up as women in private while having a sexual relationship with another man). On the other hand, some part-time male transvestites were married to members of the opposite sex and considered themselves heterosexual or 'straight'.

The Lure of a Dress

In eighteenth-century America, men were dressing as women for the fun of it. Those with power, such as the governor of New York, Lord Cornbury, donned women's clothing in public without creating too much of a stir. When he opened the Assembly in 1702, he dressed as Queen Anne, complete with ballgown, and no one complained. As with some other famous transvestites, he employed the most exclusive milliners and used the most expensive silks and ribbons.[14] However, in small local communities, it was impossible to transgress dress codes without being vilified. Sexual irregularities were considered a problem as soon as they were spotted and vigorously condemned. The Puritan Christopher Lawne established the first English plantation in the Virginian settlement of Warraskoyack around 1618. Other Puritan settlers joined him and the community grew, but it was not without controversy. After ten years, a scandal broke out after the servant Thomas Hall was caught dressing in female clothing. Although most of the villagers thought him to be a man, his employer, John Atkins, claimed that Hall was a woman. Since Hall had been found to have 'layen with a mayd', there was conflicting evidence about his true sexual identity. In order to clear up the confusion, he was ordered before a group of local midwives to have his genitalia inspected to determine his true sex. Married women or midwives were commonly called upon to inspect female bodies, usually for evidence of virginity or lack of it in proof of fornication. After the inspection the women declared Hall definitely to be a man but, humiliatingly for him, one with a very small penis – it was only an inch long. Even he admitted he had no use of it. Further confusion arose when he said he also had 'a peece of hole' representing a vagina. At first, the judge decided to call in favour of him being a woman and demanded that he should dress as one, but the female inspectors remained unconvinced and a second inspection was ordered. This time, both Hall's master and the midwives were present, but no evidence of his womanhood was found. The judge's decision was therefore reversed and Hall was once more declared to be a man and ordered to dress accordingly.

Despite the bewilderment of the villagers, Hall's predicament did not appear to have bothered him, and he would have quite willingly gone back and forth dressing how he pleased when the need arose.

Portrait of a Lady ('Manly' woman, possibly Edward Hyde, Lord Cornbury, in a dress), *c.* 1705–50, oil on canvas, artist unknown.

Although he had been brought up as a girl, at 24 he had cut his hair and dressed as a man so he could join the army. On his return home to England, he found it easier to revert to being a woman until he left the country again. When he arrived in America, he again changed his mind and decided it would be easier to settle into the local community as a man. However, this leisurely attitude to gender shifts was not greeted with enthusiasm by his neighbours, who refused to accept his cross-dressing and demanded that he define his sex once and for all. In the end, the court denied him his choice of dress and ordered him to dress in a man's basic attire but with a woman's apron and headdress, thereby stamping him as a deviant. It was

William Hogarth, *Hudibras Encounters the Skimmington*, 1726.

now obvious to anyone who saw him that he was a cross-dresser; this punishment aimed at singling him out, humiliating him and making him publicly 'different'.[15]

Enforced cross-dressing was used as a method of displaying the displeasure of the community with those who transgressed sexual boundaries – and not necessarily always those to do with gender. Sometimes an individual may simply have committed fornication, or some other sexual infraction. Around the seventeenth and eighteenth centuries, if a man had allowed himself to become cuckolded or was the victim of a shrewish wife, he would be dressed in women's clothes and paraded on an ass in a 'skimmington ride', which was intended to embarrass him into stepping up to address the issue. In 1790, one weaver who had allowed his wife to dominate him became the subject of such an exhibition. Other men from the village, fearing that their own wives might similarly rebel, gathered together to take action. They

> mounted one of their body, dressed in female apparel on the back of an old donkey, the man holding a spinning wheel on his lap, and his back towards the donkey's head. Two men led the animal through the neighbourhood, followed by scores of boys and idle men, tinkering kettles and frying pans, roaring cow's horns and making a most hideous hullabaloo.[16]

In other cases, a community came together in similar rowdy crowds in the creation of 'rough music', where men beat upon drums and women banged pots and pans to draw attention to the event and publicly embarrass the victim. The targets were often men who married much younger women, or had been adulterous. Women, too, might be subject to such humiliation, particularly if they were husband-beaters or regarded as being too masterful.

Male cross-dressing also occurred during times of political resistance. During the Rebecca Riots of 1839–43 in Wales, enraged farmers and agricultural workers joined forces to oppose the setting up of turnpikes. The Turnpike Trust collected road taxes supposedly as a means to maintain the highways, but the money was often diverted to other uses. The rioters were adamantly against the charges, seeing them as an additional financial burden on the poor. While blockading the toll gates, the men donned women's clothes as a signal to outsiders that they wanted to avoid violence in their protest. It is thought that they took the name Merched Beca, Daughters of Rebecca, from the Bible, most likely after a passage where Rebecca talks of the need to 'possess the gates of those who hate them' (Genesis 24:60). When an exchange was about to take place, the leader would call to his followers, shouting for Rebecca and 'her daughters' to come forth. Rumour was that the clothes worn by the men were borrowed from an old woman in the village who was the only woman big enough to have clothes they could fit into. Although the Rebeccas

Cross-dressing rioters: the Daughters of Rebecca attacking a toll gate in the mid-19th century.

Dan Leno
dressed for his
'You know Mrs
Kelly? . . .' act.

targeted the toll gates, this was part of a broader attack against impositions on the poor, which included the despised system of the Poor Law. This kind of cross-dressing was acceptable in the community since it muted potentially violent clashes.

During the nineteenth century, male and female impersonating became a popular form of entertainment in Victorian musical halls. The term 'drag' was in common usage in the nineteenth century, to mean men dressing in women's clothes. Eric Partridge, in his *Dictionary of Slang and Unconventional English*, believes the term is related to criminal slang of around 1850, 'to go on the drag' or 'to flash the drag', which meant to wear women's clothes for immoral purposes. In other words, its slang meaning of men wearing women's clothes pre-dates its usage as theatrical slang by some twenty years, and perhaps has its root in a common practice of male prostitutes.[17] In drag shows, comedians often took on the persona of a female gossip, such as in Dan Leno's monologue 'You know Mrs Kelly? . . .'. Although female drag artists were less common, Matilda Alice Powles made her name as Vesta Tilley, acting out various male characters. In 1870, at the age of six, she was on the stage dressed as Pocket Sims Reeves, a parody of a famous opera singer. A great success in the music halls, she reached the height of her popularity in her fifties when she ran a recruitment drive during the First World War dressed as 'Tommy in the Trench' and 'Jack Tar Home from Sea'. Actors also made their mark in pantomimes, where they wore women's clothes for comedic effect as pantomime dames. This survives right up until the present day in roles such as Widow Twanky in *Aladdin*.

Outside the theatre, wearing drag was still a dangerous occupation during the early decades of the twentieth century, so men took to various underground clubs where they could dress up at drag balls. At one club in Holland Park Avenue in 1932, police constables dressed up in drag in an attempt to infiltrate and arrest

Vesta Tilley
as a foppish
young man.

homosexuals. Numerous arrests were made and the men were hauled up in court in drag and full make-up with numbered placards round their necks.[18] However, by the Second World War, camping it up became a way to lift the morale of men in the armed forces. The Entertainments National Service Association (ENSA, popularly known as 'Every Night Something Awful') was founded in 1939 to entertain the troops. In order to avoid having homosexuals in a mainstream fighting unit, anyone who was considered 'queer' was seconded into the entertainment section – although plenty of non-drag actresses and actors also worked at entertaining them, including Joyce Grenfell, George Formby and Paul Scofield.

By the 1960s and '70s, professional female impersonators became popular in theatre, radio, television and film as British audiences took camp men to their hearts. Kenneth Williams and Charles Hawtrey in the BBC radio programme *Round the Horne* and in the *Carry On* films had huge family audiences. Drag became increasingly outlandish, with men dressing in female accoutrements with massive false breasts, fluffy, long-haired bouffant wigs, huge false eyelashes, full-length Lurex gowns and six-inch golden-heeled sandals. Danny La Rue, one of the first well-known drag artists to make drag mainstream in Britain, was a regular performer at the London Palladium throughout the 1960s. Popular and respectable enough to be invited to perform in front of the Queen, he was even awarded an OBE. In 1982, he was the first man to take over the role of Dolly Levi in the musical *Hello Dolly!* Noël Coward called him 'The most professional, the most witty . . . and the most utterly charming man in the business.'

By the 1980s, places that had been marginalized and underground in the 1970s, such as the Union Pub on Canal Street in Manchester and the Royal Vauxhall Tavern in London, were being attended by straights as well as gays.[19] A new wave of drag artists topped the bills at local clubs and pubs. Usually the entertainment consisted of drag queens miming to gay anthems such as Gloria Gaynor's 'I Will Survive' or 'I Am What I Am' from *La Cage aux Folles*, the musical by Harvey Fierstein. Based on a French play of 1973 by Jean Poiret, a production of this show won numerous awards in 1983, bringing camp to Broadway. In the 1980s, drag artists such as Paul O'Grady and Julian Clary both toured clubs and pubs before they obtained television fame; O'Grady played his alter ego Lily Savage for eight years at the Royal

Vauxhall Tavern, and Clary toured the clubs with his stage show *The Joan Collins Fan Club*, together with his pet Fanny the Wonder Dog, before he found fame camping it up on television. In the 1990s the comedian Eddie Izzard started doing stand-up routines wearing a skirt, calling himself 'a straight transvestite or a male lesbian'.[20] Yet although entertainment made cross-dressing more acceptable, at the beginning of the twentieth century it had been categorized as a medical problem.

The Rise of the Transvestite

Modern day cross-dressers were first labelled 'transvestites' by German sexologist Dr Magnus Hirschfeld – 'trans' meaning 'opposite' and 'vestis' meaning 'clothing' – in his book *Transvestites*, published in 1910. Working with a like-minded group of men, his work focused on the 'problem' of cross-dressing while fighting for better under-standing of homosexuality. In Berlin in 1897 they founded the Scientific Humanitarian Committee, a campaign group which pro-moted the idea that homosexuality should be treated as a medical condition rather than as a criminal one (in line with Karl Heinrich Ulrichs's thinking), but also supporting bisexual and trangendered people. Revolutionary thinking in its day, this was a major influence on the movement to decriminalize homosexuality. In 1919, Hirschfeld opened the Institute for Sex Research with his colleague Arthur Kronfeld; Hirschfeld's assistant Karl Giese helped out with admin-istration and gave lectures. The Institute saw about 1,800 people a year and was one of the first places people could go for advice on sex problems without being judged. Doctors offered advice on con-traception, sex education and sexually transmitted diseases, treated those with no money and advocated for the rights of both women and homosexuals. In 1933 the Institute was destroyed by the Nazis, who hauled 20,000 books and journals out of the library and burned them in the street. The Institute's administrator, Kurt Hiller, was sent to a concentration camp but he eventually managed to flee to Prague and on to London. Giese also fled, to Czechoslovakia, but later committed suicide when Hitler occupied the country; Kronfeld killed himself as the Germans approached Moscow. Hirschfeld escaped, since he was on tour in America at the time of the attack on the Institute.

Transvestite, *c.* 1896.

Hirschfeld's ground-breaking study of transvestites revealed a cross-section of people with multifarious feelings and attitudes towards their cross-dressing. Of the seventeen transvestites he interviewed, only one was a woman. Nine of the men were married; seven were fathers. Some of the men who cross-dressed were heterosexual, but others showed desire for men. Some wanted to *become* a woman, and wanted to play the role of a woman in a heterosexual relationship, one man admitting that he had 'the passing wish to complete the ideal of the condition of a woman by means of a male partner'.[21] For nearly all the men, their transvestism started in child-hood – they began by trying on their sister's or mother's dresses. Most of the men wanted to be effeminate, and wished to do fem-inine things. They spoke of acquiring the traditional feminine qualities of their day – meekness, tranquillity and being 'kittenish', modest and patient. All of them had an obsession with fashion and concerned themselves with minute details of their female dress. They often had fixations on particular items of clothing, including corsets, knickers, gloves and veils, expensive lace handkerchiefs and fine jewellery.

Studying women's fashion magazines helped many of the men to dress themselves better as women. They did not simply want to wear a frock but wanted to look and act like a woman. Female occu-pations were coveted, and men yearned to be governesses, milliners or 'chambermaid to a fine lady'. Many of the men developed female hobbies at an early age – embroidery, crochet, knitting – and enjoyed domestic housework. Female relatives sometimes offered assistance in obtaining suitable attire. One mother of a female impersonator

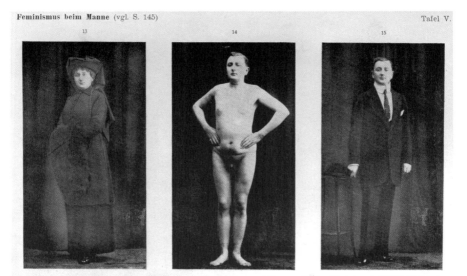

Feminismus beim Manne (vgl. S. 145)   Tafel V.

13   14   15

Der Fall stellt eine der häufigen Verbindungen von Androgynie, Transvestitismus und Homosexualität dar. Die Androgynie (Bild 14) tritt besonders in der Becken-, Brust- und Kehlkopfbildung, sowie im Gesichtsausdruck, Gestik und Mimik des 30jährigen Patienten zutage. Bild 13 zeigt ihn, wie er bei der Kriegsmusterung erschien. Er trägt Trauer, weil seine Mutter gestorben ist; ein Zeichen, wie ernst er seinen Transvestitismus nimmt. Dem weiblichen Geschlecht gegenüber besteht völlige Indifferenz, dagegen reagiert er auf männliche Personen positiv lustbetont.

Examining the links between androgyny, transvestitism and homosexuality: a case from Magnus Hirschfeld, *Sexualpathologie* (1921).

helped her son by engaging a dressmaker for him and arranged clothes swaps between him and his female cousin. His mother wrote to him, 'Gretchen is very happy about getting one of your silk dresses . . . and wants to know if you have any use for some crocheted lace and a night jacket.'[22] Others were not so lucky and experienced rejection by friends and family.

Most of the patients denied that cross-dressing caused sexual excitement or titillation in any way. One male cross-dresser said, 'Putting on women's underclothing in no way calls up sexual stimulation but rather gratifies me insofar as the feeling in my soul is given external expression.' When dressed in female attire, he acquired a feeling of peace and clarity of mind. However, this was not the case with all of Hirschfeld's patients. One patient admitted he became 'terribly excited'. At least five patients in his study had had homosexual fantasies or had experimented with sex with men. 'Mr F' told how at the age of 21 he had succumbed to anal intercourse with an Arab while on holiday. However, most denied homosexual feeling; one even asserted 'There is no sign of any homosexuality present. I deeply despise Urnings and effeminate men.'[23]

The one woman included in Hirschfeld's study expressed how she felt 'light, well and able to work' when she donned a man's cap, tie, underwear and boots, while women's clothing cramped her style and made her feel 'unfree'. Dressing as a man provided her with more opportunities to work with better pay. By the time she was 30, she had already worked as a locksmith, a miner, a butler, a barber, a house painter and in other 'male' jobs. She had even worked on a whaling ship in Arendel where 'everything would have been great if the lice had not tormented us so'.[24] Disguised as a man, she had managed to travel all over the world. Now married with children, she regretted giving up her previous independence and admitted she felt fettered. Sexually she appeared to be bisexual, but Hirschfeld thought her sex urge less strong than her urge to dress as a man. From Hirschfeld's investigations, as well as other sexologists' studies, it would seem that female transvestism was less well understood or investigated than male transvestism. This was probably because it was less obvious, and women were more cautious about exposing themselves. From the sexologists' point of view, transvestites were most generally seen either as sexually perverted in their psychology, or somehow corrupted in their physiology.

More recently, in the 1980s, scientifically controlled studies have sought to define whether transvestism elicits a sexual response or not. All those who agreed to be tested denied that their reason for dressing in women's clothes was sexual. However, after being subjected to certain stimuli under clinical observation in a controlled environment, the cohorts showed conclusive evidence of penile tumescence (blood rushing to the penis showing sexual stimulus) when they read fantasies of cross-dressing. Scientists concluded that therefore there *was* an association between the subjects' dressing up and their sexual thoughts, despite their assertion of the opposite.[25]

From Hirschfeld's study, it would seem that various types of transvestite existed: men who were homosexual but afraid to recognize the fact; men who were heterosexual who simply liked dressing as women; and those who actually wanted to change sex. From the one woman interviewed, it seemed that cross-dressing was partly used as a means to greater independence in a world which restricted women. Until then, little investigation had been undertaken on gender dysmorphia.

While people still cross-dress for fun, for sex and as part of sexual identity, transvestism has become much more diverse in the twenty-first century. With medical developments, definitions of transvestism and its understanding have became even more confused. Both society and the law have struggled to keep up with the great variance in sexuality taking place, most notably as a result of the availability of hormone drugs and the emergence of transsexual surgical realignment surgery.

Transsexuality

Although incomplete sex reassignment surgery had begun in the 1920s, it was rare in the first few decades of the twentieth century. People of both sexes struggled to come to terms with the fact that they felt as if they had been born in a body of the wrong gender. One male transvestite interviewed by Magnus Hirschfeld appears to have wanted a sex change, but there was as yet no such opportunity. He referred to a 'sexual metamorphosis' and said, 'I wish my penis would have changed into a vagina.'[26] The interviewee was an articulate physician who could appreciate his symptoms only too well; 'I feel as if I have been robbed of my own skin and am put into a woman's skin.' His feeling of being a woman from head to toe persisted and he felt as though he possessed female genitalia – 'the penis feels as though it was a clitoris'.[27]

Other individuals had similar problems and suffered as a result of negative comments made by passers-by in the streets. One young woman born in 1885, Miss Katharina T., appears to have been a possible case for transsexual surgery before the operation was available, but managed to realign her identity through cross-dressing. After the death of her mother, she had been brought up by her aunt and, from the age of six onwards, indulged in mutual masturbation with other girls. She showed no interest in boys in adolescence and by the time she was 22 she noticed her voice becoming deeper. Soon she was teased about her appearance. When she went out in women's clothing, people thought she was a male transvestite and made unpleasant comments. On cutting her hair and taking up wearing a man's clothes, the public humiliation stopped and she felt 'completely a man'. Others, however, wanted a complete physical sex change.

In an effort to help such individuals, Hirschfeld went on to develop his ideas on transsexuality, and collaborated with Dr Harry Benjamin (1885–1986), a pioneer working in endocrinology. The two men had first met in Berlin before Benjamin moved to New York in 1915 to set up practice. Benjamin was one of the first doctors brave enough to shift the topic of transsexuality to firmer ground and began seeing patients with sexual dysmorphia. In the preface to *The Transsexual Phenomenon* (1966), he described himself as 'neither surgeon nor psychiatrist' but rather as a student of sexological problems, and also as a 'long-time practitioner in sexology'. He began treating patients with oestrogen, and Alfred Kinsey and other doctors started to refer their patients to him. Patients read about his work and asked their own doctors to refer them to him. In 1968, Benjamin placed an advert in *Esquire* magazine and was inundated with letters from transvestites and transsexuals asking for help. Realizing the need for it, he founded the Benjamin Gender Identity Foundation in 1972 to help people with sex and gender conflicts. This was one of the first institutes of its kind to examine the possibilities of psychologically and surgically assisting those in identity crisis.

Many of the authors of the letters written to Dr Benjamin in 1968 and 1969 related their life stories of how their transsexuality and transvestism had left them with severe mental health problems.

Beset by guilt and the feeling of being abnormal, people were driven into states of desperation and chronic depression. One man from Iowa admitted, 'I cannot stand having two people in the same body much longer.'[28] Another desperate man from Virginia confessed, 'I am physically male but need to be cured of that desperately. I feel I am slipping over the edge of something, and I am not sure I can handle the future as a man.' In general practice, doctors were still unaware of how to best help a patient in this situation. The author of the letter added: 'My doctor is willing to prescribe hormones for me, but he is not sufficiently familiar with this type of problem to do so without further information.'[29]

Physiological differences caused just as many problems for the sufferer as psychological ones. One example can be seen in the case of one 56-year-old male who wrote to Benjamin informing him that he had developed breasts at an early age and had period-like symptoms. He wrote: 'I have a tube protruding from the rectum from which the bleeding would come from each month.' After tests at Miami Research, doctors pronounced that the tube was in fact a vagina, and declared that his testicles were 'completely dead'. At first the doctors thought him to be 'dual sex', then pronounced him a female. He was in pain from the small of his back to his head. He was prescribed oestrogen, which eased his pain a little, but was suffering from severe depression. Doctors later classified him as a pseudo-hermaphrodite, but essentially he remained a mystery to them and they wrote him off. He turned to Benjamin as a last resort and Benjamin agreed to see him.[30]

Some patients had already started the transformation of gender reassignments to become female. One man told Benjamin that he had already had his Adam's apple reduced and then had breast implants. Oestrogen treatment had assisted his progress, but he now wanted details of the best surgeon to complete the process. Although the procedure of surgical reassignment was available, the cost to many was prohibitive. One 27-year-old explained that Dr Barbosa of Tijuana was prepared to operate but wanted $4,000 – he himself earned only the equivalent of about $5 a month.[31]

Women also wrote in requesting reassignment. One eighteen-year-old Canadian, 'JA', had been tested and declared to be 100 per cent female but had always felt she was male. She offered to come in for any sort of experimental surgery Benjamin could offer. 'I would rather die in the operation than live like a half a person the rest of my life.'[32] As with many others in her position, Benjamin was her only lifeline. Benjamin always wrote back sympathetically offering sound advice, usually with a referral to someone who could treat them. After receiving his reply, 'JA' replied, 'You don't know how much it means to me to find understanding from a doctor.'[33] She started therapy at the Clark Institute in Toronto, the first female transsexual they had seen.

A man of great quality, Benjamin attracted the respect of his patients with his caring attitude. Many of them kept in touch with him for the rest of their lives. They often wrote later about how he was one of the first non-judgemental people they had come across. At this stage, few doctors knew how to treat their transgender patients and ignorance still pervaded most of the medical fraternity. Although Benjamin's priority was assisting patients, he was making conscious efforts to ensure doctors were becoming more educated in gender identity issues. He advised 'JA' to get her doctors to read *Transsexuals and Sex Reassignment* (1969) by Richard Green and John Money, two other doctors working in this area. One understanding wife even wrote in for her husband, who wanted reassignment. Through Benjamin, the husband found treatment and by 1975 could report that he was 'well on my way to the solution of my lifelong problem'.[34]

The first widely known case of a patient who had complete sex reassignment was Christine Jorgensen (1926–1989). Born George William, brought up in the Bronx, he was a frail little boy and afraid of fights, but nonetheless as an adult did a stint in the army. After taking female hormones, he saved enough to go to Sweden, where such surgery was more advanced. While on a stopover in Denmark, he was lucky enough to meet up with Dr Christian Hamburger, an endocrinologist who specialized in hormonal therapy and who agreed to help him. Jorgensen first had his testicles cut off, then had his penis removed the following year. By this time he had heard about Dr Benjamin's pioneering work, so travelled to New York to have vaginoplasty – a constructed vagina. The success of Jorgensen's sex change was to some extent a result of the additional hormone therapy that had become accessible.

Jorgensen's sex change hit the news in 1952 when the *New York Daily News* ran an article with the headline 'Ex GI Becomes Blonde

Beauty: Operation Transforms Bronx Youth'. The effect on the public was diverse: some congratulated Christine and others discriminated against her and subjected her to crude and cruel remarks. One police officer threatened, 'If you dare to use a public restroom, I'll have you picked up and examined by a board of doctors.'[35] Jorgensen walked off *The Dick Cavett Show* after Cavett made a comment about her 'wife'; she had been unable to marry the man she loved because of her status on her birth certificate. Her fiancé lost his job when it became known he was engaged to a transsexual. Nonetheless, Jorgensen used her fame to campaign for others in her position and continued to earn a living by singing and entertaining in theatres. She said in her autobiography,

> I read *The Well of Loneliness* not long ago. It made me more determined than ever to fight for this victory. The answer to the problem must not lie in sleeping pills and suicides that look like accidents, or in jail sentences, but rather in life and the freedom to live it.[36]

She rose above the derogatory comments, always carrying herself with dignity. She helped separate out the difference between transsexuals and transvestites, remarking, 'No one is 100 percent male or female . . . we all have elements of both male and female in our bodies. I just am more of a woman than I am a man.'

The Feminine Expression

Times were changing and in the 1950s, new help was offered to help transvestites and transsexuals. A transvestite going by the name of Edythe Ferguson, who lived in Long Beach, California, wrote a series of lectures for the instruction of transvestites. His aim was to provide practical advice on how to look and act like a woman. This involved changing mannerisms, vocal expression and physical appearance using the 'Julian Eltinge method of exploiting feminine expression'.[37] Ferguson produced an impressive list of 162 lectures covering topics such as 'Transvestism: Its Legal Perspective', 'A Most Important Phase of Femininity', 'Corset Adjustment and Padding', 'Would You Be Feminine? Hah?', 'The Facial Hair Problem: Its Solution', 'The Odour of Your Personality' and 'Outstanding Elements of the

Feminine Personality'. Qualified students were given individual attention, but Ferguson demanded commitment in terms of both time and
money. Students received approximately three lectures a week over
an eighteen-month period at a cost of $375. Ferguson compared the
course to a stint at college; 'the cost of the TRANSMUTATION series is
approximating attendance at a standard girls' finishing school'. He
was also very picky about who he allowed on the course:

> Applicants who are overweight or whose bone structure is
> very heavy or prominent, or who are more than 5' 10 and half
> inches in height are not encouraged for public entertain-
> ment or appearance; nor those possessing serious handi-
> caps or who anticipate a 'short cut' method of instruction.
> Triflers ignored.

Classes in dramatic instruction, ventriloquism and male/female
impersonation were also provided.

Ferguson gave reasons why he thought men wanted to dress
as women:

> This 'feel' [for female clothing] may be erotic or it may be
> aesthetic, asexual. It may also be both. But its motivating
> factor lies in an irresistible urge and impulse to more deeply
> delve into, and explore and 'know' femininity by way of self-
> expression and outward appearance.[38]

On the psychological understanding of transvestites, Ferguson was
fairly clear; the transvestite 'knows full well he is a man but feels
sorry that he has to be one and would be a lot happier were he a
woman'. This understanding does not always fit with the modern
one, where some male transvestites are heterosexual, like to be men
but find pleasure (and some say security) in occasionally dressing
as women. Ideas then were, however, fairly new and unstable. According to Havelock Ellis, many transsexuals were of low educational
standards, although Ferguson questioned this.[39] Judging from their
letters, most of the transvestites contacting Harry Benjamin for
help were articulate.

The criminalization of male cross-dressing was still a problem, as
Ferguson pointed out: 'laws have been enacted making cross-dressing

a "crime" in the case of the male but not in the case of a female – who is allowed to ape masculinity to her heart's content.'[40] Under the Municipal Code of Los Angeles section no. 52, 'any person desiring to wear any mask or personal disguise, whether complete or partial, upon any public street, sidewalk or park, shall file a written application with the Board'. The board then had to be satisfied that the person was of good moral character. The fact that women could dress in slacks with impunity while men could not wear skirts or dresses maddened Ferguson, who took up the topic in various lectures.

Gender Bending

Kinsey's survey of the 1940s and '50s complicated the hitherto straightforward historical dichotomy of the sexes between male and female. He introduced his 'Heterosexual–Homosexual Rating Scale' which ran from one to six, assessing 'femaleness' or 'maleness' within any one person. Some people were more 'masculine', at one end of the spectrum; others were more 'feminine' at the other; and there were many varieties in the middle. However, these bodily and mental varieties were further extended with the introduction of hormone therapy and sexual reassignment surgery. Those who felt they had been 'born in a body of the wrong sex' could now have sex reassignment surgery, a development that has progressed exponentially since its introduction. Now transwomen (male to female) can have newly constructed vaginas and transmen (female to male) can have newly constructed penises. The process has developed to make the change less painful and its appearance more realistic, and it is offered on a much broader scale.

Out of 5,000 people who had gender reassignment surgery in Britain by 2004, only 450 were women becoming men.[41] The country where the most operations took place was Thailand, followed by Iran, where gender reassignment surgery is accepted as a 'treatment' for homosexuality. Financial barriers preclude the poorest people from the operation in some countries, such as America, although other countries are changing their attitudes on this issue and allow the operation on their national health service. In Britain, sex changes on the NHS, which cost around £10,000, became a right in 1999 after the Court of Appeal recognized that those who believed they were born into the wrong body were suffering from a legitimate illness.[42]

Since the case in Germany in 2003 of a transsexual woman, Ms Van Kück, who was refused payment for hormone replacement therapy and gender reassignment surgery, application for medical treatment has become easier. The court found that the German medical fraternity was in breach of its obligation to supply the patient with the necessary treatment.

We now have the category of 'transgender', with which anyone can identify who does not fit with conventional socially defined gender roles. The term became popular in the 1970s to refer to people who wanted to live as members of the opposite sex without undergoing sex reassignment surgery. It can now apply to anyone who may not identify themselves wholly with their gender assigned at birth – or those who do not identify with either a male or female role but move between them, or identify with both, or neither, or as a separate type of gender. Before or between surgeries, patients could be 'in between' sexes: neither man nor woman, or both man and woman simultaneously.

Pre-operative male transsexuals with a glamorous appearance and full breasts but who also retain a penis have become a standard feature in pornography and prostitution. In the past, men wanting a sex operation who worked in the sex trade were called Ladyboys, but this term was mainly used to describe Asian people, most frequently in Thailand. In the nineteenth century in the West, the term 'shemale' was used to described assertive women, but has since been taken up more recently to describe a man with a penis and breasts who is on hormones and awaiting completion of his sex change. However, this term is reserved for those working in the sex trade and has demeaning connotations. It would be considered an offensive term to use to describe a transsexual who was not advertising themselves for business. A lesser-known term is the 'hefemale', sometimes applied to the female who has had her breasts removed and is awaiting the construction of a penis.

The area of gender and sexual orientation has therefore become much further complicated by transsexuality. There are men who want to transition to become women so they can have lesbian affairs, or women who want to become men so they can fulfil their role as a male homosexual. There are also those who have chosen to take hormones but not to realign their sex organs; they wish to remain 'in between'. As a result, a shift has occurred in the ways people perceive 'abnormalities'. Increasingly, people are calling for a way forward where bodies are accepted as they are; they argue that we should all be content to be what we all are born with, without the need to change. Demands are made for society to change its attitudes to avoid discrimination, rather than for people to change their bodies to fit a standard 'norm' of one sex or the other.

Woman with a dog: Franz von Bayros, 'Tantalus', from his *Tales at the Dressing Table*, 1908.

SIX

A Man's Best Friend: Bestiality

One thing I learned, you have to be careful in choosing your sex partner – it's difficult and dangerous to rape a horse.

Mark Matthews, *The Horseman: Obsessions of a Zoophile* (1994)

In Lucius Apuleius' *The Golden Ass* (or *Metamorphoses*, second century AD), a willing animal is depicted copulating with a beautiful woman, although it confesses to being a little nervous. The ass admits,

> I was greatly troubled by no small fear, thinking in what manner should I be able, with legs so many and of such a size, to mount a tender and highborn lady; or, encircle with hard hooves her limbs softened with milk and honey and so white and delicate.[1]

If the audience in the ancient world found it acceptable (or at least funny) in literature for an ass to copulate with a human, why do some people find it so offensive now? Often, in the present day, sex with animals is considered with morbid curiosity rather than as a terrible crime or sin, but in the medieval period, such actions could condemn a person to eternal damnation. Why was it considered so dreadful?

Most of the answers take us back to Judaism, with part of its morality being taken up by Christianity. Bestiality was considered unclean and the Torah ordered that Jews should abstain from lying with animals. Christians inherited this aversion and condemned bestiality as an unnatural act and a sin. Sex with animals was considered among the worst of crimes among Christians, alongside sex between two men, both acts being classed as sodomy. Bestiality was seen as 'against nature' and women were considered as capable as men of committing sodomy with animals. Leviticus 18:23 commanded, 'Neither shall thou lie with any beast to defile thyself therewith; neither shall any woman stand before a beast to lie down thereto', although few cases were ever brought before the ecclesiastical courts.

Today, in our secular times, can sex with animals be considered out of bounds? Even outside the context of religion and sin, it is still considered taboo. Is this because of outdated prudish concepts of immorality that still linger, or a more deep-seated feeling of abhorrence towards such acts? Attention is now shifting from the idea of human–animal sex as a problem towards the abuse of the animals themselves. The long history of sex between humans and animals suggests a deep-rooted connection between them – encompassing hunger (food), work, entertainment, pleasure and even love – and this bond is sometimes complicated by the emotions they evoke in us. In the time of ancient Greece, however, animals were closely connected to life and reproduction, and tales of sexual connection with them were part of everyday life.

Zoological Tales

In mythology and legend, people were often described as being enamoured with animals: the god Zeus turned into a swan in order to seduce Leda, and she produced four eggs which hatched as her children, Castor, Pollux, Helen and Clytemnestra. This was one of Zeus's more delicate affairs. In another, he disguised himself as a white bull in order to impregnate Europa. Most of these narratives involve a symbolically hyper-potent male animal mating with a human female: Philyra was raped by Kronos manifest as a horse, and bore the centaur Chiron; Poseidon, as a horse, mated with Demeter in Arcadia, and she bore him the horse Arion. The satyr Pan attacked the shepherd Daphnis and had frontal intercourse with a nanny goat. Occasionally, women were the instigators of bestiality: after Poseidon had cast a spell on Pasiphaë, the wife of King Minos, she fell in love with a snow-white bull. In order to enable sex to take place, she requested a wooden hollow cow to be built that she could place herself inside. She then positioned herself in such a way that her vagina was presented to the amorous attack of the bull without fear of any damage to her body. The fruit of this embrace was the Minotaur, half-bull, half-man, which was later to be slain by Theseus.[2] The ancient Romans were treated to a gruesome show

Fresco depicting a scene from Apuleius, *The Golden Ass*, c. 1575.

Léon-François Comerre, *Leda and the Swan*, 1908.

when, according to Suetonius, Nero caused the spectacle of Pasiphaë
to be enacted for real at public events.

Sex was part of religious rituals in which gods and goddesses
turned into animals and had sex with humans. Copulating with a
snake was said to produce great sons: Olympia, mother of Alexander
the Great, was a devout member of the orgiastic snake-worshipping
cult of Dionysus; it was said that Aristodama had sex with a snake
and bore Aratus. The founding of cities and families often depended

Pan copulating with a goat, ancient Roman marble statue found at Herculaneum, now in the 'Secret Room' at the Naples Archaeological Museum.

on the creation of a legend in which men are spawned or nurtured by animals. The myth of the founding of Rome is well known, with Romulus and his twin brother Remus suckled by a wolf. Less renowned is the mythical tale of the origins of the Danish royal family in which a beautiful girl was impregnated by a bear. She bore a hairy son with human limbs whom she named Ursus. After the bear was killed, she took her son back to her city where he married and sired sons of his own, one of whom in turn fathered Suens, king of the Danes. Such tales reinforced the connection between people and animals and assimilated them into everyday life. Bulls were worshipped; horses were praised for their strength and heroics; wolves and bears, which might have been regarded as a threat in the wild, were befriended and became family.

Reports of real-life incidents of a bestial nature came from Herodotus, who informed us that in ancient Egypt women copulated with goats: 'In my life-time a monstrous thing happened in this province, a woman having open intercourse with a he-goat.'[3] This activity allegedly took place in Mendes, where the goat was considered sacred, and their god was worshipped in its caprine form. Herodotus was known for his inventions and has not always been found to be accurate, though Xenophon also records sex with goats in ancient Greece. Plutarch commented on the state of Greece,

> When Nature, supported though she be by law, cannot contain your intemperance within the bounds of reason, as if it were a torrent carrying it away perforce, she often and in many places commits great outrages, disorders, and scandals against nature in the matter of the pleasure of love; for there have been men who have conceived a passion for she-goats, sows and mares.[4]

The real-life activities of women in ancient Rome were no less savoury according to Martial, who stated that women sometimes inserted snakes into their vaginas. Curiously, this was supposed to have been both for sexual purposes and also as a means of keeping cool, as it was thought to deodorize that part of the body in the heat of summer. Lucian also comments that snakes were taught to suckle on women's nipples.[5]

Satyr presents gifts to Venus, engraving by Maarten de Vos the Elder, *c.* 1580s.

This tolerance or even promotion of the imagery of sex with beasts was part of the ancient religious world, in which animals played a large role. Animals were incorporated into the universal scheme, their lives interwoven with that of humans. However, people in the Christian era were to distance themselves from animals, at least in their understanding of morality, and bestiality was condemned as a sinful act and a perversion of nature.

To Lie with a Beast

Various penances were devised for the sin of bestiality. The most appropriate punishment, according to Leviticus 20:15–16, was death. Church authorities did their best to avert such intimacy with animals by putting the fear of God into unwitting souls. One Church Father, St Jerome (c. 347–420), declared that he had seen women giving birth to satyrs after they had copulated with apes in the desert.[6] By the ninth century, Egbert, king of Wessex, deemed bestial relations worthy of 100 days of penance. However, Burchard's penitential list suggested 40 days' subsistence on only bread and water, with seven years of penance for unmarried men who had committed bestiality, and ten for married men. Just as in cases of masturbation, a single man had the excuse of his lack of access to sex, but a married man with a wife at home should not be practising sex with animals. Nonetheless, certain communities continued to include bestiality in particular rituals. Around 1188, a cleric called Gerald described a bizarre ancient rite that took place in Ireland in the tiny hamlet of Kenelcunill. When a king was appointed, he was brought before an audience of his people and was expected to copulate with a white mare while declaring himself also to be a beast. The mare was then killed and boiled in water in which the king then had to bathe. Afterwards, he and his people would eat the flesh of the mare and drink the water in which he has bathed. Gerald suggested that this ceremony was still being performed in the twelfth century.[7]

By around the year 1000, animals came to be seen as just as culpable as their human partners and were brought before the courts alongside their partners in crime. If found guilty, the pair were then hanged or burned together. In the Middle Ages, therefore, animals were considered just as guilty as the person who had perpetrated the crime. The Parliament of Paris of 1601 and that of Aix in 1679

Gustave Courbet, *Nude Woman with a Dog, c.* 1861–2.

burned the beasts involved in such crimes on the grounds that if they were allowed to live, the odious crime would live on in the memory of others. Most frequently, culprits were caught when a neighbour or fellow worker happened upon someone with a cow in the cowshed, a mare in the fields or some other large animal. Perhaps because of the size of the animals involved, these activities could not be missed. For the same reason of size, activities between cattle and humans tended to be committed by men. According to the criminal records, women tended to prefer smaller animals such as dogs and cats.[8] Because of this, it was harder to detect them. Did men and women who had sex with beasts actually prefer it or did they do it because they could not get sex from other people? Or were animals simply more available in rural areas and bestial acts merely opportunistic?

Reasons for bestiality can sometimes be gleaned by examination of trial records. Only a few bestiality cases were recorded in England in the seventeenth and eighteenth centuries,[9] but when they did come to light, they provoked shock and horror among the public. Records of bestiality often did not survive, as the trial papers were burned along with the offenders in an attempt to erase the shameful acts from history. In the sixteenth century, royal prosecutor Simon Gueulette ordered the destruction of at least 40 trial records to get rid of any trace of the misdeeds, but copies survived and found their way into the archives of the Bibliothèque Nationale in Paris.

In one trial in November 1555, the defendant appears to have made a habit of bestiality. Jean de La Soille was a 26-year-old mule keeper employed to look after the asses of Monsieur de Terron. His previous employer, the local grocer Josse Valeroin, had repeatedly told his new employer that the youth had already sodomized a favourite jenny (female ass) some time previously. Meanwhile, another witness, the local innkeeper, had caught the mule keeper sexually assaulting a jenny only the week before. With so much evidence before the judges, it was inevitable that La Soille would be found guilty and given a death sentence; the unfortunate jenny was to be burned before the prisoner and the prisoner then hanged and strangled, his body thrown on to the fire following the animal. The activities of Jean de La Soille appear not to have been merely opportunistic (although he had the perfect job to allow for the act); he had made a specific practice of seeking out mules and asses. Enough witnesses had caught him in the act to warrant him a true bestialist.

Some accusations of bestiality, however, seem to lie on less certain grounds. In the case of 35-year-old wagonmaker Antoine de La Rue, the accusation may have been a way of settling old scores. He came to trial in 1622 after visiting the apothecary for a cream to salve a strange injury – it appeared that La Rue had grazed his skin through carnal intercourse, or at least that is what he had told the apothecary who gave witness to the court. La Rue's apprentice, Thomas Le Fèvre, also gave evidence that he had seen his master sodomizing a white mare. Meanwhile, the prisoner's wife told the court that she knew her husband 'copulated daily with the mare', but felt unable to do anything about it. She was, however, enraged by the fact that her husband had earlier beaten her up, and therefore had reason to bear a grudge. Her husband had also forced her to have unnatural intercourse with him in a way 'other than is allowed by decent marital relations'. Although she refused, he came upon her while she was sleeping and fulfilled his intentions against her wishes. When La Rue came to give evidence, he admitted he had beaten his wife but said he did so because she was having an affair with the apothecary. In this case, events behind the scene provide other reasons for accusations of sodomy with animals. It may have been a ruse of Le Fèvre's wife, intended to get rid of a troublesome spouse. While it easy to see how such cases might be fabricated, the authorities did not see likewise. La Rue was hanged in the square of Montpensier and his body was burned along with that of the horse.[10]

Sometimes it was the animal itself that gave the game away, as in the case of a sixteen-year-old girl, Claudine de Culam. She was brought to trial at Rougnon in France in 1601 alongside her white spotted dog. Despite her mother's protestations of her daughter's innocence, the girl was ordered to strip naked. As the dog was brought into the chamber, it jumped on her, 'knowing her carnally', and it was obvious to all who were watching that it knew what to do. Both the girl and the dog were strangled and then burned; their ashes were thrown to the wind so that no trace would be left of them.[11] Cases of women having sex with dogs were also found in London. In 1677, a married woman from Cripplegate thought to be aged between 30 and 40 was sentenced to death for her crime. According to the summary of her case brought before the Old Bailey:

> With not the fear of God before her eyes, *nor regarding the order of Nature*, on the 23rd of June last, to the disgrace of all womankind, did commit Buggery with a certain Mungril Dog, and wickedly, divellishly, and *against nature* had venereal and Carnal copulation with him.[12]

Through several holes in the wall between her house and next door, her neighbours had been able to see her in acts of 'uncleanliness'. The dog was brought before the prisoner and 'owned her by wagging his tail, and making motions as it were to kiss her, which 'twas sworn she did do when she made that horrid use of him.' She was sentenced to death. No mention is made of what happened to the dog.

Although now it may seem unusual for people to commit bestial acts with their animals, it seems even worse that the perpetrator should die for it. Yet in the past, the act was not seen as a simple sexual transgression of society's rules, but a complete abrogation of the laws of God. It transcended normality and left a stain on society too horrendous to contemplate. The act and the culprits therefore had to be wiped out of existence.

An Abominable Sin

There was a certain reluctance by judges to convict for bestiality, perhaps because of the capital punishments for guilty perpetrators. This may also explain the unwillingness of lay people to report such crimes when they came across them, despite their aversion to the behaviour. Generally, legal authorities preferred to keep quiet about the subject. This became evident in the 1670s, when the Scottish legal advocate George MacKenzie demanded that cases of bestiality must be tried at night, and instructed that no written records should be kept of the trials. If found guilty, the perpetrator was quietly drowned at dawn in order to keep the crime hidden.

People were gradually moving to cities where acts of bestiality were more difficult to disguise. According to the London court records at least, bestiality was confined to domestic households with smaller animals, while cases in the countryside tended to involve large animals. It was not necessarily the case that there were fewer large animals kept in the city, as horses were seen everywhere, being an essential means of transport. But a sexual act with a large animal would be easy to spot by people living and working in close proximity to each other, and therefore potential perpetrators were less willing to take the risk. When men were exposed in the act of committing a bestial act, the witnesses could be male or female – at least in the countryside – but when women were caught, it was most often by their female neighbours, in towns and cities. This may have been because, as seen in the cases mentioned above, men were more likely to choose larger animals while women stuck to smaller, often canine partners. As a result, men were more likely to be caught in barns and sheds (as their targets were larger bovine or equine creatures kept outside) and women caught in their own rooms with their pets.

One case involved a woman whose activities were observed through chinks in a partition floor by her fellow tenant in a townhouse. Mary Price, alias Hartington, from the parish of 'Eling' (Ealing), was brought before the Old Bailey in London on 26 April 1704 and indicted for the 'Horrible and abominable Sin of Sodomy' committed with her dog. The nosy neighbour lived in a room upstairs from the accused, and it was reported that 'she saw her sitting in a Chair, by the Fire-side, looking backward, and took the Dog to her, which she said, acted with her as to a Bitch.'[13] The accused stated in her defence that she did nothing of the sort and it was mere malice on the part of the other tenant. Other neighbours gave evidence that there had been quarrels between the two women and the accused was acquitted.

It was mostly men who were caught in opportunistic incidents. In Geneva in 1678 an eighteen-year-old farmhand named Jean-Marc Tournier was brought to trial after being seen buggering a cow by a neighbour. The authorities took the time and trouble to interview countless residents of the village in Burgundy where the act had taken place. They all thought it suspicious that he herded the cows alone when it was usually a two-person job, but Jean-Marc gave the defence that he liked to be alone 'to think'. A wall of silence fell around the villagers after the boy's brothers threatened everyone in the village. Those brought forward as witnesses to the act said that the boy in the dock had the wrong colour of hair and hat. Although the court felt Jean-Marc was guilty, the case collapsed from lack of evidence.[14]

Another fortunate fellow was a man from Shoreditch brought before the Old Bailey on 17 June 1677. He had been seen 'amongst the Bricke-kilns [to] drive a white Mare to a small Heap of Bricks, which he had laid together, and there use most unnatural and brutish Endeavours several times, and after that to another Bay Mare'. He confessed he lately came out of Kent to seek for work, and within three or four days after his coming up was 'apprehended in this beastly Action'.[15] He too was found not guilty.

In Britain, the crime of 'buggery' was generally applied to cases of bestiality, as seen in the case in 1776 against Christopher Saunders, a cook on a ship who 'feloniously and wickedly against the order of nature did carnally know the said beast called a cow, and with the said beast called a cow did feloniously and wickedly and against the order of nature commit and perpetrate the detestable and abominable crime, not to be named among Christians, called Buggery'. One of the witnesses, Abraham Denning, was working in the cowshed on 10 March. In his evidence, he said:

> I heard the cow move; I looked through to see what was the matter, it was in another barn adjoining; it was a boarded

barn and there were chinks; I saw the prisoner at the bar
stroking the cow and patting her; I never knew the prisoner
before; this was about six o'clock in the morning; it was light
and I could see him stroking and patting her; then he went
to the other end of the barn and fetched a tub to put behind
the cow, it stood up edgeways; then he got up on the top of
the side of the tub; I saw him unbutton his breeches and
his trowsers; I saw him make motions as if he had a mind to
do; I did not see any part of his body, but he made motions
towards the cow.[16]

According to the witness, Saunders was with the cow for about ten
minutes. Another witness, John Tumey, told the court:

I knew nothing of this affair till the last witness came and
called me; I went down; he said there was a man in the barn;
I asked him what he was doing, he said come along, do not
stand, and we went there immediately; the prisoner was
standing close to the cow hustling his breeches up, he did
not get them up till we got to the door; Denning laid hold of
his collar on one side and I on the other; the prisoner asked
me what we were doing.

Despite evidence of his good character being given by Saunders's
wife and various others, and continuing to deny his crimes, he was
found guilty and sentenced to death.

From the evidence of seventeenth- and eighteenth-century
Sweden, it appears that many cases were not only opportunistic but
also involved drinking.[17] In both Switzerland and Sweden, the preference was for cows, though pigs had been common in the New
World of puritanical seventeenth-century America. In New England,
the aptly named Thomas Hogg was accused of fathering a piglet
that resembled him. At the trial, Hogg was instructed to fondle the
animal, 'and immediately there appeared a working of lust in the sow,
insomuch she poured out the seed before them'.[18] Hogg denied
having anything to do with her but failed to convince the jury. In
the end, he was charged with the lesser crimes of filthiness, lying and
pilfering, and sentenced to a whipping and hard labour.

What the Papers Say

Few cases of bestiality were reported in the newspapers of the eight-eenth century – and when they were, they were reduced to one-liners. Although the reporters seemed to want the public to know about such cases, they were not prepared to give out details. Under its 'Country News' section, the *Whitehall Evening Post* of 13 October 1789 reported that a Samuel Stretton had been arraigned for bestiality with an ewe but was discharged. According to the *London Evening Post* of 30 April 1772, a black man was tried for attempted bestiality at Hickman's Hall and found guilty.[19] The *Courier and Evening Gazette* of 23 July 1799 reported that Joseph Dewey had been found guilty of bestiality at the Assizes in Leicester and sentenced to death, but no mention was made of what happened to the animal.[20] Perhaps the newspapers wanted to encourage people to report such crimes, but were afraid to provide the details in case others followed suit.

Not all perpetrators of bestiality were given a capital sentence, and attitudes were gradually changing. Although in 1821 in Britain the Buggery Act still applied a sentence of death for acts with animals, in some cases the punishment was seen as too harsh for the crime and those found guilty were let off with a prison sentence. The law was eventually to catch up with changes in public opinion, and the punishment was amended to life imprisonment under the Offences Against the Person Act of 1861, which stated, 'Whosoever shall be convicted of the abominable crime of buggery, committed either with mankind or with any animal, shall be liable . . . to be kept in penal servitude for life.'[21] By the early nineteenth century, accord-ing to newspaper reports, guilty verdicts differentiated between actual and 'attempted' bestiality, which may indicate the reason for the lighter sentencing. According to the *Bury and Norwich Post* of 26 February 1823, a Mr Masby received only two months' imprison-ment for the latter, with the first fortnight in solitary confinement, and a good whipping.[22] The type of animal involved was not men-tioned. Robert Rose and Jonathan Burrell were both charged with bestiality at Norfolk assizes.[23] No sentence was mentioned. In York Assizes, the authorities seem to have been more lenient with those less mentally able: they let off the 'imbecile' Daniel Woodliff from Calster, who had been caught committing bestiality with a calf. John Wilkinson, being tried at the same time for the same offence with a cow, was less fortunate: he received two years' imprisonment.[24] A person's mental capacity was therefore an issue for the courts' consideration in cases of bestiality.

By 1830, newspaper reports on bestiality were starting to include extra information, such as the judge's comments and the state of the prisoner. This may have been caused by an increase in public interest in the subject, combined with decreasing censorship about the activity (and less concern about making it public). Reporters recognized the titillation value of such scandals and wanted to make the most of it. Under the heading 'Abominable Crime', the *Morning Post* of 31 August 1830 told of 39-year-old Joseph Rowbottom, who had come before the court for committing bestiality in Pendle, near Manchester. While sentencing, the judge harangued him, declaring,

> You have been convicted upon the clearest possible evidence of the perpetration of a crime which by the laws of God and Man has ever doomed the wretched individual by whom it has been committed to be cut off from his fellow-creatures . . . your mind being darkened by sin and iniquity.

The crime was still considered serious enough for Rowbottom to be sentenced to death with no hope of reprieve. Similarly, the *Liverpool News* for 16 August 1833 reported the events of the Lancaster Assizes under the heading 'Unnatural Crime'. This time the journalist reported some background details about the prisoner, 41-year- old John Haworth, a labourer who had been married twice and had two or three children. He came to court in an agitated stated and burst into tears on being sentenced to death, apparently not expecting such a harsh sentence.[25] The judge was unsympathetic, declaring the usual rhetoric, 'You have been found guilty . . . of the abominable crime, not to be named among Christians.'

Fear of the Hybrid

The antagonism towards bestiality comes in part from the fear of being associated too closely with the animal race. The spawning of hybrids became a real underlying fear when men began to travel far afield and to encounter strange animals they had never seen before. Dutch physician Jacob de Bondt (1591–1631), travelling with the Dutch East

India Company, introduced strange new creatures to the world. His work *Historiae naturalis et medicae Indiae orientalis* (1631) depicted the orangutan as an extraordinary-looking human female with fur, and reported that it wept and showed human characteristics. Bondt blamed local bestiality for the beast; he claimed that the orangutan 'was born of the lust of Indonesian women who consort in disgusting lechery with apes'.[26] His assertions were typical of a group of male travellers who saw dark-skinned 'primitives' – indigenous peoples such as Africans, Aborigines, Maoris and Indians – as akin to beasts and happily ascribed animalistic traits to them.

Sex between humans and animals also fascinated people because of the idea that it could produce curious progeny and risk corrupting the human race. Tales of human–animal hybrids were told not only in mythology but also in real-life medical publications. Physicians reported incidents of strange births to medical journals, and wrote them up in casebooks. One remarkable book of curiosities was *On Monsters and Marvels*, written by the sixteenth-century physician Ambroise Paré, who explained, 'There are monsters that are born with

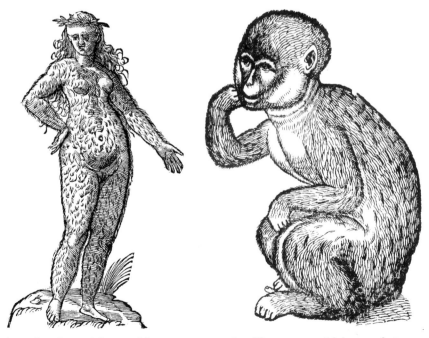

'Foemina cinnaminiae gentis', woman with excess body hair, from Ulisse Aldrovandi, *Monstrorum historia* (1642).

Ape-like creature with human features, woodcut by Conrad Gesner, *Historiae animalium* (1551–8).

Apes attacking two naked women: illustration by Jean-Michel Moreau for
Voltaire's *Candide*, c. 1803.

a form that is half-animal and the other [half] human, or retaining
everything from animals, which are produced by sodomites and
atheists who "join together" and break out of their bounds – unnat-
urally – with animals.'[27] From these unions, hideous monsters were
born. One example, in a chapter headed 'An Example of the Mixture
or Mingling of Seed' relayed the birth of a creature in 1493 that came
about as a result of a union between a woman and a dog. The upper
part of the creature's body resembled its mother but the lower part

had the hindquarters of a dog. The hybrid was allegedly sent to the Pope. Paré also wrote about a shepherd named Cratain in Sybaris who, 'having exercised his brutal desire with one of his goats', produced offspring with the head of a child and the body of a goat. Another of Paré's tales involved a woman who gave birth to a daughter as hairy as a bear because she had looked upon a picture of St John in a bearskin. Such tales continued to reverberate well into the eighteenth century.

In 1726, the infamous case of Mary Toft, a 26-year-old servant girl from Godalming in Surrey, was on everyone's lips after she asserted that she had given birth to eighteen rabbits (the number varied in each account). In search of fame and fortune, she had inserted various rabbit parts into her vagina with the intention of duping her doctor. She had called in her local physician, claiming to be in labour, and, to his astonishment, out popped the various bits of rabbit. He reported, 'I waited for the coming of the fresh Pains, which

'Youth with the lower body of a canine', from Ulisse Aldrovandi, *Monstrorum historia* (1642).

hapned in three or four minutes, at which time I deliver'd her of the entire trunk, strip'd of Skin.' All of the parts were partially formed: 'They were all broken in Pieces, and much in the same Manner . . . First the four Paws with the Fur on; then the Liver and the Intestines; the Trunk and Shoulders in another Part.'[28] The king sent his own surgeon to investigate and Toft continued to successfully outwit most of the medical fraternity, relating her tale to anyone who would listen. Although she may not have heard of the various strange phenomena being regularly reported in the Royal Society's pamphlet 'Philosophical Transactions', she would have been familiar with local folklore. People still believed that a pregnant women's imagination could stamp monstrous marks – either birthmarks or some sort of deformity – on her baby's body.[29] Toft played on such beliefs to add credulity to her case, saying she had craved rabbit meat during her pregnancy. In the end, she confessed her fabrication to investigating doctor Sir Richard Manningham and was sent to Bridewell Prison, where she served four months.

White male Europeans wanted to distance themselves from supposedly inferior, primitive men and animals. Darwin frightened many a Victorian when he spoke of a common ancestor between man and beast in his *Origin of Species* (1859) and *Descent of Man* (1871). His idea had been popularized as the theory that man had

William Hogarth, *Cunicularii; or, The Wise Men of Godliman in Consultation*, 1726: Mary Toft gives birth to numerous rabbits.

descended from the ape, with an unknown 'missing link' between men and animals. These 'links' were leapt on as evidence of the possibility of man-beasts or hybrids, so when travellers found astonishing children in the wild they were taken as examples of this missing link in the stage of evolution. Journeying through the kingdom of Oude in the 1840s, William Henry Sleeman, an officer of the East India Company, described the wolf-child cases he had heard about. After being raised by wolves, these children were then rescued and returned to the human world, by which time they were incapable of behaving like humans. They refused to wear clothes, lapped water like dogs, growled like wolves and walked on all fours.

A general interest in man-beast stories developed. Wild children were a feature of popular books such as Thomas Henry Huxley's *Man's Place in Nature* (1863) and Rudyard Kipling's *The Jungle Book* (1894). A strong sexual element emerged, incorporating eroticization of the animalistic, and attached itself to stories in which the crossing of boundaries was feared, but nonetheless explored. While the stories focused on a central erotic character, the subtext was sex and horror. Books such as Bram Stoker's *Dracula* (man into bat, 1897) and Robert Louis Stephenson's *Strange Case of Dr Jekyll and Mr Hyde* (man into beast, 1886) became best-sellers. Werewolf tales, which had been around for centuries in Scandinavian folklore, re-emerged in novels such as Guy Endore's *The Werewolf of Paris* (1933). In literature, the oft-used theme of humans falling in love with beasts could be seen in such stories as Honoré de Balzac's *A Passion in the Desert* (about a love affair between a soldier and a female panther, 1830) and David Garnett's *Lady into Fox* (1922), and fairy tales including *Beauty and the Beast* and *The Frog Prince*.

Similarly, love between humans and animals were taken up in film. The gigantic gorilla *King Kong* (1933) with his love for a human heroine kick-started a cinematic fascination with hairy beasts in romantic lead roles. Many years later, the French film *Max, Mon Amour* (1986, dir. Nagisa Oshima) took this idea one step further in a remarkably non-judgmental cinematic exploration of love and sex between a woman (played by Charlotte Rampling) and a chimpanzee. More explicit was the prolonged horse-mating sequence in Walerian Borowczyk's film *La Bête* (The Beast, 1975). America had its own bizarre comedy take on bestiality with Woody Allen's *Everything You Always Wanted to Know About Sex* (*But Were Afraid to Ask)* (1972), in which

Lucas Cranach the Elder, *The Werewolf*, c. 1510.

a psychiatrist played by Allen falls in love with a winsome sheep named Daisy. The discovery of the affair drives him to the gutter, to drink 'Woolite' in despair.

Towards the end of the nineteenth century, there was increasing interest in why people wanted to have sex with animals. The question of whether this was abnormal or not arose. The answers came with the emergence of psychiatry, psychology and sexology, and a raft of new scientific views to provide reasons as to why people might commit acts of bestiality. In his *Three Essays on the Theory of Sexuality*

(1908), Freud suggested that such people were timid and were unable to find suitable sexual partners. Krafft-Ebing considered bestiality to be connected to a low moral standing and a strong sexual drive. He distinguished between zoophilia and zooerasty: the first was a kind of fetish connected to a love of animals which might or might not manifest itself in a sexual way, but involved a need to caress and fondle animals that might act as an erotic stimulus; the second was a pathological condition, a sexual perversion which manifested itself in an insurmountable urge for sex with animals. However, acts of bestiality might occur which involved direct contact with animal genitals but with no pathological content when a great sexual desire existed but no suitable partner was available. There have also been cases of *mixoscopic zoophilia* – sexual pleasure experienced while watching copulating animals.

Avisodomy, or Sex with Birds

One 'new' obsession that arose in the eighteenth century was copulation with birds (although cases may yet be found to prove it existed earlier). The act entailed a man putting his penis into the cloaca (posterior opening) of the bird, then strangling it. As the bird's sphincter contracted, it would squeeze the man's penis and produce an ejaculation. According to the Marquis de Sade, Parisian brothels catered for the predilection (now called avisodomy), which he describes in a scenario of one of his novels: 'the girl holds the bird's [turkey's] neck locked between her thighs, you have her ass straight ahead of you, and she cuts the bird's throat the same moment you discharge'.[30] Havelock Ellis noted this desire for sex with birds in his analysis of sexual perversions during the nineteenth century. Much as Sade had envisaged, Ellis recorded that on their visits to prostitutes, men took live pigeons to be strangled just before the men had intercourse with the women. He also mentions a woman who could only orgasm after catching and stroking a chicken and wringing its neck.[31] This last case, however, seems more in the realms of sadism as a sexual stimulus rather than any sort of true bestiality.

By the mid-nineteenth century, the practice had become well known in military circles, according to a case reported in the *Gazette Médicale* in 1849. Non-commissioned soldiers became suspicious after they were being served duck for dinner somewhat more

Gerda Wegener (1886–1940), girl with swan, from *Les Délassements d'Eros*,
c. 1925.

frequently than they would normally expect. Apparently the quarter-
master was sodomizing the ducks, splitting open their cloaca, then
serving them up for meals.[32] Another case, *United States v. Lebel*,
was tried by general court martial in Oxford and involved a soldier
copulating with chickens. The defendant was charged around 10
October 1944 with violating the 96th Article of War. Although he
denied the crime, the soldier was dishonourably discharged with
two years' hard labour. On 2 February 1960, Ricardo Sanchez was
brought before court martial by the U.S. Army after he was accused
of copulating with a fowl, 'penetrating the chicken's rectum with his
penis with intent to gratify his lust'.[33] He had also molested a three-
year-old girl. He was found guilty and given a dishonourable discharge with three years' confinement.

Krafft-Ebing uncovered two cases of avisodomy both reported
in 1889; the reasons for each were different. The first only came to

a Boileau Despreaux

Penis-headed ducks accost a young woman, Martin van Maële, *La Grande danse macabre des vifs* (*The Great Danse Macabre of the Quick Prick*, 1907–8).

light after chickens had been dying one after another. The culprit was eventually apprehended red-handed. When asked by the judge why he had committed such an act, the culprit replied that his genitals were so small that normal coitus was impossible. On examination, this was indeed found to be the case – but he was found to be mentally sound. The second case was that of a sixteen-year-old shoemaker's apprentice who was caught with his penis in a goose. He was found to have had a cerebral disease. Krafft-Ebing, in line with his thoughts on other perversions, believed that the boy's mental deficiency led him to commit the acts.

Reasons to be Fearful

Although bestiality might be tried out opportunistically or as a result of mental incapacity, people also experimented out of simple curiosity. Havelock Ellis provided a case of one pretty, well-educated country girl from Missouri who, on examination, was found to have a profuse offensive discharge emanating from her genitals. When questioned, the patient confessed that she had been playing with the genitals of a large dog, which had become so excited that she thought she might try 'slight coitus'. On close inspection of her vagina, she was found to be bleeding from three large tears. The animal had hung on so tightly with his forelegs that she had been unable to get him off – the dog's penis had become so swollen that the dog could not extract itself.[34] If a dog is separated from its partner before ejaculating, it can cause pain and serious damage. A dog's penis has a bone, the baculum, as well as a small bulb at the base, which swells up to five times its normal size once inside the vagina. The bitch's muscles tighten and 'lock on', which means that two dogs become stuck together. In this case, the young woman from Missouri suffered considerable physical harm.

Alcohol continued to feature in twentieth-century bestiality cases. In 1944, one 33-year-old cement worker from northern Sweden confessed to police that he had stumbled into a stable and attempted to put his penis into a cow, but fell off the stool he was standing on, unable to complete the act, before groping his way home to bed. He later retracted his confession and the court acquitted him. Jens Rydström, the historian who uncovered the case, believes that the period from 1880 onwards in Sweden was a time when views were changing on bestiality. People who committed bestial acts (*tidelag*) were no longer seen as 'sinners' but as 'perverts'. Police tended to regulate the sexual behaviour of the poor more frequently, and bestialists brought before the courts were most often from the lower classes, mostly farm-hands. Swedish authorities eventually abolished the law on bestiality as they thought it outdated and considered

Girl stuck to a dog,
Martin van Maële,
*La Grande danse
macabre* (1907).

that a person who committed such activities was in need of treatment, rather than punishment.[35] Many perpetrators were also now being classed as insane, although it seems obvious in some cases the acts committed were merely opportunistic. These types of acts were still most frequently committed by adolescent boys working on farms.

Another problem arose for the u.s. Army (*u.s. v. Malone*) during the Second World War, when an American soldier was caught sodomizing a cow in Ipswich. A British farmer chased him through a field and called the police. Rushing to the spot, when the police snapped on their headlights, they found him mounting the cow. As mitigating evidence, the soldier said he was intoxicated – he could hardly deny the charge as his erect penis was encrusted with dung.[36] According to the police witnesses, the hindquarters of the cow were imprinted on the defendant's thighs. His case came to trial on 8 September 1943 and he was sentenced to a dishonourable discharge and three years' hard labour.

In other cases, sexual acts took place with an animal because the owner felt a real emotional attachment to it. Such a case of zoophilia was aired on the Jerry Springer show in the programme entitled *I Married a Horse*. The story followed the commitment of marriage made between Mark Matthews (a pseudonym) and Pixel, his pony. Matthews had already tried marriage to a woman and had two children, but he preferred his pony. Springer's comment was 'This is pretty sick', to which Matthews retorted, 'A psychologist called it an unusual adjustment to a unique situation.' The programme was not aired on some channels as it was considered too obscene. Matthews wrote about his experience with his own version of 'My Little Pony' in *The Horseman: Obsessions of a Zoophile*, published in 1994. While in college, he fell in love with a pony called Goldie that lived nearby and began having sex with her. The man who looked after the horse caught him with Goldie but was surprisingly non-judgemental. As Matthews explained, 'Loe surprised me alright. He was the first adult outside of Dad who found out about my desires and not only accepted but condoned them.'[37] The relationship of such men and women with their animals was not merely sexual, but emotional, with loving attachments formed, apparently on both sides. In these relationships, the human partner frequently declared that the love was reciprocated.

The Love of Furry Friends

Attraction to animals appears to be gender-biased, with most studies concurring that women were less prone to bestiality than men. In investigations of past trial records, this bias is seen to pre-date modern times. In one study of bestiality involving the examination of 1,200 cases in seventeenth- and eighteenth-century Sweden, only nine of the cases that came to trial involved women.[38] Kinsey's study of sexual behaviour in the 1940s and 1950s found that only about 8 per cent of all men interviewed had had sex with animals, most in adolescence. However, when it was narrowed down to farm boys it was as high as 50 per cent. In Kinsey's study, among women, the rate was only 3.5 per cent. Just as with most of the eighteenth-century cases, men usually went for larger farm animals, whereas women opted for smaller animals such as dogs.[39] Furthermore, according to Kinsey, men opted for vaginal or anal copulation whereas women liked general body contact or preferred masturbation of the animal. Only a small minority experienced cunnilingus from the animal, or coitus. Morton Hunt undertook a similar investigation in 1974; his sample showed higher percentages of oral contacts for women, with no actual female–animal coitus. He found a similar desire for certain animals as Kinsey had uncovered, but over twenty years, there had been a decrease to just under 5 per cent for males and nearly 2 per cent for females who had sex with animals. This drop he attributed to a declining rural environment in the United States, as people were moving to the cities.[40] Also, the sexual revolution of the 1960s allowed for greater opportunity for sex with other people and less inhibition about sex generally. Both studies show that actual incidents of bestiality were infrequent, and rare after adolescence.

More recently, a new kind of sexual activity has arisen which connects sex, animals and humans among people who call themselves 'plushies' or 'furries'. Plushophilia is a modern concept and describes an obsession with stuffed animal toys. For some people, plushophilia also extends to a fascination with large, furry animal suits. These men and women may don life-size costumes, and plushie groups meet up to share their obsession and to find a likely partner in plushiness. This understanding has been extended to the love of large furry animal suits

Stalking Cat (Dennis Avner).

– men and women don life-size costumes and whole communities meet up to share their obsession and to find a likely partner in plushiness. The costumes are often inspired by Disney-type caricatures, covering the whole body. In contrast to the plushies, the furries take on animal characteristics and disdain plushies. Furries argue that being 'furry' is an identity and furries often say how they feel anthropomorphized – they feel part animal with human characteristics. They partly dress as animals, the rest of their transformation completed by using makeup to transform their features to look animal-like; at least one man has had plastic surgery to define his features in the shape of a cat. Plushies and furries meet at conferences such as ConFurence and Further Confusion. These meetings attract around 5,000 people at a time, providing them with the opportunity to openly display their fetishes. Furries have defined their role-playing behaviour as 'scritching', which involves embraces, scratching and combing one's hand along a partner's chest, head, scalp or back. Making noises in response shows appreciation of a scritch. One observer pointed out, 'It should be worth noting that heterosexual males and females within Furry Fandom also participate in this social body language between members of the same sex without any apparent threat to their sexual identity as a heterosexual.'[41] In a survey of 360 furries taken in 1998, nearly half of those furries who responded said that they were bisexual.

So in secular Western societies, should people be taking a different view on bestial activities? Is bestiality hurtful or harmless fun? Can animals consent? Is it important that they do? How do we know when they do and when they don't? In more recent years, with the work of animal rights campaigners, a new caring attitude to animals has emerged. Questions have arisen as to whether it is acceptable or not to allow humans to have sex with animals (be it vaginal intercourse, sodomy, cunnilingus or fellatio, and so on). These sorts of acts usually take place in secluded places or behind closed doors and so are difficult to detect. Bestial activists argue that there should be a possibility of accepting cases of shared affection between humans and animals where boundaries can be crossed, whatever our personal feelings towards the idea.

In seeking answers, governments and campaigners have come together to change laws and provide more protection for animals, particularly in the light of the exposure of human–animal sex farms.

In Britain, under the Sexual Offences Act 2003, a man is deemed to have committed an offence if he 'intentionally performed an act of penetration with his penis' and 'what is penetrated is the vagina or anus of a living animal'.[42] For this, he can be imprisoned for up to two years. Nothing is said about female bestialists. In November 2008, Sweden discussed new sex laws concerning bestiality after the uncovering of an animal sex ring where men met on a farm regularly to have sex with a variety of animals. Concerns were raised after the Swedish Animal Welfare Agency registered 115 cases of bestiality between 2000 and 2005.[43] Sweden is perhaps more advanced than most countries in addressing the matter.

More worryingly, animal–human sex 'farms' are emerging in the U.S. and people are even travelling abroad to find places where they can indulge in bestiality more easily. In most Western societies cruelty to animals is against the law, but some campaigners think the penalties are neither harsh enough nor enforced as strictly as they should be. One case involved a woman who was convicted of bestiality in Britain in 2011 after police found photographs of her having sex with her Rottweiler. The picture of the 42-year-old woman was taken by her 41-year-old boyfriend. According to the *Liverpool Echo*, police found a CD of 33 'vile images' in a raid on their Liverpool home after he was suspected of arson and voyeurism. Officers also uncovered 61 indecent images of children. The woman, who had two teenage daughters and one grandchild, admitted at Liverpool Crown Court to having had sex with the animal. Judge Robert Warnock called her a 'troubled and damaged individual' and imposed a two-year community order with supervision. The pair hid their faces as they fled court. A neighbour said they still own the dog, adding: 'It's disgusting. They seemed a normal family.'[44]

Our attitudes towards bestiality might therefore vary depending on the person and animal involved and the individual case. Cases involving cruelty are obviously quite different from situations in which, say, an animal willingly licks its owner's genitalia in a show of mutual affection, with both animal and human enjoying the act. The dog in effect is consenting by being the 'active' partner. Some cases seem to have arisen from opportunity (working on a farm) and lack of outlet for sex with a human partner; we might think that these cases unfairly exploit the animal that has been subjected to such an act. Certainly where small creatures, such as birds and mice, are involved, and the act results in the death of the creature, it can be considered cruelty, and legal penalties can thus be levied. The questions around bestiality should therefore surely be ethical rather than moral. In cases where the animal is consenting, does it really matter? The difficulty is in trying to prove consent.

SEVEN

The Ties that Bind:
Sadomasochism

Hurt, and be hurt, and, at the same time, experience the exquisite pain of
orgasm until the pain becomes one great climax, or the sight of pain inflicted
grows into the organs.

Marquis de Sade (1740–1814)

The enjoyment of inflicting pain, or taking pleasure in punishment, has been experienced for centuries. All sorts of equipment
used in real historical torture and punishments has since been put
to use for sexual pleasure, including ropes, whips, canes, chains,
manacles and spiked collars.

According to the *Oxford English Dictionary*, sadism is a desire
to inflict pain, suffering or humiliation on others, a specific psychological disorder characterized by sexual fantasies, urges or behaviour
involving the subjection of another person to pain, humiliation or
bondage.[1] Masochism, frequently defined as the opposite of sadism,
is seen as the urge to derive pleasure, especially sexual gratification, from
one's own pain or humiliation. Types of sadomasochistic behaviour
range from primary sadism (desire to inflict pain) to moral masochism
(seeking punishment, often unconsciously and non-sexual), male or
female sadism/masochism, homosexual sadism/masochism, extreme
non-consensual sadism, extreme consensual sadomasochism, self-
inflicted pain and sadomasochistic role-play.

Although sadism was reasonably well known in the ancient world,
we have less evidence of masochism; perhaps people had less desire
to feel pain as a sexual pleasure because pain was more commonly
experienced. Before modern medicine, people felt more pain, since
there were few possibilities of easing suffering. Apart from the odd
medicinal herb or two, little was available in the way of anaesthetics.
In addition, more injuries were experienced, either through fighting in hand-to-hand combat or accidents in the field or at home – life
was simply less safe. Effective anaesthesia during surgery was non-
existent until 1847, when chloroform was introduced. Prior to then,

any operations or amputations saw the patient in agony, although opium, alcohol and hypnosis were used in attempts to alleviate suffering. In recent times, with the advent of analgesics such as chloroform, gas and air, and opiate-based drugs, people suffer less pain. Nowadays, the absence of pain makes it more unusual when it is suffered. This therefore makes the experience, for some people, more exciting and exotic.

Pain in the Classical World

The Greeks and Romans were well versed in other people's suffering, having enjoyed centuries of domination during which they thrashed their slaves and beat their prostitutes. One of their unusual methods of foreplay involved slapping a partner with a sandal. More serious infliction of pain – such as severe whippings and burning parts of the body with oil lamps – was undertaken only by men on women, not vice versa.[2] The demarcation of such inflictions depended on where a person stood on the class ladder, and whether they were a man, woman or child. If they were a freeborn and high-bred citizen, they would be unlikely to suffer pain at the hands of another man or woman. Slaves and non-citizen women, however, were more than likely to be harmed in some way by irate masters or more seriously sadistic owners, either through being whipped as a form of chastisement or subjected to someone else's sexual enjoyment. In ancient Greece, both

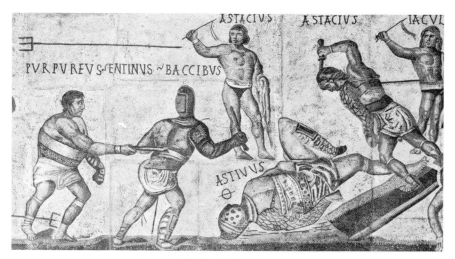

Gladiatorial games.

high-class courtesans known as *hetairai* and street-walking prostitutes, *pornai*, might be slaves. Both might have pimps, panderers or be self-employed but either might be beaten for sexual pleasure or as a means of control. Slaves could be sold to brothels or abused by their owners; one Greek husband, Euphiletus, for example, was accused by his wife of manhandling his female slave while drunk.[3]

Few people fared better under the regime in ancient Rome, a slave society powered by slaughter and sex. Essentially brutal, Roman society paid tribute to victory in strength and adulated the 'manly man'. Aggression was part of everyday life and became a key element in successful entertainment in the Roman amphitheatre. People flocked to the gladiatorial games to watch spectacular shows of cruelty where criminals and Christians faced lions and gladiators fought each other to the death. The Roman audience revelled in the sight of blood and took their pleasure in the pain of the victim as he received injury after injury. Here, the bloodthirsty spectators experienced the tyrannical delights of sadism, albeit by proxy. In this context, pain was undoubtedly linked to power.

Despotic Roman emperors such as Caligula and Nero excelled in inflicting pain on others and epitomized the sadism of the times.[4] Caligula demanded people worship him as a god, and killed people on a whim; when presiding over the gladiatorial games, he ordered an entire section of an audience to be thrown into the ring to be eaten by lions merely because he had became bored after they had run out of criminals. He was, however, as a young man, obsequious to his adoptive grandfather and the imperial household. Suetonius wrote that people said of him, 'Never was there a better slave, or a worse master!'[5] He possessed a natural brutality, and he loved watching torture and executions. Once he watched the manager of his gladiatorial games being flogged with chains for several days, only having him killed when the smell of his suppurating brains became insufferable. Nero prowled the streets and taverns looking for men to attack, stabbing them if they resisted, then dropped their bodies in the sewers. He kicked his wife Poppaea so badly that she died from her injuries. He also used his power to sadistically abuse others sexually; he raped the Vestal Virgin Rubria[6] and seduced freeborn boys. Roman sex was taken rather than asked for, a concept neatly summed up by Ovid in his *The Art of Love*:

It's all right to use force – force of that sort goes down well with
The girls: what in fact they love to yield
They'd often rather have stolen. Rough seduction
Delights them, the audacity of near-rape
Is a compliment . . .[7]

The idea that women (and 'inferior' men) should be subjected to
sex with violence pervaded parts of everyday life in much of the
world for the next two millennia. A new religion was about to emerge
which would perpetuate the belief in the natural submissiveness
of women and promote physical disciplining as a method of growing closer to God.

A maenad defends herself against a sexual assault by a satyr. Red-figure cup by
Makron, c. 480 BC.

The first generation of Roman men abducting neighbouring Sabine women to take as wives. David, *Rape of the Sabine Women*, 1799.

Sin and Suffering

In the Christian era, the concept of pain was linked to blood and suffering. This was encapsulated in the image of the crucified Jesus. A new world of pain opened up to allow for a succession of masochistic saints to endure terrible torments. Heaven-bent on taking up the burden of Christ's torment, they were covered in boiling tar, engulfed in the flames at the stake, tied to cartwheels and had their bodies pulled apart with ropes. Monks and nuns yielded themselves before Christ's image in prayer, while flagellating themselves in obeisance. It was no longer good to feel pleasure except in suffering for one's sins.

The necessity for Christian discipline was passed on to parents educating their children. Rather than pampering their offspring, parents were advised to beat them. A disciplined child was a God-fearing one and the phrase 'Spare the rod and spoil the child' became a Christian mantra. Derived from Proverbs 13:24, the saying declared, 'he who spares the rod hates his child, but he who loves the child is careful to discipline him'. In fact, the Book of Proverbs was full of such advice for disciplining children and pointed to beating as the only way to lead a godly life. To be blunt, the Judeo-Christian tradition sanctioned physical child abuse.[8]

Albrecht Dürer, *The Martyrdom of St Catherine*, 1497–8.

Christian Idea of the Torture Wheel, woodcut
by Nicolas le Rouge, 1529.

From *Tortures and Torments of the
Christian Martyrs* (1903).

In early Christianity such violence was not merely applied to children; sadism was part of early medieval life. More often than not, sexual sadism was inflicted on women and more vulnerable men, usually by men of higher social status who wielded power over them. Men were well placed in society – socially, sexually and legally – which made it easier for them to inflict pain on women without retribution. In law, a man was allowed to beat his wife if she strayed from the conditions laid out for her in her subservient role as a chaste wife. But for many, the concept of sadism was recognized only in the eighteenth century, after a man who investigated every conceivable aspect of sadism in his novels created the ultimate in a grand sexual philosophy.

The Exquisite Pain of the Marquis de Sade

The Marquis de Sade unwittingly gave sadism its name, and it was he who was responsible for pushing sexual sadism to its fictional extremes. Laying out scene after scene of all the types of pain and pleasure imaginable, Sade believed he would write about 600 perversions, but in the event managed only 30. While he was imprisoned in the Bastille, he explored every aspect of sexualized pain in his novel

Justine, written in 1787 and published in 1791. His heroine, Justine, was the prototype of the pure submissive masochist. Virtuous and innocent, she is subject to various torments, beatings and rapes. In contrast, the heroine of his mirror novel *Juliette* (1797) actively seeks out every perversity known to man. These two novels, along with *Les 120 journées de Sodome* (written 1785), *Aline et Valcour* (written 1785–8) and *La Philosophie dans le boudoir* (1795), were the best of his outpourings but his literary influence was not widespread in his own times – *The 120 Days of Sodom* was found belatedly in a huge scroll left behind in the Bastille but was only published in 1904. Although his fictional work was highly imaginative, Sade himself played out some of his fantasies in real life. Indeed, he ended up in prison for his perverted practices, which included, among other things, torturing his maid and poisoning prostitutes.[9] His life story provides an insight into why an intellectual aristocrat such as Sade might enjoy sadism.

Marquis Donatien Alphonse François de Sade was born in Paris on 2 June 1740 into a noble family and was brought up and educated by his uncle. He started to write when he was about 23 years old, by which time he had already gained a reputation among the bawds of the Paris brothels for his violent behaviour. Eventually, the extremity of his violence towards prostitutes came to the notice of the police. One Inspector Marais complained about Sade,

> He has been pressing Madame Brissault to provide him with girls for his petite maison supper revels. Fully aware of what he is capable of, she has consistently refused his requests but he has apparently applied to others who are either less scrupulous or who do not know him and we may thus be certain that before long we will be hearing about him again.[10]

In October 1763, Sade was imprisoned for abusing a woman who had been supplied to him by Madame Brissault. The woman was Jeanne Testard, a fan maker by trade, who sold sex as a sideline. During the encounter, not content to have conventional sex, Sade threatened her with pistols and sodomitical rape but, worse still in the eyes of the law, masturbated over a crucifix while spouting a stream of blasphemy. Although he was released after fifteen days, his arrest marked the beginning of his brushes with the law. Another incident was to

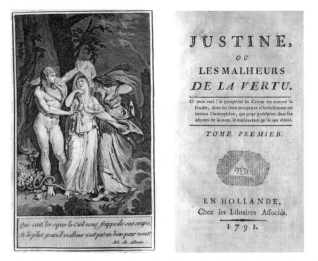

Frontispiece and title page from the Marquis de Sade, *Justine* (1791).

H. Biberstein, *Fantasy Portait of the Marquis de Sade*,
19th century.

Spanking scene from the Marquis de Sade, *Justine* (1797 edition).

put him behind bars for much longer. In April 1768 Rose Keller, the 36-year-old widow of a pastry baker, approached Sade in the street for alms. Instead of giving her a handful of change, he took her back to his chateau at Arcueil, stripped her naked, whipped her until she bled and poured hot wax on her. He then locked her up, but she eventually escaped and later brought a prosecution against him – she dropped the case after being given a vast sum as a pay-off. Five years later in June 1772, Sade once again encountered the law when he was accused of 'poisoning' a group of prostitutes by adding cantharides ('Spanish fly', which was alleged to act as an aphrodisiac as a result of its irritation of the genito-urinary tract, but was also toxic) to their drink.

Despite being ostracized by his peers for his flagrant behaviour, Sade had managed to find a woman of good status to marry: the daughter of President de Montreuil, a magistrate at the Court of Aids. The situation may have settled down, but once again Sade antagonized those closest to him. Having fallen in love with his wife's younger sister, he enraged the rest of the family by eloping with her, and with these actions sealed his fate. His disgusted in-laws used their influential contacts to force the couple to return home and had their son-in-law thrown in prison for a variety of minor offences. After further indiscretions, Sade was detained under a *lettre de cachet* that stated that he should be kept in jail indefinitely at the king's pleasure. His in-laws never forgave him and would manage to keep him incarcerated on and off for the rest of his life. He was first kept in the Château de Vincennes for seven years, then removed to the Bastille for a further five, released only after its storming in 1789 during the French Revolution. In all, he spent around thirteen years in prison, passing through frustration, despair and psychosis. As a result of his attacks on the Church and the state, he made countless enemies in powerful positions. He made no secret of his hatred of these institutions, along with those who ran them – priests, bishops, judges and army generals were all vilified in his books. Indeed, his hatred of his own class and his portrayal of them was at least part of the reason for his persecution.[11]

Despite the force of his writings and his vivid descriptions of sexual sadism, Sade himself did not necessarily indulge in all the perversions he wrote about. Philosophers, psychologists, psychiatrists and sociologists, as well as historians, have all tried to pinpoint

Illustrations of sexual torture from the Marquis de Sade, *Juliette* (1797).

his predilections, but attempts to retrieve the thoughts of such an intellectual have proved problematic. However, his military life may go some way in explaining the fluency and vitality of his descriptions of violent scenes. While in the army as a young man, Sade had witnessed brutality and slaughter on a mass scale, and had seen the slaughter of villagers by the conquering army during the Seven Years War. Such profound experiences are bound to have left a vivid impression.

Yet Sade went further than merely marking out territories of boundless physical pain and pleasure, and invented an inverse moral code by which anything is possible. In his novels, he dispenses with the usual dividing lines of normality and abnormality. Active and passive sodomy, paedophilia, gerontophilia, necrophilia, coprophilia and a host of other acts that would later be labelled perversions were all explored in *The 120 Days of Sodom*. Sade also exposed many different types of sadism – infantile sadism (cruelty inflicted on babies and young children), murderous sadism (involving sex before murder), necrophilia (involving sex after death) and blood-sucking sadism. His understanding of perversion contradicted that of contemporary commentators, who pointed to how sex between men and women was 'natural' and all other sexual acts – sodomy, necrophilia, coprophilia and so on – were 'unnatural'. Sade turned this viewpoint on its head when, in the epigram to *Juliette*, he defended its publication stating that he saw 'unnatural vices' as 'the strange urges inspired by Nature'.[12] 'Natural' for Sade were all the perversions he described. His philosophy stated that we sense pleasure when we act according to nature and with our own nature, and that thus all acts must be natural. It was a pamphlet against Napoleon that finally ensured his fate. In 1801, he was arrested again and in 1803 he was locked up in Charenton as a lunatic. He was 74 when he died in 1814, still in the asylum.

The Ultimate Masochist: Sacher-Masoch

Sade's antithesis was Leopold von Sacher-Masoch, considered by most people to have been the man who gave rise to the concept of masochism. He created a stir both with his book *Venus in Furs* (1870) and because of his relationships with his lovers Anna von Kottowitz and Fanny von Pistor. Born in 1836 in Galicía, he studied at the universities of Vienna and Prague and, like Sade, fought as a cavalry officer.

THE PLEASURE'S ALL MINE

As a child he had been attracted to depictions of cruelty in paintings, executions and the sufferings of martyrs. But it was his Aunt Zenobia, whom he adored, who was to be the crux of all his later fantasies. His sexual predilections revolved around her after an impressionable event in his childhood – his beloved aunt had beaten him after discovering him watching her having sex with her lover. At the time, she was completely naked but for her fur-lined dressing gown, a *kaza-baika* – an item of clothing which would forever feature in his fantasies.

In 1861, his first love affair with Anna von Kottowitz scandalized the town of Graz, Austria. He was only 25 at the time, and she was a doctor's wife eight years his senior. She left her husband to live with Sacher-Masoch and, at first, they were happy. As time went by, Sacher-Masoch began to find fault with her and complained about her excessive expenditure on luxuries. When asked about it, she flew into a fury and hit him, startling him, but leaving him begging for more. Since she also seemed to have enjoyed the experience, they embarked on increasingly sadomasochistic behaviour. At first he asked her merely to whip him, but he quickly graduated to a lust for humiliation. He therefore suggested she have an affair with another man in order that he might experience the pain of 'betrayal'. To fulfil his fantasy, they searched for someone to fulfil the role and landed upon 'Count Meciszevski', who was not a count at all, but a man wanted back in Russia for theft. Unfortunately for Anna, he gave her syphilis; in revenge, Sacher-Masoch arranged to have the count deported. Sacher-Masoch went on to describe his relationship with Anna in his novel *The Separated Wife*, which was published in 1865, thereby creating further waves of gossip.

It was Fanny von Pistor who completely fulfilled Sacher-Masoch's masochistic fantasies. They met in 1869 after she had sent him a thick bundle of manuscripts, signing herself 'Baroness Bogdanoff' from Baden. She had read *The Separated Wife*, so had more than an inkling of his masochistic personality. Since they pleased each other, they made a formal written agreement about the type of relation-ship they would have: he would act as her footman and she would humiliate him while they travelled around the world. They signed a written contract to that effect: 'Herr Leopold von Sacher-Masoch gives his word of honour to Frau Pistor to become her slave and to comply unreservedly for six months, with every one of her desires and com-mands.' For her part: 'The mistress has the right to punish her slave in any way she thinks fit for all errors, carelessness or crime of lèse-majesté on his part.'[13] Part of the contract included her promise to wear furs as often as possible in order to indulge his obsession. On their trip to Italy, he again began to fantasize about being subjected to betrayal and insisted she have an affair. This time, unable to find a suitable aristocrat (pretended or not), they ended up with a third-rate actor, Salvini, who was only too willing to have an affair with Pistor. Salvini, knowing nothing about the type of relationship she had with Sacher-Masoch, could only congratulate himself on finding such a rich

Leopold von Sacher-Masoch (1836–1895).

mistress. Although the six-month agreement between Sacher-Masoch and Pistor proved a success, both had had their fill at the end of the period. The contract was not renewed.

In 1873, Sacher-Masoch married 27-year-old glove maker Angelika Aurora Rümelin (she later called herself Wanda, after his heroine in *Venus in Furs*). She also wrote a series of letters to him under a pseudonym, obviously a method guaranteed to pique his interest. She was a young woman of humble background who knew he was rich and was no doubt attracted by his high status. A friend had already drawn Wanda's attention to Sacher-Masoch when she had presented her with his book *The Heritage of Cain* and told her, 'He needs a woman who will drag him under the yoke – who will chain him up like a dog and kick him when he growls.'[14] As Wanda intended, the mysteriousness of her letters fascinated Sacher-Masoch so much that he went out of his way to find her. Initially, their marriage was a happy one but the death of their first child left them both consumed by grief. A continued lack of finances and Sacher-Masoch's demands for beatings on a daily basis left Wanda drained – Leopold was only satisfied if she wore her fur dressing-gown and treated him as her slave. Once again, he turned to the idea of forced adultery in order to enable himself to revel in the pain of betrayal. He told her: 'It is necessary to love a woman to the point of madness – as I love you – for her infidelity to make one suffer a martyrdom as excruciating as that which I will suffer when I see you in the arms of another man.'[15] For a young Catholic woman used to regular confession, the idea was all too much. In her memoirs, she relates an occasion when they visited friends on their estate in Hungary and her husband insisted that they all indulge him in his favourite game. He would make all the women dress up in furs and run around the grounds of the estate playing hide-and-seek, chasing him like a pack of wolves. Once they had captured him, they were instructed to fall on him and bite him. He eventually absconded with the children's governess in 1887, and had two children by her. He died in 1895.

Sacher-Masoch was one of the first people to write constructively about masochism and his sexual fantasies involving masochistic behaviour. Sade's revelations also exposed the connection of pain and suffering to heightened lust and desire. The work of both men was to become the basis of explorations into sadomasochism that would change medical thinking in the twentieth century.

Algolagnia, the Love of Pain

Although pain, pleasure and suffering had been linked together for centuries before, it was Krafft-Ebing who linked the names of Sade and Sacher-Masoch in his explanation of sadomasochism. He was among the first to examine sadism and masochism in the 1890s as sexologists began to make the connections between pain and sexual pleasure a subject of medical concern. He described sadism as 'the experience of sexually pleasurable sensations (including orgasm) that is produced by acts of cruelty and bodily punishments, either self-inflicted or witnessed in others, whether animals or human beings. It may also consist of an innate desire to humiliate, hurt, wound, or even destroy in order to create sexual pleasure in oneself.'[16] According to Krafft-Ebing, sadism was a form of sexual perversion, whereby 'an act of cruelty is practised by a man on the body of a woman, not so much as an act preparatory to coitus in the case of a shrunken libido or potency, but as an end in itself, as the satisfaction of a per-verse vita sexualis'. Masochism, on the other hand, he described as 'Where, the man, because of his sexual sensations and impulses, permits himself to be mistreated by the woman and prefers to take the part of the pursued rather than the pursuer.' From that time, sadism became known as the pathological pleasure enjoyed by some people by inflicting pain, masochism its opposite. Such acts came to be seen as illnesses of the mind rather than merely exotic paths to sensual pleasure.

As the study of pain associated with sexual pleasure spread, in 1892 the German doctor Albert von Schrenck-Notzing (who inciden-tally also had an avid interest in the paranormal, examining both telepathy and hypnotism) coined the new descriptive term 'algo-lagnia' to describe the lust or craving for pain which included sexual excitement or gratification obtained by suffering pain. In reasoning that was advanced for its time, he recognized that the organs for sensing pleasure and pain need little stimulation and that some-times the two sensations meshed together. Up until then the similarities between the sensations of pain and pleasure had not been explored.

The investigations of sexologists at the end of the nineteenth century threw up three main themes: first, the idea that women were more prone to masochism because of their 'natural' submissiveness;

second, the debate about the causes of sadomasochism – whether a result of inherited congenital defects or an acquired or learned behaviour; and third, the notion of sadomasochism as an urge which could not be resisted, an 'irresistible impulse' (by implication thereby rendering the sadomasochist not culpable for his or her actions). Victorian and Edwardian values permeated the work of sexologists with a prominent perception of women as naturally passive and men as natural aggressors. An ideal was envisaged where men were the heads of the household and the material providers for their families and women were the domestic angels of the hearth and instructors of moral values. This was, after all, an era when science had 'proved' that women had inferior brains, inferior skeletons and inferior bodies.[17] Women were thought to be irrational, impulsive and unable to control their feelings. This was exemplified by Ellis in his work *Love and Pain* (1903), which categorized men as the sadists and women as the receivers of pain. As in Krafft-Ebing's work, sadomasochism only became a major issue when men chose to receive pain. For women it was considered more 'natural' to be submissive and only became pathological if it got out of hand. Ellis surmised, 'While in men it is possible to trace a tendency to inflict pain, or the simulacrum of pain, on the women they love, it is still easier to trace in women a delight in experiencing physical pain when inflicted by a lover, and an eagerness to accept subjection to his will.'

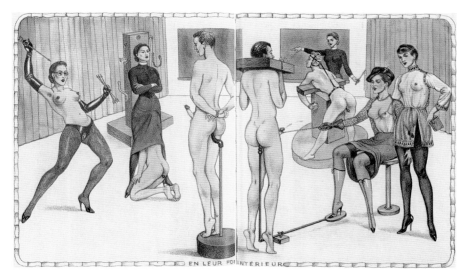

A spot of bondage, illustration by Bernard Montorgueil, 1930s.

In *Love and Pain*, Ellis more specifically explored the theme of sadism and its 'normality'. In trying to further the cause of sexual liberation, he used 'science' to argue that pain was related to normal sexual desire and therefore should not be considered a 'perversion' at all.[18] His description is very much based on what we would now call 'evolutionary biology' – that in courtship, it is nature's way to cause pain: male animals treat females roughly and females respond by surrendering. A woman as well as a man could prove cruel in this love process, as she 'delights to arouse in the highest degree in the male the desire for her favours and to withhold those favours from him, thus finding on her part also the enjoyment of power in cruelty'.[19]

Ellis believed that ordinary male and female relationships involved an aspect of sadomasochism. He observed the cries 'of a woman in the ecstasy of passion, when she implored the man to desist, though that is really the last thing she desires'.[20] Thus for Ellis, the male and female sexual impulses in courtship involved a non-pathological type of sadomasochistic tendency which he considered to be 'normal'. He does at least qualify this notion by refuting the idea that women actually enjoy pain, professing, 'As regards physical pain, though the idea of it is sometimes exciting, I think the reality of it is quite the reverse.'[21] He believed that even a small amount of pain would destroy a woman's enjoyment completely.

Like Ellis, Charles Féré believed that women, by their very natures, wanted to be subjugated. In *The Evolution and Dissolution of the Sexual Instinct* (1904), he described masochism as 'the seeking of real or imaginary suffering, whether for the purpose of exciting and facilitating sexual pleasure, or for obtaining an actual equivalent of sexual excitations that provoke orgasm'.[22] Unlike Albert von Schrenck-Notzing (who thought the condition was acquired through auto-suggestion), Féré believed that the desire was congenital, asserting 'the need of association between cruelty and violence with sexual enjoyment, such violence or cruelty not being necessarily exerted in the person himself who seeks pleasure in this association'. As with homosexuality, the congenital versus acquired debate was applied to sadomasochism.

Many sexologists agreed that sadism was part of normal sexual instincts and was only problematic when carried to its extreme.[23] The psychiatrist Albert Moll asserted that 'the sexual impulse consists of the tendency to strike, ill-use and humiliate the beloved person.'[24] In

1902, Albert Eulenburg wrote on algolagnia in his book *Sadism and Masochism*. Here he plays on the evolutionary theory, speaking of the 'irresistible impulses' and 'brutality of human nature'. He asks, 'Is the inclination towards cruelty deeply implanted in human nature as one of the fundamental instincts?' and whether it is 'peculiar only to humans'.[25] As a professor of neurology, he was interested in physiology, although his explanation of the need to inflict pain seems to concur with the idea of a primitive type of reaction described by other sexologists. He saw sadism as an act of cruelty and believed that the negative feelings that men felt for women after sex were inherent, a result of 'the bodily and spiritual reaction of regaining one's dignity after sexual enjoyment (at times in man) frees itself in antipathy towards the partner'. He may have surprised some of his readers when, by way of an explanation of the feelings of sadism, he declared, 'Many men look upon the sleeping woman at their side with whom they have just had intercourse with a feeling as if they could at least thrash this lovely or even unlovely women, if not stab her or choke her to death in cold blood.' Luckily for the Edwardian woman, this appears to have been only a 'momentary seizure, a fleeting upheaval of flaring up' which ceases after a moment.[26] For Eulenburg, man's 'desire for power' is caught up with the need to inflict pain on others. However, in an unusually insightful revelation for his day, he upbraided men for keeping women in a state of perpetual servitude, a tradition that had continued over thousands of years. He asks whether rape can be committed by non-sadists. Rapists do not necessarily have sadistic motives. The primary action is undertaken not because of the perpetrator's love of inflicting pain but his need for the 'disgraceful humiliation and maltreatment of his victim'.

Sigmund Freud's contribution was to shift the understanding of sadomasochism away from the idea of congenital causes and evolutionary theory, and explain it in terms of his Oedipal theory of sexuality. Freud refuted the idea that sadomasochism had an evolutionary basis and thought it stemmed from incidents in childhood. At the beginning of the twentieth century, Freud identified violence applied to children as part of the adult masochistic make-up, a hypothesis promulgated as part of his work on the Oedipal complex. In his essay 'A Child is Being Beaten: A Contribution or the Study of the Origin of Sexual Perversion' (1919), he explored the concept of a child being beaten in his patient's fantasies; this discipline awakened simultaneous feelings of sexual pleasure and disgust. In his *Three Essays on the Theory of Sexuality* (1905), he blamed boys' rough games such as wrestling and tumbling for causing sexual excitement. The connection between sexual excitement and dangerous physical activities was seen as one of the reasons for higher rates of 'crimes against the person' in young men (a result of 'high testosterone'). In the 1960s, Freud's psychoanalytical theory influenced psychiatric thinking and psychiatrists began to use Freud's analysis to explain every sexual perversion. Unusual or 'abnormal' sexual impulses were related back to childhood experiences. Yet even this late, doctors of mental health were talking of 'the evils of sensuality and sadism, with their attendant vice – masochism'.[27]

Although sexologists were responsible for giving us the definitions of sadomasochism and went some way to explaining the behaviour, many of the meanings are far too narrow to encompass the vast array of understanding and experiences of S&M that evolved during the twentieth century. Sexologists tended to define sadism and masochism through representations of the assertive male (the sadist) and the passive female (the masochist), but there are of course exceptions to this. The sexologists also tended to concentrate on S&M in heterosexual sex and did not generally explore homosexual sadism or masochism to a large degree, although there was the occasional mention of the homosexual sadist.

Hirschfeld noticed a connection to childhood experiences and the discovery of pleasure in pain, but explained it in a quite different way. He noticed that his transvestite patients who had experienced a masochistic pleasure in childhood grew up with tendencies towards penetration of parts of their body, such as piercings or tight corseting. One transvestite even mentions the pleasure of the extremes of humiliation expressed through dressing as a woman, asking 'Is there a greater humiliation than when a physically stronger man is forced to take on the form of the woman?'[28] The enjoyment of self-inflicted harm of parts of the body has since developed into a fully ritualized element in sadomasochistic activities, although some psychiatrists say that such activities are a result of a lack of self-worth or a result of depression and self-destruction. Legally, inflicting harm on others has been seen as a criminal offence, regardless of consent.

Stabbing and Cutting

Cutting and stabbing as acts of sexual sadism appears to have been a fairly common crime, at least as far back as the eighteenth century. These sadists tended to enjoy stabbing their victims – most frequently young women – with sharp instruments such as blades, pins or scissors. One eighteenth-century London case hit the news after a man known as the 'London Monster' took to cutting women's dresses as he passed them in the street. He made his first appearance in 1788, shouting obscenities and stabbing women in the buttocks. Some years later, a series of attacks sprang up in Paris in 1820 where a group of men known as the 'piqueurs' strolled round the boulevards and the Palais Royal making random assaults on women by stabbing their buttocks and ankles, causing the blood to flow. These incidents died out without anyone being apprehended. Similar attacks were reported as having taken place in London, Brussels, Hamburg and Munich.[29] In Metz, the 'Hip Stabber' attracted attention by wounding at least 23 women with a needle-like instrument. Another stabber followed suit in Trier; this time, he aimed at the genitals. Meanwhile in Kiev on 23 October 1901, eighteen-year-old Ivan Kaprovitch was apprehended after he attacked a number of young girls, stabbing them in the throat and lower abdomen in the street with a penknife. Many of the women had to undergo serious operations as a result. When asked in court the reason for his crimes, he answered, 'I cannot stand the women. Their appearance gives me cramps . . . I must stab them until the blood runs.'[30]

Less common but equally confounding were attacks carried out by women on young girls. One sadistic female attacker was reported on in *Alienist and Neurology* in 1907. The culprit had stabbed and mutilated the genitals of a young girl whom she had adopted from 'a Home'. The woman was not found to be insane or normally violent; on the contrary, she gave the appearance of being modest, chaste and even prudish. She carried out over a hundred attacks using scissors, forks and similar instruments, although the wounds on the girl were kept fairly superficial. Significantly, the woman used domestic weapons, something not usually indicated in other cases. Although she was married, she was said to be an 'invert', her pathological tendencies brought out because of the repression of her true feelings.

Isaac Cruikshank, *The London Monster*, 1790.

Self-inflicted S&M was another problem with which sexologists thought they had to grapple. In the 1950s, the psychiatrist Frank Caprio attempted to explain the behaviour of one of his patients, who experimented with almost every form of painful equipment on his own body. His favourite experience was to feel scratches, and he enjoyed the feeling of pricking on his penis, scrotum, anus and buttocks. He

admitted, while out on his forays in isolated woods: 'I often delib-
erately brought my scrotum into contact with briars while in a state
close to the sexual climax.'[31] This invariably gave him a strong orgasm.
He continued to follow other avenues in attempts to replicate the
pleasure, telling his doctor, 'Later I pushed pins and needles through
a fold of the scrotum, foreskin and the lower abdomen and achieved
the same response.' A hairbrush pressed against his scrotum or anus
had the same effect. After inserting a thermometer into his urethra,
although he found the painful sensation erotic, he gave it up for
fear of injuring himself. He moved on to experimenting with bind-
ing his body up with straps and belts, then with rubber bands around
his erect penis. He also tried suction with rubber hoses and water
aspirators. According to Caprio, his patient responded successfully to psychotherapy, resolved his sexual conflicts and was finally
happily married.

When a patient self-harmed, psychiatric treatment was often
sought to uncover the reasons – usually given as untoward influences
in childhood – and therapy was given to attempt to prevent the patient
continuing the action. Where injury was inflicted on or by a third party
and the actions were consensual, the ethics of the activity became a
public matter.

A Case of Supposed Sadism

On Saturday 7 August 1920 at about four thirty in the afternoon, a Mr
McM., who was walking in an easterly direction through a vacant lot
adjoining the large High Park in Toronto, noticed a boy of about
eight lying on a path, almost hidden by weeds. The weeds were pat-
ted down in the vicinity and there was no indication of a struggle.
The boy was breathing slowly, his mouth was opening and shutting
and his eyes were fixed and staring; he was bleeding and apparently
insensible. Two buttons of his knickerbockers were undone, and his
right knee protruded from a hole in his torn clothes. Seeing a person
(afterwards identified as Frederick L. Davis) moving slowly some 40
or 50 feet away, McM. called to him; Davis quickened his speed, but
was overtaken by McM. running. Davis had his hands in front of
him, apparently closing the flap on his trousers. McM said to him,
'There is a little boy fell. Will you stay by him till I get help?' Davis inter-
rupted him: 'I didn't do nothing; I was just urinating.' McM. asked him

to stay with the boy till he got help, and Davis went towards the boy. On returning with help, Davis was nowhere to be seen. The clothes of the boy had been buttoned up, but the boy was dead.

The post-mortem found that the boy's skull was fractured and his throat had been cut from ear to ear. The rectum was gaping and patulous; three gloved fingers could be inserted without difficulty. There was a tear about one-third of an inch long in the mucous membrane of the posterior wall of the rectum, indicating recent violence; the other conditions indicated long-term passive pederasty. Davis absconded before the police had a chance to apprehend him. He pawned his tools and a stolen bicycle and went by boat to Rochester, New York. He was eventually caught and the case came to trial in Toronto in January 1922, where he was found guilty.

Despite the conviction, when Canadian William Renwick Riddell, a lawyer, judge and historian wrote about the case, he called it *A Case of Supposed Sadism.* Whether the term 'supposed' was inserted because he was unsure about the sadism involved is unclear. But it seems that the term 'sadism' was used as an alternative word for sexual abuse before rape and paedophilia became separate emotive issues. Here, sadism is directly connected to lust-murder. Sadism at this time was therefore connected to rape and murder rather than seen as a stand-alone sexual pleasure. Riddell believed that 'Sexual inclinations towards children are especially apt to be associated with sadistic acts and in a comparatively large proportion of cases children are the victims of lust murder.'[32]

Certainly Davis's background suggested possibilities for the making of an unstable character. His father was unsociable and died when Davis was only six years old, leaving his mother free to marry again. For four years thereafter, he was separated from his mother and lived with his grandfather, but later joined her and his stepfather in Chicago. After his mother died when he was eighteen, disturbing his development still further, he took up an itinerant life. He contracted syphilis at twenty after intercourse with a prostitute. He married seven years later but his wife left him after another seven years. In statements to the prison surgeon, he denied sexual perversion of any kind. He said he had been initiated into homosexual practices when he was under ten by an adult man. Although he had normal sexual relations with women, he did not enjoy their company and preferred young boys. He was a chronic alcoholic and his mental age was classed as eleven years and ten months. He alternated his story as he saw fit. On conviction he said, 'Under the eyes of god, your Lordship, to the best of my knowledge, I am innocent', yet admitted that he had murdered the boy to the prison warden. He said he had no knowledge of what made him do it as he had no ill towards the boy, but nonetheless expressed no remorse. Riddell stated 'that cerebral syphilis will produce a state of mental disorder leading to sexual offence against children is as well recognized as the similar effects of chronic alcoholism'. In other words, Riddell thought Davis's mental reduction to be a 'general paralysis of the insane', a disorder caused by syphilis and a common argument of sexologists. The prisoner was convicted of murder but died in prison on the day set for his execution.

As a non-consensual act, sadism becomes an act of violence, which, as Eulenburg pointed out, does not necessarily have a sexual context. Eulenburg saw the fullest extent of sadomasochism realized in lust-murder and necrophilia, which he places under the category of 'violent unlawful non-consensual sexual intercourse', but recognizes that 'not every lust-murder arises from purely sadistic motives' (as perhaps in the Davis case).[33] In most countries the law covers a non-consensual act as violence against another person in one form or another (grievous or actual or bodily harm with or without intent, common assault, attempted murder and so on), murder being the ultimate violent act. However, as indicated, not all murders are sadistic. Types of non-sadistic murder can range from torture used in order to extract confessions to mass genocide – the point being that for sadism to occur, the perpetrator must derive some sexual pleasure from the activity. There are equally many reasons given why certain people might enjoy sadomasochism: not only mental derangement or incapacity, or even having been molested as a child, as was the case with Davis.

The Question of Consent

A prime example of the problems of establishing the difference between consensual sadomasochism and bodily harm can be seen in the 'Spanner Case', when in December 1990 sixteen gay men were sentenced to up to four and a half years or fined for engaging in consensual S&M activity. Their activities were exposed as a result of a police investigation called 'Operation Spanner', and a chance finding of a videotape of the men's activities. Although S&M was not 'illegal', anybody involved in such activities could be prosecuted for assault. In this case, those involved were convicted. Despite their later appeal, their convictions were upheld by both the Court of Appeal in the UK and the European Court of Human Rights in Strasbourg. All of the defendants stated that they had consented to the acts, but the standard offence of assault occasioning actual bodily harm was applied and their convictions were upheld.

Police stated that they had become involved after watching the videotape, in which a group of men were seen to be involved in heavy beatings and genital lacerations. The injuries inflicted were great enough for the police to have believed that someone had been murdered. During their investigation, they interviewed dozens of gay men to try and track down the people involved. In all, the investigation is rumoured to have cost £4 million, and at this stage the police must have felt the pressure to go ahead with a prosecution. Summing up in a complex legal argument, Judge Rant decided that the activities in which the men had engaged fell outside the exceptions to the law of assault. The problem lay in the fact that, in law, a person cannot consent to an assault, although there are exceptions. For example, a person can consent to a medical practitioner touching and possibly injuring their body; a person can consent to an opponent hitting or injuring them in sports such as rugby or boxing; and a person can consent to tattoos or piercings if they are for ornamental purposes. But in the 'Spanner Case' there was no exception to the rule. The judge explained that any bodily harm applied or received during sexual activities was not unlawful if the pain it caused was 'just momentary' and 'so slight that it can be discounted'. Bodily marks such as those produced by beatings or bondage must not be of a lasting nature. In this case, he decided that the injury, pain or marks were more than trifling or momentary and therefore deemed them illegal and to be considered an assault under the law. However, many groups campaigned against the decision and supported the right to freedom of choice for the individuals involved.

The Philosophy of Pain and Pleasure

Trying to explain the enjoyment of experiencing pain has been problematic. Although sexologists provided us with ideas – some believing

(urolagnia), scatophilia or coprophilia, bondage, flagellation, clamping, asphyxiation and so on.

The last words on the subject I leave to the philosopher Edmund Burke (1729–1797), who summed up his thoughts about pain and pleasure in *A Philosophical Enquiry into the Origins of Our Ideas of the Sublime and Beautiful*:

> Pain and pleasure are simple ideas, incapable of definition. People are not liable to be mistaken in their feelings, but they are very frequently wrong in the names they give them, and in their reasoning about them. Many are of the opinion that pain arises necessarily from the removal of some pleasure; as they think pleasure does from the ceasing or diminution of some pain. For my part, I am rather inclined to imagine, that pain and pleasure, in their most simple and natural manner of affecting, are each of a positive nature, and by no means necessarily dependent on each other for their existence.[37]

EIGHT

Loving the Dead

Living or dead, the prize that I have in view shall be mine.

Charles Brockden Brown, *Ormond* (1799)

Necrophilia literally translated from Greek means 'love of the dead' (from *necro*, dead, and *philia*, love) but the term is usually understood as the sexual attraction to corpses.[1] Sex with the dead has existed at least as far back as the ancient world. Herodotus tells us that in ancient Egypt, men from elite families guarded the corpses of female relatives until they started to decompose in order to put off unscrupulous morticians from copulating with their wives and daughters:

> The wives of men of rank when they die are not given at once to be embalmed, nor such women as are very beautiful or of greater regard than others, but on the third or fourth day after their death (and not before) they are delivered to the embalmers. They do so about this matter in order that the embalmers may not abuse their women, for they say that one of them was taken once doing so to the corpse of a woman lately dead, and his fellow-craftsman gave information.[2]

Greek mythology gives us a glimpse of necro-passion, after the Byzantine scholar Eustathius of Thessalonica added to the story that, when Achilles kills Penthesilea, queen of the Amazons, he consummates his desire by having sex with her corpse.[3] Periander, a tyrant of Corinth who ruled during the seventh century BC, was possibly one of the first recorded rulers to have murdered and had sex with their wives. Describing Periander's necrophilia, Herodotus wrote: 'Periander baked his bread in a cold oven.'[4] But why did sex with the dead create such an aversion for the majority, but such an appeal for a few? And did this happen at particular times in history? If so why, and how has it changed, if at all?

The actual practice of necrophilia is more difficult to uncover than its myths. Throughout history, few people have been caught copulating with dead bodies and, as with so many other marginal sexual acts, it remains very much hidden. The dead tended to be laid out in enclosed, private places, so when the act took place, it was unlikely to be seen accidentally by others. When cases did come to the attention of the authorities, records may well have been burned (as with the bestiality cases), as they were considered too offensive to remain in existence. Necrophilia is therefore harder to detect than other 'perversions' and our understanding of it is skewed to the few extant records. Cases emerge in anecdotal accounts, in medieval Church investigations, in nineteenth-century hospital asylum

The Egyptian god Anubis prepares a body for mummification, c. 1280 BC.

J.H.W. Tischbein, *Death of Penthesilea*, 1828.

records and in reports of twentieth-century psychiatrists. These later cases show that necrophilia came to be treated as a medical problem rather than a legal one (although touching the dead had been a taboo for centuries). Because of the relative scarcity of cases, we therefore have to make some assumptions based on societal reactions to dead bodies. Incidents were exposed when the body had been disrupted somehow (for example, if there was evidence of semen or damage to the flesh or body parts of the corpse); or gravediggers,

The Amazon Penthesilea killed by Achilles. Athenian cup from
Vulci, c. 460 BC.

morticians or others working in proximity to the dead detected it. In
some cases, these were the very people committing the act.

Another reason for the lack of evidence of necrophilia is that in
many countries, up until recently, necrophilia itself was not specifically named as a crime. This lack of legislation could indicate a
variety of feelings about necrophilia. Perhaps some people considered it unimportant; it may have been considered too awful to
mention; or maybe it was considered in a completely different way
from the way we see it now. Since sexual predilections have been
known to be partly related to taboo – forbidden acts being the most
exciting ones – if dead bodies were not taboo, then was there less
necrophilia? Were dead bodies as much a taboo in the past as they
are now?

From Herodotus' reports, it would seem that necrophilia was
taken seriously and considered an offence to extant family members of the dead. This seems to hold true throughout the ages. Most
people feel protective of their dead relatives and do not want their

corpses violated by strangers. However, the dead body itself was also seen as unclean. The Israelites considered touching a corpse as defilement and the person in contact with the dead body was seen to be in need of immediate purification. Sexual intercourse with a corpse would be considered the ultimate taboo by both Jews and Christians. The Book of Numbers 19:13 states, 'Whosoever toucheth the dead body of any man that is dead, and purifieth not himself, defileth the tabernacle of the Lord; and that soul shall be cut off from Israel: because the water of separation was not sprinkled upon him, he shall be unclean; his uncleanness is yet upon him, he shall be unclean.' There are more scriptures that make it abundantly clear that contact with the dead was forbidden. Leviticus 21:11 stipulates of a priest, 'Neither shall he go in to any dead body, nor defile himself for his father, or for his mother'. While the phrase '*go in to* any dead body' could be interpreted literally (as in male penetration of a female corpse), the New English Bible translates it as 'He shall not *enter the place* where any dead man's body lies.' The only exception to the rule of not touching the dead was when they were being interred, with the proviso of purification afterwards. Veneration of the dead, disturbing grave sites and touching and interacting with corpses for any other reason was likewise prohibited in many ancient societies. This prevalent idea that the dead were unclean may have kept some attempts of copulation with corpses at bay.

By the medieval period, although dead bodies may still have been taboo, people could be on open display when they were in their death throes. Just as they had in ancient Greece and Rome, people continued to die early and easily in domestic brawls and wars. Mass deaths also occurred in the plagues that repeatedly swept through Europe – the Black Death is believed to have killed one-third to one-half of Europe's population during the fourteenth century. Rotting bodies were thrown into the streets for the corpse collector to pick up, piled on to handcarts and wheeled away to be burned. Death was exposed even further in public executions. Everyone from the richest nobles to the lowest peasants witnessed the spectacle of the latest traitor or murderer being killed. Indeed, public executions became well-established as popular forms of entertainment. Laying-out of the dead meant that relatives, both young and old, came to visit the dead before they were buried. Death was therefore a common sight and people were introduced to it at an early age. Was this the reason that necrophilia was rare – that death was simply not taboo enough?

A Medieval Necrophile

Continual wars meant that many men observed mass slaughter at first hand. For some soldiers, the aftermath of war meant a search for peace and tranquillity, but the constant and bloody hand-to-hand combat and the sight of scene after scene of body-strewn battlefields left others obsessed with death. As a result, for some, the connection between euphoria and brutality became embedded, leading to what we would now diagnose as psychiatric disorders. This was the problem of nobleman Gilles de Rais (1404–1440), one of history's most infamous necrophiles. As with many cases of sexual atrocities, his predilection involved more than one vice, taking in paedophilia as well as necrophilia. Known for fighting bravely alongside Joan of Arc during the Hundred Years War, he debauched, tortured and murdered around 800 children; many of their bodies were never recovered. The tale is remarkable in that he left a personal testimony to the crimes, now preserved in the Nantes archives.

After a long series of battles, Charles VII of France decided to disband his armies and a period of calm ensued. Nobles such as de Rais, who had experienced the excitement of leading bloody battles, were told to either enjoy court life or retire to their estates. After mass slaughter and the thrill of battle, a quiet life was perhaps not what de Rais had in mind. At first, he retired to his castle in Tiffauges and set about spending his family fortune, holding debauched parties and surrounding himself with sycophants. Property was sold off piecemeal to pay for his extravagant lifestyle, and he eventually turned to alchemy in an attempt to turn his finances around. It was rumoured that his first murder of a child occurred when he slit a boy's throat, cut out his heart and eyes, and used his blood for the purpose of an agreement with the Devil. However, in reality, it would seem that his abuse and slaughter of children had little to do with the black arts; instead, these acts were crimes undertaken purely for his own sexual gratification.

The first murders began at Champtocé, where he was living at the time of his grandfather's death. There he managed to murder 40 children without attracting too much notice. His status as a wealthy

Gilles de Rais by Eloi Firmin Féron, 1835.

lord and marshal of France, as well as his spectacular military career, provided him temporarily with immunity from suspicion. The fact that many of his victims came from peasant families or were orphans meant that they were hardly missed. In a time of great poverty in France, swathes of orphaned children scoured the countryside looking for food. Even children with parents were urged to seek work wherever they could. Luring the children to his castle in promise of a job would have been simple. De Rais' cousins, Gilles de Sillé and Robert de Briqueville, acted as his procurers, venturing into nearby villages, ostensibly to search for a boy who could come to work at the castle; but the boy never returned home. The first victim to alert suspicion was a young apprentice called Jeudon (although there were so many murdered children that it has been impossible to document the complete facts). It was only because the child worked for a local furrier that it became known he was missing.

When de Rais moved to Machecoul, he built his own chapel, which he called the Chapel of the Holy Innocents, and filled it with beautiful children, all dressed in bonnets, furs and robes of the finest cloth. Two of his favourites, the boys with the finest voices, André Buchet and Rossignol, were purchased from their parents. He would later debauch them and then draw them into his secret life. Here in his castle, a further 40 bodies would later be found.

When the evidence was brought in court, de Rais' page, Etienne Corrillaut, otherwise known as Poitou, bore witness to his master's crimes. He revealed that de Rais' favourite trick was to have a servant hang up a child by a hook, enter the room feigning horror at the child's plight, then sit the child on his knee. He would then gently wipe away the child's tears and slit its throat. The page told the court that,

> in order to practise his libidinous pleasure and unnatural vices on the said children, both boys and girls, first he took his member in his hand and stroked it until it was erect, then placed it between the thighs of the said girls, rubbing his member on the bellies of the said boys and girls with great delight, vigour and libidinous pleasure until the sperm ejaculates on their bellies.[5]

The children were subjected to further violent sexual assaults as they lay dying; sometimes they were already dead.

The reason de Rais was finally caught was more to do with an interest in his property than in the murders themselves. De Rais had already ploughed much of his money into his luxurious chapel full of choirboys and decided to mount a huge theatrical production there. This was to be a mystery play in which he was to perform the central role, acting out all the heroic deeds he had undertaken in his earlier days. The play was to be presented on 8 May 1435 in Orléans, but his family, seeing him rack up all manner of debts, were not prepared to sit back and watch him squandering the family fortune. They therefore called a clandestine meeting to discuss how best to stop him and decided to take his estate at Champtocé by force. On hearing of his relatives' intentions, in a panic, de Rais ordered his henchmen to recover as many corpses as possible under cover of night, and to shift them to his estate at Machecoul. Hidden in the tower of the castle, the bodies first had to be prised out of the shafts before they could be encased in strong chests with ropes wound round them to prevent them inadvertently falling out. However, other bodies were hidden elsewhere – so many that his servants had forgotten where to look for them. No sooner had de Rais moved his entourage to Machecoul than children started to disappear in that vicinity. By the time an official inquiry was launched, hundreds of children had been murdered.

De Rais was put on trial in both a secular and ecclesiastical court in 1440, but at first he refused to confess to his crimes. Witness Henriet Griart reported that de Rais had not only raped the children but had taken his greatest enjoyment in playing with the severed heads and limbs of his victims. He said,

> When the said children were dead he kissed them and those who had the most handsome limbs and heads he held up to admire them, and had their bodies cruelly cut open and took delight at the sight of their inner organs; and very often when the said children were dying he sat on their stomachs and took pleasure in seeing them die.[6]

It was only under the threat of torture that de Rais finally confessed. When asked why he had committed such atrocities, he admitted he did them 'in accordance with his own imagination . . . solely for his pleasure and carnal delight'. His sentence was to be excommunicated and burned to death but in the event his body was only symbolically passed through the flames and his intact body was given back to his family for a Catholic burial in the churchyard of the Carmelites.

De Rais' case served as a perfect medieval example of sexual perversion in its connection to moral and spiritual corruption. His crimes were acted out as a result of diabolical desire, an inversion of moral consciousness, rather than simply a negation of the law, and were seen as a form of radical evil.[7] Why de Rais committed such atrocities is more difficult to understand. It was suggested at his trial that Gilles de Rais had started his crimes as early as 1426 but he himself stated that he had begun his assaults on children after his grandfather died – sometime between spring 1432 and spring 1433. His grandfather's death therefore appears to have made a dramatic impact on his inner emotional life, snapping the final thread connecting him to reality – since his grandfather had exercised at least a semblance of parental control over the young de Rais. Coming so soon after the execution of Joan of Arc (she had been burned to death in 1431), perhaps the death of his grandfather was the last blow which sent de Rais over the edge. His victims were small, beautiful, fair-haired children, the image of himself as a child. Those who might try to explain his adult behaviour in terms of childhood trauma would describe this as a sort of self-murder by proxy after some psychological affliction had taken hold, the veracity of which is impossible to know. His experience of blood, gore and death in battle had provided him with a euphoria he could only recapture in a sexual assault on freshly mutilated corpses.

Similarities appear in comparisons between Gilles de Rais and the Marquis de Sade. Sade had a similar background to de Rais in that he was an aristocrat, cosseted as a child, separated from his parents while still young and had been subject to bloody battles during his time in the military. Curiously, they played out similar fantasies. In his novels *Juliette* and *The 120 Days of Sodom*, Sade explored a heady mixture of sex, torture, pain and death. Throughout his stories, he uses the method of graduating his sexual atrocities from the least sexual abominations to the worst, necrophilia being among the latter. In some stories, he spoke of carving new orifices in the dead bodies to create a wound to penetrate. In one scene in *Juliette*, Durand, Juliette and Clairwil visit a cemetery where they have an orgy with a pile of rotting corpses. Gruesome details include how she uses a skeleton bone as a dildo and how Durand uses a severed hand with which to masturbate Juliette. On coming across a cadaver, Juliette declares, 'It occurs to me that these bones, shaped as they are, might serve in the stead of pricks.'[8]

While de Rais carved out a world of necrophilia for himself in his castles, Sade experienced necrophilia vicariously through his novels. Although Sade indulged in sadism, as far as we know he did not commit necrophilia but merely wrote about it. He did, however, admit to knowing a Parisian who ordered corpses to be brought to his house in order to indulge in necrophilia.[9] In de Rais' case, his desire to experience closeness to death meant copulation with fresh corpses. Murder was an essential part of the ritual. If not, he would merely have dug up corpses, as did the 'regular' necrophile.

Doctoring the Dead

By the time of the Enlightenment, ideas about dead bodies were shifting. The new science of anatomy meant that surgeons were dissecting and displaying the interiors of corpses in ways that had not been seen before. The public were left with a strange sense of unease, as most people felt they wanted their dead to be buried intact. The Church preached that come the day of the Resurrection, the faithful would be bodily restored to life. It was therefore important to keep the body in one piece. In this light, aversions to dissection can be seen as a reasonable fear, since people wanted to retain all their limbs and visceral organs in heaven. These anxieties were realized in popular prints such as Hogarth's depictions of the dissecting table in 'The Reward of Cruelty' (1751), the fouth plate of *The Four Stages of Cruelty*. As the corpse is stretched out on the table, it undergoes the onslaught of the surgeon pulling out its entrails. Rowlandson's print *The Persevering Surgeon* adds a sexual dimension to dissection. Here, the lone debauched surgeon leers over the naked torso of a beautiful young woman.

While such prints reflected the public's aversion to dissection, medics at the Royal College of Surgeons and groups such as the Royal Society were moving in the opposite direction, increasingly exploring the interior workings of the body. For this they needed more corpses; interest in anatomy grew. The surgeon William Hunter began a series of lectures on the subject in 1746 and provided specimens for display. As a result, more students were influenced to join the expanding profession, which meant an increased demand for cadavers. Since few people wanted to donate their bodies to scientific investigation, surgeons were left with a shortage of corpses on which to work. Stealing bodies therefore became a profitable occupation. The problem was significant enough to be satirized by Rowlandson in his drawing *Resurrection Men* (1775), which shows two dubious-looking characters digging up a corpse, assisted by a gruesome skeleton representing death. As Death holds a lantern, egged on by his friend, one of the men lies atop the prone female corpse as if about to copulate

William Hogarth, *The Four Stages of Cruelty*, plate IV, 'The Reward of
Cruelty', 1751.

with it. In a similar vein, another picture by Rowlandson, *Death in
the Dissecting Room* (1815), shows a pretty young corpse lying on
the floor, about to be sliced open by an unscrupulous surgeon as
another man brings in another corpse in a sack. At least the idea of
sex with the dead was therefore present in the Enlightenment mind.
Reflecting public anxieties over death and sexual violation, dissection also became a topical subject in magazines. In a letter to the
Gentleman's Magazine in 1747, one man expressed his concern over
stolen bodies: 'The affair which lately happened to the vaults at St
Andrew's, Holbourne . . . [the] body was taken away by the sexton,
the very night of its interment and sold to a surgeon', believing it to

be 'a common practice with these fellows'. In order to try and prevent such crimes while freeing up more corpses, pressure was exerted on the authorities to allow the bodies of executed murderers to be used for the purpose of dissection, culminating in the Murder Act of 1752.

Since money could be made selling bodies to surgeons for dissection, ruthless villains turned their hand to murdering for profit. Although accounts of Burke and Hare's activities are comparatively well-known, few know about Dr Robert Knox and the corpse of Mary Paterson. Both are connected in a series of events entailing the murder of vagrants and prostitutes, and involved the possession of the body of a young woman in the dissecting rooms of Dr Knox. The gruesome case of Burke and Hare came to court in Edinburgh in 1828 after the murder of sixteen people (it is a popular misconception that they were grave robbers). William Hare ran a boarding house with his wife Margaret Laird in the West Port area of the city. Nearby, the

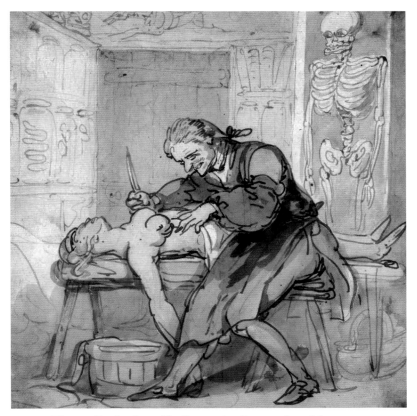

Thomas Rowlandson, *The Persevering Surgeon*, late 18th century.

Edinburgh Medical School was suffering from a shortage of cadavers on which to practice – only two or three bodies of executed criminals were available for a large number of students. According to Burke's testimony, after one of their tenants died of natural causes, owing £4 in rent, Hare and Laird hit on the idea of selling the corpse to the medical school. They received £7 10s. for the body, a handsome sum, considering that a pint of beer cost one and a half pence and a loaf of bread weighing 2 lb cost fourpence. With such easy profits to be made, Laird and Hare, along with their accomplices William Burke and his partner Helen McDougal, began murdering drunks, prostitutes and anyone whom they thought would not be missed. At first

Thomas Rowlandson, *The Resurrection Men*, 1775.

Surgeons fuss over a male cadaver with undue interest in Thomas
Rowlandson's *The Dissecting Room*, 1775–80.

they murdered their tenants, but later moved on to luring men and
women from the street, getting them drunk and smothering them.
When the case came to light, it was evident that the bodies had been
sold on to a surgeon for dissection.

The person who had been receiving the bodies was the famous
Edinburgh anatomist Dr Robert Knox, a graduate of Edinburgh University. It was said that after being presented with one female corpse
he thought it too lovely to dissect and kept it in a tub of whisky for
three months before dissection.[10] The body was that of Mary Paterson,
a teenage prostitute who had been lured to her death in Burke's
brother's house. Scores of students scrambled to Knox's dissecting
rooms to view the pickled woman. The fact that she was both beautiful and naked no doubt helped swell the numbers signing up for Knox's
classes. Once Burke and Hare came to trial, Dr Knox was implicated
by connection and his activities were exposed. The Royal College of
Surgeons immediately demanded his resignation, resulting in the loss
of his teaching job as well as his lucrative lecture tours. Gossip festered
around him for years to come, and he would never again find a position as a surgeon.

Rowlandson's depiction of the Burke and Hare story.

Hare and Laird were let off for turning King's Evidence and giving witness against Burke and McDougal. Burke was hanged, watched by enormous crowds. Perhaps in a case of poetic justice, his body was later taken for dissection. The two wives of the men escaped without charge, but only narrowly missed being attacked by an angry mob. As soon as the case came to court, gossip about the Burke and Hare murders spread through word of mouth, broadsheets and pamphlets. The story fed into public concerns about grave robbers and body-snatching, with the lurid details laid out for all to see. The case reinforced what people had suspected: that doctors were unscrupulous lechers delving into areas that should not be seen. The case helped influence the introduction of the Anatomy Act of 1832, which expanded the legal supply of cadavers for medical schools.

Meanwhile, scientific experiments and demonstrations of new findings continued to instruct interested audiences at public lectures. Fresh, exciting displays were on offer in 1791, when scientist Luigi Galvani used electricity to charge life into otherwise seemingly dead body parts. In packed lecture rooms, he brought frogs' legs 'back to life' using the trick of electrocution to make the legs dance. Men and women watched, entranced by the fact that bodies could be made to move even though they were dead. Galvani's ideas captured the imagination of Mary Shelley. His experiments would inspire her some years later to write her *Frankenstein* (1818), a sad tale about the creation of a human-looking monster pieced together with body parts scavenged from executed criminals and brought to life by electricity. The monster wandered the woods looking for love but, unable to find anyone suitable, demanded his master make him a female counterpart. Thus necrophilia reached it apotheosis in the image of dead bodies having sex with dead bodies. The theme was explored in depictions in film such as *Frankenstein* (1931) and *Bride of Frankenstein* (1935). Since then, zombie movies such as *Porn of the Dead* (2006) have taken sex with the dead to its ultimate form in celluloid.

Feminizing Fatality

The feminizing (and sexualizing) of death was apparent in images, news reports and pamphlets where the female body was closely linked to lust and death. An example can be seen as early as 1517 in the image *Death and the Maiden* by Hans Baldung Grien. By the

Dr Knox was implicated in the Burke and Hare murders, portrait *c.* 1830.

Elsa Lanchester and Boris Karloff in *Bride of Frankenstein*
(dir. James Whale, 1935).

eighteenth century the female body was objectified and passified in doctoring, in death and in sex. Women, sex and death melded together in a display of a sort of macabre exoticism.[11]

Nowhere was this more evident than in the eighteenth-century execution of Mary Blandy. Her story was recounted in the pamphlet *A Genuine and Impartial Account of the Life of Miss M. Blandy* (1752) after she had poisoned her father at her lover's instigation. Blandy was convicted and sentenced to hanging, a spectacle that attracted an exceptionally large crowd. In the pamphlet, the narrator gave a general description of the incidents leading to her trial, but languished most lovingly over the intimate details of her execution and her bodily appeal. Her clothes were described down to the ribbons and bonnets she wore; her female form was outlined with care – even in death, it seemed, her figure retained its pert bosom, its shining hair and its trim waistline.[12] The author tells us Blandy 'begged to be hanged decently', not too high, so the crowds could not see up her petticoat. In the event, when her body was cut down it was passed among the crowd, revealing all.

Fewer women than men were hanged and there were therefore fewer female corpses available to dissect. In response to this lack of

Hans Baldung Grien, *Death and the Maiden*, 1517.

female corpses, some doctors took to ordering their own human dummies of wood or wax, making them available as a tool for teaching. These life-sized models were anatomically correct and could be pulled apart to expose the insides of the female body, complete with visceral organs. Indeed, some were clearly made with the intention of exposing female sexual features and reproductive organs; or as one historian put it, they 'delighted the sight and invited sexual thoughts'.[13] Ostensibly educational, the figures had real hair and were even given eyebrows and eyelashes. These models were invariably shown lying down on a table, passive, their bodies open to the eyes of the male investigator; contrarily, male models tended to be shown standing and assertive. Such models were exhibited all over Europe, the most famous of which were displayed in La Specola in Florence and the Josephinium in Vienna. The extraordinarily gifted modeller Clemente Susini (1754–1814) was chiefly responsible for their technical construction. The models were produced in Florence between 1784 and 1788 and then brought to Vienna in costly transportations. By the nineteenth century, the models were being openly exhibited to the public. However, owing to the exposed nature of the bodies, men and women attended on different days – it was evidently thought too intimate an exhibition to have shared viewings.

Clemente Susini, Anatomical Venus, late 18th century, now in the Josephinium medical museum, Vienna.

Wax anatomical
model by
Clemente Susini
(1754–1814), in La
Specola, Florence.

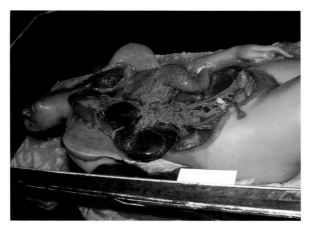

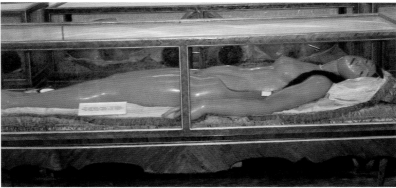

The idea of extreme female passivity was to infiltrate Victorian
culture at all levels. The Pre-Raphaelite artists made a huge contribution to the romanticization of death. John Everett Millais's painting
of Lizzy Siddal as the drowned Ophelia reinforced the Victorian
connection of women to submissiveness, sex and death.[14] This popular painting also triggered rumours about the model's own death.
Gossips suggested that her health was damaged as a result of catching cold while lying in a bath for hours posing for the artist. This
fanciful image of the ideal dead woman was enhanced by the impulsive action of Siddal's husband, the artist Dante Gabriel Rossetti. They
had been had been romantically involved from around 1852, but
their relationship was erratic. They parted in 1858, but married two
years later. Her death by overdosing on laudanum a few years later
sealed her image in the public imagination as the Queen of Death.
In a spate of grief, Rossetti encased a book containing the only copies

John Everett Millais, *Ophelia*, 1851–2, featuring the artists' model Lizzie Siddal.

of some of his poems in the coffin with her body, only to regret it some years later. In 1870 her coffin, buried in Highgate Cemetery, was exhumed at Rossetti's request so that he could retrieve the poems.

The romanticized dead featuring the adored female lover was also encapsulated by Robert Browning in his poem 'Porphyria's Lover' of 1842. Here, he portrays a man who has strangled the woman he loves because he cannot possess her except in death.

> About her neck: her cheeks once more
> Blushed bright beneath my burning kiss:
> I propped her head up as before . . .
> And thus we sit together now,
> And all night long we have not stirred . . .[15]

Browning recognized the idea that necrophilia was sometimes inspired by the fact that the body is a subject of deep affection. Unrequited love in this case was just too much to endure.

Understanding the Necrophile

Such desire for extreme forms of passivity can similarly be seen in a necrophile who admits to being unable to socialize with women properly. Psychiatrists have claimed that sex with dead bodies is related to the feeling of insignificance experienced by the necrophile. In interviews, the necrophile has often shown up as a particular type, with a certain sort of childhood background – timid, bullied at school and unable to have successful relationships with women. Necrophiles often admitted to being unable to attract women, so they found non-resistant sex attractive. In these cases, the body on which the necrophile focuses his (and it is usually *his*, not *her*) attention is objectified. The corpse was a body that would not refuse him, so any fear of rejection was removed. The body in these cases could belong to anyone. However, in other cases of necrophilia, the person to whom the body belonged was important to the necrophile. Who that corpse once was, and the feeling of love for that person, was closely connected to desire of that specific dead body and it was not simply about the ease of copulating with a non-resisting corpse.

In some cases, mere caressing or even having coitus with a corpse was not enough. Mutilating, dismembering or destroying the cadaver in some way was necessary for a necrophile to gain the most intense pleasure, often through violent orgasms. Dr Auguste Ambroise Tardieu wrote graphic accounts of patients who had dug up corpses to have sex with them. One of his most detailed cases was that of Sergeant Bertrand, a French army officer who confessed to his crime in 1849. Bertrand was 25 when he was arrested. He was considered a slight man 'of delicate constitution' who admitted to being prone to solitude in his childhood. Perhaps in recognition of the rejection he felt, he confessed that his parents stopped buying him toys, as he broke everything. By the age of nine, he was fantasizing about murdering and having sex with female corpses (sometimes even fantasizing about men, but he felt revulsion at this). As was often the case with necrophiles (and indeed, lust-murderers), his love of death began by mutilating and killing animals. By the time he was fourteen he was masturbating up to seven or eight times a day, later saying, 'The mere sight of an article of feminine attire was enough to cause an erection.' He admitted, 'I would in my mind torture them [the women] in every possible way, according to my desire. I would imagine them as dead before me, and would defile their corpse.'[16] The mere closeness of a graveyard sent his pulse racing and his heart beating.

By 1847, he had exhumed his first corpse and mutilated the body, experiencing orgasm while he sliced it into bits. By way of explanation, he simply said, 'I felt in need of mutilating dead bodies.' He began to target newly dug graves, knowing there would be a fresh body recently interred. On 10 March 1848, he went to the cemetery, having to climb a wall and swim across an icy ditch to get there. He described the incident:

> No sooner had I entered the cemetery than I began to disinter a young girl who might have been from 15 to 17 years of age . . . I have kissed this dead woman in all parts of her body, I pressed her against myself as if to break her in two; in a word I lavished on her all the caresses that a passionate lover could on the object of his love.[17]

He then started to press out her entrails, replaced the body in the grave and went back to his barracks. Bertrand also admitted to having dug up male cadavers, but with those he restricted himself to masturbation. With females he would have full coitus.

Bertrand told his doctor, Marchal de Calvis, that he would not have risked digging up corpses merely to have sex with them, but that his overwhelming desire and pleasure was to mutilate and destroy them. Although Bertrand described himself as a Lothario, alleging to have had many women whom he had satisfied sexually (according to him, many even wanted to marry him), his doctor believed this to be a delusion. It may also have been a pretence made up to protect himself from his own lack of confidence – self-aggrandizing is often undertaken by those least likely to achieve the heights they say they have. He was finally caught and sentenced to a year in prison.

Cases of unrequited passion and continual rejection led some men to copulate with the female dead. Under his pseudonym Stendhal (1783–1842), Marie-Henri Beyle described in his thinly disguised autobiography how he was drawn to a cemetery and dug up a decomposing body of a girl of twelve or thirteen, removed her entrails and mutilated her genitalia. But his original passion had been an incestuous love of his mother. He confessed, 'I wanted to cover my mother in kisses even when she had no clothes on. She loved me passionately and hugged me often. I returned her kisses with such a fire that she often was obliged to run away. I hated my father when he used to come and interrupt our kisses. I always wanted to give them on her bosom.'[18] Stendhal seems to have had a confused sexuality (whether fantasy or reality) combining necrophilia with incest, but such cases seem to be rare. However, necrophiles sometimes developed unusually strong feelings – of either love or aversion – for their parents.

By the turn of the nineteenth century, sexologists were interviewing and assessing patients who were confessed necrophiles, trying to understand their behaviour. Krafft-Ebing interviewed countless perverted patients, but admitted to being stumped when it came to necrophiles. He left few words on the subject in his book *Psychopathia Sexualis* but summed up his feelings on the matter: 'This horrible kind of sexual indulgence is so monstrous that the presumption of a psychopathic state is, under all circumstances, justified.' While showing compassion for many of his cases, he could not muster sympathy for the necrophile. In order to be able to have sexual congress with corpses, he believed people had to be mentally unstable; that a perverse sensuality was necessary to overcome the natural repugnance that ordinary men have for corpses.

On assessing Victor Ardisson, a French grave robber and necrophile, Krafft-Ebing blamed mental incapacity for his crimes, describing him as a 'moron void of any moral sense'. Ardisson had earned the nickname 'the Vampire of Muy' because of his predilection for sucking on his victims' body parts. His case came to light when he was arrested in 1901 for robbing graves and mutilating corpses; his job as a gravedigger provided him with the perfect opportunity to indulge his passion. While some necrophiles appear not to care what the corpses look like, Ardisson's desire was only for beautiful young women. William Stekel reported that Ardisson admitted that he drank his own semen after masturbation, 'because it would be too bad to have it go to waste'.[19] As with other necrophiles, Ardisson was socially inadequate with women and all his marriage proposals had been rejected. In compensation, he masturbated as he watched women urinate. He admitted that his inadequacies led him to pay for one beggar woman to have sex with him. While he had problems with women, he continued to fellate men for money. He claimed to have copulated with his mother after her death but Stekel believed this to be mere fantasy (this fantasy bears a striking resemblance to Stendhal's desire for his mother). His method of assault on female bodies, whether dead or alive, was first to suck their breasts, then to perform cunnilingus on them. Albert Moll identified his behaviour as 'passivism', a behaviour typified in a certain type of self-disregarding person. Ardisson spent the rest of his life in the psychiatric hospital of Pierrefeu du Var.

Incidences of necrophilia have been associated with narcolepsy, where perpetrators of the crime suddenly fall into a deep sleep after fulfilling their sexual obsessions with the dead. One example can be seen in Henri Blot, who was arrested in 1886 for raping a number of exhumed corpses. His first act of necrophilia had been with a ballet dancer buried in the Saint-Ouen cemetery, after which he fell into a deep sleep. It was only after his next excursion, when he was found in this coma-like state next to the corpse, that he was apprehended.

The female necrophile is uncommon in fact or fiction. Perhaps this is due to physiology – it is more difficult for a woman to copulate with a corpse unless the male cadaver is in the throes of rigor mortis. However, one strange case emerged in 1848 of a royal lady who had allegedly secreted the corpse of her lover in her home. The woman was Princess Cristina Trivulzio di Belgiojoso, who was to become the sweetheart of Paris intellectuals and counted Chopin, Liszt, Victor Hugo and Alexander Dumas among her friends. Known as a revolutionary, her book *Della Condizione Delle Donne e del Loro Avvenire* (*Of Women's Condition and of their Future*; 1866) was a proto-feminist tract. The princess was also a neurotic and apparently suffered from epilepsy, a condition thought by sexologists to be common in necrophiles. After the Italian Revolution of 1848 she fled her home in Locate but left behind the body of her 27-year-old lover Gaetano Stelzi, who had died of tuberculosis earlier that year. He was found completely preserved, dressed from head to toe in black. The coffin in which he had been supposedly buried was dug up and found to contain only a log. It is believed Stelzi had died suddenly of a lung haemorrhage in the presence of the terrified princess in her house in Milan. From there she had his newly embalmed body transferred to a vault on her estate. How his corpse ended up in her cupboard was never revealed. After fleeing the country she ended up in Turkey, living in a tent; she eventually returned to Italy where she died in 1871.[20]

By the twentieth century a new way had been found to bring death and dead bodies into people's daily lives and viewing space to replace eighteenth-century public hangings and nineteenth-century funeral displays. The American television company HBO aired a special documentary, *Autopsy*, in 2005, about one of the most infamous cases of necrophilia from the 1930s. The programme focused on Carl von Cosel (sometimes called Carl Tanzler), a radiologist living in Florida who treated a young, beautiful tuberculosis patient, Maria Elena Milagro de Hoyos. He looked after her and tried to save her life, buying her medicines and visiting her regularly, but the disease finally killed her. By this time he was in love with her. Unable to accept her death, with her parents' permission, von Cosel had her exhumed and placed her body in a mausoleum specially built for her. Unbeknown to anybody, he took the opportunity to clean and re-embalm the body, writing about his experience in his memoirs: 'Decay had set in a most disheartening manner. Only with the greatest care was I able to peel the pieces of textile from her body; this took hours.'[21] He sponged her face with a specially prepared solution, spread her clean body on to a white sheet and sprayed it with preservatives.

Hoping that he might be able to slow down the inevitable process of decay, he thought it preferable to keep her body above the ground. He visited the corpse every day, taking her presents – flowers, a comb, a shawl. Soon he could no longer bear to be parted from her so he decided to transport her secretly from the mausoleum to the cabin of an old aeroplane he kept at the back of his hospital. Now he could spend more time with her. As he undid the casket once more, he saw she was 'pure, despite the mud and slimy rags in which she had been lying for so many months'. He kissed her lips and breathed deeply into her body so her bosom rose. He carefully redressed her in a wedding gown – she was now his 'sweet wife'.

Two years after her death, with her body still inside it, he moved the plane to a hanger at South Beach where he could rest happily at her side. Here, he built a laboratory in which to keep the equipment he needed to preserve her – her incubator, sterile tissues, chemicals and wax to keep the remnants of her flesh together. As the years passed, he had to keep her bones together with piano wire and performed the time-consuming task of daily applying new wax and slathering perfumes on what was left of the body. He also made wigs of her hair to keep as much of her genuine as he could. He loved her even though she was patently rotting: 'I looked deeply into the fallen cavity of her eyes, like deep, empty black holes. I saw her dried lips, slightly

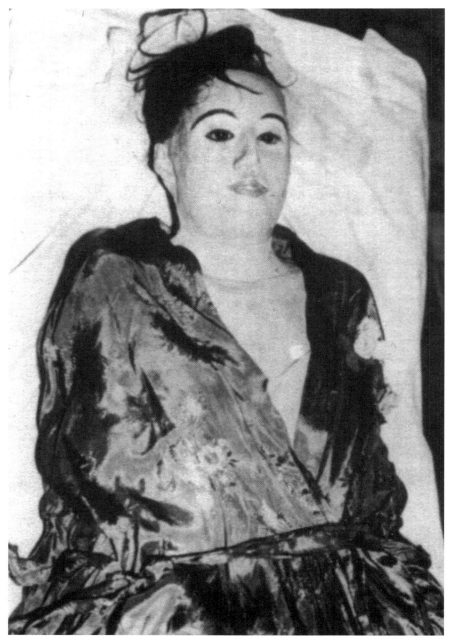

The corpse of Maria Elena Milagro de Hoyos (1910–1931) encased in wax and plaster, c. 1940.

parted with her white teeth gleaming between them.' Eventually he found an old house to rent where he could place her in a proper bed. Not wanting to leave his home, he received huge deliveries of the wax and sprays, until his neighbours started to become suspicious.

Rumours were circulating around town because of the amount of purchases he made of perfume, wax and other objects necessary to keep the corpse fresh. Gossip eventually reached Maria's sister, Nana, who insisted on seeing the body, which she thought was still resting in the mausoleum. Von Cosel managed to convince her not to go to the mausoleum, but instead to come to his house where the body now lay. He may have thought Nana would have been happy to see her sister again, but she was horrified at what she saw and reported him to the authorities. On investigation, they found that along with daily love letters to Maria Elena, the technician had consistently had sex with what was left of her body – basically bones and silken packing material, as there was no flesh left. Dr DePoo, who made the autopsy on Maria, stated: 'I found a tube wide enough to permit sexual intercourse. At the bottom of the tube was cotton, and in an examination of the cotton, I found there was sperm.' Von Cosel had gone to the trouble of inserting a tube where her vagina had been in order to allow himself to penetrate what was now essentially her skeleton.

Although the events were not pleasant for Maria's family, Dr von Cosel was never a violent man and his love for Maria was unquestionable. His love story provoked an outpouring of sympathy for him and letters of support poured in. Strangers as well as friends visited him in prison, bringing him food and gifts. He was fined but released, since, after being examined by a psychiatrist at the order of the judge, he was found to be sane despite his obsession. The court returned the body to Maria's sister, who took it to be buried in an undisclosed location, presumably to keep publicity (and Cosel) at bay. Von Cosel returned to his hometown in Germany, where he died in poverty.

From the late 1940s onwards, Western societies were at a stage where the sight of death was becoming less common and therefore more taboo; so, did cases of necrophilia increase as a result? Although sexologists had identified necrophilia as a paraphilia, there were remarkably few known cases for them to discuss. Necrophilia seems to have been an aside in terms of sexually perverted behaviour.

Recent research has shown a worrying trend that the act of murder undertaken in order to obtain a body for the purposes of sexual violation is increasing. A pair of psychiatrists working at the Department of Psychiatry at Cleveland Metropolitan General Hospital, Ohio, investigated necrophilia and published their findings in 1988. In this study, Rosman and Resnick found that 42 per cent of their sample of necrophiles had murdered in order to obtain a body. They established that there were three types of true necrophilia – necrophilic homicide (where the necrophile murders in order to have sex with a body), 'regular' necrophilia (where the necrophile copulates with an already dead body) and necrophilic fantasy (where the necrophile imagines having sex with a dead body but does not act upon it). Psychosis, mental retardation and sadism do not appear to be inherent in necrophilia. The researchers stated: 'The most common motive for necrophilia is possession of an unresisting and unrejecting partner. Necrophiles often chose occupations that put them in contact with corpses. Some necrophiles who had occupational access to corpses committed homicide nevertheless.'[22]

In the U.S. there is no federal legislation specifically barring sex with a corpse. Fewer than half of the states have their own laws, and many of them class necrophilia only as a misdemeanour. Sexual penetration or 'interference' of any part of a corpse became illegal in the UK only with the Sexual Offences Act 2003, although prior to that it might be considered 'indecency with a corpse' under common law. In Britain, the Criminal Justice and Immigration Act 2008 states that it is also illegal to possess physical depictions of necrophilia, electronic or otherwise. Necrophilia pornography falls under the governmental description of extreme pornography, possession of which is classed as illegal under the Act. If the person is role-playing, the picture is no longer illegal. But how might the authorities detect that a person is really dead merely from pornographic photographs? Is this law worth anything?

The DSM V of the American Psychiatric Association classifies necrophilia, also called thanatophilia and necrolagnia, as a paraphilia. Its British equivalent, the ICD-10, calls it a 'disorder of sexual preference', which puts it in the same category as bestiality. However, while attitudes towards sodomy, homosexuality, lesbianism, sadomasochism and bestiality have changed, necrophilia stands out as being continually condemned as a 'perversity'. But what is the 'crime' of necrophilia, if murder or stealing of corpses is not involved? The 'crime' of necrophilia surely lies not so much in having sex with a corpse as in not having gained consent prior to the person's death.

The incestuous couple: Nero and his mother Agrippina as she crowns him with a laurel leaf; *c.* 54–59.

NINE

Too Close for Comfort: Incest

Incest is like many other incorrect things, a very poetical circumstance.
Percy Bysshe Shelley (1792–1822)[1]

Having sex with one's closest kin – a brother, sister, father or mother – has been seen as a prominent taboo throughout most of the Western world. More distant connections, say aunts and uncles by marriage or cousins, have been more contested. Generally speaking, though, the closer the blood tie, the greater the aversion. Incest was, and is, unlawful in most Western countries, but legal conditions and sentencing vary enormously.

The Oldest Loves

In the past, incest was not only permitted, in some cases it was positively encouraged. Members of the royal families in Egypt were seen as gods. It was therefore considered unacceptable for them to procreate with commoners. Royals needed to find other gods and goddesses with whom to copulate and this invariably meant keeping procreation in the family. This ensured that the bloodline remained pure but also kept the family wealth intact. These incestuous marriages set the royal family apart from the rest of society, as commoners did not tend to marry their sisters or daughters. Proof of this can be seen in the census returns in Roman Egypt during the first three centuries AD.

In Egyptian royal families, the line of succession ran through the eldest daughter rather than the eldest son. Pharaohs who wanted to make a claim for the throne therefore had to legitimize themselves by marrying a sister or half-sister. Both Cleopatra VII's brothers, Ptolemy XIII and subsequently Ptolemy XIV, became co-regents when she married them. Amenhotep III's daughter, Satamun, was known as 'king's wife' and even 'king's principal wife', along with her

Zeus and his sister Hera by Annibale Carracci, 1573.

Albrecht Altdorfer, *Lot and His Daughters*, 1537.

mother Tiy. Their son, Akhenaten, married the beautiful Nefertiti, and also married at least one of their daughters. The fact that they had offspring indicates that these unions were consummated.

In Greek mythology, gods and goddesses who were related frequently bore children together. The brother and sister Kronus and Rhea were married and produced the leader of the Heavens, the brother and sister couple Zeus and Hera. In reality, incest was not

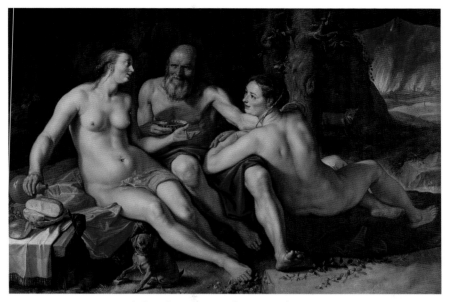

Hendrik Goltzius, *Lot and His Daughters*, 1616.

allowed, and Greek tragedies were full of the problems it might cause. In Athens in the fifth century BC, Sophocles' play *Oedipus Rex* warned audiences about such domestic drama, with the hero Oedipus known as the exemplar of familial incest. Having killed his father (unaware of who he really was) in a brawl at a crossroads, he unwittingly marries his mother, Jocasta. After a plague of infertility sweeps the city of Thebes, Oedipus consults the Oracle at Delphi and asks what he should do. The messenger of the oracle tells him he must avenge the murder of Laius – which, of course, he himself had committed. On discovering that Laius is his father, and that his wife is actually his mother, Oedipus bewails, 'Incestuous sin! Breeding where I was bred! Father, brother, and son; bride, wife, and mother confounded in one monstrous matrimony! All human filthiness in one crime compounded!'[2] Jocasta hangs herself, while Oedipus pokes the pin of her brooch into his eyes and is left to wander blindly throughout the country. In this Greek tragedy, it is the very closeness of the blood ties that is the problem, quite the opposite of the understanding of the ancient Egyptians.

While ancient Roman society also considered incest as forbidden, Rome's history is littered with incestuous families. According to Cicero, the Roman politician Publius Clodius prostituted himself dressed as a woman but also committed incest with his sisters.[3] Caligula committed incest with each of his three sisters in turn and loved Drucilla so much that he treated her as his wife.[4] He so adored her that he is said to have gone insane after her death. Caligula's sister Agrippina the Younger supposedly lured her son Nero into sex. Nero's passion for his mother was so great that her enemies feared that if it was consumated, she would become even more powerful and ruthless. However, Suetonius tells us, 'some say that he did, in fact, commit incest with Agrippina every time they rode in the same litter – the state of his clothes when he emerged proved it'.[5] Notwithstanding, her overbearing ways became too much for him and he had his henchmen slaughter her.

For Christians the Hebrew Bible provided the law. Scholars have argued that the laws of Leviticus developed to separate the lifestyle of the Israelites from the sinful lives of the people of Canaan. Leviticus (18:6–18) outlines the types of kinship that are allowed and those that are forbidden. A man should not commit incest with his mother, father's wife, sister, granddaughter, aunt, daughter-in-law or sister-in-law. Although the list does not include daughters, this is implicit in verse 6, which comands 'none of you shall approach to any that is near of kin to him, to uncover their nakedness'. Ostracization is suggested as the appropriate punishment for incest with one's own sister – 'they shall be cut off in the sight of their people' (20:17); if a man lies with his aunt or sister-in-law (as did Henry VIII), they shall die childless. Other crimes were more serious; if a man commits incest with his wife's mother, he should be burned to death. Incest with a daughter-in-law was punishable by death for both those involved. However, despite the fact that the Bible condemned incest, the Old Testament depicts it in the book of Genesis. When Lot left the city of Sodom to live in a cave alone but for his two daughters, no other men were available to impregnate them. The elder daughter tells the younger, 'Come, let us make our father drink wine, and we will lie with him, that we may preserve the seed of our father' (Genesis 19:32). In their favour was the fact that they did not see him naked. Lot's excuse would have been that he was drunk at the time.

Incest Laws

From the beginnings of Christianity, the main discussions around incest tended to be focused on consanguinity (how close a person was related to another in blood) or affinity (ties by marriage) rather than child abuse by a family member as they tend to be today. Laws and customs were mainly concentrated on marriage and stretched way beyond the nuclear family. In the West, the incest taboo related to most of the extended family and anyone related by blood or marriage to the sixth or even the eighth degree (second and third cousins – each degree accounting for one generation from a common ancestor).[6] A person could not marry their in-laws or even the in-laws of their in-laws, nor their godparents or godchildren.

Church authorities were, however, divided on the matter of permissable relationships. St Ambrose (339–397) claimed that divine law forbade the marriage between brothers' children 'joined in the fourth degree', while St Augustine suggested it was not divine law but imperial law which made such unions illegal. Meanwhile, the Code of Justinian allowed marriage between first cousins (*consobrini*), but the Greek Church in 692 at the Second Trullan Synod condemned such marriages. According to Theodore Balsamon, a twelfth-century Greek Orthodox Patriarch of Antioch, even those of second cousins (*sobrini*) should not be allowed. Pope Gregory III (732–41) forbade marriage to the seventh degree of consanguinity, whereas the *Roman Penitential of Halitgar* (*c.* 830) stipulated that a man's stepmother and his uncle's wife were out of bounds. Debate continued into the second millenium. In 1215, the Lateran council decided that the law was too harsh and reduced the degree of consanguinity from seven to four. Yet around 1440, *Jacob's Well*, a treatise on the 'cleansing of man's conscience', advised: 'Contract of matrimony in kynrede in-to be fyfte degree is forfendyd',[7] disallowing marriage up to (but not excluding) the fifth degree. If the Church authorities seemed to contradict themselves, it must have been even more confusing for the layperson.

The word 'incest' was introduced into Middle English around 1225 as a term to describe the sin of familial incest, but was not widely used.[8] Although incest was not a civil crime, it was regulated by the Church. The ecclesiastical courts placed incest in the same category as adultery and fornication (all sex outside marriage was illicit) and doled out penances accordingly. Usually plenty of warnings were given beforehand and penalties were light. Incest was not considered as bad as sodomy – even when undertaken with one's closest relative, procreation was at least still possible. Capital punishments were meted out in some cases of incest, but usually such severe sentences were reserved for situations where the culprit was also accused of bestiality or sodomy. For example, in the 1490s in Ferrara records show 'a peasant burned to death for impregnating his sister and for bestiality with asses, a 17-year-old youth from the suburbs burned for sodomy, another peasant hanged for theft and incest with his sisters . . . [but] an 80-year-old draper convicted of sodomy and sentenced to death by burning was spared his life'.[9]

Kissing Cousins

The Church authorities had referred back to Leviticus in decision-making about incest and cousin marriages. To clarify the situation, the Fourth Lateran Council of 1215 defined incest as sexual intercourse between relatives of the fourth degree, which included cousins.[10] This also allowed the Church authorities to introduce a fee-based dispensation for marriages taking place between first, second or third cousins.[11] In other words, an individual was allowed to marry a first, second or third cousin but had to pay off the Church for the freedom to do so.

In 1540, a statute of Parliament did little to change the situation. It decreed, 'all persons be lawful that be not prohibited by God's laws to marry; and that no reservation or prohibition, God's Laws except, shall trouble to impeach any marriage without the Levitical degrees'.[12] The list of prohibitions on incestuous marriages in Leviticus was therefore still the ruling on such matters. First cousins were still not specifically mentioned on the list of prohibited relationships, nor were they mentioned at the Council of Trent in 1563 when a list of forbidden marriages was drawn up. The degrees of consanguinity and affinity in reference to cousins therefore continued to remain cloudy and were not stated explicitly in canon law – that of 1606 simply referred back to the ecclesiastical table of 1563. Adding to the confusion, canon law and civil law counted the degrees of consanguinity differently, so cousins-german (or first cousins) would be considered second-degree cousins under the former and fourth-degree cousins under the latter.

Meanwhile, over half a century later, the little-known Puritan scholar Andrew Willet (1562–1621) provided a litany of examples of why it was best to avoid first-cousin marriages, as they were not only 'inconvenient', but also possibly illicit under divine law. Yet it was common for European aristocrats at this time to marry cousins or fairly close family to keep wealth in one family – even among English squires, cousin marriage was so frequent that it had become meaningless in terms of patronage, as everyone was related to someone else nearby.[13] In England, while marriages between first cousins were not illegal, the rest of the family closely oversaw them. Lydia DuGard wrote regular letters to her first cousin, Samuel DuGard, between 1665 and 1672, which tell a touching story about courtship and romantic love between cousins. She wrote to him, 'I did not think such reports would have bin spread abroad from our Whitford Journy. A year or two since it would have troubled me much, but now since I am so used to hear people talk of you and mee.'[14] At first, she tried to conceal their relationship from the rest of her family. The family had a say in the way the matter progressed, with the couple's behaviour regulated by a code of social conduct defined by ties between its members, but the couple eventually were allowed to marry.[15]

The anxieties about incest between cousins remained and were sometimes expressed in concerns about the possibility of diabolical creatures being born from such unions. Written anonymously, *A Most Strraunge and true discourse . . . of incestuous copulation* (1600) acted as a warning to all those contemplating similar behaviour. It tells of a young girl named Frances Browne who gave birth to a strange-looking child in the Malvern Hills. Two years earlier, she had gone to work for her uncle, living in his house along with two of his sons. She started an affair with one of them, 'their lust was so hot, that soon after the same began to be kindled, it was so set on fire that the divill had blinded the eies of these two, they lay together and she was gotten with child by him.'[16] When the child was born, it was extremely deformed. Although it was fed and tended, it never stopped crying and they thought it had no eyelids. Three days later, it died. Such cases of incest became more public around the seventeenth century as small pamphlets were published in London issuing

Limbless child, illustration from the *British Medical Journal*, 8 June 1889.

details of the sin, which were then hawked all over the country. The moral of the story, and similar ones in the same vein, shows a conjunction where medicine met religion – the deformity did not happen by chance but was taken as a sign of 'God's will' against incest.

Warnings were no less frightening by the eighteenth century, but for different reasons. Gentlemen's magazines were providing incest as means of sexual titillation for their readers, but within these stories there was an implicit suggestion that cousins should be guarded against. The *Rambler* for Saturday 2 November 1751, carried a piece entitled 'The History of *Misella* debauched by her relation', a title intended to pique every reader's interest. The article came in the form of a letter allegedly from a girl who had been ravished by her cousin. In it, she relates how he took advantage of the familial ties to complete her ruin, backing her into submission while acting as her benefactor.[17] Intended as a cliffhanger, in the following week's journal, she related her decline in 'Misella's description of the life of a prostitute'.[18] Her cousin continued to visit her and was bent on her complete defilement; 'but I now saw with horror that he was contriving to perpetuate his gratification, and was desirous to fit me to his purpose, by complete and radical corruption'. He eventually deserted her, fleeing with his family to Ireland, leaving her destitute and without any apparent means of supporting herself. After an elderly man invited her to a tavern, she was initiated into prostitution and ended up on the street: 'In this state I have now passed four years, the drudge of extortion and the sport of drunkenness; sometimes the property of one man, and sometimes the common prey of accidental lewdness.' The readers are provided with full details of the sordid life into which she had been forced – all this as a result of her male cousin.

By the nineteenth century, marriage between cousins and in-laws was becoming a common practice, a strategy of the new bourgoise, undertaken to bind families together. The Darwin and the Wedgwood families used multiple first-cousin marriages to make useful family alliances, and it was common for brothers and sisters to marry other brothers and sisters to create a double bond.[19]

Incestuous 'Marriages'

While cousin marriages were becoming less threatening (at least in Victorian England), marriages between in-laws and step-relations remained a problem for the authorities. In recently settled America, Samuel and Rebekah Newton of Marlborough had their marriage broken up when the courts discovered she was the widow of his uncle, Isaac Newton. Although they had two children together, they were prohibited from cohabiting any longer.[20] Yet in the United States, in Massachusetts and Plymouth, there were no incest laws, which meant that magistrates were left to deal with incestuous marriages as they saw fit. In this case, ultra-puritanical New Haven enacted the incest laws verbatim from the Old Testament. These lapsed when the state joined with Connecticut, which had no incest law until 1673, when laws were introduced for father–daughter and mother–son relationships. Courts dealt with other incest according to its perceived seriousness.

Among the lower ranks, the reason for marriage was often based on basic economic and domestic needs. Plebeian widows looked for financial security, while plebeian widowers needed a housekeeper and someone to look after their children. In the rural British county of Somerset between 1730 and 1835, most incestuous births resulted from a relationship between a stepdaughter and stepfather. It would have been less costly to cement a relationship this way rather than dividing the household after the death of a wife and mother. Any clergy marrying a couple had to rely on a couple's declaration that they were legally entitled to marry. Yet step-relatives still attempted to marry. Revd Holland wrote in horror about his discovery of an incestuous relationship between a stepfather and his stepdaughter which had resulted in the birth of a child. He complained, 'that shocking Sinner Old Porter . . . had a child by his own Wicked Daughter . . . [and] did not seem to have much sense of guilt on his mind, but I spoke to him in Strong Terms'.[21] Holland considered the young woman as guilty as her stepfather, but it is unlikely that a poor girl in her situation would have had anywhere else to go. In another case, the same reverend apparently had more sympathy for a man who had children with his sister-in-law. Nonetheless, he refused to marry them. It would seem that little distinction was made by the clergy between affinity and consanguineous incest.

Cases of incest were still unusual enough to be reported in newspapers. The *Oracle Bell's New World* for Tuesday 28 July 1789, reported: 'A French manufacturer by the name of Warrin in Artois has been convicted of incest with two of his daughters, and an attempt to debauch a third.'[22] This newspaper seems to have been keen to expose the perpetrators of such indiscretions; a month later, it reported another incest case, this time that of a British man from Littlehampton, 55-year-old Richard Glazemark. He had been living in incest with his daughter Jemima for over fifteen years but, enraged by jealousy upon her marriage, he stabbed her husband and set fire to his house. For reasons that were undisclosed in the newspaper, the jury acquitted the father, but he continued to storm around the village, threatening to burn down houses and barns. He also threatened to kill the children he had had by his daughter. Finally, after forcing his daughter to meet him in a public house, he took her to a field and mutilated her. He stayed with her until she died, then made a failed attempt to cut his own throat. He was finally picked up at his house and taken to court where, after five hours of deliberation, the jury found him guilty of murder.[23]

Meanwhile, gossip flourished when Fanny Burney's brother eloped with his half-sister in 1798. The courts were powerless to prevent them, as no civil law against their activities existed; nonetheless, the

Eugène Delacroix,
*The Bride of
Abydos*, 1857.

couple shocked polite society by living together for the next five years. Lord Byron similarly attracted scandal when his wife spread rumours about his affair with his half-sister Augusta Leigh. In his original idea for his epic poem *The Bride of Abydos* (1813) he celebrated a love affair between a brother and sister, but lessened the impact when he changed their relationship to one of cousins for publication.[24]

Incest came to be seen as a serious sexual perversion, which led to the corruption of society and the downfall of queens. Henry VIII notoriously blamed his incestuous marriage with his brother's widow for his lack of an heir to the throne. Close familial incest was associated with witchcraft in some countries, and sexual depravity in others. With the coming of Cromwell, new puritanical measures were introduced in 1650 for 'supressing the detestable sins of incest, adultery and fornication'.[25] A short-lived English statute was introduced in 1650 which declared incest to be a felony, but this did not live past the Restoration in 1660. Surprisingly, in Britain incest was not made illegal until 1908.

Discussion around the problem with marrying a close in-law continued unabated throughout much of the early nineteenth century.

In England, only with the Marriage Act of 1835 were the laws about the degrees of kinship in marriage firmed up. Marrying one's sister-in-law became legal only with the Deceased Wife's Sister's Marriage Act of 1907, although this had been a hard and long battle waged in Parliament on a yearly basis. It took another fourteen years before the Deceased Brother's Widow's Marriage Act 1921 was passed.

Meanwhile, as a result of the rise of the new middle classes, a new target for pornography emerged and incest in the family became a main theme.

A New Pornography

The use of incest as a subject in pornography had already taken off in France. In the *Histoire de Dom Bougre, portier de Chartreux* (1741), attributed to Jean-Charles Gervaise de Latouche, by the fourth page the narrator is anxious to commit incest with his sister Suzon: 'I kissed her and she slapped me on the cheek; I forced her to the ground and she writhed like a snake. I held her tightly in my arms, kissing her breasts through her bodice.'[26] The Marquis de Sade took the subject much further, devoting a whole novella to incest. Although his novella *Eugénie de Franval* (1800) is less well known than most of his other works, it provides an intriguing account of an incestuous relationship, the manipulation of a young daughter Eugénie by her father, Monsieur de Franval. As soon as she was born, he 'conceived the most detestable designs on her'. In an early case of grooming, he first separates her from her mother, then from all other guidance except his own. Franval admits, 'I love my daughter, I love her passionately, she is my mistress, my wife, my sister, my confidante, my friend, my sole god on earth – she is in short all the titles which can win the homage of a heart.'[27] She in turn loves him as no other, refusing to be with any other man.

The English were proving to be more reticent than the French in their depictions of incest in pornography. At the beginning of the eighteenth century, incest was merely mentioned rather than being explored in any depth. *A New Description of Merryland* (1741) pointed out the drawbacks of maternal incest, since 'to enter again in that Part they were born in, is looked on as an infamous Crime, and severely punishable by Law; yet some have been hardy enough to do it.'[28] Initially, the English took to inserting incest into translations of

A brother watches as his sister fornicates with a priest. Anonymous engraving
from *Histoire de Dom Bougre* (1741).

Laisse moi donc
tranquille, sal cocu
(à Mr La Perle)

An illustration typical of 19th- and early 20th-century pornography: a father figure molests a young girl. Martin van Maële, *La Grande danse macabre* (1907).

French pornography, the translators adding bits here and there as they chose. In the dialogue between two women in *The School of Venus* (*L'Ecole des filles*), one remarks, 'incest is counted no sin, for they put it off with a jest, saying it makes the top of their prick look redder if they dip it in their own blood'.[29] Yet there was no mention of incest in the French original. There was, however, an increasing move towards portraying scenes of incest, as new predilections were explored in English pornography from around the 1770s onwards.

By the Victorian period, incest was littering the pages of the gentleman's erotica collection. This shift occurred at the time of growing concentration on the nuclear family in which the home was to be the haven of peace, set apart from the bustle of the outside world. 'Home', wrote William Thayer (1820–1898) in *Pastor's Wedding Gift*, 'is the harbinger of all that is good . . . and a panacea for all ills . . . a sweet bower of peace and joy in this desert world'. Within this idyllic family set-up, the father was the disciplinarian, the mother the nurturer of their children; their offspring were blessed gifts from God, their innocent natures guided by the strict but loving hands of their parents. This happy family was a prototype depicted by moralists and pornographers alike, but for widely different reasons. While the Victorians were peddling the patriarchal family as the Christian ideal, pornographers were striving to parody them, thereby attacking the ideals of bourgeois society. The pornographer's aim was to shatter this illusion of purity and to replace it with sexual perversion – sadism, sodomy, fellatio, cunnilingus, lesbianism and coprophilia all served to displace the procreative process that led to family life.[30]

British pornography pursued the incest theme with passion. Books such as the anonymous *Romance of Lust*, privately printed around 1873, explored sex between various family members. Readers knew exactly what sort of treat they were in for as by the third paragraph, the hero and his sisters were experimenting with each other's genitals: 'My sisters and I all slept in the same room . . . we had discovered that mutual handling gave a certain amount of pleasing sensation; and latterly, my elder sister had discovered that the hooding and unhooding of my doodle, as she called it, instantly caused it to swell and stiffen as hard as a piece of wood.'[31] The fact that the British middle-class family was such an esteemed social institution made the breaking of its boundaries even more transgressive, and therefore more exciting.

Tainted Families

Incest in the Victorian and Edwardian periods was becoming a new focus for consideration. While pornographers were experimenting with the fantasies about the Victorian libertine, nineteenth-century philanthropic investigators such as Henry Mayhew, Charles Booth and William Acton were busy exploring London's labouring poor and uncovering the harsh realities of life.[32] They noticed that incest was connected to poverty, and saw overcrowding as the underlying cause; mothers, fathers and children were all forced into small living areas. In the towns, hovels were so overcrowded that there was no other place to sleep than to huddle together in one bed. It was also a convenient way to keep warm in a chilly, uninsulated home. Where few had the fuel to keep their fires lit all night, the warmth of each other's bodies was a comfort. Similarly, in rural hovels, the whole family might sleep in one bed: the daughter slept against the wall in order to safeguard her chastity in case of intruders, then the mother, followed by the father with the son on the outside. With so many people in the same bed, the real danger was suffocating one's child, not its sexual molestation.

Andrew Mearns, secretary of the London Congregational Union, assisted by W. C. Preston, undertook his own inquiry into the conditions of the abject poor in *The Bitter Cry of Outcast London* (1883). Initially published anonymously as a penny pamphlet, it reported:

> One of the saddest results of this overcrowding is the inevitable association of honest people with criminals. Often is the family of an honest working man compelled to take refuge in a thieves' kitchen . . .Who can wonder that every evil flourishes in such hotbeds of vice and disease? . . . As if the men and women living together in these rookeries are married, and your simplicity will cause a smile. Nobody knows. Nobody cares . . . Incest is common; and no form of vice or sensuality causes surprise or attracts attention . . . The low parts of London are the sink into which the filthy and abominable from all parts of the country seem to flow.[33]

Attitudes against incest began to firm up in the nineteenth century as studies were published proving that 'idiots' were born as a result of close blood unions. In 1846, the American Medical Society brought out an influential study concluding that close marriages led to mental deficiencies in resulting offspring. By the 1870s, pioneering American anthropologist Lewis Henry Morgan was suggesting that people should avoid the evils of the consanguineous marriage altogether and look for a partner outside the family.[34] As a result, thirteen American states outlawed cousin marriage by the 1880s; double that number had done so by the mid-1920s.

Although studies of poverty helped to convince the public of the environmental influences leading to incest, sexologists added their own views. From the mid-nineteenth century onwards, sexologists, psychiatrists, anthropologists and sociologists began to attempt explanations of why incest occurred and why it was prohibited. They incorrectly assumed that incest was forbidden in all cultures and societies, and that incest was commonly seen to be a danger to society. Furthermore, they did not adequately explain why societies might want to prohibit intimacy between close relatives in the first place. What they did debate was why a person might want to commit incest.

Nearly all of the sexologists took it for granted that incest was a perversion and not 'natural'. The Finnish sociologist Edvard Westermarck in *The History of Human Marriage* (1891) stated that people have a natural biological mechanism to avoid incest. Of women, he reported: 'There are certain facts which cannot be explained as either the direct or indirect results of feminine coyness, but indicate a close connection between sexual modesty and the aversion to incest.'[35] Krafft-Ebing thought mental deficiency was to blame, asserting that 'only great sensuality and defective ideas of law and morality can lead to incest', although he recognized that both conditions may be present in 'tainted families'.[36] In men, drinking alcohol encouraged incest, as did weakness and lack of shame in women. Incest was also more likely to occur in the lower classes because of 'defective separation' and their inability to keep the sexes apart. Interviewing patients, he found both men and women were riddled with angst because of their incestous desires. Some of the more desperate among them threatened suicide when their offspring threatened to leave. One 44-year-old 'nymphomaniac' (as Krafft-Ebing described her) attempted suicide because of unrequited love for her son; 'She pestered him with kisses and caresses and tried one night to force him to engage in coitus, which he refused.'[37]

Ellis believed that any incestuous desire tended to be found in children and died out naturally as a person grew up, 'when stronger stimuli from outside are applied'. He claimed 'for children there is only love for an object of affection, not incestuous desire'.[38] Taking a psychoanalytical approach, Sigmund Freud examined childhood complexes more deeply in a series of essays in 1905, adding to them in later editions his theory that children's desires for the parent of the opposite sex was normal. These desires needed to be redirected to people outside the family if a child was to grow up to become a healthy adult. He blamed a combination of the biological urge of sex and the mother's nurturing of the human infant as the reason for the emergence of an incest taboo. Opposing Krafft-Ebing's early ideas, he argued: 'It is the fate of all of us perhaps, to direct our first sexual impulse towards our mothers and our first hatred and our first murderous wish against our father.'[39] As an example, he developed his now famous theory of the Oedipus complex, according to which a boy, via his suppressed unconscious, desires to sexually possess his mother and kill his father. His colleague Carl Jung took this idea further, establishing the concept of the Electra complex, by which a girl desires her father and directs her anger towards her mother. The successful resolution was supposed to take place when the child finally identified with the same-sex parent. In his *Totem and Taboo* (1913), Freud published four essays, one of them tackling the subject under the title 'The Savage's Dread of Incest'. Here, he examined the complex social organization of Australian Aborigines, which had been put in place in order to prevent incest, and allied this totem system to the Western nuclear family. The system was applied to prevent sexual relations not only between relatives but also those who were not blood relatives but were members of the same family. To some extent, the psychoanalytical theory pandered to the Edwardians, who were eager to distance humans from other animals and see themselves as culturally and intellectually significant.

Anthropologists saw incest and its taboo in terms of the relationships between individual human nature (through evolutionary biology) and society. At least one asserted, 'The taboo on incest within the immediate family is one of the few known cultural universals.'[40] The

288

anthropologist Claude Lévi-Strauss in *The Elementary Structures of Kinship* (1949) suggested that the incest taboo emerged because it violated the inherent social design of society. Like some sexologists before him, he believed the incest taboo to be universal, but for him the problems of the behavioural urge lay in the social context of human societies, not in the human psyche. Broad sexual interaction and marriage was needed to prevent a family becoming isolated. In this way, the incest taboo served a purpose – it was not simply a means by which a community policed undesirable sexual behaviour but it encouraged people to go elsewhere to find a mate. Meanwhile, the evolutionary biologists developed a new theory based on biology. They pointed to the incest taboo as a way humans evolved to avoid reproducing bad genes – it was intended to encourage the spread of the gene pool outside the immediate family or community. This would prevent defective genes concentrating in a small community and producing increasingly defective individuals. Arguably, though, everyone in the family staying together could better serve social cohesion, and it is more likely that the incest taboo arose from an attempt to prevent the breakdown of harmonious relationships. If there was a father–daughter or mother–son sexual relationship, it was problematic for the other spouse, causing friction in the family. The ensuing imbalance in domestic equality would contribute to the breakdown of the family.

From the anthropologist's perspective, the incest taboo existed to promote social function and interaction. Other social scientists believed that there was no reason for societies to prohibit intimate relationships between close relatives. In contradiction to the evolutionary biologists, the anthropologist Conrad P. Kottak asserted, 'There is no simple or universally accepted explanation for the fact that all cultures ban incest.'[41] However, these sexologists and anthropologists got it wrong:[42] incest taboo never has been universal, and this really is the point. Although some may regard incest as taboo, it has been committed the world over. One aware investigator declared 'It is incest itself – and not the absence of incest – that has been universal for most people in most places at most times.'[43]

With the introduction of the Punishment of Incest Act 1908 for the first time in England, perpetrators could be prosecuted under the criminal law. Yet only a handful of incest cases came in front of the Old Bailey between 1908 and 1913, the individuals involved usually accused of 'unlawfully carnally knowing'. Three years' penal servitude seemed to have been the usual punishment, as indicated by the case of 53-year-old John Daniel, who pleaded guilty to raping his adult daughter Caroline Drain on 12 October 1909. The age of the girl at the time of a rape seems to have made no difference to the length of sentence. When 51-year-old Charles Bennett came up on rape charges, although he 'pleaded guilty of carnally knowing Jane Bennett, his daughter', who was around fourteen or fifteen, he still only received three years' penal servitude in 1910. It also seems to have been regarded as less serious if a sister was involved rather than a daughter. Twenty-two-year-old labourer William Morley only received eighteen months' hard labour when he pleaded guilty to indecently assaulting his sister in 1913.[44]

By the 1950s, studies of incest were being undertaken to assess the reasons why it was happening. American Professor of Sociology at Roosevelt University, Dr S. Kirson Weinberg studied over 200 cases. He concluded that different types of incest occurred in different types of household. Father–daughter incest was prevalent in father-dominated households; sibling incest was apparent where the father did not take the dominant role; and mother–son incest occurred where the mother was the dominant figure.[45] The pathology of the perpetrator included drunkenness, being highly strung, nervousness, irritability, loneliness and moodiness.

Changing attitiues resulted in the Marriage Act of 1949 in the UK, which prohibited sexual relations with adopted daughters. Families were no longer organized merely along ties of blood, but were increasingly based on newly emerging love and living arrangements. More recently, because of the rising divorce rate, remarriage and the rise in the number of second families, the nuclear family has become one which includes half-brothers, stepsisters, second husbands, third wives and so on. Gay couples also sometimes have extended families involving friends as egg or sperm donors, further complicating the modern-day model of the family. Because of this, blood ties matter less in terms of incest than the context of the relationship. In a world where families are made up of children from different marriages and partners are unrelated to the children in the house, it is sexual desire between adults and children which becomes the overriding factor of concern. Anxiety is now focused on control and power within the family.

In cases of separations and sperm and egg donorships, often children are unaware of those to whom they are related. They might meet their parents later on in life, and see them as viable sex partners without ever knowing the true connection. Brothers and sisters who have been separated at birth and share the same biological parents have met up later in life as adults and fallen in love. One of the recent cases of sibling incest arose in Germany after the separation at birth of a brother and sister. Patrick Stübing had been taken into foster care when he was three years old and was later adopted. He found out about his natural parents when he was 23 and made contact with them. This was when he first met his biological sister, Susan Karolewski. He moved in with his natural family and around six months later he became sexually intimate with her after their mother died. The pair had a child together in 2001, the first of four, three of whom were born mentally and physically disabled. As a result, their children were taken into care, and a battle began between the family and the authorities. Their wish to remain together has brought into question the nature of incest and its illegality. Stübing has already served two years in prison as a result of their incest but the couple say they are happy together. The main problem in this particular case was that Karolewski was only sixteen and thought to be mentally impaired. Could she therefore be seen as having consented? Since Stübing underwent a vasectomy and there was no evidence of coercion, there was no reason for concern about genetic problems and seemingly little point in pursuing further prosecution.

Various studies have also shown how people choose to mate with those who look like themselves – which increases the likelihood of being attracted to a family member. Indeed, studies have shown that sibling incest has become more common more recently.[46] Although Stübing took his case to the European Rights Commission, they ruled that it was acceptable for a country to have laws against incest.[47]

There has been a shift in thinking from the idea that incest was a rare occurrence to the idea that it is (and was in the past) more commonly taking place than originally thought. During the 1980s in America, the public were shocked to be informed that incestuous child abuse was rife in many of their communities. Celebrities came out in droves to speak about their childhood abuse stories, tales of familial torture and abductions. From the investigations of sociologists to the increasing number of confessional books, there has been an attempt to understand the 'survivor's' story. Therapists introduced new ways to uncover and retrieve 'lost memories' of abuse. In many of these cases, the victim was ashamed at having been abused, and saw it as their own fault. As Toni McNaron and Yarrow Morgan, both 'survivors' themselves, stated, 'We feel shame at having been abused by those we know are supposed to love us, and the horror of that abuse and shame turns inwards as the victim tries to learn what she has done wrong, why this is happening to her.'[48] They feel that keeping silent has led to suicide attempts.[49]

In response to public exposés of incestuous abuse, family members who said they had been wrongly accused formed a backlash organization called the False Memory Syndrome Foundation. The adults who via various forms of therapy had 'retrieved' childhood memories of abuse were now accused of 'false memory syndrome'.[50] Occurrences of father–daughter incest are most common among fathers who have been absent for long periods of time, when the child was growing up elsewhere, and between non-biological relations, such as stepfathers and stepdaughters.

On the subject of incest taboo, questions have been posited about how laws are made; have laws been created by those in power, or do they come from so-called 'natural' aversions, be it from individuals, groups or societies? Legalization of incest is now openly discussed and allowed in certain cases. In Brazil, for example, a blood-related uncle and niece or aunt and nephew may have a relationship provided they undergo health checks. In Argentina, Austria and Italy, the same relationship is allowed. Currently in England and Wales, sexual relationships are illegal between a person and their parent, grandparent, child, grandchild, sibling, half-sibling, or a blood-related uncle, aunt, nephew or niece. Under the Sexual Offences Act 2003, the maximum sentence for adult incest is two years' imprisonment.[51] In America, it varies from state to state: in New Jersey incest is not illegal for consenting adults, whereas Massachusetts can hand out twenty-year prison sentences. Most countries still do not allow marriage between siblings, the exception being Sweden, which allows marriage between half-siblings.[52] What is incest in one country therefore is not incest in another.

Incest is a taboo in most countries, but people still violate these restrictions, just as they do with other forbidden sexual activities. And although incest may be taboo, that taboo is not universal. Whereas cases have emerged of incest being tolerated between father and daughter, siblings, step-relations, in-laws and cousins, no mother and son incest has ever been seen as acceptable, as far as my research has revealed, although cases from the past may well eventually be uncovered. The case of incest with underage children, or paedophilia, is an entirely different matter, as we shall see in the next chapter.

Anthony van Dyck, *George Villiers, Second Duke of Buckingham, and His Brother Lord Francis Villiers*, 1635.

TEN

Child Love or Paedophilia?

It is quite difficult to lay down barriers [particularly since] it could be that the
child, with his own sexuality, may have desired the adult.

Michel Foucault

Sex with children is one of the most contentious topics of modern
times. The word 'paedophilia' creates a reaction that overrides all
other concerns about sexual deviation. The term comes from the
Greek παίς (*pais*), meaning 'child', and φιλία (*philia*), the word for
love or friendship. The meaning has since been corrupted and is
now taken to mean the sexual abuse of children. Because of this,
most people have difficulty thinking rationally about child sexuality, particularly in their own children. But was this always the case?
There was no legal or medical classification of 'paedophilia' right
up until sexologists defined it at the end of the nineteenth century.
Was desire for the young not a problem in the past? And how did it
come to be placed at the top of society's concerns?

To understand these concerns – if there were any – in the more
distant past, we need to understand how those who lived around
children saw them, and how parents and employers treated them in
the household and at work. In legal terms, and in medicine, this can
be seen in marriage arrangements and in debates about the age of
consent and the desexualization of the childhood body. The ways
in which child victims and perpetrators have been treated in court
reveal whether the society of a certain time and place saw the act
of sex with children as a serious matter or not.

A Child's Place

From antiquity up to the eighteenth century, unwanted babies
were routinely thrown off cliffs or exposed to the elements. With no
reliable contraception, plenty of children were born; plenty died
from accidents and diseases. The wanted Greek child was, however,

carefully guarded, and considered so unruly as to need nurses and pedagogues to watch him or her constantly. Girls were kept out of public view under the supervision of their mothers, while boys were sent to school once they reached a certain age. They did, however, have to be supervised or accompanied when going out, as Xenophon explained: 'When children are able to understand what they are told, at that time slave-pedagogues are appointed and they are sent to school.'[1] As we have seen, youths were prey to the attentions of adult men and to some extent this was accepted and understood, but strictly within certain rules. The fact that girls were kept at home and boys had to have guards indicates a real fear for their moral and physical welfare once they were in the outside world.

In ancient Greece, children of slaves automatically became slaves themselves and were routinely bought and sold into prostitution. Some ended up in brothels, with the more fortunate becoming *hetairai* or courtesans, who entertained citizen men. The well-known courtesan Neaira, who was born in the decade after Athens lost the Peloponnesian War to Sparta (404 BC), was sold into prostitution as a child, along with six other young girls. They were bought by Nikarete, a freewoman of Charisius of Elis, who spotted their beauty and recognized that it could be turned into profit. In order to obtain the highest price from the men wanting to have sex with them, Nikarete pretended that the children were freeborn, calling them 'daughters'.[2]

Roman citizen children were brought up by slave nurses (although they may also have had pedagogues, a practice influenced by the Greeks), but not everyone thought this a good idea. Writers at the time frequently criticized Roman parents for handing over their children to foreign and corrupt nurses; Favorinus, for example, attacked mothers who did not suckle their own children but instead handed them over to a wet-nurse. The bad nurse was thought to be unchaste, vulgar and drank too much; she failed to take proper care of her charges, who then ended up morally weak and degenerate. Nurses were even portrayed as procurers who perverted the sexual behaviour of the young girls they were meant to be protecting. The bad nurse, it seems, personified the general decline of Rome and its degeneracy.[3] Despite the care taken over children, some emperors nonetheless managed to corrupt them. Suetonius condemned Tiberius because he taught 'little boys who he called "his minnows" to chase him while he went swimming and get between his legs and lick and nibble him'. Suetonius also condemned the emperor for letting unweaned babies 'suck at him', calling him 'a filthy old man!'[4]

By the medieval period, there was little reticence about mentioning sexual matters in front of children. Louis XIII's father played with his son's genitals until the child was three years old and made jokes about them. Sex came early for young royals: at the age of fourteen, Louis was married off, placed into bed with his wife and expected to perform.[5] As the next monarch, he would have been closely protected throughout his childhood. Girls were even more closely guarded. Just as in ancient Greece and Rome, their virginity was vital if they were to find a marriage partner. Nobles had a distinct moral code; the male head of the household had a duty to look after the women in the family and preserve their chastity. Yet children were dressed as mini-adults, further complicating judgement on their sexual maturity. Children of higher birth might be sent away to live with other noble families as a form of education and patronage. This practice was presumed to be safe, as it was a matter of honour for those fostering the noble children of their peers to ensure that they were protected and treated as members of the family.

Labouring adults concentrated on getting their children to work as soon as possible. Children took up menial tasks, and then gradually took on more responsibility as they became more able. In rural families, children would help their fathers or mothers either in the fields or the home. Later, around puberty, they might go into an apprenticeship or domestic service. This was when children were usually at their most vulnerable, as the court records show, with assaults made on domestic servants and apprentices. Not only did they leave the family household, but they also had to deal with being newly aware of their sexuality and sexual attractiveness.

However, parents and municipal courts did their best to protect children from molestation. In 1339, when one man assaulted a fourteen-year-old girl, he was forced to pay £40 to the chamberlain in recompense, to keep for the girl until she was married or came of age. Similarly, when Robert Trenender, a brazier from Byrstow, and his wife Issabell complained that Philip Rychard had deflowered their daughter, the case was taken to arbitrations and Rychard was told to give the child Agnes either a pipe (a large storage container) and a half of woad or £20 in compensation. Adolescents themselves

Pederasty: a man titillates a youth. Red-figure cup by Brygos Painter,
c. 500–47 BC.

were recognized as developing their own sexual desires, and the
onset of puberty was seen to be a worrying time of 'lust-longing'
when they needed to be watched.[6] Generally, close-knit communities in the country had their own form of policing – neighbours would
look out for other neighbours' children, and children old enough to
work were overseen by their masters in apprenticeships (although,
occasionally, as we shall see, these masters were themselves abusers).

298

From the eighteenth century, as the urban centres of Europe grew larger and more anonymity was possible, there was a breakdown in community networks; with this came more opportunities for unsupervised access to young girls and boys.

Age of Consent

The legality of sex hinged on the age of consent. If a child was considered under the age of consent, an adult could be prosecuted for having sex with them. Above a certain age, an individual was no longer considered a child and therefore could consent to sex. Yet the age at which a child was responsible for its actions was something of a conundrum to the medieval layperson. In law, a child was only considered capable of deception at the age of seven. Their legal responsibility came into play only between the ages of twelve and seventeen; this varied depending on the issue at hand. In 1118, Henry I ordered that the earliest age at which a child could bring legal action or sit on a jury was fifteen. From the Church's point of view, if a couple having sex were unmarried, they were committing fornication, which was illicit at any age. The age of consent therefore depended on the permissible age for marriage.

During the medieval period in England, the marriageable age was twelve for a girl and fourteen for a boy, although they were often betrothed before then. Noble families were particularly keen to unite their fortunes as soon as possible. Occasionally the children were still young, even prepubescent, when they were married, although close relatives frequently refused to allow consummation to take place until the girl was older. How far the law was implemented and successful was another matter. Lady Margaret Beaufort, the mother of Henry VII, was particularly keen to protect her granddaughter from an early marriage because she herself had gone through one in 1450 when she was only six years old. This marriage was later dissolved, since she had not been of age. As soon as she was twelve, however, she was forced into another marriage and widowed a year later, only to find herself seven months pregnant. This was by no means unusual. The idea of young love was common, as seen in the theatre audience's understanding of Shakespeare's *Romeo and Juliet* – Juliet was only thirteen when she fell in love with Romeo and her father was already trying to find a husband for her.

Because of the importance placed on female chastity, early British law made attempts to establish some sort of protection for children regarding rape, abduction and sexual assault. If a girl had been raped, her prospects of marriage were grim. When the rape of prepubescent girls occurred, it was therefore taken extremely seriously and was a capital offence. Similarly, the abduction of underage girls was punishable by death, with no exceptions. There was, however, no understanding of 'paedophile' or 'paedophilia', just adults who 'ravished' children. In 1275, in England, part of the rape law made it a misdemeanor to 'ravish' a 'maiden within age' (this was taken to be around twelve), punishable by two years' imprisonment, whether with consent or not. In Elizabeth I's reign, rape and carnal knowledge of a girl under the age of ten were made felonies in 1576.[7] If a girl was abducted, restitution was usually paid to a girl's parents, since she belonged to them, just as restitution was made to a raped woman's husband. Children up to puberty were still considered 'infants' right up into the eighteenth century; this can be seen in the terminology used in trial records. For example, when Stephen Arrowsmith was indicted in 1678 for ravishing and abusing Elizabeth Hopkins, she was referred to as 'an Infant of the age of eight years'.[8] Meanwhile, the ravishment of boys did not come under the same law, but came under the general laws against sodomy.

By the seventeenth century, little had changed when English jurist Sir Edward Coke made it clear that 'the marriage of girls under twelve was normal, and the age at which a girl who was a wife was eligible for a dower from her husband's estate was nine even though her husband be only four years old.'[9] But the situation in which a man had consensual sex with a girl between ten and twelve was a grey area (twelve or over was considered acceptable). Any sexual intercourse in such cases would more likely be considered a misdemeanour than a felony, while sex with a girl under ten years old was a felony regardless of consent. Whether a girl agreed or was coerced was harder to prove, and when rape charges were brought against a man, it was difficult to obtain a conviction.

Age of consent differed between centuries, and between countries. In Norway during the Viking age (c. 800–1050), the age of consent for heterosexual sex was from the onset of first menstruation, but in some regions this changed during the Lutheran Reformation to twenty years of age. In 1875, England raised the age to thirteen years, making an act of sexual intercourse with a girl younger than thirteen a felony. In countries which fell under the French Napoleonic Code, the age of consent was set at eleven in 1791 and raised to thirteen in 1863. In countries which did not take the Napoleonic Code, age was set by statute law, or as local custom determined.

The Changing Notion of Childhood

Church teachings had seen children as having original sin, which had to be beaten out of them. It was advised that children should not be mollycoddled or pampered by their parents but should be disciplined to keep them on the path of virtue. Elder children were expected to play a part. In sixteenth-century Germany, Thomas Platter remembered being beaten as a boy; 'my cousin Paulus would walk along behind me, armed with a stick or a pike, and would beat my bare legs, for I had no breeches and only a bad pair of shoes.'[10] It became a matter of moral responsibility for masters of schools to ensure their charges were regularly thrashed. In order to fulfil this commitment, at Winchester College in England during the seventeenth century, pupils were flogged every Saturday to keep them in line, the day known as 'the bloody day'.[11]

Anxieties about children's susceptibility to corruption further surfaced in instruction manuals from seventeenth-century Jesuit boarding schools in which the Jesuits suggested that children should not be left alone at night. Nor should they be left in the company of domestic servants who might have a negative influence on them. The potential for domestic servants to corrupt their charges was reiterated throughout the eighteenth century; the French cardinal De Bernis stated, 'nothing is more dangerous for the morals and perhaps for the health than to leave children too long in the case of servants.'[12] This fear of servants corrupting children was a concern that would continue to filter down through the ages.[13]

The question of 'innocence' in childhood was discussed in the French Enlightenment, and the notion emerged that children were naturally good but corrupted by society.[14] This turned the old idea of original sin on its head. One influence on people's perceptions of children was the French philosopher Jean-Jacques Rousseau, whose book *Emile* (1762) established the idea of a separate period that existed prior to puberty, a time in which a child remained

George Cruikshank, birch discipline for the Child Dunce, 1839.

untainted and uncorrupted. This ideal was to become common-place in the Victorian family and broader society a century later. Despite the fact that the industrial revolution was a time of great exploitation of child labour, a time when children were forced to work in unsavoury conditions down mines and in cotton mills as well as in brothels, it was also a time when the wider public under-standing of childhood and adolescence was shifting. After centuries of ignoring, starving or working children to death, children were now seen to be in need of protection, and broader laws were intro-duced to safeguard them.

Meanwhile, the idea that poverty was responsible for early sex-ual encounters in childhood was gaining ground. Concern about

Schoolmaster applies the birch.

302

Learning in the Enlightenment; sketch by William Hoare (1707–1792).

childhood prostitution had started to emerge in the eighteenth century, with philanthropists and police alike eager to get rid of it, but for essentially different reasons. Philanthropists were concerned for the welfare of children, observing that they were bought and sold into sex, while police simply wanted to clear the streets of prostitution altogether, since they saw prostitutes as a nuisance. Magistrate John Fielding, founder of the modern justice system, was perhaps more concerned than most when he pondered the plight of young girls brought up in the slums: 'they often become Prostitutes, even before their Passions can have any share in the Guilt'.[15] He believed that children lacked that innate lasciviousness which adult women were thought to possess, a desire that drove them into prostitution. At least Fielding recognized that most young girls had been coerced into prostitution because of poverty. Boys, on the other hand, he suggested, went on the streets to become thieves. However, evidence suggests that boys, too, were forced into prostitution or raped, or suffered attempted sodomy.[16]

One twelve-year-old boy, Benjamin Taylor, became the victim of Michael Levi, as told in court on 23 May 1751 at some length. Levi lived in London's Holborn and ran an alehouse from a stall in Baptist's

Child labour in the United States, *c.* 1900.

Head. Most nights he would carry up the boxes left over from his night's sales after shutting up his stall and go up to the room he had in the house in the same yard. On the night in question, around dusk, after shutting up the stall as usual, Levi asked Taylor to help him get the boxes inside. He then proceeded to assault him. The boy told the court, 'he unbutton'd my breeches and threw me down on the bed on my face, he unbutton'd his breeches and put his c – k into my backside.'[17] This carried on for about quarter of an hour. Taylor admitted he had been too ashamed to say anything about the incident, although he told one of his friends, who in turn told his father, and the father told Benjamin's father. Levi was sentenced to death for sodomy. Although when caught the perpetrators were dealt with harshly, often there was difficulty in making the accusations stick.

Catching the Abuser

Looking back to the seventeenth and eighteenth centuries, in incidents of sexual assault, it was usually the parents or guardians of the child victims who were responsible for bringing the case to the notice of the courts. Even so, many of the cases brought before the courts were dismissed because of lack of evidence and witnesses. If the child had developed venereal disease since the attack, it was more likely that this would be taken as evidence that an attack had taken place, especially if the perpetrator was known to be 'poxed'. One such case of 1680 was that of William Harding, tried for 'ravishing' Sarah Southy, a girl of about seven or eight years of age. He had enticed her down into a dark cellar with the promise of some apples. The court recorder verified that he then 'accomplished his detestable Villainy, not only giving the Child the foul Disease wherewith himself was infested, but likewise by forcibly penetrating her Body, so abused her secret parts'.[18] She was left in a distressed condition, but was afraid to complain to her mother in case she was beaten by her.

The fear of a parent's reaction might make a child unwilling to reveal an incident of rape. It explains why in some cases the child might have felt it was easier to let the matter go. Those who did go through the unsettling procedure of informing their parents then had to give witness in front of many hostile adults in court – judges were unwilling to send a man to his death on the word of a child unless there was a cast-iron case. Sarah Southy finally told her mother, who procured a couple of surgeons to examine her daughter. Both physicians found that she had been forced into intercourse. Witnesses at court denounced the perpetrator as a 'debauched fellow' who 'was wont to Act carnally with his own mother, threatening when she refused to permit his incestuous desires, to Fire the house about her Ears'. When he was examined, he was found to have 'several Simptoms of the Venereal Distemper', which allowed the jury to find him guilty of rape. The fact that he had passed on venereal disease to his young victim acted as evidence in proving his guilt.

In other cases, perpetrators simply disappeared, which seems to show that the attitude of the law towards child rape was rather lax. On Saturday 6 January 1722, the *Weekly Journal or Saturday's Post* reported that an 'old gentleman' accused of raping and thereby murdering a three-year old-child had disappeared. In another case of rape, reported in Tunbridge Wells on 5 August 1727, the *Weekly Journal or British Gazetteer* pronounced that Lord Lateran, 'who had for many Years been highly honour'd and distinguish'd by the

Quality, and others who use the Wells', was caught in an attempt to rape a child of seven; rather than facing trial he had also absconded.[19] It seems that the authorities were more cautious about immediately apprehending a man of any standing or taking him into custody for fear it might go against them and that they would gain a powerful enemy. However, when the perpetrator was convicted, the law came down heavily upon them. Unsurprisingly, lower-class men were more easily caught, and more of them suffered the death penalty.

Others managed to escape execution or got off with a whipping. On Friday 10 April 1730, George Roufon was tried at Hicks Hall for raping a child of nine and sentenced to be 'Whipt twice from Islington Turn-pike to the Church. And to be kept on Hard Labour at Clerkenwell Bridewell for one Year.'[20] Some prisoners were sentenced to the pillory at Palace Yard, Westminster, like Henry Herbert, who in 1731 had attempted to rape an eight-year-old girl.[21] This at least gave the public a chance to express their opinion. When James Allen stood in the pillory at Charing Cross in 1737 for attempted rape of a six-year-old, the crowd pelted him viciously.[22]

Despite the existence of capital punishment for rape of under-age girls, few cases were ever brought to justice during the eighteenth century. Believing a child's word against that of a grown, and often respectable, man, was hard for most judges. More importantly, there was a 'normalization' of heterosexual rape – a prevalent public (and male) belief that it was a fact of life for a man to desire sex with a young girl.[23] As we have seen, in Victorian and Edwardian pornography, images of incestuous sex with children were common. Youngsters were portrayed as responsible for sexually enticing their elders. A cult of defloration flourished in which having sex with a virgin was viewed as something desirable, a result of a shared understanding between libertine men. Various men's clubs paid procurers to bring virgins for their members to deflower; cracking a hymen was a glorification of a man's sexual prowess. Rumours also floated around that sex with a virgin would cure a man of the pox. As a result, diseased men flocked to brothel-keepers – who themselves were often women – who could supply them with young virgins. Men had no need to rape to find young victims; they merely needed a few pence in their pockets and an eye for a starving child.

The age of the girl in rape cases made a marked difference to the attitudes of the judges. A fifteen-year-old girl would have been classed

'Presto Agitato'
from Martin van
Maële, *La Grande
danse macabre*
(1907).

Presto Agitato, M. Georges

as any other adult woman, as shown in the case of Stephen Cooper, who had raped fifteen-year-old Elizabeth Child and was reprieved before the judges even had the chance to return home.[24] Doctors' evidence was provided in court where they had examined the woman, girl or boy involved in rape or sodomy charges. If there was evidence of rupture, scatches, bruising or other signs of violence, it assisted the case. In Newcastle, on 17 May 1736, William Johnson went into the house of George Atkinson of Bishop-Warmouth and, finding everyone else out of the house, he attempted 'in an unnatural manner' to rape (sodomize) Atkinson's seven-year-old daughter. The injuries were so great that the surgeon took her into his care.[25]

Character witnesses went a long way in swaying the court against conviction. In Dublin, a man called Keely escaped sentence for raping a ten-year-old girl because of the positive testimony on his character provided by the witnesses.[26] Indeed, there was a history of doctors believing that it was impossible to rape a child of ten or under because of her physiology – she was deemed simply too under-developed for penetration. In one case of the rape of a nine-year-old girl at the Old Bailey in 1678, an apothecary told the court that in his opinion, 'a Child of those years could not be Ravished'. This notion held into the nineteenth century and was repeated in Alfred Swaine Taylor's *Medical Jurisprudence* (1844).[27] Generally, the forensic evidence of rape or abuse was to check whether a girl's hymen had been broken, the concentration being on the investigation of the abuse of girls. Sometimes 'female searchers' were brought in to examine a girl in the presence of doctors, but generally female physicians were not used, even after 1865, when women were allowed to qualify as doctors. Doctors used various texts when trying to establish child abuse, such as Thomas Percival's *Medical Ethics* (1803) and Michael Ryan's *A Handbook of Medical Jurisprudence* (1831).

The courts recognized that offenders frequently escaped because of the difficulty in establishing proof of ejaculation in sodomy and rape cases. The Sexual Offences Against the Person Act was therefore passed in 1828, making it easier to prosecute: evidence of ejaculation was no longer necessary and penetration, even partial, was enough to bring about a prosecution of sodomy.[28] Nonetheless, this did not seem to discourage the perpetrators of such crimes. According to the child rape cases of the Middlesex sessions between 1830 and 1910 at the Old Bailey, 67 per cent of sexual assault victims were children; the majority of these cases involved the children of the poor working classes and lower-class artisans.[29] However, rape ceased to be a capital offence in 1841, and from then on the number of prosecutions, particular successful ones, rose dramatically.[30] The nineteenth century was a confusing time in respect of attitudes towards children and child abuse. It teemed with contradictions; although many statutes were introduced in an attempt to protect children, men continued to molest children and escape the consequences.

By the 1850s, two French physicians, Adolphe Toulmouche and Ambroise Tardieu, undertook an investigation into signs of abuse on boys,[31] using their exceptional knowledge of forensic medicine to investigate maltreatment of children. Tardieu even provided a detailed description of the 'pederast':

Hair curled, face made up, neck bared, waist cinched to accentuate his curves, the fingers, ears, and chest covered with jewels, the most penetrating perfume wafting from the whole person, and in his hand a handkerchief, flowers or some needlework: such is the strange, repulsive, and by all rights suspect physiognomy that betrays pederasts.[32]

This pederast not only preyed on youths, but also sold his effeminate body. Tardieu published his studies of child abuse cases as *Etude medico-legale sur les attentats aux moeurs* (Forensic Study on Offences against Morals) in 1857, thereby bringing the problem to the attention of the medical and legal world. Even so, most doctors seem to have been extremely reluctant to admit to signs of abuse. Since then forensic science has developed considerably, with various methods of 'testing' abuse, but it was years before it was possible to properly protect children from it.

So how are we to apply the shifting notions of childhood to paedophilia? There is plenty of evidence to suggest that parents cared greatly for their children and were anxious about their children's welfare – and they had need to be.[33] People perpetrated sexual rapes and assaults on young children because they were attracted to children, not simply because there were no suitable or willing adults about, and such attacks were taken extremely seriously. People, including those of the law, recognized that children were seen as easy targets, more vulnerable than adults, and in need of protection. Men regarded as pillars of society, such as Lord Melbourne, Queen Victoria's first prime minister, enjoyed sexually abusing children. He not only beat his wife and mistresses but also took an unhealthy interest in whipping children.[34] His interest was patently sexual: he cut out pictures of children being beaten from a collection of French erotica called *Les Dames gallantes* and sent them to his mistress, Lady Elizabeth Brandon. In return, she sent him pictures of children being flogged for 'reasons of discipline'.

Concerns around paedophilia have led to questions about why a person would seek out children for sex. A flurry of scientific studies has emerged over the last 30 years or so in an attempt to understand the reasons for paedophilia.[35] One recent line of thought suggests that a paedophile's prior cognition about children as potential sexual partners plays a role in their searching out children for sexual behaviour; their conception of children plays a pivotal role in their attitude towards them in relation to sex. There must therefore have been a conception of the young child as a sexual object in the past for the attacks to have taken place.

The Golden Age of Childhood?

The cult of the girl child emerged in the 1850s and was to morph into the golden age of childhood at the turn of the century. Alluring images of children were painted, photographed and written about by artists and authors, all seemingly acceptable to those around them. Millais's Pre-Raphaelite, euphemistically titled painting *Cherry Ripe* provided the provocative picture of a prepubescent girl, her cheeks flushed and her hands pointing to her pudenda. The 28-year-old painter Philip Wilson Steer used the eleven-year-old Rose Pettigrew and her sisters as models for his paintings of prepubescent girls, depicting them naked or with their clothes in disarray. Steer and Rose kissed, danced and drank wine together; he even proposed to her and gave her a ring. The relationship went on uncontested until she was eighteen years old, when she left him after a quarrel at a dance and refused to see him again.[36]

The sexually ambiguous cult of the girl child saw a period of seemingly innocent adoration of pre-pubescent girlhood by adult men. Edgar Jepson wrote, 'There was at Oxford in the eighties a cult of little girls, the little daughters of dons and residents: men used to have them to tea and take them on the river and write verses to them.'[37] How innocent these relationships were is questionable. Lewis Carroll (Charles Dodgson), author of *Alice's Adventures in Wonderland* (1965), entertained girls aged between five and eleven in his rooms at Christ Church, Oxford University, where he was a mathematics don. During these friendships, he took photographs of them naked, but broke off connections when they reached twelve – an age at which they evidently lost their appeal for him. Carroll's provocative photographs of the prepubescent Alice Liddell, the girl who inspired 'Alice', were considered acceptable at the time but Carroll evidently had a penchant for little girls even if he did not act on it sexually. Another admirer of young girls was the poet Ernest Dowson, who became obsessed by Adelaide Foltinowicz. When he first set eyes on her in her parents' cafe in Soho, she was nearly twelve. Although he never

John Everett Millais, *Cherry Ripe*, 1879.

had sex with her, he adored her and wrote poems to her, but she never took as much interest in him. He waited and waited (as was his way – Dowson was a known procrastinator), but when she reached the age of eighteen she found another suitor and married him instead. Although Adelaide was always Dowson's one true love, she was not the only subject of Dowson's devotion; he also adored and wrote poems about other young girls.

311

Between 1890 and 1910, a so-called 'golden age of childhood' developed from an ideal espoused by writers and artists who believed in the basic innocence of children. Kenneth Grahame wrote *The Golden Age* (1895) and *The Wind in the Willows* (1908), J. M. Barrie, *Peter Pan; or, The Boy Who Wouldn't Grow Up* (1904) and E. Nesbitt, *The Railway Children* (1905) as part of the movement of the glorification of childhood. In America, Katharine Forrest Hamill cemented this type of sentimentality towards childhood innocence in her book *The Golden Age of Childhood*, published in 1906, an illustrated book of children's poems accompanied by pretty pictures of children.

Philip Wilson Steer, *The Black Hat*, a picture of Rose Pettigrew, *c.* 1900.

Lewis Carroll's photograph of Alice Liddell.

Barrie was known to be inordinately fond of children. In the opening to chapter Nineteen of *The Little White Bird*, published in 1902, the narrator described how he undresses the boy: 'David and I had a tremendous adventure. It was this – he passed the night with me . . . I took [his boots] off with all the coolness of an old hand, and then I placed him on my knee, and removed his blouse. This was a delightful experience, but I think I remained wonderfully calm until I came somewhat too suddenly to his little braces, which agitated me profoundly . . . I cannot proceed in public with the disrobing of David.' Despite its obvious description of sexual allurement, the reviewer for the *Times Literary Supplement* wrote: 'If a book exists which contains more knowledge and more love of children, we do not know it.' Meanwhile, Barrie indulged in dressing his favourite boy, one of the sons of the Llewelyn Davies family, as Peter Pan.

The golden age of childhood was in contradiction to the tawdry realities of life for some children. In some cases of sexual abuse, doctors such as Lawson Tait were pronouncing children 'virulent little minxes', set up by their mothers to cry rape in exchange for money for keeping quiet. However, Victorian campaigners realized that child abuse permeated society. The NSPCC (which had developed from the London Society for the Prevention of Cruelty to Children, founded in 1884) had increasing success in bringing about prosecutions for child abuse. Their most notable success was the uncovering of a Baptist minster in 1905 who was found indecently assaulting three young girls in his charge. Again, the blackmail ruse was presented by the defence, but the girls gave their own account and described how the minister had invited them to extra Bible

Cover of Kenneth Grahame, *The Golden Age* (1895).

classes. Their testimony was supported by a policeman who witnessed that the minister had been 'suspected of immorality for years'.[38]

The supposed golden age of childhood had brought with it some of the definitions and examples of serious child abuse, which we now term 'paedophilia'. The 'discovery' of sexual abuse in England started from around the 1860s, with the campaigning movements for child welfare and the social purity movement. The emphasis, however, was on rescuing fallen women and girls rather than concern over adolescent boy prostitutes.[39] Howard Vincent of the Metropolitan Police told a Select Committee of the House of Lords in 1881 that female prostitution abounded around the Haymarket and Piccadilly, with children of fourteen, fifteen and sixteen openly soliciting. But the biggest scandal was about to erupt as a result of the work of the journalist W. T. Stead, after he undertook a clandestine operation to try and expose the 'white slave traffic'. It was thought that women and young girls were being abducted and sold as sex slaves abroad. The results of his investigation were published in a series of articles in the *Pall Mall Gazette* in July 1885 under the heading 'The Maiden Tribute of Modern Babylon'. Here, he declared, 'It is, however, a fact that there is in full operation among us a system of which the violation of virgins is one of the ordinary incidents; that these virgins are mostly of tender age, being too young in fact to understand the nature of the crime of which they are the unwilling victims.'[40] He claimed to be revealing just how easy it was for a man to purchase a child for sex. In fact, he had tried for weeks to do so unsuccessfully and in the end had to hire a known procuress, who lied to the girl's mother, saying the child was going into service. Once the mother found out what had happened, she went to the magistrates and Stead was arrested.

However, Stead had good intentions. He had long been an ardent advocate of civil liberties, world peace and women's rights, a defender of the oppressed and a supporter of the social purity movement by the time he set up a secret committee to investigate child prostitution. His comrades included the social purity campaigner Josephine Butler and members of the London Committee for the Suppression of the Traffic in British Girls for the Purposes of Continental Prostitution. In order to publicize the subject, in May 1880 Butler wrote a letter to the *Shield*, a weekly newspaper for the Campaign Against the Contagious Diseases Act, where she complained about

Victorian idealized view of children in a wood engraving after William Small
(1843–1929).

the extent of child prostitution in European brothels: 'in some of
the houses in Belgium there are immured little children, English
girls of some twelve to fifteen years of age, lovely creatures (for they
do not care to pay for any who are not beautiful) innocent creatures
too, stolen, kidnapped, betrayed, got from English country villages by
artifice and sold to these human shambles . . .'.[41] Butler, along with
the rest of the Committee, supported Stead's proposals to procure an
underage girl as means to expose the ease of such a purchase. Indeed,
Butler herself pounded the street with her son Georgie, pretending
to be a madam procuring girls, spending £100 in the process. However,

Two girls kissing,
Julia Margaret
Cameron, *The Turtle
Doves*, 1864.

it was Stead who managed to purchase an underage virgin for £5 through various contacts. Despite the fact that he had undertaken the operation only to expose the crime, once the fact became known, Stead was prosecuted and served three months in jail. Nonetheless, the exposé was to have a profound effect on the public and would help to effect a change of law. The Criminal Law Amendment Act was introduced in 1885 as 'an Act to make further provision for the Protection of Women and Girls, the suppression of brothels, and other purposes'. It raised the age of consent from thirteen to sixteen, just as the social purity reformers had wanted, and with it Stead had at last accomplished his aim.

The Making of the Paedophile

Krafft-Ebing first coined the term 'paedophilia' in 1886 to describe sexual attraction to children. He explained the process; 'the sexually needy subject . . . [is] drawn to children not because of a degenerated morality of psychic or physical impotence, but rather because of a morbid disposition, a *psychosexual perversion*, which may at present be named as *erotic pedophilia*.'[42] Although the perpetrator of such crimes was labelled a 'pervert', the classification of the paedophile was that of a person with a mental disorder – and, indeed, still is, medically speaking. Although the concept of paedophilia was introduced in the medical arena in the early twentieth century, it was not taken up by the public until much later.

According to Krafft-Ebing, one-third of all cases of 'sexual atrocities' that came before the criminal forum for the period 1856–60 were committed on children; he said such crimes were on the increase in Western European countries. In France, for example, the rate of rape of children rose dramatically from 136 cases in 1826 to over 800 in 1867. Similar trends were seen in England, rising from 167 during a four-year period from 1830 to a staggering 1,395 for the three years 1855–7. Yet Krafft-Ebing personally knew of only a handful of paedophiles, and considered it to be mainly a condition of men, a state which he saw as a 'platonic love' (something which paedophiles commonly assert) stimulated only by little girls. All of the patients were 'tainted' by heredity and developed emotions towards little girls either early on in their own childhood, or as young men in their early twenties. He insisted that the men were a danger to society and should be placed in an insane asylum, and blamed 'coital impotence and moral decay (senile dementia)' for their acts.[43]

Few women were thought to have similar sexual obsessions with children. Sexologists reported a few cases, but they thought them unusual. Krafft-Ebing reported on one 29-year-old woman who had a strong desire for sexual intercourse with one of her five nephews, the first when he was only five. She could not explain the inclination, but transferred her desire to the youngest of each of them in turn as they grew up, and would orgasm at the sight of them. Havelock Ellis found a similar disorder in another female patient, a 48-year-old schoolmistress who went out of her way to seek physical contact with her young charges. She would take two or three of them and 'lie on the bed naked with them and make them suck her breasts and press them to every part of her body'.[44] She was caught after other children peering through the keyhole saw her, and she was placed under the care of a doctor. Sometimes a patient who had been diagnosed with

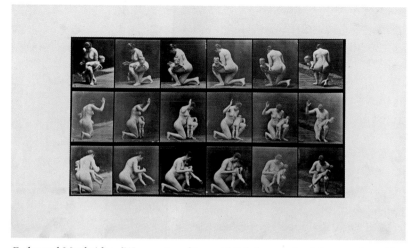

Eadweard Muybridge, 'Woman Spanking a Child', from *Animal Locomotion*, 1887.

one sexual disorder also had others; one married woman with two children was a female invert (lesbian) and before marrying had had sex with a dog. She was also a sadist: after adopting a girl from a children's home, she inflicted over 300 wounds on the girl's breasts, labia and clitoris and half starved her. According to Ellis, the woman was curiously 'pruriently prudish', which he deemed was 'often the case with sadists'. The woman was sent to a hospital for the insane and afterwards served two years in prison.[45]

Sexologists gave little consideration as to why it was mainly men and not women who were thought to be so prone to paedophilia, but took it as given. The general thrust of the understanding of the sexologists was linked to the ideology of the time; women were thought to be more passive, less sexual and less aggressive than men and therefore less likely to commit such crimes. They did, however, give much thought to the type of man who might become a paedophile.

Krafft-Ebing categorized two different types of sex offenders against children: men who use children as a substitute for an adult partner; and paedophiles who have a disorder. When Freud investigated child abuse, he took a different path. He believed that for every case of hysteria there was a case of childhood incestual abuse behind it. He later replaced this with his Oedipus theory in which he classed reports by women of abuse as subconscious fantasies. In other words, he believed that women reporting childhood rape were suffering from delusions as a result of a fixation with their fathers. In certain cases, Freudian psychoanalysts did not consider the abuse as a real problem. Frank Caprio mentioned a case of father–daughter incest in the 1950s to which he had been alerted when the mother came into his office for a consultation. She told him that she had caught her husband performing cunnilingus on their eleven-year-old daughter. For Caprio, this perversion represented for the man 'a psychological return to the sex life of his own childhood'. The molested child herself was given less consideration, the male adult patient being the doctor's main concern. About the paedophile, Caprio surmised, 'as a rule they masturbate to excess. Not all of them are dangerous.'[46] He later took up the case of a young married man who had been charged with sexually molesting children and, confident of his own ability, testified in court that the man could be cured by therapy.

So where did the current concept of paedophiles as violent child abusers come from? During 1960s Britain, there was no mention of paedophilia in the course of everyday life. Mothers warned their children not to talk to strangers but no one talked of 'paedophiles'. 'Flashers' or male exhibitionists were known to operate in the local parks, but they were not generally considered to be rapists. Children were instructed not to look and to run home as quickly as possible. The topic on everyone's lips was the case of Myra Hindley and Ian Brady who had abducted and murdered several children on the Saddleworth Moors. The other notorious case was that of eleven-year-old Mary Bell, who was convicted of murdering two children in 1968.[47] As it turned out, Bell herself had been the subject of cruelty from her sadistic mother and had been sexually abused by various men who came to the house. This cycle of being abused, and then abusing others in turn, was for some psychiatrists the answer to unlocking the mind of the paedophile. While this may have been the case in some instances, it does not answer the questions about how child abuse surfaces in those who have *not* been abused themselves. Also, not all people who have been abused themselves automatically go on to become child abusers.

In the 1960s, although there was considerable attention paid to battered, physically abused or murdered children, the topic of their sexual molestation was not at the forefront of the discussion. But from the late 1970s onwards studies attempted to understand and 'cure' the paedophile and to understand childhood sexuality.[48] Certain studies have made the case that most children have no innocence to lose, and that most children are already aware of their own socio-biologically inherited sexuality. William O'Donohue argues that we need to understand the types of harm sexual acts can do to children; that children do not have the capacity to consent by virtue of being children; and that adults have a duty not to harm but to protect children.[49] It has also been suggested that some professionals' reactions to paedophilia, with their interventionist approach with children, are more harmful to children than the abuse. Fear is ingrained in children and any subsequent medical investigations of their body can be more intrusive and traumatic than the act itself, adding further stress to the child and leading to anxieties as an adult.

Historically, there has been an innocence ascribed to children in most Western societies where prevention of any form of sexual behaviour for young people is the norm. Yet Kinsey gave detailed and extensive physiological examples of arousal and even orgasm in infants and prepubescent children. However, the data relating to this issue was decidedly suspect, as it was taken from a self-admitted paedophile who had been operating over many years. He gave data of his sex episodes with children to Kinsey's researchers, but they questioned much of the statistical information. Also, some of the researchers questioned the morality of including data provided by a paedophile.[50]

In 1974, paedophiles set up their own organization, the Paedophile Information Exchange (or PIE) in Britain, ostensibly to campaign for their rights, as they claimed they were misunderstood. In 1978, they brought out a pamphlet containing questions and answers, which provided an insight into how they viewed themselves and their activities. They asserted that 'those involved represent no special threat to society but on the contrary are often a force for social good.' Since many people disagreed, they should have perhaps added an explanation of their reasoning. The authors use the words 'sexual love' to describe the sexual relationships of paedophiles with young people, a description claimed by other paedophiles elsewhere. In answer to the question 'would most paedophiles like to be normal?', they argue that sexuality is natural, harmless and an integrated part of their personality and they would not want to change, even if it were possible. Nor do they approve of the use of drugs as 'treatment', as it 'is not desirable to destroy a paedophile's love for children'. The authors assert that the child is often 'a willing partner' and the adult 'gentle, fond of children and benevolent'.[51] On 16 July 2011 the *Guardian* newspaper reported that detectives found over 3,000 drawings of children being raped at the home of the former leader of PIE, alongside thousands of pictures and films that were described as 'vile and disgusting'. As a result, he was jailed, becoming the first person to be prosecuted under the Coroners and Justice Act of 2009. This in itself highlights problems in the law, since 'prohibited images of children' under the Act includes 'a moving or still image (produced by any means)'. Regardless of what we think of paedophiles, how can a drawing, the making of which has not involved any illegality, be illegal? If an artist depicts a paedophile rape scene but no actual abuse has taken place of any child, how can this be deemed illegal? Also, artists who have been placed in an abusive relationship may portray the event in their own work – is this then also illegal?

However, it took the sordid case of the Vatican's cover-up of mass paedophilia within its ranks to outrage both those in the Catholic faith and those on the outside, and bring paedophilia to the centre of public concern. In 1984, the case of Father Gilbert Gauthe in Lafayette, Louisiana, led to numerous revelations of similar cases of abuse all over America. Church officials routinely refused to believe victims, intimidated them into silence or failed to act upon complaints – not once, but repeatedly. By 1985, the victims had begun to take up the matter in civil courts. Action spread throughout the U.S., Canada, Ireland and the UK. Under pressure, investigations were eventually commissioned in the U.S. John Jay College of Criminal Justice and the National Review Board found that dioceses had reported almost 4,500 clerical perpetrators since 1950 and at least 10,000 victims were involved. The National Review Board report places blame for the widespread scandal directly on the negligence of bishops.[52]

A further flurry of concern about paedophilia hit the newspaper headlines around the 1980s with reports of paedophile sex rings operating in Amsterdam. Child murder was now beginning to be more closely associated with the sexual abuse of children, and the term 'paedophilia' was becoming more widespread. The Belgium police came under attack after a widely publicized case during the 1990s when Marc Dutroux, formerly an electrician, kidnapped and abused six girls aged between eight and nineteen years of age, four of whom he killed. He had been known to the police for years before he was finally arrested in 1996. The police had even searched his house and heard the screams of two of his victims but did nothing, choosing to believe the noise came from children playing outside. They later discovered that he had been let out of prison in 1991 after serving only three and a half years of a thirteen-year sentence for multiple rape. Because of the catalogue of 'mistakes', the public believed that there had been a major cover-up and that police were involved in the paedophile ring. The prison authorities even briefly allowed Dutroux to escape from prison. He was then nearly released on human rights grounds as it had taken the police so long to bring a case against him. He was finally jailed for life in 2004.[53] His accomplices, Martin and Lelièvre, were also jailed for 30 and 25 years respectively, but no further paedophiles have been exposed in the network. It was such cases of murder, abduction and violent child abuse that moulded public perception of paedophiles and shook the legal systems in Europe and the U.S. into bringing out new laws.

By the 1990s, concern about child abuse was at a historic high when 45 million viewers tuned their televisions to watch a documentary about the subject, *Scared Silent*, which aired on 4 September 1992 in the U.S.[54] By 1997, steps were taken by the police to monitor the movements of convicted sex offenders but the information was kept from the public and shared only between the police, probation officers and the local Member of Parliament. Under the British Sex Offenders Act of 1997, convicted paedophiles were obliged to register their names and addresses at their local police stations within fourteen days of their release. Increasing public reaction against paedophiles led to campaigns for more openness about their whereabouts. In the U.S., community notification laws were enacted throughout the country in the 1990s following the murder of seven-year-old Megan Kanka; popularly known as Megan's Law, public disclosure of the identity of convicted sex offenders was allowed to the local community in which the paedophile lived. A similar public campaign to introduce 'Sarah's Law' was launched in Britain after the murder of eight-year-old Sarah Payne in 2000. Because of the prominence and violent public reaction to horrific child murder cases, all paedophiles have now come to be considered as sex abusers who might potentially go on to murder children. Treatments have been applied to paedophiles in attempts to alter their sexual interests.

These have ranged from surgical castration (although this is no longer used) to drugs (effectively chemical castration) and aversion therapy, and they can be administered without the patient's consent. Paedophiles can be incarcerated for life, particularly if they do not admit that what they have done is wrong, since an admission is seen as part of their 'treatment' and shows that they are 'getting better'. More recently, some paedophiles have declared themselves incurable and that attempts should not be made to 'cure' them. They have claimed that their feelings are merely another sexual orientation.

Public perception and anger has since concentrated on the more severe end of the spectrum of paedophilia. Public emotions were further stirred up in the tabloids in 2000 when *News of the World* editor Rebekah Wade (later Brooks) created a controversial 'naming and shaming' campaign attacking convicted paedophiles. She declared, 'The fact is, that if you have paedophiles in society that aren't monitored they will strike again.'[55] Her statements about 'protecting children' encouraged the establishment of a vigilante movement. In 2000, in Newport, South Wales, a mob, in their ignorant frenzy, targeted a paediatrician's house for attack because they had confused the word with 'paedophile'.[56] Public fury was understandable, though, when the police admitted to 'losing' four convicted paedophiles. Scotland Yard said that the perpetrators had served their jail sentences but had gone missing after failing to report to their local police station under the terms of their release.

The public perception of a paedophile is of a stranger who abducts young girls (or sometimes, but less often, boys). Yet the idea that the paedophile is always unknown to the child is misplaced. More commonly, the abuser is an adult already known to the child. Research in the U.S. indicates that 40 per cent of children who are raped are victims of family members.[57] Studies of father and daughter incest in child abuse cases show common features existed within families where such abusive relationships took place. Generally, the father is extremely dominant with a mother resigning from the role of caring for her daughter. Older daughters are usually the targets. As a result of childhood abuse, a woman (or man) may develop psychological problems in later life, often being unable to connect to their partner. The majority of American rape victims (61 per cent) are raped before the age of eighteen; furthermore, 29 per cent of all rapes occurred when the victim was less than eleven years old. Eleven per cent of rape victims are raped by their fathers or stepfathers, and another 16 per cent are raped by other relatives.[58] The perpetrators involved were fathers, stepfathers and uncles. Even when the wrong-doing was explained to them, they refused to stop the abuse; they not only failed to recognize how they had used their power to make the children submit, but identified their abuse as caring for the child. Half of those interviewed claimed that the love was mutu-al.[59] Yet public anger over paedophilia has made discussion about its prevention extremely difficult and debate about children's own sexuality is virtually non-existent. Better sex education at all ages and increased awareness is needed.

Feminists shifted the perspective of child incest to some extent when they argued that it was not a rare occurrence as previously thought, but was a common experience. Most victims were girls and most perpetrators were men. Twenty-nine per cent of incestuous child abusers were birth fathers and a quarter were stepfathers.[60] To this extent, it has been argued, the acts express masculine norms of power and control and feminine norms of passivity within a patri-archy system.

ICD-10 defines paedophilia as 'a sexual preference for children, boys or girls or both, usually of pre-pubertal or early pubertal age'. According to the DSM paedophilia is a paraphilia, in this case a form of sexual arousal or gratification which is extreme or atypical in which a person has intense and recurrent sexual urges towards and fantasies about prepubescent children (usually considered to be thirteen years old or under), and on which feelings they have either acted or which cause distress or difficulty. The person must be at least sixteen years old, and five years older than the child in the case of adolescent paedophiles, for the act to be classified as paedophilia. However, some paedophiles never act out their fantasies and just masturbate, so can these people be deemed harmless? The last point has also been made by several researchers who have remarked that a so-called 'contented paedophile' – an individual who fantasizes about having sex with a child and masturbates to these fantasies, but does not commit child sex abuse, and who does not feel sub-jectively distressed afterward – does not meet the DSM criteria for a paedophile.

There has also been increasing discussion about the age a young person is thought able to consent, particularly relating to young

Wilhelm von Gloeden, male youth in classical pose, from his *Taormina* series, *c.* 1900.

teenagers. This opens a whole area of debate about erobophiles, those who are attracted to young men. Groups such as NAMBLA (the North American Man/Boy Love Association) argue that such relationships are mutually consensual and beneficial to both parties, and independent research has found the same.[61]

If an adolescent agrees that they have consented and not been in any way coerced, and that they have enjoyed the experience, can their older partner be seen as a paedophile, particularly when what is considered acceptable varies from country to country? What is considered acceptable in Spain, with an age of consent of thirteen, for example, would result in a prison sentence in Britain, where it is sixteen.[62] Technically, therefore, what is acceptable in one country is classed as paedophilia and an imprisonable offence in another.

Jules Scalbert (1851–1928), *The Bathers*.

ELEVEN

The Games People Play

There are rules against shitting that way; you should at least have given us notice; you know damned well that we are prepared to receive shit at any hour of the day or night.

Marquis de Sade, *The 120 Days of Sodom* (1785)

Over the centuries, people in search of erotic experiences have generated various methods of sex play. These games have had different origins and often arose from complicated feelings; some people were influenced by social conditioning in childhood or adolescence and needed to replicate as adults a sensation they had felt in the past. Yet others were simply adults on the look out for new sexual adventures – sometimes straightforward sex was simply no longer enough.

New ideas were conjured up in the form of openly displaying, or passively watching, the sexual activities of others; there were watchers and doers, actors and spectators. The more aggressive forms of exposure were seen in public exhibitionism. For the more passive personality types, voyeurism often gave equal pleasure – the eighteenth-century female dominatrix might play the role of governess to the pupil; Victorian men and women experimented with slave and master relationships (although this game did not necessarily follow the path of current sadomasochistic role-play); in the twentieth century, nurse and patient games developed, or mother and child games in adult-baby play. People in same-sex relationships played different games – cops and robbers, cowboys and Indians – or dressed up as public servicemen or tradesmen such as firemen or builders. These forms of play might involve 'extras' such as coprophilia and urolagnia, sometimes known colloquially as 'shit-loving' or 'golden showers'. These roles and games also varied throughout history – but when did they arise, how were they defined and how they were played out?

Playing games, from the Marquis de Sade, *Juliette* (1797).

More games, from Sade, *Juliette* (1797).

Exhibitionism

Exhibitionism has taken various forms throughout the ages. According to Herodotus, the Egyptians who travelled to Bubastis to celebrate the festival of Artemis exposed themselves to those they passed by. They came on barges in great numbers and on the way the men would play flutes and the women sing, clap and clatter castanets. As they passed by a town on the riverbank, they would bring their barge close into the shore and the women would 'shout abuse at the women of the place, or start dancing, or hitch up their skirts'.[1] These activities were an expected part of the procession. However, there were a variety of reasons and opportunities for showing off, and not all fitted neatly into patterns.

People have also exposed themselves as a form of insult. One woman called Mara from sixteenth-century Dubrovnik had gone to the house of Fiorio Petrovich and condemned him as a sodomite, calling him a 'horned goat' while gesticulating with lewd gestures. Afterwards, according to Petrovich, 'to spite me, she lifted her clothes,

A female dancer exposes herself to a satyr. Martin van Maële, *La Grande danse macabre* (1907).

showing her private parts'.[2] Such displays of intimate body parts were later to become recognized by twentieth-century anthropologists as methods of challenging or aggressive behaviour in 'primitive' people. As Evans-Pritchard remarked of the Azande women of Central Africa, 'unusual action of the female genitalia is considered unlucky.

331

It is injurious to a man if a woman provokingly exposes her vagina to him, and it is yet more serious if she exposes her anus in the presence of men.'[3] This belief gave women an innate power over men. Yet this type of exposure was obviously undertaken not only by tribal people but was also a common form of expression made with the intention of frightening the onlooker.

Some exhibitionistic acts undertaken in the past do not fit into a category of serious sexual deviance but were intended to shock with a laugh. Chaucer's 'Miller's Tale' in his fourteenth-century *Canterbury Tales* told of one man involved in an incident in which he bared his buttocks:

> And so he opened window hastily,
> And put his arse out thereat, quietly,
> Over the buttocks, showing the whole bum;
> And thereto said this clerk, this Absalom,
> 'O speak, sweet bird, I know not where thou art.'
> This Nicholas just then let fly a fart
> As loud as it had been a thunder-clap,
> And well-nigh blinded Absalom, poor chap . . .

However, the seventeenth-century libertine was equally capable of intentionally insulting other people by showing off his buttocks, as Samuel Pepys was to record. He reported an incident of lewd exposure in his diary after the infamous Sir Charles Sedley had been celebrating at the Cock in Bow Street in June 1663, along with a party of friends that included Lord Buckhurst and Sir Thomas Ogle. Drunk as lords, they went out on the balcony, and according to one observer, 'putting down their breeches they excrementized in the street: which being done, Sedley stripped himself naked, and with eloquence preached blasphemy to the people.'[4] He was heavily fined for his actions.

More innocuous acts involved tempting bets from friends who urged each other on to expose themselves. The *Observer* newspaper reported that on the evening of Friday, 5 July 1799, at seven o'clock, a naked man was arrested at Mansion House, the official residence of the Mayor of London. From there he was sent to the Poultry Compter, the small prison run by the Sheriff of London. The prisoner confirmed that he had accepted a wager of ten guineas (worth about £750 in

Thomas Rowlandson (1856–1827), *The Congregation*.

today's money) to run naked from Cornhill to Cheapside.[5] While these types of exhibitionism were not taken too seriously (although there were sometimes small fines involved), laws were introduced to deal with more obvious intentions to shock, frighten or insult.

The Vagrancy Act of 1824 enabled the prosecution of 'every person willingly, openly, lewdly and obscenely exposing his person with intent to insult any female'.[6] It was thereby deemed to be an act perpetrated by a man towards a woman. Henceforth the perpetrator would be deemed 'a rogue and a vagabond' according to the law. However, men continued to exhibit themselves. On 2 January 1843, 43-year-old George Herridge was indicted 'for indecently exposing himself'; he pleaded guilty and was jailed for twelve months. However, when 31-year-old John Daniels was found guilty of the same offence nine months later on 23 October, he only received only one month in jail; there is nothing in the records to indicate why there was a disparity in sentencing. Some years later, on 2 July 1849, 62-year-old William Joiner was confined for four months for indecent exposure. Without more in-depth knowledge of the incidents, it is impossible to understand why some were treated more seriously than others, but other mitigating circumstances may have been involved. Then again, sentencing was, and is, notoriously inconsistent from one court to another.

In any case, given the low sentences passed, the activity was evidently not regarded as being too threatening. Even when the case of exposure took place in public places, it was often difficult to obtain a conviction. When, on 5 January 1857, Felix Hue exposed himself to Elizabeth Williams, it was on a public highway. Nonetheless, he was found not guilty, so presumably there were no witnesses. Even when there were witnesses, it seems to have still been problematic to ensure a conviction. On 27 February 1860, 31-year-old Giuseppe Pugno was accused of exposing himself to Margaret Stafford in the presence of William Henry Crocker. The incident had taken place in a railway carriage used for conveying passengers along the South Eastern Railway. Crocker's defence argued that the carriage was not in a public place and suggested the carriage 'might then be lying under some shed, or undergoing some repair in the carriage-house'. The indictment was squashed on a technicality as 'although it alleged the exposure to be in the presence of another person, it did not allege that it was within the view of that person; who, though present, might have been blind or sleeping'.[7]

'Streaking' or 'mooning' became new terms for old activities. 'Mooning' as a popular term originated in the U.S. only around 1968 and was specifically used to apply to the act of publicly displaying the bare buttocks. It was usually done for fun rather than erotic arousal. Although the term 'to streak' had been used since medieval times to mean 'to rush or run around', it only came to imply nakedness from around 1973 onwards; this occurred after a mass nude run by 533 people took place at the University of Maryland. It seems to have been a particularly popular pastime at sports grounds – at cricket, rugby, football, tennis, snooker, golf and even the Olympic

Games in 2006. One of the most famous female streakers (mainly because of the size of her breasts) was Erica Roe, who ran across a rugby match during an international tournament, showing off her forty-inch chest. Thousands of people saw the incident as it made headline news. Exhibitionism and its prohibition or acceptance therefore is, to a large extent, dependent on time and place.

The Medical Invention of the Twentieth-century Exhibitionist

The French physician Charles Lasègue first described exhibitionism in 1877 as the act of receiving gratification by exhibiting sexual organs to persons of the opposite sex, commonly to children or 'innocent' people. Overall, sexologists classed exhibitionism as a perversion and recognized it as an illness, a psychological disorder. Lasègue thought these types of acts were performed mainly by men.

Krafft-Ebing defined exhibitionism as acts 'exclusively those of men who ostentatiously expose their genitals to persons of the opposite sex . . . without, however, becoming aggressive'. The cases he described generally involved older men (not youths) who exposed themselves mainly to young children. Many of those he interviewed were married and had suffered from some sort of brain deterioration. He therefore concluded – as with most other sexual perversions – that those who committed such crimes were men of moral or mental weakness, degenerates or idiots.

Once the law was involved, exhibitionism officially became 'indecent exposure'. An example of this can be seen in Krafft-Ebing's Case 210 in *Psychopathia Sexualis* (1886):

> At nine o'clock at night in the spring of 1891, a lady, very much in great trepidation, went to a policeman in the city park of X. and stated that a man, his front absolutely naked, had approached her from the shrubbery, after which she has run away frightened. The officer went at once to the place indicated and found a man who exposed his naked belly and genitals. Although the man attempted to escape, he was overtaken and arrested. He stated that he had been excited by alcohol and had been at the point of going to a prostitute.[8]

While the ages and excuses of the perpetrators varied, this case was fairly typical of reported incidents. Many of those caught exposing themselves claimed to have been urinating, others that they had forgotten to do up their trousers. Also known as 'lewdly exposing', and later 'flashing', exhibitionism was just one of the fixations that men and women experienced – sometimes compulsively, according to sexologists.

Various sexologists, including Iwan Bloch, Sigmund Freud and George Merzbach, interviewed and assessed exhibitionists and concluded that their behaviour was a weakened form of sadism.[9] In other words, the exhibitionist was forcing himself or herself on to unwilling victims who had no option but to watch. Only when the exhibitionist's own behaviour became a problem to himself was it classed as a psychological disorder.

Certain physical ailments such as epilepsy were connected to exhibitionism and sexologists believed that its onset usually took place while a patient was still young (mid-teens or early twenties). They noticed that the exhibitionist frequently felt decidedly uncomfortable with his actions, but was compelled to go through with them. This was attributed to a feeling of guilt on the part of the perpetrator. An example can be seen in a case reported by Albert von Schrenck-Notzing involving a loving husband and father who, unable to stop himself, exposed himself to women in the street and suffered terrible guilt thereafter.

Guilt was associated with an emotional feeling that was expressed by a person when they had committed a moral offence for which they bore responsibility. The appearance of this emotion came as a result of a shift from public shame to private guilt.[10] Prior to this, in the medieval period in rural areas, people had been shamed into conformity, which prevented them from acting in a way that might be considered as out of the ordinary. In these incidents, there was not necessarily any guilt involved on the part of the perpetrator, only shame, and then only after he was found out. As rural communities broke down and people moved to urban centres, there was less supervision of public morals from the local neighbourhood. The Lutheran Reformation also shifted attitudes towards sin, encouraging the development of a more internalized world of personal guilt. An inner, closer God who made a person responsible for his or her own sins replaced an omnipotent, retributive God. These sins were no longer so easily absolved by a local priest but elicited strong inner feelings about moral responsibility for one's own actions. This new feeling of inner personal guilt was partly responsible for giving an added frisson to exhibitionism.

As the licentious eighteenth century gave way to the more reserved Victorian period, exhibitionism became more prevalent. Although the whole argument around the great Victorian cover-up has been questioned, the increase in the middle classes and the emergence of a more 'polite' society meant there was more potential for shocking people. Evangelicals in particular were 'consistently anti-sensual as was humanly possible', with a restraint placed on revealing dresses for women, dancing and reading novels. One shocked London footman remarked on women's dress, 'they are nearly naked to the waist . . . the breasts are quite exposed except a little bit coming up to hide the nipples'.[11] By the twentieth century, the German sociologist Hans Freyer was reporting entirely different reasons for exhibitionism than the early sexologists had. A 35-year-old barber had the usual array of 'tainted' family members: his father was a drunk and his mother and sister both suffered from nervousness. As a child of between seven and eighteen years old, Freyer's patient had suffered from convulsions, but he had managed to achieve sexual intercourse from the age of sixteen. At 21, his behaviour began to change and he started to display unusual symptoms: he passed a playground and began to urinate there. When the children noticed him, he admitted he obtained a sexual thrill, leading to an erection and ejaculation. From then on, he found it difficult to have sexual intercourse with women. His exhibitionism was only detected when he was caught and imprisoned after inviting a young girl to touch and feel his penis. On physical examination his penis was found to be smaller than average but he was of sound mental condition. The diagnosis was that his complex had arisen due to his small penis size.

Unlike Freyer's case, other reported cases of exhibitionism found that the size of genitalia was not an issue. In the 1950s book *Sexual Perversion and the Law*, Porter Davis found that the size of the penis of exhibitionists varied widely – some had very big penises and some very small. Their display was more likely to be based on feelings of inadequacy. Davis believed that 'the exhibitionist is usually a less virile person and less intelligent than the flagellant. His sexual impulse is much weaker and he is often a degenerate.'[12] According to Davis, indecent exposure rarely went further than exhibitionism. A man did not approach or want to touch the woman to whom he had exposed himself. His excitement was gained merely from the look of disgust his actions evoked on the woman's face.

Explanations of exhibitionism were still relatively new and sometimes contradictory. While some doctors believed that the behaviour was a result of a physiological defect, others began to explain exhibitionism as a result of a psychological problem, increasingly so with the development of psychoanalysis. The law was less ambiguous and tended to recognize it as indecent behaviour. Nonetheless, exhibitionism was not taken particularly seriously. In the 1950s, the New York Penal Law outlined its stance on indecent exposure: 'A person who willfully and lewdly exposes his person or the private parts thereof, in any public place, or in any place where others are present – is guilty of a misdemeanor.' However, it would seem that unreported crimes of exhibitionism were far more widespread than police statistics indicate. When interviewed by doctors, many victims were found never to have reported the incident to the police.

In his *Variations in Sexual Behavior* (1957), Frank Caprio argued that exhibitionism was one of the most common sexual offences, yet displayed a misunderstanding of what it was. When he declared that 'Exhibitionism was a widespread phenomenon among primitive people', he was failing to recognize the urge behind the perversion. Nakedness or exposing one's genitalia among 'primitive' people cannot in itself be considered exhibitionism, since the intention is not to shock but to insult. When tribal people want to exhibit themselves, they use different methods and it means different things. They might flaunt their bare bottoms to another person, but this was considered an aggressive act, or even witchcraft – their behaviour was not necessarily to do with genitalia or sex.[13]

In an equally ill-conceived statement, Caprio asserted, 'Among adult groups we find vicarious expressions of exhibitionism in today's nudist camps.'[14] Again, nudism in the West cannot be seen as exhibitionism, since nudists have no intention to shock or disturb other people or to elicit attention. Frequently they congregate with likeminded people – and in an enclosed, private colony rather than in public. Naturists tend to just want to take a break with a group of people taking part in normal daily activities – pitching tents, playing volleyball, swimming and so on. These forms of nakedness therefore would not generally be considered as sexually perverted or as paraphilias, although they might well be considered deviances in law. However, certain forms of flaunting one's naked body, such as burlesque, strip shows (which Caprio also mentions), and lap and pole dancing, are legally acceptable as 'entertainment' but nonetheless *can* be seen as exhibitionism, but only in as much as any other form of public dancing is. This shows just how confusing the Western concept of exhibitionism is.

By the mid-twentieth century, the psychological profile of the male exhibitionist had been fleshed out. He was thought to be a man who feels inferior, is insecure and needs attention; he was driven to exhibitionism as a means of proving himself a man by provoking a reaction. Because this insecurity was deeply ingrained, the prospect of legal penalties did not deter him from committing the illegal act again and again. In contrast to Krafft-Ebing, who had found his patients to be men of moral or mental weakness, in the 1950s, Caprio found his patients to be overly moralistic and often well-educated. Nonetheless, the old sexologists' idea that these people possessed hereditary problems continued to linger. Discussing one nineteen-year-old who had displayed his genitals since the age of fourteen, Caprio noted that the family history was 'heavily tainted', since both his parents had been neurotic. His father was religious and had attempted suicide. One uncle was in a lunatic asylum; another had been dismissed from his job as a teacher for exposing himself. Caprio thought the reason for his young patient's trauma was that his mother had showered in the same bathroom while her son was cleaning his teeth; we would hardly consider this traumatic now. In another case, Caprio commended one wife who chose to stand by her husband after he confessed the full story to her, but only after he had been caught exposing himself while driving around in his car. But, according to Caprio, 'Many wives become quite hysterical when they learn their husbands have been arrested for indecent exposure and immediately run to an attorney for a divorce.'[15]

Frotterism was seen as a sort of progression of exhibitionism, described as a man's irresistible urge to rub his penis against a women's body, the target usually being her buttocks. The behaviour was usually carried out in crowds in a public place, say on a crowded train.

One man was caught at a bus station in the act of rubbing his penis on a woman's bottom. He repented deeply, but admitted that it was the woman's noticeable posterior that made it irresistible. Although he admitted to becoming 'confused', he was apprehended and sent to an asylum. But prejudices against women reigned in the 1950s and '60s, with men blaming women for not taking enough care of themselves and wearing provocative clothing. One author, in a book on sexual deviation published in 1964, suggested that such sexual advances, 'though distasteful to many women, are not always repelled' – all men, it would seem, are likely to have felt the urge.[16] He even blamed women who walked alone over heaths and commons for seeking out exhibitionists, grumbling, 'the woman who complains that this experience often happens to her may generally be justly accused of seeking it out'.[17]

Other erroneous statements were made about exhibitionism, too. One writer discussing sexual perversion and the law claimed, 'True exhibitionism never involves any actual sexual connection such as rape.'[18] More recently this has proved not to be the case at all. In a series of studies undertaken by psychologists and behavioural scientists, it has been found that extreme sex crimes such as rape have often been preceded by the lesser crime of indecent exposure. In 1998, Freund and Seto undertook a study based on a sample of 127 rapists. Twenty-two per cent admitted voyeurism, with the same number admitting exhibitionism. Whether this shows an escalation from exhibitionism to rape, or that exhibitionism is just another sign of sexual deviance, is unclear. However, a further study under-taken by Rabinowitz-Greenberg and his colleagues provided a clearer picture when they assessed 221 exhibitionists between 1983 and 1996. They compared recidivists and non-recidivists in order to examine the probability of escalation in the offence chain, and to clarify the differences between hands-on and hands-off sexual offenders. The results indicated that indecent exposure was often a recurring crime, with the same offenders brought before the court again and again. Of the 41 sexual recidivists, fourteen went on to commit more severe hands-on sexual crimes (sexual assault). In a follow-up on the same offenders (thirteen were 'lost') in 2006, the investigators found that 'It is apparent that approximately 39 percent of our sample went on to commit other offenses, with approximately 31 percent committing a sexual or violent offense', which points to escalating patterns of offending behavior from non-contact sexual offending towards more serious sexual assaults.[19]

If in the past the motivation behind exhibitionism was the desire of men to reveal their penises to passing female onlookers, what might sexologists make of it today? In Sweden in 2006, as many women as men reported having exposed their genitals to total strangers and to have become sexually aroused by it. Again, the people subjected to these displays were ususally children and ado-lescents.[20] The question as to why this happens in a Scandinavian country which generally takes a much more liberal attitude to nakedness shakes the idea that more exposure and exhibitionism might take place in countries where bodies are less on show. If bare flesh, including genitalia, is available for viewing, why is there a need for exhibitionism – indeed, what is the difference? Again, the answer must be in the shock value, the reaction of the victim and the lack of consent from the innocent party.

Generally, though, when women display their genitals in public, most men are less upset than women are when men expose their inti-mate body parts to them. There is an apparent disparity between the sexes about how offensive exposing parts of the body can be (and which body parts). The contrived exposure of flesh in the striptease act illuminates the difference between men and women's reactions. When men go to a strip club, or to watch pole dancing, they go to experience sexual pleasure and to become excited by watching women take off their clothes or dance naked. Women, on the other hand, go to see male strippers such as the Chippendales for a bit of fun, usually along with a gaggle of girlfriends. For hen parties or all-female nights out, these strip clubs are arguably a spectacle of mirth rather than taken as any sort of serious eroticism. Nowadays we see a huge amount of exposure of the body, including genitals, in the theatre, on television, in popular magazines and at the cinema – does this make us all voyeurs?

The exposure (and the watching) of bodies also seems to be gender-biased in the media. Arguments currently circulate about the sexualization of our media and culture and its 'pornification'. But generally it is women rather than men who have become in-creasingly sexualized in popular culture.[21] And if we examine the equivalent in the past – for example, erotic prints and drawings – they consisted of mainly sexualized women rather than men, so perhaps things have not changed so much after all. This concentration on showing female genitalia has extended itself to television, which shows vaginas and labia, though erect penises are still taboo. This is generally the case throughout the media in most Western countries, including America and Britain. Those concerned about censoring the over-virile member use as their guideline the 'Mull of Kintyre' rule, a crude benchmark which says that you cannot display a penis at any greater angle of erection than that of the Mull of Kintyre against the coastline of Scotland. But why should an erect penis so offend, particularly when most people watching it have already seen one? Post-television watershed, what does it matter?

The dividing line between naturism or nakedness and exhibitionism therefore depends to a large extent on the attitudes of the people around that naked person and where the act takes place. Certain beaches in parts of Europe have become known over the last few decades for their leniency towards nakedness, and generally there is a tendency to accept nakedness where there is an established tradition. However, this all depends on the morality of the people on the beach and they could well be within their legal rights to condemn someone for exhibitionism in an area where everyone else is clothed. The naked person on a naturist beach would not be welcomed (or ignored) so easily in a town supermarket. As a result of this confusion, and the ever more liberal attitudes to nakedness in countries in the West, cases of nakedness have proved problematic for the police. Nudism lacks a shock element – the nudist does not have any intention to shock, and the person observing the nudist is not shocked either. So where then does the law stand?

The Case of the Naked Man

When Stephen Gough decided he wanted to walk naked from Land's End to John O'Groats in 2003, the police were at first baffled about what to do with him. Previously, he had worked as a lorry driver and had been involved in environmental groups and communal living. After moving to Vancouver for a year with his partner and children, he had an ephinany. He revealed, 'I realised that at a fundamental level I'm good, we're all good, and you can trust that one part of yourself.' He realized if he was good, his body was good – 'the human body isn't offensive' he says. 'If that's what we're saying, as human beings, then it's not rational.'[22] On his return to his home town of Eastleigh, he asked the police if it was legal to walk the streets naked, but they were unable to give him a definite answer. He was to test the theory out for himself.

He set out on his quest to walk the length of Britain wearing only hiking boots and a rucksack. On his first venture, he kept off main roads and slept in fields and barns, and attracted little attention. However, on his second attempt, which was undertaken with his then girlfriend Melanie Roberts in 2005, media attention on him had increased significantly, and so had the interest of his followers and the police. At every stop he was arrested, imprisoned, fined, told to put his clothes back on and released. Bemused officers would turf him out of the station on the sly by the back door. On release, he would undress and carry on with his trek. Frequently police took him to the border of the next jurisdiction so they would not have to deal with him. He was usually taken into custody for Breach of the Peace, for 'conduct which does, or could, cause the public to be placed in a state of fear, alarm or annoyance'. Yet the police found it difficult to rustle up witnesses willing to testify that Gough's nakedness had that effect on them.

Scottish sheriffs twice found in Gough's favour and declared that no crime had taken place – either appearing naked in public, or in court (he had decided to defend himself so he could not be refused permission to enter court naked). Eventually, after further arrests, he refused to put his clothes on at all, so was not let out of prison. Because he refused to wear clothes in prison, he was not allowed to move freely about but was only let out of his cell for 30 minutes a day in order to undertake daily chores – post letters, empty his rubbish and have a shower. While such a stance for one's principals can be admired, the law does not take a similar view and continues to see naked bodies as potentially threatening to society. In March 2012, Gough was still in Her Majesty's Prison in Perth, Scotland, serving 657 days for Breach of the Peace and contempt of court. This was his seventeenth conviction in ten years and effectively he had been in custody for six years. He says he will only be released when he is allowed to walk home naked.

Voyeurism

Sexologists described voyeurism as the opposite of exhibitionism: watching people in the desire to glimpse their sexual organs or to see them having sex. Voyeurs often benefit from watching people who are unaware that they are being watched, the very secrecy providing an added frisson. In ancient Roman friezes and paintings, depictions of men and women having sex often included someone watching, standing behind a door or peering through a window; in paintings from Campania, someone else, usually a servant, is nearly always around in the pictures depicting couples having sex. The Roman poet Martial appreciated voyeurism when he advised one woman, 'Always with doors wide open and unguarded, Lesbia, you receive your lovers; you do not hide your vices. The beholder gives you more pleasure than the lover.'[23]

Peering through keyholes and gaps in walls seems to have be a pastime with a long history, if eighteenth-century bestiality and lesbianism trial reports are anything to go by. Many an upright citizen gave witness to the debauched behaviour of their neighbours after secretly peering through holes in their walls into adjacent homes. Richer families shared their homes with a bevy of servants who might sweep in at any time without a moment's notice. Domestic servants were particularly well versed as witnesses at trials because of their close proximity to the rest of the household. Servants sleeping in overhead garrets were often party to the sexual activities of the inner sanctum of the boudoir of their mistresses. No doubt this created a sense of danger; the possibility of being caught in a clandestine relationship merely heightened the excitement.

Watching sex was also used as a method of instruction for young people, who were encouraged to witness couples having intercourse. John Cleland was worldly enough to have known about the regime of brothels when he wrote *Memoirs of a Woman of Pleasure* (1748). He shows how the fictional heroine Fanny Hill began her sexual experience as a voyeur, watching through a hole in the wall while a couple had sex in the next-door room at the brothel where she was living. John Cannon (1684–1743) showed that this was not only a fiction. At sixteen, he drilled holes in a privy wall so he could masturbate while viewing the genitals of a maidservant living in the house next door. Similarly, a bunch of eighteenth-century libertines from

A man in the background watches a woman as a couple have sex through a glory hole. Illustration by Paul Gavarni in *The Places of Pleasure*, c. 1840.

Norwich planned their voyeuristic activities after they had drilled holes in their guests' bedrooms in order to watch them. They also peered through keyholes to watch the sexual activities of others.[24]

During the twentieth century, voyeurs were sent to psychiatrists for assessment and treatment,[25] but most doctors seemed to consider them harmless (if excessive masturbators). As with exhibitionism, women were even blamed for men's problems. One contemporary commentator of the 1960s exclaimed: 'Some men provoke complaints from women; but some women invite such attentions by dressing and undressing with needless publicity.'[26] During the 1950s and '60s, voyeurs were thought of as people who hung about parks, beaches and swimming pools hoping to catch a couple having sex or obtain a glimpse of genitalia. Others, known as Peeping Toms, peered through windows under cover of night, lurking in gardens. The term 'Peeping Tom' comes from the legend of Lady Godiva, when in 1044 Leofric, Earl of Mercia and Lord of Coventry, imposed excessive taxes on his tenants which his wife, sympathetic to the townspeople, asked him to remove. He agreed to do so only if she would ride naked through the town. Lady Godiva did so, but all the townspeople averted their gaze, except for Tom the tailor, who peeped though his window and was struck blind as a consequence.[27]

In the twenty-first century, voyeurism is no longer necessarily conducted outside the home but can be quietly indulged in while sitting at a computer. In the comfort of an easy chair, it is possible to watch adults copulating, overhear schoolgirls chatting with each other about sex, watch women undress, see men urinate or all manner of acts which involve a state of undress – none of it illegal. Housewives have set up webcams to expose themselves and get paid for their services by the minute. Home videos now compete with the higher end of the porn market: teenage girls masturbating, single women having sex with their boyfriends, suburban married couples sharing partners with their neighbours – all are easily accessible to view online. The concept of voyeurism has therefore been eroded to a large extent, although there are still those who seek their pleasures in a more 3D form. Striptease acts, pole dancing and naked bars all offer full frontal viewing for the price of a couple of pints. The acceptability of voyeurism now comes down to a matter of consent.

One of the most recent forms of displayer/spectator sport can be seen in a more equitable form of exhibitionism–voyeurism. Called 'dogging', this activity takes place in parked cars in public or semi-public places. It seems to have started in the UK in the 1990s when people began to visit a particular area such as a car park or lay-by in order to have sex in the car, but left on their lights so that other people could watch. This also indicated to other doggers that they

The Devil copulates with sleeping women while other devils watch, by Achille Devéria, c. 1835.

were part of the scene. The phenomenon has spread all over the West and several websites have sprung up to organize meetings between strangers to have sex in public places.

Strangely, non-consensual voyeurism did not become a criminal offence in the UK until 1 May 2004, and in Canada not until 2005. These laws also cover the offence of secret filming. In the U.S., the Video Voyeurism Prevention Act of 2004 amended the federal criminal code to provide that whoever knowingly videotapes, photographs, films, records by any means or broadcasts an image of a private area of an individual, without that individual's consent, shall be fined or imprisoned for not more than one year, or both. Increasingly the laws have had to be amended and updated to take into account new ways of becoming voyeuristic. Meanwhile, exhibitionists and voyeurs were to introduce new games to their sex play.

Coprophilia and Urolagnia

Coprophilia (or coprolagnia) and urolagnia are among the 'extras' that are involved in watching and displaying. Once again Sade tops the list in the exploration of perversions, describing coprophilic activities in *Justine, Juliette* and *The 120 Days of Sodom*. He was perhaps the first to mention rimming (licking of the rim of the anus) in *Philosophy in the Bedroom* (1795): one character, Dolamance, says, 'I am going to glide over this pretty little arsehole with my tongue.'[28] Sade's coprophilia has been seen as the ultimate expression of a sadistic superego, which represents an inversion of moral values, 'his ultimate challenge to the social order and to the authority of texts and tradition'.[29] Although Sade was said to have personally indulged in coprophilia, other authors were merely enthralled with it in their literature.

Jonathan Swift, author of *Gulliver's Travels* and Dean of St Patrick's Cathedral in Dublin, has had his writings on faecal matter dissected. Some critics have suggested that his descriptions of women defecting and urinating not only show Swift's obsession with those bodily excrements, but delineates his misogynism. An example can be seen in his poem 'The Lady's Dressing Room' (1732), in which Swift writes, 'Celia, Celia, Celia shits', as he imagines the woman he admires defecating. He sets her in her toilet scene in order to lower her status in his own mind and in the reader's imagination – he deflates the idealization of woman by her own bodily functions. In 'Strephon and Chloe' he similarly shows women in a poor light. He describes the misadventures of a wedding night, in which the bride's reticence towards sex results from a need for urination rather than any maidenly innocence, as is first assumed by her lover. Critics have suggested that the sound of 'drippings and droppings' in *Gulliver's Travels* may have originated from the overly intense preoccupation with his toilet functions as a child, which then infiltrated his ideas. But these analyses relied heavily on Freud's ideas on the perverse. Freud believed that obsession with faeces and urine stemmed from childhood events, a fixation taken into adulthood called 'psychosexual infantilism'. Other critics have suggested that Swift's misogyny possibly resulted from a rejection of marriage in 1696 by a woman he called 'Varina', who was thought to be Jane Waring, a respectable local girl who had inherited a small fortune. Swift wrote to her,

John Collier, *Lady Godiva, c.* 1897.

'Surely Varina, you have but a very mean opinion of the joys that accompany a true honourable unlimited love?'[30]

By the twentieth century, the psychiatrist Albert Moll was outlining his patients' cases of coprophilia; one youth hid in closets in order to catch young girls defecating, this desire having been with him since childhood. Another patient of Moll's described his desire in more detail, 'No-one can imagine what demonical joy I am possessed with at the thought of a beautiful naked boy whose abdomen is filled as the result of long abstinence from stool. To observe defecation would still further increase this pathological enjoyment.' He had the idea that he would feed the boy potable and coarse spread, which delayed defecation, and would thereby derive greater excitement when at last he watched it emerging from the boy's anus.

The association between faeces fixation and olfactory enjoyment was first noticed by Wilhelm Fliess (1858–1928), a specialist in otolaryngology, or ENT (ear, nose and throat), who associated many disorders to the nose. Fliess had developed a theory connecting reflex nasal neuroses to various pathological disorders, an idea which influenced Freud. In Freud's view, smell was most closely linked with faeces and with the 'anal phase' of psychological development. A few decades later, in the 1950s, Caprio applied the same theory

349

when he analysed a patient who had become fixated on faeces; as a ten-month-old child, he would smear his legs and thighs with faecal matter and expose his buttocks through the window. By the time he was between the ages of six and eight, he had developed a fixation with buttocks, while playing with little girls. It was then that he developed his olfactory fetishes, first picking up and sniffing his sister's underwear while masturbating, then graduating to sticking pencils up his anus and sniffing them. He admitted to becoming sexually aroused when he saw the buttocks of a naked woman. Caprio perversely labelled this behaviour 'masked homosexuality', though he does not give an explanation as to why homosexuality had anything to do with the case.[31] Sexologists were obviously still having some problems with their categorizing and labelling, even at this late stage.

More recently, coprophagia, or the eating of faeces, has been celebrated in an act called the 'Hot Lunch', where one person defecates into the mouth of another. There are variations on this activity: one – devised as a result of the invention of cling film – entails a person defecating on to cling film which is stretched over someone's open mouth. Then, on masturbating to ejaculation, he bursts through the cling film, giving the recipient a mouthful of faeces and sperm. Such coprophilic activities are no longer always regarded as a sexual perversion but are seen as an experience shared by gays and straights in sadomasochistic behaviour. Faecal-based activities may be taken up in adulthood as part of a preferred lifestyle choice rather than a result of strange childhood experiences: one study informs us that the 'participants were socially well-adjusted and that sadomasochistic behavior was mainly a facilitative aspect of their sexual lives, most participants being flexible in both sexual activities and sadomasochistic role-taking'.[32] Coprophilia is no longer necessarily always considered a perversion, but an alternative sexual predilection.

Others have shown an inclination for urolagnia (the love of urine), either through watching someone urinate or being urinated on. This activity is now sometimes referred to as a 'golden shower' or 'water sports'. This sort of attraction is evidently nothing new. In *My Secret Life*, supposedly written by a 'Victorian gentleman' and privately printed in 1895, the narrator, 'Walter', tells of his delight in watching women urinate. He combined his fetishism with voyeurism, drilling holes in the walls of hotels in order to watch, but frequently holes were already there, indicating that others had taken up the pastime before him. Although there were 'holes in doors as big as small peas', the women seemed oblivious to them.[33] There was therefore at least an understanding of such sexual pleasures in the nineteenth century.

Yet Krafft-Ebing said he had never known anyone who liked this activity. He had been unaware of the fact that his fellow sexologist Havelock Ellis was an urolagnist, although most of Ellis's women friends seem to have known about it. His companion in later life, Françoise Lafitte, called Ellis's urolagnia a 'harmless anomaly', defending it against objectors. Lafitte became his 'Naiad' (water nymph) and they both enjoyed the water play. She told a friend that Ellis liked to have her urinate as they walked down the street in the rain, and he once persuaded her to do it in a bustling crowd in Oxford Circus.[34] Unsurprisingly, therefore, Ellis was much more verbose on the subject in his writings. In *Analysis of the Sexual Impulse* he explained the special and intimate connection of sexual feelings and the energy of the bladder; 'in men . . . distention of the bladder favours tumescence by producing venous congestion . . . in women . . . a full bladder increases sexual excitement and pleasure.'[35] Ellis referred to this preference as 'undinism' and connected his urolagnia to an incident in his youth. At the age of twelve his mother took him to a zoological gardens and while walking down a solitary path he heard 'a very audible stream falling to the ground'. His mother had urinated on the ground and he instinctively turned round to see it. He admitted that many of his happiest moments were associated with being close to women when they urinated. In his *Studies*, he explored how a man might manage to urinate while inside a woman, bringing them both immense pleasure. He devoted over 100 pages to the subject of urolagnia.[36] In his book *Fountain of Life*, he eulogized urine when he wrote about the woman H.D. (probably the poet Hilda Doolittle), as he watched as 'a large stream gushed afar in the glistering liquid arch, endlessly it seemed to my wondering eyes, as I contemplated with enthralled gaze this prototypical statue of the Fountain of Life.'[37]

Usually there has been a distinction in sexologists' writings between being urinated on and drinking a woman's urine. Ellis's own experiments with urine no doubt led him to a better understanding

A case of coprophilia, from Marquis de Sade, *Juliette* (1797).

The artist as voyeur on a defecating man: Bernard Picart, *The Perfumer*, 16th century.

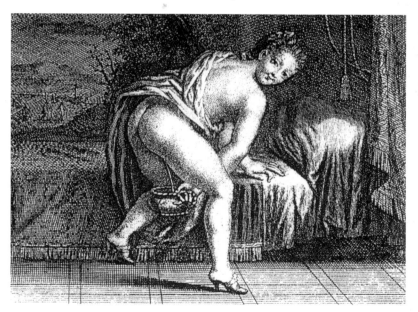

The Piss-pot, 17th century.

Woman urinates in pot. Attributed to Peter Fendi, *The Sovereign's Entrance,*
c. 1835.

of his patients. He commented on one patient, a healthy young
man who connected sexual excitement with ingesting urine. The
patient was diagnosed as a neurotic who had masturbated until he
was sixteen. By the time he was 30, he had graduated to drinking
women's warm urine. If a woman left his presence to urinate, he

felt compelled to follow her and would become greatly excited and ejaculate. He was oblivious to the taste; his fascination, according to Ellis, was based around erotic symbolism. For Ellis, the act took place when 'the lover's attention is diverted from the central focus of sexual attraction to some object or process which is on the periphery of that focus, or is even outside it altogether'. In other works it diverts the person away from its true course of 'sexual conjugation'.[38] This is revealing in that it shows that this was a time when heterosexual vaginal penetrative sex was seen as the only normal type of 'real' sex – even for the more enlightened sexologist. Anything other than this was classified merely as a 'diversion'. Yet drinking urine was not always necessarily connected to any sexual predilection. The practice of *amardi*, or ingesting one's own urine, has been a form of therapy for centuries, well known to Yogis. German doctor Johann Heinrich Zedler listed the many properties of urine: for example, 'inflammation can be helped by gargling with urine to which a bit of saffron had been added.' In the case of Ellis's patient, though, drinking women's urine seems to have been undertaken as a sexual obsession rather than for any health reason.

Although most of the cases of both coprophilia and urolagnia involved male subjects, some women indulged in a passion for faeces and urine. One of Albert Moll's cases was an extremely intelligent lesbian 'with various masculine tastes' and a feminine build. Although she had lived exclusively with one woman, finding her sexual satisfaction through cunnilingus, later her tastes developed to include coprophilia and urolagnia, as well as being bitten and whipped.[39]

Coprophilia and urolagnia also occurred in paraphilic infantilism, otherwise known as baby role-play or 'adult baby syndrome', and still continues today. This involves the participant dressing up and acting like a baby, usually donning giant nappies and sucking on large dummies. Lacy bonnets or romper suits are sometimes worn. The role-player may defecate or urinate into outsized nappies, thereby incorporating 'shits and showers' into fetish baby play. Adult babies crawl about on the floor and sometimes large cribs are involved to cater for their fantasies, which may also involve an adult or 'parent' role, played by another willing partner, who may bathe, dress, feed, scold or nurture the 'baby'. Paraphilic infantilism has been seen as reflecting the participant's underlying need to surrender adult responsibilities and be cared for for a short period of time, and are often seen as a welcome respite for men in high-powered jobs. Renowned brothel keeper Cynthia Payne reports that she threw 'specialized parties' at 32 Ambleside Avenue in Streatham, London, where judges, barristers and top professional men were among her best 'baby' clients.[40] The first public event for adult babies was celebrated at a 'Baby Week' occurring in San Francisco in the early 1990s. This suggests that it is a fairly new sort of sexual role-play. The DSM classes it as sadomasochistic, but the fetish does not necessarily take that path (although it can). Little is known about it in history but its very association with nappies and dummies indicates that it is a twentieth-century phenomenon. So far, no mentions of this activity have come to light further back in historical records.

Both coprophilia and urolagnia were, and still are, well-known in pornography. Offerings of 'golden showers' or 'water sports' are advertised on calling cards left by prostitutes in public telephone boxes. This method of advertising services has declined with the increase in mobile phone use and the corresponding dwindling numbers of telephone boxes. Now it is more common to meet like-minded people on the Internet.

The Flagellant and the Supplicant

Spanking or flogging has its own history, with all manner of weapons incorporated into its application – cat-o'-nine-tails, nettles, birches, riding crops, leather whips and switches among them. They have been applied to backs, buttocks, shoulders and loins in equal measure. Flogging has been used as a medicinal cure, as a penance for one's sins and as a punishment for a variety of crimes used everywhere from the nursery to boarding schools, the British Navy and European prisons. However, it was also used as a means of sexual gratification, with the scenarios involved often connected to religion, childhood beatings or some form of sadomasochistic fantasy. One of the earliest depictions can be seen in an erotic painting found in an Etruscan tomb, which shows a man caning a woman while he copulates with her from behind and she fellates another man. Another group to the right of the scene depicts a naked man and youth wielding a whip over a woman. At times of fertility festivals such the Lupercalia, young men chased women, whipping those who wanted to conceive.[41] Although whipping may be classed as part of the perversity of S&M

role-play, in the past it could be used with the aim of increasing fertility or by religious fanatics as a form of self-mortification.

From medieval times, flagellation was used on a regular basis as a penance for sins. Abbott Peter Damian seems to have inspired his fellow brothers in self-mortification during the eleventh century – so much so that he eventually had to intervene to prevent them from harming themselves. He was particularly concerned about sodomitical leanings within his abbey but seems not to have

A man watches excitedly as a woman urinates. From *Gathering Mushrooms*, 1930s.

357

recognized that the punishment itself might have the opposite effect to the one he intended and elicit erotic feelings. Other religious leaders, such as St Francis of Sales, displayed equal fervour for the whip. In 1604, he wrote to advise his friend Madame de Chantal, a member of the French aristocracy,

> As a third remedy, it would be good once in a while to take fifty or sixty strokes of the discipline, or only thirty, depending on what you can take. It's surprising how effective this measure has been for someone I know. Undoubtedly that's because the physical sensation distracts from interior suffering and calls for the the mercy of God.[42]

Some penitents, however, preferred more public admonishment. In Spain and Portugal it was common for a procession of flagellants to walk through the streets wearing high sugar-loaf head coverings, flagellating themselves as they went. Countess Marie Catherine D'Aulnoy described them during her trip to Madrid in 1685: 'They make terrible wounds on their shoulders, from which the blood flows in streams.'[43] Women gazed on in admiration and it was considered a blessing if the blood flew from the flagellants and landed on a lady's clothes.

Flogging was advocated as a medicinal cure for impotence by the sixteenth-century German physician Johann Heinrich Meibom (1590–1655). In his book *A Treatise of the Use of Flogging in Venereal Affairs*, first published in Latin in 1629, he explained how the stimulation of the circulation of blood helped no end in encouraging the penis to engorge. As an example, he related the story of fifteenth-century Count Pico della Mirandola, who hardened his whip in vinegar to make it all the more tormenting. The Count declared that a man has cause for complaint if a woman is 'too lenient with him, and is not fully satisfied of his desire unless the bloods flows'.[44] By the eighteenth century, the fantasies of the libertine gentleman were being accommodated in specialized brothels to cater for the increase in demand for flagellation. One contented customer wrote commending the actions of the particular flagellants offering their services – Mrs Brown, whom he found to have 'a pretty strong arm', Mrs Chalmers, who had 'a very experienced hand' and Mrs Wilson of Marylebone, who 'was no chicken at all'.[45]

Flagellation scene from Marquis de Sade, *Juliette* (1797).

Hannah Cullwick dressed as a slave.   A 19th-century birching.

During the nineteenth century, sexologists explored flagellation as a perversion, grouping it under the category of sadomasochism. One woman confessed to Krafft-Ebing that when she was only five she had been placed over the knee of her father's friend, who playfully pretended to whip her. From then on, she had fantasies about being a slave to the man she loved: 'I revel in the idea of being whipped by him, and imagine different scenes in which he beats me.' Nowadays, such slave-and-master relationships tend to involve sadomasochistic role-play, but in the past they were a stranger affair. One such was that of Arthur Munby and Hannah Cullwick. Munby was an upper-middle-class educated man, a barrister who typified the respectable Victorian gentleman. However, there was another side to him. In his spare time, he loved nothing more than to stroll around working-class areas to meet and to interview shop girls, rag-pickers, milliners, maids and prostitutes – all were of interest to him. He particularly liked those who undertook physical labour that made them dirty – faces, clothes and limbs covered in coal suited him just fine. Meanwhile, Cullwick was looking for a man to tell her what to do. Daughter of a Shropshire saddler, she took up menial jobs as a scullery maid. While employed in one large house in 1853, the cook urged her to see a play of Byron's called *Sardanapalus*, about a king who falls in love with his slave. This was to have a great influence on Cullwick and for ever after she took a delight in self-abasement. After she bumped into Munby on the street on her twenty-first birthday, they quickly became lovers. She wrote to him, 'I kissed you first when yo' axed me. It was to see what you mouth was like.' They quickly fell into their self-appointed roles in which she called him 'Massa', her interpretation of how a Negro slave would address his master. She would wash his feet 'for being useful and for showing humility and that I never wanted to be set up'. She did not want to be 'set up' as his mistress; her humility was her gift to him. Munby's reaction was to have her black up, naked but for a slave collar, and take photos of her. Both of them loved dirt. She took joy in cleaning the toilet, used her bare hands to clean the foot scraper free of horse manure, and licked Munby's boots clean while kneeling between his legs. She wrote: 'Stripp'd myself quite naked and put on a pair of old boots and tied an old duster over my hair and then I got up in the chimney.'[47] She loved to clean the kitchen and sweep the chimney, and he liked to hear about her chores. Their relationship was based on true affection, however, even though to the outside world it may have seemed a little bizarre. 'I showed my strength with carrying him around the room', she declared with gusto. Because of his position, they had to continue their affair clandestinely, but they married in secret and a deep and lasting love was established.

Munby and Cullwick enjoyed the roles of slave and master, but they did not fit the standard type of S&M relationship. Indeed, the slave-and-master roles were not mere enactments of sadomasochism play but were embedded in their whole relationship – he was a Victorian gentleman and she was a domestic servant. Munby was no sadist, but wanted the best for Cullwick. Nor was beating or violence part of their relationship, as far as we are aware. Cullwick liked to undertake subservient behaviour, yet she was a strong character and was by no means always passive. The class division between them added a dynamic to their relationship – rather than keeping them apart, it brought them together.

Sexual role-play is astounding in its diversity and its ability to brighten up languishing sex lives. Yet most of the applications of exhibitionism, voyeurism, coprophilia, urolagnia, flagellation and slave-and-master relationships have been considered sexually perverse. Surprisingly, though, the supposedly most innocuous of acts within this book – exhibitionism and voyeurism – were in the past the ones which were most likely to be practised without consent.

TWELVE

On Body Parts: Fellatio, Fetishism, Infibulations and Fisting

Then sticking closely to the Text,
He fairly *tipt the Velvet* next;
And straight the warm salival Juice,
Did wonderful Effects produce
Her Pulse beats High, her Blood's inflamed,
Symptoms so plain her Love proclaim'd . . .

The Ladies' Miscellany (1718)

Our genitalia are usually the first areas that come to mind when we think about having sex. The clitoris, labia and penis are all erogenous zones considered prominent sites of sexual stimulation. Yet at times in the past, in the Western world, touching these areas in certain ways was taboo. The ancient Greeks, for example, thought that fellatio and cunnilingus were unspeakable crimes, particularly when the object of desire – the clitoris or vagina – was attached to a menstruating woman. Similarly, in ancient Rome oral sex was seen as distasteful. Sextus Cloelius, the scribe and secretary to the Roman politician Clodius Pulcher, was criticized for performing cunnilingus on menstruating women; and Quintus Apronius, chief henchman to the corrupt magistrate of Sicily, Gaius Verres, was accused of having bad breath – in those days, a sure sign of a fellator or cunnilictor.

A gender distinction existed in relation to oral sex: it was considered much worse for a man to provide fellatio or cunnilingus than for a woman to provide the same service. Men should not go down on other men or women, as it would undermine their status. Yet both fellatio and cunnilingus, despite being considered vile, commonly took place. In Pompeii, good fellators were congratulated: 'Myrtis, you suck well', complimented one graffiti writer on the walls in the street; 'Secundus is an excellent fellator', declared another, although in truth these comments may just as well have been intended as insults. Prostitutes offered fellatio but it was not always cheap – it usually cost two 'asses', an 'ass' being the equivalent of an ounce of silver in ancient Rome. One prostitute, Euplia, thought it was worth more and requested five asses for her oral expertise.[1]

By the Middle Ages, oral sex was regarded as sinful both in Christian pastoralia and canon law, so it was basically off-limits. Any good Christian had to find other ways of sexual fulfilment. One Irish penitential suggested that seven years of penitence was appropriate for

Fellatio depicted on the rim of an Attic red-figure kylix, *c*. 510 BC.

A man performs cunnilingus on a woman. Roman fresco from the Suburban Baths in Pompeii, 1st century AD.

those who had committed fellatio. Yet little about actual oral sex is mentioned in history, although there are a few references in English sodomy and pornography trials in the seventeenth and eighteenth centuries. At a time when few people washed regularly and hygiene was at a low, oral sex was probably not an exciting prospect. A few jocular references were made to it in bawdy ballads, but these were usually about the bad smell.

By the nineteenth century, the verb 'gamahuche' was used for oral sex, possibly from the Greek *gamo*, 'to fuck', and the French *hucher*, 'to call' ('fuck call', although just like the English colloquialism 'blow job', it does not mean what it says). 'Gamahuching' had become rife in both French and British pornography and although pornography cannot be taken as actual proof of the practice, it does mean that there was an understanding that these events were taking place. According to the pornographic *The Lascivious Hypocrite* (*c.* 1891), boys in boarding schools reported 'plenty of details concerning mutual friggings, and pointed out pretty boys who could be found in each other's beds, and had been detected in gamahuching and every kind of excess'.[2] Likewise, in *The Quintessence of Birch Discipline*

A woman fellates
a man, Roman
oil lamp found
at Pompeii,
1st century AD.

('1870'), privately printed in London in 1883, the character Mrs M. receives cunnilingus from Sir F., 'gamahuching me most rapturously as he swallowed every drop as eagerly as a bee sucking honey'.[3] The anonymous *Romance of Lust* (*c.* 1876) similarly described the central characters' oral activities. 'We immediately began with a gamahuche, I taking Mary's cunt, while Lizzie crossed her legs over her head, and was gamahuched by Mary.' Likewise, the Victorian narrator 'Walter' in his 'memoirs' wrote of gamahuching but did not think it the best form of activity, claiming, 'I had early in life and indeed till middle age as told, been indifferent to having my cock sucked or gama-huched, had indeed forbidden French women – who do it as a matter of course, either as a preliminary or finish – to operate on me.'[4] His exception was licking 'virgin cunts'. There were therefore varied opinions on just how pleasant or unpleasant oral sex could be.

By the end of the nineteenth century, views had shifted slightly, but not to any great extent. Like some of the Greeks, Krafft-Ebing found oral sex repugnant, although he seems to have thought it was not too disturbing. He declared, 'Cunnilingus and fellatio (putting the penis into a woman's mouth) have not thus far been shown to depend upon psychopathological conditions', adding in apparent disgust, 'These horrible sexual acts seem to be committed only by sensual men who have become satiated or impotent from excessive

Fellatio and cunnilingus scenes from the Marquis de Sade, *Juliette* (1797).

Woman fellates man, from Peter Fendi, *Die Vorstellung im Theater* (1910).

A man fellates a woman in a group sex scene by Achilles Devéria for Alfred de Musset, *Gamiani*, c. 1848.

indulgence in a normal way.'[5] How far his feelings about oral sex were indicative of those of other Victorian and Edwardian men is hard to judge, but from the extant sources it is clear that there continued to be a wide variation of opinion. Certainly for sexologists it was not seen as befitting behaviour for an upstanding gentleman. Rather, it was seen to be the practice of men of low morality or those who were mentally unbalanced or already sexually satiated. Ellis linked cunnilingus to the activities of foreigners (those from Zanzibar, or the Slavs from the Balkans) and lesbians. He did, however, concede that 'cunnilingus and fellatio as practised by either sex, are liable to occur among healthy or morbid persons, either in heterosexual or homosexual relationships'.[6] Nonetheless, he warned that these oral activities became perversions if they were practised to the exclusion of 'normal sexual relationships'. Little had changed by the mid-twentieth century, when one psychiatrist stated of one of his patients, 'The wish to degrade women is evidenced in his wanting to have women perform fellatio which he links up with his incestuous relationship to his mother and sisters.' It made him feel as though he was 'the man and the master'.[7] Krafft-Ebing would no doubt have been surprised at the extent of current-day practice of oral sex, which is now seen as part of a natural, healthy sex life.

Fetishism

Any obsession with certain parts of the body – such as fat, hair, hands, feet, neck and so on – was labelled as fetishism by sexologists. These fetishisms could lead to licking, stroking, sucking, infibulating or otherwise inserting into or ejaculating on to the focus of lust. Many fetishists felt a complete lack of the control over their impulses, and many sought help from psychologists and psychiatrists.

It was the French psychologist Alfred Binet who first identified sexual fetishism in 'Le Fétichisme dans l'amour' (*Revue Philosophique*, 1887) and saw it as a predominant or exclusive interest in inanimate objects or a particular body part, a type of deviation in which 'the person's libido becomes attached to something that constitutes a symbol of the love-object'. He remarked, 'in the life of every fetishist, there can be assumed to have been some event which determined the association of lustful feeling with the single impression.' He believed that fetishism was normal, declaring, 'everybody is more or less a fetishist in love'. Identifying between the *petit* and the *grand* fetishism, he saw the latter as a type of 'genital madness'. Both Krafft-Ebing and Binet examined many fetishists and believed that a fetish could be traced back to one's youth. Usually, the connection with the love object happened at the time of first sexual stimulus, or first masturbation. Krafft-Ebing claimed that in fetishism 'the pronounced preference for a certain portion of the body of persons of the opposite sex, particularly for a certain form of this part, can attain great psychosexual importance.'[8] He also identified two sorts of fetishists: *body* fetishists, who are obsessed with particular body parts such as hands, feet or hair; and *object* fetishists, who might have an obsession with anything from shoes, boots, stockings and underwear to materials such as fur, leather or velvet. He stated that we should not regard the fetishist as a monster of excess, but a monster of weakness. More often than not, people were worried about having their fetishes revealed, which made them feel guilty. The problem often led to depression and suicidal feelings.

Initially, medico-legal experts opined that fetishism was a hereditary predisposition, and that acts were involuntary, impulsive and overpowering. A fetishist had no option but to follow his inclinations.[9] Many sexologists, including Krafft-Ebing, believed fetishism to result from a psychopathic constitution which could arise in combination with other paraphilias, such as sadism, masochism or inversion. As with other acts perceived as perverted by sexologists, frequently patients' case notes refer to epileptic sisters, nervous mothers, insane uncles and domineering fathers. Echoing many of his fellow psychologists, Krafft-Ebing surmised that 'pathological fetishism seems to arise only on the basis of a psychopathic condition that is for the most part hereditary, or on the basis of existent mental disease', although, significantly, he did believe that there was a 'single impression which had determined the association of lustful feelings with the object of desire'.[10]

While Krafft-Ebing had outlined two kinds of fetishism, Havelock Ellis went further and described three different classifications of what he called 'erotic symbolism':

1 Parts of the body (normal) – hands, feet, breasts, nates
   [buttocks], secretions

Parts of the body (abnormal), lameness, squinting,
    smallpox scars, paedophilia, presbyophilia [love of the
    old], necrophilia
2 Inanimate objects – gloves, shoes, stockings, handker-
    chiefs, underwear
3 Acts (active) – whipping, cruelty, exhibitionism
    Acts (passive) – being whipped, masochism, voyeurism

For body fetishists, sexual intercourse was not necessarily the main aim. They could ejaculate by merely placing the object next to their body or their genitals and masturbating. On the other hand, some male fetishists were despairing that they could not have 'normal' intercourse with their wife because their fetish had such a hold over them. Some men took the object of their fetishism to bed with them in the hope that it would stimulate them if they felt it while having intercourse with their wives. In the case of the object fetishist, the item did not need to be connected to a particular person. Further explanations were to come in psychiatry, when Freud developed an interest in explaining fetishism. He followed the line that fixations developed in childhood rather than believing that they developed as a result of inherited family traits, or 'taints'.

Although the labelling of fetishism occurred only at the end of the nineteenth century, all kinds of fetishisms have been described over the years, involving everything from handkerchiefs, corsets and knickers to shoes, ribbons and buttons. In the medieval period, people would not have had a name for desires for a particular body part or object, although they may have experienced them. The Church's guide to illicit sexual acts as used in penitentiaries made no mention of any sort of sexual behaviour which could be identified as fetishism. Since the Church authorities expressed prohibitions on most other sexual acts (dorsal sex, fellatio, masturbation, anal sex and so on), this lack of interest might indicate the Church's ignorance of such possibilities. However, the Church often feigned ignorance of some sexual behaviour of which it disapproved so long as it brought on 'normal' vaginal penetrative sexual intercourse between a married man and woman. This may have been the case with fetishism; if a man or woman had a fetish, the Church would be unconcerned so long as the protocol of ejaculation into a vagina was followed and conception ensued.

One constant fetishism, stretching from medieval times to its labelling, was an obsession with hair. Fetishism around a woman's hair can be seen in the legends of King Arthur. Chrétien de Troyes' *Lancelot, or the Knight of the Cart*, written in the 1170s, was one of the first books to describe the story of Lancelot's adulterous love for Guinevere, but it also describes his love of her hair. After finding a comb and discovering that the hair on it is Guinevere's, Lancelot nearly faints. He extracts the hairs from her comb, careful not to break any of them:

> Never will the eye of man see anything receive such an honour as when he begins to adore these tresses. A hundred thousand times he raises them to his eyes and mouth, to his forehead and face: he manifests his joy in every way, considering himself rich and happy now. He lays them in his bosom near his heart, between his shirt and the flesh. He would not exchange them for a cartload of emeralds and carbuncles.[11]

Can this fascination with a part of the body of his loved one be called fetishism, or is it merely adoration? Was Guinevere's hair a fetish object? In the end, Lancelot was not fascinated with anybody else's hair, only Guinevere's – and the hair only became a love object when he discovered it was Guinevere's. From his position as a knight, he could only love her from a distance, so her hair became a sexual substitute for the whole of her body (although, of course, the lovers would break this code of honour). Since the relationship of Lancelot to Guinevere is the one of a subject to his queen, a position of subservience should be taken up by him; a knight must revere his lady. Courtly codes dictated behavioural rules; men were subject to obeying the seemingly capricious whims of ladies in order to win their love, and knights were continually given dangerous quests in order to prove their dedication. Adoration of Guinevere's hair could be safely undertaken from a noble knight's position without the idea of 'fetishism'.

Yet similar obsessions with hair were detected in the late 1890s, when sexologists established a long list of similar sexual focuses on particular body parts. One of the first people to be recorded as having a problem with hair fetishism was a patient of Krafft-Ebing's.

As a ten-year-old boy, he began to have erotic feelings at the sight of a woman's hair, particularly the hair of young girls. He was soon taught to masturbate by his schoolfriends. His sister's twelve-year-old girlfriend would kiss and hug him and her hair pleased him enormously. The connection between hair and erotic feeling became established in his mind and grew more powerful with his advancing years. Thick, black, luxuriant hair made him particularly excited, especially if he could kiss and suck it. While out on the streets, he began to kiss women's heads, then hurry home to masturbate. Once he was compelled to cut off a lock of a girl's hair. His obsession eventually led him into alcoholism, resulting in an epileptic attack, and he was hospitalized. This patient was something of an anomaly for his doctor. Previously, Krafft-Ebing had believed that most of his 'perverted' patients had to have some sort of hereditary disability, but this man was from a healthy family.

More easily explained was another of Krafft-Ebing's cases, a man who took sexual gratification from despoiling women's hair. He fitted perfectly with Krafft-Ebing's psychological profile for fetishists, as both his parents suffered from mental disabilities – his father was temporarily insane and his mother was of a nervous disposition. After suffering a febrile disease, the patient's nervous system had been badly affected. Soon after his illness in August 1889, he was arrested in the Trocadéro in Paris with a pair of scissors in his pocket, forcibly cutting off a lock of a young girl's hair. On searching his home, police found 65 'switches', or tresses of hair, neatly sorted into packets. He admitted that when he held the tresses he had cut from the women's heads, he became sexually excited. Another hair fetishist admitted that it did not matter what a woman looked like so long as she had ravishing tresses, preferably 'a woman with over a yard of jet black hair'. He fantasized about women pulling each other's hair and liked to pull his wife's hair during intercourse. For the medics, the fact that he performed cunnilingus was proof of his masochism. Bizarrely, his fantasies of lesbians performing cunnilingus were given as evidence of his latent homosexuality.[12]

A more historically specific fetishism had been in vogue with the wearing of nosegays and carrying of handkerchiefs. In the eighteenth century a glove or a flower was enough for a person to be overcome with sexual desire. Monstrous bouquets of flowers worn on the lapel could make both men and women swoon. One prostitute known for running a flagellation brothel told of a scene with another woman: 'Then she began kissing me again, and smelling at my nosegay, or rather my sweet broom, the scent of which seemed to augment her lust: she passed her hands all over my body, and in fact acted with me as men do with women to excite their desire before they enjoy them.'[13] Nosegays were explicitly connected to sex, the larger the better. Huge bouquets worn on the lapels, known as 'nosegays of lechery', became a sign of the female flagellant.

By Victorian times, ladies' handkerchiefs were of particular erotic value, presumably because of their connection with gentility. Psychiatrist Albert Moll provided an example of the power the wave of a hanky could produce. One woman told him, 'I know of a certain gentleman, and when I see him at a distance I only need to draw out my handkerchief so that it peeps out of my pocket, and I am certain that he will follow me as a dog follows its master.'[14] One 32-year-old baker's assistant was more persistent. He admitted to stealing between 80 and 90 ladies' handkerchiefs, but cared only for handkerchiefs belonging to attractive women. When arrested in August 1890, on searching his house, police found over 400 ladies' handkerchiefs and he confessed that he had already burned two bundles of them.[15]

Foot fetishism is probably one of the most common fetishes to persist through the ages. Closely connected to obsession with shoes, it is found more or less exclusively among men (although the obsession of many women with shopping for shoes has been the butt of jokes – Imelda Marcos was particularly noted for her gigantic shoe collection). As with so many other predilections, this one can be found in antiquity. In ancient Greece, Antiphanes finds pleasure in a woman rubbing his feet. Lucius, the son of the Roman emperor Vitellius, carried round one of Messalina's sandals. Suetonius tells us that Lucius 'begged Messalina to grant him the tremendous privilege of removing her shoes; whereupon he would nurse the right shoe inside his gown, and occasionally take it out to kiss it'.[16] In medieval literature, the courtly poem *Le Roman de la rose*, immensely popular in thirteenth-century France, rhapsodizes about the loveliness of some women's feet – the ideal foot was narrow, high-arched and long-toed. The character of the jealous husband recognizes the delight a woman's feet can evince when he berates his wife for showing off her feet to other men, 'Besides, you wear your shoes so tight that you often raise your dress to show your feet to those knaves.'[17]

By the eighteenth century, shoe fetishism had taken hold and many men and women admired other's perfect feet. Restif de la Bretonne (1734–1806) admitted to an admiration of girls' shoes, and in his first literary success, *Le Pied de Fanchette*, the narrator is attracted to a girl he sees in the street sporting charming shoes. Bretonne traced his fetishism (although he did not call it such) back to when he was four and found himself admiring the feet of a young girl where he lived. He preferred his girls neat and clean and

A scene of leather-and-PVC-clad S&M play.

was especially entranced by a young girl from another town 'whose shoes were of a fashionable cut, with buckles, and who was a charming person besides'. The love of his life, Collette Parangon, provided him with the perfect opportunity for admiration of her feet. She 'possessed a charm which I could never resist, a pretty little foot; it is a charm which arouses more than tenderness'. He went into raptures about her shoes, with descriptions of 'green heels and a pretty rosette'. On one occasion it became too much to bear, and when she left the room he masturbated into her shoe. He confessed, 'my lip pressed one of these jewels, while the other, deceiving the sacred end of nature, from excess of exultation replaced the sex object.'[18]

By the end of the nineteenth century, foot fetishism had been categorized by sexologists and was seen as a worthy topic of medical exploration in its own right. One 29-year-old man described exactly how his obsession had developed. Like so many others, his family had a medical history – his mother was a neuropath, his father was a diabetic and he himself was a nervous man. He remembered distinctly that at the age of six he had had his first sexual stirrings when watching women's feet. By the age of sixteen, he was creeping into his sister's bedroom to kiss her feet. At eighteen, he had full sexual intercourse with a woman. At 25 everything suddenly changed and he became homosexual. 'The naked foot was his charm. He often felt impelled to follow men in the street, hoping to find an occasion to take off their shoes.' His doctor saw his constant masturbation as problematic, suggesting that 'excessive masturbation brought about neurosis and invert sexuality'.[19] As a cure, the patient was subjected to hydrotherapy (cold-water treatment) at a specialist institute and, as a result, regained some of his inclination towards women. He was advised to use his fetish as a 'bridge', which meant that he was allowed to indulge his fetishism for feet while having 'normal' intercourse with a woman, but only if he abstained from masturbation and 'perverse connection with men'. Unsurprisingly, his treatment had no long-term effect and he relapsed into being irresistibly attracted to farm labourers and tramps 'whom he paid for the favour of kissing their feet'.

More sadistic methods of enjoyment were found by employing feet as a weapon. One man told Ellis how he liked to be stepped on by a woman's foot. The desire was not for intercourse but to lie on the floor and be trampled on. The patient admitted,

The treading should be inflicted for a few minutes all over the chest, abdomen, groin, and lastly on the penis; which is, of course, lying along the belly in a violent state of erection, and consequently too hard for the treading to do damage to it. I also enjoy being nearly strangled by a woman's foot.[20]

Another patient confessed to having been trampled underfoot by at least 100 women of good social standing who would never have dreamt of having intercourse with him.

By the mid-twentieth century, a new group of researchers were questioning these fetishisms and trying to uncover what caused them. In a study in 1965, sex researchers suggested that the origins of fetishisms were to be found in restrictive childhood sex play by female peers, the fetishism developed by way of compensation. People have different degrees of fetishism, from a slight preference to a strong extreme obsession which overtakes their lives, where sexual functioning is no longer possible without the fetishistic quality. The fetishist traditionally was found to be a loner, usually male, someone who feels inadequate and who is lacking in social skills with the opposite sex.[21] Meanwhile, in the 1980s, societies and clubs were set up in adoration of the foot, such as The Foot Fraternity, an organization for homosexual and bisexual foot fetishists. This organization was the subject of a survey in 1995 in which 262 of its members (all men) were interviewed. This study is invaluable in that it summed up many previous studies ranging from the 1950s through the 1980s tracing the profile of fetishists. It is also important in that it negates some of the earlier studies. Fetishism was no longer seen to be a result of hereditary mental disease, but to have emerged through learned behaviour and experience.[22] Other analysts found that in cases of sexual deviancy, men tended to come from repressive families. A compulsion overtook them, forcing them to undertake the deviant behaviour, followed by a feeling of shame, guilt and anxiety, a fact already revealed in the many cases by earlier sexologists. Yet over 80 per cent of the interviewees believed that foot fetishism did *not* relate to negative experiences in childhood; 45 per cent thought that the fetishism was linked to pleasurable experiences during childhood. Many men had their first feelings of sexual pleasure with a member of the family's feet (fathers, uncles, brothers), the experience connected to innocent activities such as tickling or washing feet, or through experiences with the feet of others in their peer group. Masturbatory fantasies reinforced their fetish.

Other items of clothing besides shoes could also be the focus of fetishistic tendencies. Male transvestites have been obsessed with beautiful dresses since at least the seventeenth and eighteenth centuries.[23] However, the item of obsession has changed according to fashion. What was de rigueur in the nineteenth century – say corsets, handkerchiefs and gloves – has changed for the modern-day transvestite to stockings, suspenders and knickers from Victoria's Secret or similar lingerie stores. Cases of specific underwear preferences – for example, the wearing of lace knickers, bras and suspenders – were more common in the twentieth century than in earlier periods. In his study *Transvestites* (1910), Magnus Hirschfeld found that transvestites were often obsessed with items of women's clothing, such as corsets, gloves or jewellery. Some collected buckles and belts, or veils. All had an obsession with women's clothes in general rather than one item in particular. Hirschfeld himself saw the obsession of transvestites as dressing as a woman from 'head to toe'. It was not the item itself in its abstract form that was the object of attraction, but the whole ensemble, which was 'loved as part of themselves'.[24]

Often various sorts of fetishism were mixed and were not always confined to one particular item, as seen in Jerome Henry Brudos, who became both a shoe and an underwear fetishist. His fetishes were so intense that they resulted in murderous behaviour and he became known as 'The Shoe Fetish Slayer'. His problems started from the day he was born, 31 January 1939, as his mother had wanted a girl. To indulge her fantasy, she dressed him up in little girl's clothing, belittled him, abused him and generally treated him with disdain. Initially the family moved around but eventually settled in Salem, Oregon. It was here, when he was only five years old, that Brudos began to fetishize shoes after finding high heels in a junkyard. He began to steal underwear from his neighbours and spent his adolescence undergoing psychotherapy in various psychiatric hospitals. He then moved on to attacking women, choking them and stealing their shoes and underwear. After threatening to stab a woman if she did not comply with his orders to perform certain sexual acts, he ended up in Oregon State Hospital. Doctors concluded that his sexual fantasies stemmed from his hatred of his mother and he was diagnosed as schizophrenic. Despite his mental instability, he was released and went on to graduate from high school. When he was about 21, he married a seventeen-year-old girl who bore him two children. His eccentricities began to show when he started to make her do housework naked except for high heels while he took photographs of her. He began stalking women, and soon graduated to murder, hiding the bodies in his garage – he bludgeoned four women between 1968 and 1969 while dressed in women's clothing. In order to try out the shoes he collected, he kept the left foot of one of his victims.[25] Even after he was in prison, he continued to collect shoes, writing to shoe companies to ask for pairs. He died from liver cancer in prison on 28 March 2006. This sort of murderous extreme is, however, relatively rare and fetishism is usually an innocuous activity.

The fetish object has often been associated with a particular time and place. Hence gas masks became a fetish object for those who had experienced unusual or unexpected sexual experiences during or just after the Second World War. In the case of fetishism of fur, leather, rubber, plastic, rubber, pvc, latex and so on, fetishists revel in wearing the specific material. Clothing made out of these materials has become particularly popular in s&m sex play. Such play might combine multiple fetishisms, such as the wearing of masks made of leather, shoes of suede and silk underwear.

'Chubby-chasing' became a hobby for those obsessed with fat. Whether this has to do with the after-effects of post-Second World War rationing or with the current preoccupation with diet has yet to be ascertained. In certain poorer countries, fatness is connected to wealth but in the West it is thinness that is usually admired. Some fetishism for particular body parts is more problematic and can be dangerous. Neck obsessions, for example, have led to choking or strangling. Known as hypoxyphilia, strangulation for sexual pleasure has been classed as a paraphilia in a sub-category of sexual masochism in psychiatrists' diagnostic manuals. Consenting controlled strangulation was introduced into s&m role-play as it induces a semi-hallucinogenic state called hypoxia. Combined with orgasm, it provides a rush akin to a cocaine high, so pleasurable that it is highly addictive. Also known as asphyxiophilia, or sexual asphyxia, this potentially lethal sexual practice refers to sexual arousal that is produced while reducing the oxygen supply to the brain. These activities have frequently been known to lead to fatalities and can be traced back at least as far as the eighteenth century.

Leather bondage hood.

Studded leather codpiece.

Jonathan Swift wrote of 'Swinging by session upon a Cord, in order to raise artificial Extasies', but this seems to have been referring to non-asphyxial swinging. Sade also wrote about hanging in *Justine* where Roland hangs the heroine, wanting her to enjoy the pleasures he has experienced through strangulation. He declares, 'it's the rope that's waiting for me: 'tis the same delight I am pleased to have women savour: that's the one will serve my undoing; I am firmly persuaded as I possibly can that this death is infinitely sweeter than cruel.' He is still at the stage of experimentation, but appears to have discovered the method of erotic auto-asphyxiation, 'I want to find out whether it is not very certain this asphyxiation impels, in the individual who undergoes it, the erectory nerve to produce an ejaculation.' He insists on hanging himself, assisted by Thérèse, who describes as she watches as 'rapid jets of semen spring nigh . . . without any assistance whatsoever from me'.[26]

Few cases of real-life auto-asphyxiation have been passed down to us in history. It is possible that public hanging put people off the idea of trying it out for themselves in great numbers (the last public hanging in England was in 1868). Seeing the victims evacuating their bodily fluids and writhing and jerking could not have been a pleasant sight. However, there are two interesting cases of self-strangulation in the eighteenth century. One involved the Czech musician and composer Frantisek Kotzwara, who famously died after asking a prostitute to hang him. Unfortunately, she left him too long and he died. The other case related to a 'Reverend Manacle', who administered to those awaiting death sentences. He showed one female prisoner how exciting hanging could be, but later died after trying it one too many times.[27] There may well have been more cases of auto-asphyxiation that were were mistakenly judged to be accidental strangling of a non-sexual sort. It seems that the practice only took off in any significant numbers in the twentieth century.[28]

Sometimes auto-asphyxiation was a shared activity, but even then it was dangerous. When 62-year-old actor Albert Dekker was found dead in his Hollywood home on 5 May 1968, he was naked, kneeling in the bath, with his head in a noose hooked up to the shower rod. Although the coroner ruled a verdict of autoerotic asphyxiation, it is unlikely that Dekker had undertaken the task alone. There were no signs of forced entry, but money and camera equipment had been stolen, indicating that he had brought someone to his apartment.

Also, he was blindfold, gagged and handcuffed and had sexually explicit words scrawled on his body in red lipstick, hardly an act of a solitary man.

Sexual advice manuals such as Alex Comfort's *The Joy of Sex* (1972) warned against the activity, while magazines like *Hustler* published letters from individuals who had tried it out. One woman wrote in to the 'Advice and Consent' column telling how her lover had taught her to apply pressure to his neck with her knees until he lost consciousness. The editorial warned against 'The Orgasm of Death' in a two-page article on the subject, saying it 'kills 200–300 people a year in the U.S.'[29]

Strangulation to orgasm was often undertaken by men alone in their apartments or hotels and sometimes involved cross-dressing. One such case of auto-asphyxiation took place on 7 February 1994 when Stephen Milligan, the Member of Parliament for Eastleigh, Hampshire, was found dead in his flat in Black Lion Lane, Chiswick. He had self-bondaged with an electrical flex bound round one ankle. It ran up his body and was wound around his neck with the other end close by one hand. He was naked but for a pair of stockings and suspenders and a cover over his head. A piece of orange was found in his mouth. Such deaths occur usually as a result of a failure of the get-out strategy – when people misjudge their dizziness or state of semi-consciousness and fail to act quickly enough to release themselves. Generally, at the scene of death, sexual paraphernalia or pornography has been found – bondage-gear hoods, masks, blindfolds, gags, enema tubes, electric wires or mirrors in which to watch what is happening.

Love of Inanimate Objects

A desire for a relationship with an inanimate representation of a human figure is described in the story of Pygmalion, in which a sculptor falls in love with the statue he has carved and names her Galatea. He prays to Venus, the goddess of love, requesting that she bring his statue to life, and Venus grants his wish. According to one anecdote, Klisyphos of Samos was known to have sexually assaulted the statue of a goddess. The 'Statue Syndrome', otherwise known as agalmatophilia, was recognized when sexologist Krafft-Ebing recorded a case in 1877 of a gardener falling in love with a statue of the Venus de Milo and being discovered while attempting coitus with it. But at least one sex researcher denied that it ever existed, except in pornographic fantasy.[30]

The passion for statues was replaced with more pliant models. Full-bosomed life-size latex or rubber dolls were produced to provide passive sex for lonely men. The dolls had open spaces for penetration to take place in either the 'mouth' or 'vagina' orifices. Perhaps one of the most ingenious rubber dolls is described in the pornography *La Femme endormie* (1899), which purports to be the story of Paul Molaus, a wealthy man of about 40 from Bois-Colombes. Inspired by the story of Pygmalion, and having become disillusioned with his mistresses (and with women generally, one assumes), he asks a designer to make the perfect lover. The creator himself describes her perfection:

> I paid particular attention to her interior, which is fitted with three basins, several boxes and cylinders, and a number of little ducts, so as to permit the circulation of all sorts of products that it would please the experimenter to introduce into the silent goddess's body. By pulling certain curls of her hair, her eyes and lips can be made to move. One can place her in every imaginable position: standing up, seated, kneeling, lying prone, lying on her back. By pushing the navel, one provokes indulations in every part of her body. Her sexual organs are as perfect as those of any live woman. To warm up her body, all one had to do is to pour boiling milk or hot water in sufficient quantities into the different receptacles located under her head, behind her breasts, in her buttocks, stomach, leg, etc.[31]

Similar lifelike dolls were recorded by Iwan Block, who knew of a manufacturer of rubber dolls, both male and female. He claimed,

> More especially are the genital organs represented in a manner true to nature. Even the secretion of Bartholin's glans is imitated, by means of a 'pneumatic tube' filled with oil. Similarly, by means of fluid and suitable apparatus, the ejaculation of the semen is imitated. Such artificial human beings are actually offered for sale in the catalogue of certain manufacturers of Parisian rubber articles.[32]

A basic model of blow-up doll.

A more life-like, silicone sex doll.

Since then all sorts of variations of sex dolls have been produced, from cheap plastic inflatable ones (which barely resemble dolls, let alone humans) to life-size ones made out of silicone, which appear amazingly human. They can be brought online from specialized companies. These 'real life' dolls have human hair and are covered in a material that feels like human skin to the touch.

The relationship between people and rubber dolls was made all the more poignant in the film *Lars and the Real Girl* (2007). The lead male character, the lonely, girlfriendless Lars, invests in a lifelike doll, takes her everywhere and treats her as a real girlfriend. For the sake of Lars, everyone in the community treats her as his real girlfriend, tolerating his taking her for nights out drinking, going bowling with her and voting her on to various committees. He eventually discards her when he finds a real girlfriend.

More recently a new kind of sexuality has made the news with people who call themselves 'objectum sexuals' (os), or 'people who have loving relationships with objects'. The British television documentary *Married to the Eiffel Tower*, directed by Agnieszka Piotrowska (2008), claimed that there are only about 40 such people in the world, but this may be because they keep quiet about their inclinations as a result or from fear of persecution. Three women who classified themselves as os were interviewed about their sexual orientation in this documentary, each of them telling how they had fallen in love with objects. Erika LaBrie became a world-champion archer after she fell in love with her archery bow, which she called Lance. She says she was 'attracted to him because of his looks'. Her close relationship with her bow allowed her to become a champion archer but her expertise in archery began to fail when her attraction for her bow diminished. She then fell in love with the Eiffel Tower and went through a marriage ceremony with it in 2007, which was performed on the tower itself in front of a group of her friends. She took the married name of Erika La Tour Eiffel. Before this she had a three-year relationship with the Golden Gate Bridge in San Francisco. She then fell in love with the Berlin Wall. When challenged about her behaviour on *The Tyra Banks Show*, she asserted: 'I am not broken.'[33]

Objectum sexuals say they have been derided and treated as if they were mad. In the documentary, all of the women were portrayed as profoundly distressed and shown to have suffered some sort of rejection or familial dysfunction in their childhood. Erika was discharged from the army for post-traumatic stress disorder. In the programme, she admitted that she identified with the Berlin Wall and had been built up only to be torn down. She received no love from her parents and was rejected all her life. To encourage herself, she says, 'Stand up and be yourself. I am the Berlin Wall.' Identifying with the thing she loves, she tells the Wall, 'I wish I were an object like you.' Aurita from Sweden was at first competition for Erika, as she was also in love with the Berlin Wall (it had replaced her affections for a guillotine). However, although they were initially jealous of each other, Aurita and Erika made friends and, since they are both polyamorous (having multiple lovers), they have agreed to share the Berlin Wall as a lover. Another polyamorous objectum sexual, Amy, fell in love with the Empire State Building and the World Trade Center, and grieved her loss of the latter as one would a lover. She also admitted to coming from a dysfunctional family. Her sexual encounter with a church organ upset one pastor, who banned her from the congregation, but the succeeding cleric was more understanding of her love of the church banisters, even allowing her to cut part of one out and take it home.

Professionals have classified the 'condition' as a paraphilia, but the people themselves prefer to see it as an orientation. Erika has since gone on to found OS Internationale, an organization aimed at educating people about objectum sexuality and offering support. She dismissed the documentary as misleading, saying that she was manipulated into confessing a childhood trauma. She says that her OS was evident before this trauma, which she believes has nothing to do with her sexual orientation. She continues to strive for an acceptance of objectum sexuality.[34]

Infibulations and Insertions

Historically speaking, dildos were perhaps the inanimate objects most commonly inserted into body parts. Such insertions were considered sodomy and seen as a perversion of 'natural' sex. Given the responses of judges in lesbian trial reports, such objects were regarded as the height of obscenity in the eighteenth century. As seen in the case of Katherina Hertzeldorfer, women 'acting the male role' showed ingenuity in designing their own dildos.[35] They used wooden poles wrapped in material, or stitched leather stuffed with old rags.

One tribade's self-fashioned dildo was described at some length in *The True History and Adventures of Catherine Vizzani* (1755). After Vizzani's death, the book tells us, 'The leathern Machine, which was hid under the Pillow, fell into the Hands of the Surgeon's Mates in the Hospital, who were immediately for ripping it up, concluding that it contained Money, or something else of Value, but they found it stuffed only with old Rags.'[36] Glass dildos show up in pornographic depictions, usually consisting of glass injectors, filled with milky, warm liquid, with a bulb attached to allow for the simulation of ejaculation. Adverts for machines thought to be disguised vibrators were sometimes placed in respectable women's magazines of the 1950s, with pictures of gadgets that looked like Bakelite hairdryers. A more advanced vaginal manipulator called the 'Sybian Saddle' was invented in the 1980s: it is a machine that simulates sex for women. A motorized rod protrudes from a hole while the woman sits on the saddle accepting it. At the cost of £1,265, despite free next-day delivery, it is one of the more expensive options. One of the most popular dildos is a vibrator dubbed the 'Rabbit', which was introduced in the 1990s and pulses in various ways to give stimulation to the clitoris at the same time as providing stimulation inside the vagina. Nowadays,

Dildos and a penis assister, 19th century.

gone are the perceptions of vibrator use as a perversity, and many a modern woman keeps one in her bedside cabinet.

Other objects have been used as attachments to the genitals and erogenous zones for both convenience and pleasure. In the West, infibulations took a different form. For example, in ancient Greece, athletes used penis infibulations with string through the foreskin mainly in order to tie the penis out of the way when they exercised naked. These were known as *kynodesmes*, or dog ties.[37] Romans used infibulation as a method of preventing an erection, closing the foreskin off with their equivalent of a large safety pin or ring, or thread. Singers, athletes and entertainers were often infibulated to prevent an untoward erection disturbing their artistic performances. Generally, though, the Greeks and Romans did not go in for body modification through piercing, tattoos or resculpting. Instead they went for a more protracted form of body alteration that they inflicted on small children, confining them in jars or small cages, stunting their growth and turning them into midgets. Midgets and dwarfs were considered comical but were also thought to be good at oral sex. Indeed, Pliny believed a man could easily develop an obsession with dwarfs.[38]

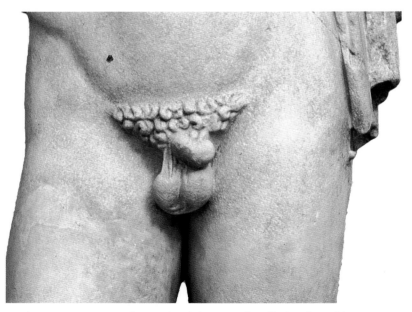

The poet Anacreon is depicted with his genitals infibulated. Marble statue, Monte Calvo, Italy, 2nd century AD.

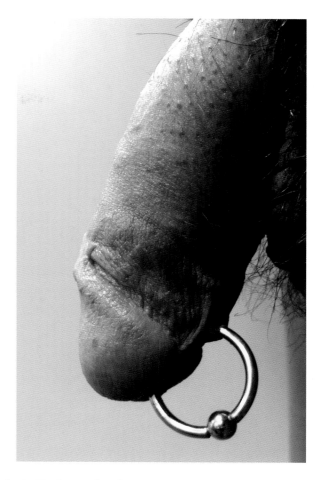

A 'Prince Albert' piercing.

More recently, infibulation has been seen as a perverse practice undertaken in S&M as a form of torture, such as stabbing with needles, hammering in nails or stapling folds of the body. This desire for the insertion of objects into genitalia has spawned a whole new industry in piercing, tattooing and even surgery. Professional piercings took off with the 'Prince Albert', one of the most well-known infibulations for male sexual enhancement, which involves a ring-style piercing that extends along the underside of the glans from the urethral opening to where the glans meets the shaft of the penis. Clitoral rings and nipple piercing have also become popular. As a result of their concerns over penis size, some men resort to surgical enhancements, paying thousands of pounds for penis extensions. Cutting the ligaments that hold the penis in place so that the penis hangs lower can extend length; weights are then attached to it for a few months to stretch the organ to ensure the enlargement is permanent. Men can also extend the girth of their penis with fat taken from other parts of the body transplanted into its sides – however, since the penis head cannot be fattened this way, the results sometimes look a little odd. Silicone injections can also be used to enhance the size of the penis and can cause amazingly fast results, increasing the penis girth by up to five times. For this reason, the procedure has been used in the pornographic film industry, despite the dangers of damage and desensitization. Surgeons have on occasion suggested penile implants, which involve inserting a rod or a pipe in cases where a man may have had difficulty in obtaining erection. A pump is attached to the groin and the penis is pumped up when he wants an erection. For women there are all sorts of methods available to enhance their sexual organs – breast-enlarging serums such as 'Lady's Secret', vaginal tightening and oestrogen creams have become money-spinners worldwide.

Surgery for breast augmentation or reduction is now common-place, with hundreds of thousands of women worldwide undergoing cosmetic breast procedures. Operations for making the labia look smaller and 'tidier' are now increasingly fashionable. But have obsessions developed beyond the interest of the psychoanalyst or sexual psychologist? Is it a case of mass body dysmorphia, or are we all merely taking advantage of new opportunities offered to us? People who have experienced Body Integrity Identity Disorder (BIID), a severe type of body dysmorphia in which people desire an amputation, have requested the removal of limbs – and in some cases doctors have complied with their wishes. But is this ethically acceptable? New fixations and methods of sex develop with new types of surgery. Apotemnophilia, a paraphilia in which the subject is aroused by their being or imagining themselves as an amputee, is related to BIID: amputation has now become part of the erotic ensemble, with stumps of arms and legs being used for penetration (acrotomophilia refers to an erotic interest in amputees).

John Money and his colleagues examined apotemnophilia in the *Journal of Sex Research* in 1977, summarizing as follows:

> The findings in two cases show that self-demand amputation (apotemnophilia) is related to erotization of the stump and to overachievement despite a handicap. The apotemnophiliac obsession represents an idée fixe rather than a paranoid

delusion. It may be conceptually related to, though it is not identical with transsexualism, bisexuality, Münchausen syndrome, and masochism. As with most paraphilias it undoubtedly occurs more frequently, if not exclusively, in men. The two patients related apotemnophilia to recalled experiences of childhood which were necessary but not sufficient for a causal explanation. The precise etiology of the condition is not known, and there is no agreed upon method of treatment.[39]

One researcher, F. Tomasini, described the condition BIID in an ethics journal in 2006:

> Self-demand amputees are persons who need to have one or more healthy limbs or digits amputated to fit the way they see themselves. They want to rid themselves of a limb that they believe does not belong to their body-identity. The obsessive desire to have appendages surgically removed to fit an alternative body-image is medically and ethically controversial.

He provides a number of normative and professional ethical perspectives on whether or not it is possible to justify surgery for self-demand amputees. He concludes that no explanation can fully incorporate an understanding of what it is like to be a self-demand amputee.[40] Other researchers, such as Tim Bayne and Neil Levy, have added to the debate, arguing that request for self-demand amputations of healthy limbs should be agreed to if patients 'are experiencing significant distress as a consequence of the rare psychological disorder named Body Integrity Identity Disorder'.[41] The actual use of amputated limbs in sex for penetration (whether self-elected amputees or not) has possibly derived from fisting, but little research has been undertaken on this development.

Fisting

One of the earliest mentions of fisting comes in Aristophanes' *Peace*, where he uses sporting metaphors for rough sex. In this surreal comedy of 421 BC, the hungry vine grower Trygaeus shares his fantasies of sex with Lady Festival, whom he has just met:

Now that you have her, You can straightaway conduct a
very nice athletic competition tomorrow:
wrestle her to the ground, set her on all fours
throw her on her side, bent forward, onto her knees;
then well oiled up for the pancration,
strike out with vigour, fist burrowing in with the cock.

This might well be hitting or spanking her at the same time as
entering her but more likely, since she has been 'well oiled', it refers
to intercourse while simultaneously fisting her anus or vagina.[42]
Another source in history where we can find anal fisting – no surprise
here – is the writings of Sade. In *La Philosophie dans le boudoir*
(1795) he describes a scene in which the character Dolmance urges
Madame Saint-Ange to insert her fingers into his anus, 'drive them
in further. To the wrist.'[43] There was therefore at least an understanding of the act in the eighteenth century, even if was rarely
mentioned. However, if Sade imagined fisting, there is every likelihood that he experimented with it.

Although the term 'fisting' (or 'handballing') is not used, the
concept was mentioned in 1949 in Larry Flint's *Hustler* magazine.[44]
This practice involved inserting the whole hand or arm into the
anus or vagina. As a commonly practised anal activity, it grew popular sometime in the 1960s in gay leather biker groups in California.
In 1975, a member of the Fist Fuckers of America opened up one of
the first gay male fisting sex clubs, The Catacombs, in San Francisco
where a person could enjoy everything leather and fisting had to offer:
any night a person might see (by reservation only) '40 men variously
hanging in leather slings, tied down on restraint tables with their
legs raised by shackles, or laid back on waterbeds and mattresses
while 40 other men massage Crisco up their fists to start the one
finger march to a full fist gliding up the asshole to the elbow'.[45] The
gay male subculture of fisting was also evident in 1960s gay men's
s&m porn in which naive young men were tortured by rugged
manly brutes with huge penises and 'even bigger fists which they
sink up to the armpits in our quivering hero's sweetly puckered
virgin ass'.[46] In male gay bondage bars in the late 1970s, finger
hygiene was at its best: 'You cut your nails, then you cut your nails
again, and then you filed them.' Then you did it again before putting on your surgical gloves. The cover of a 1983 issue of *Anal Sex*,

published in Copenhagen, although aimed at heterosexual men, showed one woman fisting another. Although the lesbian magazine *Quim* featured fisting between women in 1992, the activity was less well known in lesbian circles.

Discrimination against fisting came out in the form of DVD censorship in 2011, when it was made illegal in America to film the act of fisting.[47] In response, aficionados of fisting porn banded together on 25 October for an International Fisting Day. Those against censorship wondered how the censorship board came to the conclusion that it was permissible to film a penis (or even two) in a vagina but not a hand. Some lesbians and gays saw this as yet another form

An early case of fisting? 19th-century sketch of two figures from Michelangelo's *Last Judgement*.

of social control over their private behaviour. More recently, doctors and surgeons have investigated the problems presenting in those who enjoy fisting: rupture of the anal sphincter, perforation of the colon, the spread of rectal and colon disease and disturbance of heart rhythms due to vagovagal response. With precautions, these risks can be minimized.[48]

It is now reasonably common for people to incorporate fellating, fetishism, infibulating or fisting (or at least one of these activities) into their usual role-play. What was previously 'abnormal' has become 'normal'. After conducting interviews in Finland with 164 men and 22 women from two sex-oriented clubs, one researcher concluded, 'For many gay men leather is not only a style-item, but also and especially a sexual fetish.'[49] It could similarly be argued that what was once a fetish is now a fashionable pastime. The only time any of these activities becomes a problem is when it negatively affects someone who has not consented to inclusion in the activity. More often, people go to conferences around their predilection and celebrate it openly, sharing their particular desires with other like-minded people. For many people at the beginning of the twenty-first century, few body parts or activities are seen as out of bounds.

Epilogue: A Limit to Tolerance?

Are we to accept a fundamentalist, oppositional approach towards those sexual preferences we consider strange, or are we to embrace more unusual sex acts wholeheartedly? Is there a way forward to a more tolerant society, or is there a limit to tolerance?

Some of our old ideas have followed us down the ages and resulted in the persistent persecution of minorities who are merely following their inclinations. In many countries, lesbians, homosexuals, transvestites and transsexuals continue to be persecuted. Incest between consenting siblings is still prosecuted in some countries, yet there is no reason for it to be illegal. Some people might even argue that it should be acceptable for incestuous couples to have children despite the risk of disability of the newborn – but is disability such a crime? After all, older women are in greater danger of producing babies with disabilities, but they are not forbidden to do so by law.

While the more liberal-minded might be tolerant of sadomasochistic practices (and may even indulge in a little of the milder kind themselves behind closed doors), it might be more difficult for them to accept other sorts of sexual acts. Negative reactions to bestiality and necrophilia have been fairly consistent throughout the ages in most countries in the West. In the 1980s, paedophiles tried to come out alongside gays, but they were told to go back in the closet, and remained criminals. If anything, attitudes towards paedophilia have hardened in recent years.

There is no doubt that when observing the sexual behaviour of people in history sexual perversion is found to be mutable. Laws and punishments have changed throughout the centuries to reflect shifting opinions on sexual behaviour. The idea of what is and what is not 'sexual perversion' is based on our perceptions of what is

397

right and wrong. Whether these perceptions are created by the state, the Church or the community, the idea of acceptability is filtered downwards, with the working classes generally more accepting of 'different' behaviours, and the poorest being most often caught and punished for acting them out. In cases where a 'perversion' has been upsetting to these institutions, the method of controlling it has traditionally been through punishment – hanging, burning, flogging, the pillory, incarceration or fines. This changed at the end of the nineteenth century to allow for the introduction of 'treatment' for the individual, rather than punishment. Over the last couple of centuries, in cases where a 'perversion' is upsetting to the individual who undertakes such behaviour, psychiatrists have traditionally investigated what it was that 'made' them this way, and which particular experience in their past (notably focusing on their family background, their childhood and their adolescence) made them 'abnormal'; medics have strived to make those who indulge in these deviant acts become 'normal'. Yet if society did not see these sexual practices as 'abnormal', it is unlikely that the person undertaking the acts would see themselves in this way. A move towards a more accepting attitude around consensual sexual activities would mean less persecution of individuals and groups, and greater equality in their human rights.

Although changes have been made throughout history regarding what was perverted or not – for example, sodomy, masturbation and oral sex were thought of as heinous sins in medieval times but are now accepted sexual behaviour – the long-established Christian tradition of guilt over many sexual acts has continued. Bestiality, incest, necrophilia and all those other acts deemed forbidden by the Church remain taboo. In a secular society, it is time to re-evaluate the position and consider why any activities between consenting adults should be criminalized. Where acts are not harmful to others, there is no reason for legislation.

People have changed their minds about sex from one era to the next. Nothing, therefore, is set in stone. There is no reason why people should be marginalized for their desires. However, three areas of contention need discussing: first, harmful sex, to the degree of death or bodily harm between consenting adults (sexual cannibalism or sadomasochism); second, vulnerable adults; and third, the age of consent.

A commonly cited example of the first area is that of Armin Meiwes, who advertised on the Internet for someone to share in his fantasies of cannibalism. A young man, Bernd Jürgen Brandes, came forward; they met and discussed what they both wanted to do. With the young man's consent, Meiwes cut off the youth's penis and cooked it, and they ate it together. Meiwes then stabbed the man to death, dissected his corpse and ate bits of it over the next ten months. The whole scenario was videotaped. Meiwes was arrested in December 2002 after a college student found details of the killings and an advertisement for a new partner on the Internet. Since there is no law against cannibalism in Germany, and Brandes consented, Meiwes was sentenced to eight years imprisonment for manslaughter.

So what should we do about these sorts of cases? Many people would suggest that both Meiwes and Brandes were 'sick' or mentally unstable. But there was no proof of this when the case came to court. If a person is making a rational choice – albeit one thought strange by society's standards – should they be left alone? In most societies, an act which results in the manslaughter or murder of another individual is against the law, regardless of whether sexual activities are involved or not. The problem here is first whether the law can establish that there was consent once the person involved is dead. If this can be established, the question arises – does society have a duty to protect people from their own self-destructive urges? But then what about euthanasia, or assisted killings? While many of us agree with this in cases of painful terminal illness, we may not agree with allowing death by sexual cannibalism, even where the adults are consenting.

However, if we believe people should be stopped from chopping off body parts, then prevention of self-demand amputation is called for. But amputation of parts of the body is considered acceptable in law in many cases, such as breast reduction or transsexual operations. Here the law and medicine in many Western societies see it as acceptable to chop off a body part; it is considered that an individual has the right to change their body how they see fit. Yet some amputations or removal of body parts – such as female circumcision – are illegal in the UK and U.S., even when requested by the patient themselves (though they continue to take place in secret). This is an area fraught with difficulties; while female genital mutilation is opposed in law, male circumcision is still allowed, with some private clinics dedicated to its practice.

If we allow the amputation of some parts of the body, what about the person who demands that a healthy limb be removed? In some cases of body dysmorphia where doctors have agreed to amputate an arm or a leg of their patient in favour of their mental health, they have been severely criticized. This consideration then pushes us back to evaluate self-harm or consenting harm by another person for sexual pleasure, as in the Spanner Case discussed in chapter Four, and whether grievous bodily harm should be permitted in S&M activities or whether it should be illegal. Should we prosecute or not? The distinctions become increasingly blurred.

The second outstanding issue is around people with learning difficulties and the matter of consent. It has been deemed that some such vulnerable people cannot give consent and therefore they are prevented from having sex, even though they want to. What about a 26-year-old couple with Down's syndrome – shouldn't they be allowed to have sex if they both want to? They have the same lusts as other young men and women of their age, and it is unfair that they cannot find sexual fulfilment. There is no reason why relationships between vulnerable adults should not be facilitated so they too can enjoy sex. The ground may be fraught with problems, but just because a subject is difficult, it does not mean we should ignore it. Laws are already in place to protect vulnerable adults or children from non-consensual acts.

Finally there is the matter of the age of consent. Most people would agree that there should be a cut-off point when sex is not acceptable for a child, who is unable to consent as an 'adult'. The age of consent has shifted in different periods and between countries. Usually it has hovered somewhere between the ages of twelve and 21. The difficulty, of course, is that each person matures at a different age, and that what might be acceptable for one adolescent would not be for another. The problem occurs when there is an abuse of power or relationship manipulation. The law rightly comes down heavily on those who have forced young boys and girls into rela-tionships against their will.

More worrying are the cases of institutional abuses on a mass scale which have been ignored for years in places where young people should have been protected. Such abuses have taken place in children's homes and within the Catholic Church and other religious organizations, such as the Church of Jesus Christ of Latter-day Saints in Utah. Places with a veneer of respectability seem to have often been the most dangerous. Better communication routes are needed to ensure that children and vulnerable young adults are able to complain. Even when there have been grievances aired, those complaints have often been ignored. There therefore need to be procedures through which the responsible adults are forced to follow up these complaints, either by regular inspection from outside agencies or some other method of protective monitoring.

Meanwhile, for those adolescents in a comfortable relationship in a secure environment, facilitation of sex makes the experience safer and more enjoyable. They are less likely to be abused, suffer unwanted pregnancy or catch sexual diseases if they are properly informed and able to protect themselves. Young people should be taught about all sex methods available to them (not just intercourse). Coercion, manipulation and bullying is all too easy and education and support are the keys to its prevention – this means supporting *all* young people and vulnerable adults who want to explore sex, be they heterosexual, homosexual, bisexual or transgender. Dedicated groups are needed to supply support and advice.

Under the Sexual Offences Act 2003, bestiality and necrophilia became specific offences in the UK for the first time. Anal and vaginal penetration of, or by, an animal or of a corpse is illegal, and carries a sentence of up to two years' imprisonment. Historically, an unspecified range of acts was illegal, but the Act, which followed a major review of all sexual offences in UK law, clarified this, removing ambiguities. Possession of extreme pornography was criminalized in the Criminal Justice and Immigration Act 2008. The law on pornography is broader than that of actual acts: it applies to dead animals as well as living; and images may be illegal even if they are faked. Thus it may be illegal to possess an image of a legal act. The first prosecutions for bestiality pornography occurred in 2009.

Yet the ever-expanding vista of sexual exploration in the global age comes at a time when procreation is no longer a sexual necessity (or hazard); this equalizes sex acts and renders them all of approximately equal value. With in vitro fertilization, when even vaginal penetrative sex is no longer needed for conception, the *need* for vaginal penetrative sex is no longer there, even if the desire remains.

But if sex between men and women is not calculated to produce children, what is the difference in the value between vaginal penetrative sex, lesbian oral sex, male–female sodomy, male–male sodomy or the penetration of men by women using a strap-on (called 'pegging')? It simply becomes a matter of choice which type of non-procreative sex a person wants.

The end of the twentieth century heralded an era of global sex. The ease of international travel and world commerce has eroded national differences; cultures merge in the airport lounges, hotels and shopping malls that make up the landscape of great cities in countries from Iceland to Nairobi. The same sexual imagery is available for viewing online in any part of the world, be it from a village cyber café in Siem Reap or a lavish home computer in the U.S. Forty per cent of all traffic on the Internet has to do with sex and pornography. It is not so much that the Internet has contributed to sex in the twenty-first century; to a large extent it *is* sex. People who do not know each other, and never will – except as a series of electronic impulses – have cybersex, pretending to be what they are not: more beautiful, richer or even a different gender. The Internet has facilitated the possibility of meeting up with like-minded people to share similar preferences in cities all over the world. In virtually unregulated Internet traffic, the only boundaries are those which users place on themselves from time to time: whether today it will be s&m sex; whether today they will be gay or straight, male or female.

Only so much can be covered in one book, and the history of sexual perversion is still in its infancy. Greater exploration and discussion is needed about sexual diversity, both in history and in the contemporary world, if we are to understand how and why sexual activities and sexuality have emerged in the ways they have, and how we are to get rid of prejudices against individuals with sexual desires that are different from our own. This book is but a small offering to equal rights in the hope of the creation of a less phobic world.

REFERENCES

Introduction

1 See section on 'Problems with the Current Diagnostic Criteria', in *Sexual Deviance: Theory, Assessment and Treatment*, ed. D. Richard Laws and William T. O'Donohue (New York, 1997), p. 4.

1 Taking it Straight

1 The current sociological argument is that heterosexuality is a learned behaviour, not a natural occurrence. A hetero–homosexual binary exists, but this framework also categorizes types of heterosexual behaviour in a hierarchical way. As Ingraham argues, 'Thinking straight is understanding heterosexuality as naturally occurring and not as an extensively social arrangement or means for distributing power and wealth.' For a more in-depth sociological understanding of the development of heterosexuality, see Chrys Ingraham, *Thinking Straight: The Power, the Promise and the Paradox of Heterosexuality* (London, 2005).

2 Pseudo-Demosthenes, 'Oration', *Against Nerea*, 59.122.

3 Wilhelm Adolf Bekker, *Charicles; or, Illustrations of the Private Life of the Greeks* (London, 1866), p. 463. Although this is not entirely true as some Roman women have been found to exercise a good deal of financial independence in practice; see for example Suzanne Dixon, *Reading Women* (London, 2003).

4 Suetonius, *Tiberius*, 43–44; David Mountfield, *Greek and Roman Erotica* (Fribourg, 1982), pp. 43.

5 King Priam had many children born of consorts, according to Homer's *Iliad*, but by the classical period, having a concubine and a wife under the same roof was ruled out; see Susan Lape, 'Heterosexuality', in *A Cultural History of Sexuality*, vol. 1: *In the Classical World*, ed. Mark Golden and Peter Toohey (London, 2011), p. 18.

6 John Younger, 'Sexual Variations: Sexual Peculiarities of the Ancient Greeks and Romans', in *A Cultural History of Sexuality*, vol. I: *In the Classical World*, ed. Golden and Toohey, I, pp. 71–3.

7 It must be noted that not all the works ascribed to Hippocrates were actually written by him. Helen King, 'Sex, Medicine and Disease', in *A Cultural History of Sexuality*, vol. I: *In the Classical World*, quoting Virgil 8.468L. See also Helen King, *Hippocrates' Woman: Reading the Female Body in Ancient Greece* (London, 1998); and Helen King, ed., *Health in Antiquity* (London, 2005).

8 Hippocrates, *On the Diseases of Women*, Book 1.

9 Aristotle, *Generation of Animals*, 1, 1, 730a25.

10 These ideas were circulating at least as late as the seventeenth century; see Helkiah Crook, *Misocosmographia* (London, 1615), p. 216.

11 Peter Lewis Allen, *The Wages of Sin* (Chicago, IL, 2000), p. 11.

12 John Davenport, *Aphrodisiacs and Anti-aphrodisiacs* (London, 1869).

13 See Virginia Burrus, *The Sex Lives of the Saints: An Erotics of Ancient Hagiography* (Philadelphia, PA, 2004), pp. 12–13; Joyce Salisbury, *Church Fathers, Independent Virgins* (London, 1991).

14 St Augustine, *De bono coniugali*, c. 1 (PL 40, 373); c. 3, n. 3 (PL 40, 375).

15 St Jerome, *Against Jovinian*, quoted in Vern L. Bullough and James A. Brundage, *Handbook of Medieval Sexuality* (New York and London, 1996), p. 86.

16 See Thomas Aquinas, *Summa theologica*, article 1, 12.

17 Louise M. Sylvester, *Medieval Romance and the Construction of Heterosexuality* (Basingstoke, 2008).

18 Pierre Bayle, *Letters of Abelard and Heloise*, trans. John Hughes, at www.gutenberg.org.

19 See Judith M. Bennett, 'Writing Fornication: Medieval Leyrwrite and its Historians', *Transactions of the Royal Historical Society*, XIII (2003), pp. 131–62; quote from Faramerz Dabhoiwala, *The Origins of Sex: A History of the First Sexual Revolution* (London, 2012), p. 10.

20 Martin Luther, 'The Estate of Marriage', trans. Walther I. Brandt, in *Luther's Works*, vol. XLV (Philadelphia, PA, 1962), 9.13.

21 According to Lawrence Stone, the shift from parental decision-making to a couple's own choice in marriage had already taken place by 1660, except among the highest ranks of aristocracy: Lawrence Stone, *The Family, Sex and Marriage in England, 1500–1800* (London, 1977), p. 183.

22 Thompson mentions around 400 cases of wife sales: see E. P. Thompson, *Customs in Common* (Harmondsworth, 1993),

pp. 404–62; PRO, National Archives, Kew, HO27/1 Criminal Register for England and Wales 1805.

23 For examples see Julie Peakman, *Lascivious Bodies: A Sexual History of the Eighteenth Century* (New York, 2005), pp. 46–72; and Julie Peakman, *Mighty Lewd Books: The Development of Pornography in Eighteenth-century England* (London, 2003).

24 See Julie Peakman, *Whore Biographies, 1700–1825* (London, 2008).

25 Jonathan Katz, *The Invention of Heterosexuality* (Chicago, IL, 2007), p. 17.

26 Quoted ibid., p. 86.

27 R. J. Brodie and Co., *The Secret Companion: A Medical Work on Onanism or Self-Pollution* [1845] (London, 1985), p. 37; Richard Freiherr von Krafft-Ebing, *Psychopathia Sexualis*, reprint of 12th edn [1903] (Berkeley, CA, 1999), p. 15. This is the edition used throughout.

28 Others, such as H. J. Löwenstein in 1823, Joseph Häussler in 1826 and Heinrich Kaan in 1844, all made early contributions to the subject.

29 Harry Ooserhuis, 'Richard Von Krafft-Ebing's Step-children of Nature', in *Sexualities in History*, ed. Kim M. Phillips and Barry Reay (London, 2002), pp. 271–91.

30 'Foreword', in Krafft-Ebing, *Psychopathia Sexualis*, p. xxi.

31 Krafft-Ebing, *Psychopathia Sexualis*, p. 418.

32 Ibid., pp. 420–21.

33 Chris White, ed., *Nineteenth-century Writings in Homosexuality* (London, 1999), pp. 66–7.

34 Quoted in Chushichi Tsuzuki, *Edward Carpenter, 1844–1929: Prophet of Human Fellowship* (Cambridge, 1980), p. 72.

35 Havelock Ellis, *My Life* (London and Toronto, 1940), p. 269; see also Phyllis Grosskurth, *Havelock Ellis: A Biography* (New York, 1985).

36 Ellis, *My Life*, p. 289.

37 Kinsey dedicated *Sexual Behavior in the Human Male* 'to the 12,000 people who have contributed to this data'; and dedicated his *Sexual Behavior in the Human Female* 'to the nearly 8,000 females who contributed to the data on which this book is based'.

38 As well as my own research below, see Liz Stanley, *Sex Surveyed, 1949–1994* (London, 1995).

39 'A British Sex Survey', File Report 3110B, Mass Observation Records (MO), University of Sussex Archives.

40 MO, diary of female teacher born in 1891, living in Chepstow, Monmouth, Wales, 1941.

41 MO, diary 5010, 1939, Image 20, p. 36.

42 Ibid., Image 25, p. 48.

2 From Onanism to Spending

1 See Rachel Maines, *The Technology of Orgasm* (New York, 1998), but her ideas have been criticized: see Lesley Hall, 'Maines' Martyrdom and Vibratory Censorship' (July 1999), at www. lesleyahall.net; and Helen King, see reference 4 below.

2 Frig: 'To move about restlessly. To agitate the body or limbs; to rub, chafe': *Oxford English Dictionary*. In one eighteenth-century case, the word was used when one young boy reported that an older man had attempted to seduce him, the man asked him if 'I never frigged myself.' The boy confessed, 'I did not know what it meant' – but then denial, in this case, was of course to his benefit, since sodomitical acts were still a capital crime. The word became more commonly used in the nineteenth century. Randolph Trumbach, *Sex and the Gender Revolution* (Chicago, IL, 1998), p. 59.

3 Plutarch, *Morals*, 1044b.

4 Helen King, 'Sex, Medicine and Disease', in *A Cultural History of Sexuality*, vol. I: *In the Classical World*, ed. Mark Golden and Peter Toohey (London, 2011), pp. 107–24; Helen King, *Hippocrates' Woman: Reading the Female Body in Ancient Greece* (London, 1998), pp. 221, 233; Helen King, 'Galen and the Widow: Towards a History of Therapeutic Masturbation in Ancient Gynaecology', *EuGeStA: Journal on Gender Studies in Antiquity*, I (2011), pp. 205–35.

5 King, *Hippocrates' Woman*, pp. 221, 233; King, 'Galen and the Widow', pp. 205–35.

6 King, 'Sex, Medicine and Disease', p. 113.

7 Thomas Aquinas, *Summa Theologica*, II–IIae, q. 154 a. 11 co. (in Latin).

8 Walter O. Bockting and Eli Coleman, eds, 'Masturbation as a Means of Achieving Sexual Health', *Journal of Psychology of Human Sexuality*, XIV/2–3 (2002), pp. 5–18.

9 Pierre Hurteau, 'Catholic Moral Discourse on Male Sodomy and Masturbation in the Seventeenth and Eighteenth Centuries', *Journal of the History of Sexuality*, IV/1 (July 1993), pp. 1–26.

10 Quoted in Jean Stengers and Anne Van Neck, *Masturbation: The History of a Great Terror* (Basingstoke, 2001), p. 19.

11 David Stevenson, 'Recording the Unspeakable: Masturbation in the Diary of William Drummond, 1657–1659', *Journal of the History of Sexuality*, IX/3–4 (July 2000), pp. 234–9.

12 Ibid.

13 Peter Wagner, *Eros Revived: Erotica and the Enlightenment in England and America* (London, 1998), p. 11.

14 Laurence Stone, *Family, Sex and Marriage in England, 1500–1800* (London, 1977), p. 513.

15 On Beggar's Benison, see Julie Peakman, *Lascivious Bodies: A Sexual History of the Eighteenth Century* (New York, 2005), pp. 129–47; Jean-Jacques Rousseau, *Confessions*, quoted in Vernon A. Rosario, *The Erotic Imagination: French Histories of Perversities*, (London, 1997), p. 3

16 Nicolas Venette, *Tableau de L'amour* [1686] (London, 1818), p. 134; 'La femme n'a pas la puissance de se polluer comme l'homme, ni de se décharger de la semence superflue: elle la garde quelquefois fort longtemps dans ses testicules ou dans les cornes de sa matrice, où elle se corrompt et devient jaune, trouble, ou puante, de blanche et de claire qu'elle étoit auparavant.'

17 Roy Porter and Lesley Hall, *Facts of Life: The Creation of Sexual Knowledge in Britain, 1650–1950* (New Haven, CT, and London, 1995), pp. 6–7.

18 Robert Burton, *The Anatomy of Melancholy* [1621] (London, 1855), p. 555.

19 Jean-Paul Guillebaud, *The Tyranny of Pleasure* (New York, 1998), p. 178.

20 Peter Wagner, *Erotica and the Enlightenment* (Frankfurt, 1991), pp. 17–19.

21 Tom Laqueur, *Solitary Sex: A Cultural History of Masturbation* (New York, 2003), p. 32.

22 Stolberg also argues that the date previously assumed by historians of 1710 is incorrect and the correct date is 1716. I have used the date as given in the British Library catalogue. Michael Stolberg, 'Self-pollution, Moral Reform, and the Venereal Trade: Notes on the Sources and Historical Content of *Onania* (1716)', *Journal of the History of Sexuality*, IX/1–2 (January–April 2000), pp. 37–61; Peter Wagner, 'The Veil of Medicine and Morality: Some Pornographic Aspects of the *Onania*', *Eighteenth-Century Studies*, V (1983), pp. 179–84; 'A Clergyman', *Onania; or, The Heinous Sin of Self-pollution, and All Its Frightful Consequences in Both Sexes Considered with Spiritual and Physical Advice to Those Who Have Already Injured Themselves by this Abominable Practice and Seasonable Admonition to the Youth of the Nation of Both Sexes*, 8th edn (London, 1723).

23 MacDonald believed this eighteenth-century book to have been pivotal in altering thinking about masturbation, whereby the act came to be seen as a cause of mental and physical disability. He asserts that its author had been influenced by Jen Frederick Osterwald, *The Nature of Uncleanliness* (1707). Robert H. MacDonald, 'The Frightful Consequences of Onanism: Notes on the "History of a Delusion"', *Journal of the History of Ideas*,

XXVIII/3 (July–September 1967), pp. 423–31. Lancashire physician Edward Baynard also advocated cold baths.

24 'A Clergyman', *Onania*.

25 *Onanism Display'd* was another anonymous pamphlet, the only copy being the second edition kept in the National Library of Medicine in Bethesda, Maryland.

26 Robert James, *A Medical Dictionary* (London, 1743–5), vol. I, pp. 153–63.

27 *Critical Review*, XVIII (1760), pp. 304–05.

28 Paul-Gabriel Boucé, 'Imagination, Pregnant Women and Monsters in Eighteenth-century England and France', in *Sexual Underworlds in the Enlightenment*, ed. George Rousseau and Roy Porter (Chapel Hill, NC, 1988), pp. 86–100.

29 Laqueur has suggested that the sudden eruption of anxiety about masturbation in the eighteenth century was because it became related to the imagination, privacy and solitude, yet desire was at the heart of the commercial system. Masturbation was therefore a threat. The question was 'whether sociability, or indeed any form of public virtue, could survive the frenzy of private desire and private gain'. But this is perhaps an over-complication – the issue was always about self-control throughout history, just that now it was new medics rather than old clerics who were setting the standards. Laqueur, *Solitary Sex*, p. 277.

30 S.A.D. Tissot, *Onanism; or, A Treatise Upon the Disorders Produced by Masturbation* (London, 1766), pp. 41–2.

31 Rousseau cites various French editions, two in 1771; one each in 1772, 1778 and 1784; a French edition that appeared as 'Published in London', 1789; and two English translations for 1775 and *c.* 1840; G. S. Rousseau, 'Nymphomania, Bienville and the Rise of Erotic Sensibility', in *Sexuality in Eighteenth-century Britain*, ed. Paul-Gabriel Boucé (Manchester, 1982), pp. 95–119. I have found eight French-language copies and three English copies in the British Library catalogue, one for 1775 and two for 1840; I have used the former. Another English language copy for 1766 has been destroyed. There is also one Italian and one German edition for 1760.

32 Ibid., p. 50.

33 M.D.T. Bienville, *Nymphomania, or, a Dissertation Concerning the Furor Uterinus* (London, 1775), p. 36. Tissot met with Rousseau and was aware of his novel *Emile*, and the physician sent him a copy of his own treatise.

34 Peter Lewis Allen, *The Wages of Sin: Sex and Disease* (Chicago, IL, 2002), p. 97.

35 Benjamin Rush, *Medical Inquiries and Observations Upon the*

Diseases of the Mind (Philadelphia, PA, 1812).

36 *Dictionnaire des sciences médicales*, XIII, 2nd edn (Paris, 1878), p. 732.

37 Allen, *Wages of Sin*, p. 97.

38 Reveillé-Parise, *Revue medicale française et étrangère*, III (1828), p. 98.

39 Dr J. B. Fonssagrives, *L'Education physique des garçons* (Paris, 1890), pp. 302, 313.

40 For a more in-depth look at French attitudes, see Stengers and Van Neck, *Masturbation*, pp. 1–36.

41 Quoted ibid., p. 4.

42 Lallemand, *A Practical Treatise on the Causes, Symptoms, and Treatment of Spermatorrhoea*, trans. and ed. H. J. McDougall, 2nd edn (London, 1847), p. 2.

43 See Lesley A. Hall's assessment in her article 'Forbidden by God, Despised by Men: Masturbation, Medical Warnings, Moral Panic, and Manhood in Great Britain, 1850–1950', *Journal of the History of Sexuality*, II/3, Special Issue, Part 2: The State, Society, and the Regulation of Sexuality in Modern Europe (January 1992), pp. 365–87.

44 Michael S. Patton, 'Masturbation from Judaism to Victorianism', *Journal of Religion and Health*, XXIV/2 (1985), pp. 133–46.

45 Samuel Bayard Woodward, 'Remarks on Masturbation: Insanity produced by Masturbation; Effections of Masturbation with Cases', *Boston Medical and Surgical Journal*, XII (1835).

46 P. R. Neuman, 'Masturbation and Madness, and the Modern Concept of Childhood and Adolescence', *Journal of Social History*, VIII/3 (Spring 1975), pp. 1–27.

47 Quoted ibid.

48 Priscilla Barker, *The Secret Book: Containing Information and Instruction for Young Women and Girls* (Brighton, 1889), p. 25.

49 Alan Hunt, 'The Great Masturbation Panic and the Discourse of Moral Regulation in Nineteenth- and Early Twentieth-century Britain', *Journal of the History of Sexuality*, VIII/4 (1998), pp. 575–615.

50 Ibid.

51 Joseph William Howe, *Excessive Venery, Masturbation and Continence* (London, 1883), p. 63.

52 Edward Kirk, *Talk with Boys About Themselves* (London, 1905), p. 3.

53 Robert Anderson, 'Speech at a Purity Rally', *Alliance of Honour Record* (January 1911), quoted in Hunt, 'Great Masturbation', p. 203.

54 J. H. Kellogg, MD, *Plain Facts for Old and Young: Embracing the Natural History and Hygiene of Organic Life* (Burlington, IA, 1892).

55 Alfred Kinsey et al., *Sexual Behavior in the Human Male* (Philadelphia, PA, 1948), p. 499; *Sexual Behavior in the Human Female* (Philadelphia, PA, 1953), p. 142; Michael S. Patten, 'Twentieth-century Attitudes to Masturbation', *Journal of Health and Religion* (1986), pp. 291–302.

56 John Hunter, *A Treatise on Venereal Disease* (London, 1786), p. 200.

57 Sir James Paget, 'Sexual Hypochondriasis', *Clinical Lectures and Essays* (London, 1879), p. 292.

58 Ralcy H. Bell, *Self-amusement and its Spectres* (New York, 1929), p. 39.

59 M. Gerressu, C. H. Mercer, C. A. Graham, K. Wellings and A. M. Johnson, 'Prevalence of Masturbation and Associated Factors in a British National Probability Survey', *Archives of Sexual Behavior* (2007), http://eprints.soton.ac.uk/198459.

3 From Ganymedes to Gays

1 D. Halperin, 'Sex Before Sexuality', in *Hidden from History*, ed. M. Duberman, M. Vicinus, M. and C. Chauncey (London, 1989), p. 39. This theory has been queried by Simon LeVay, who wrote, 'It seems to me quite artificial to make the existence of homosexuality dependent on the coinage of a term to describe it.' In LeVay's view, people can formulate the concept of homosexuality without the word, and even the ability to formulate the concept is irrelevant to the existence or nonexistence of homosexuality; see his *Queer Science: The Use and Abuse of Research into Homosexuality* (Cambridge, MA, 1996), pp. 56, 297. Broader coverage of the social constructionism versus essentialism debate has been covered in Edward Stein, ed., *Forms of Desire: Sexual Orientation and the Social Construction Controversy* (London, 1990).

2 This simplistic version of the older penetrator and the receptive youth has been questioned by James Davidson, *The Greeks and Greek Love* (London, 2007). He believes that there was much more variety of relationships between men than previously thought.

3 Aeschylus, *Myrmidons*, fr. 135 Radt.

4 Plato, *Symposium*, 178a–180b; Homer, *Iliad*, 11.78b; W. M. Clarke, 'Achilles and Patroclus in Love', *Hermes*, 106 (1978), pp. 381–9.

5 Aristotle, *Physiognomonica*, 808a12–6.

6 Suetonius, *Galba*, 22, in *Roman Sexualities*, trans. and ed. Judith Hallett and Marilyn B. Skinner (Princeton, NJ, 1997), p. 56.

7 St Peter Damian, Rule 15, *Book of Gomorrah* [c. 1048] (Waterloo, Ontario, 1982).

8 See articles by Bernd-Ulrich Hergemöller, 'The Middle Ages', and Helmut Puff, 'Early Modern Europe, 1400–1700', in *Gay Life and*

Culture: A World History, ed. Robert Aldrich (London, 2006), pp. 57–77 and 79–102.

9 This was written by Geoffrey le Baker of Swinbrook, *c.* 1350. Stowe in his *Annales* (1605) and Stubbs in 1883 both believed that Baker's *Chronicon* was a translation into Latin of a French chronicle by Thomas de la More, one of Baker's patrons. More was witness to Edward's deposition but not his death. No one knows what actually happened; just that Edward was murdered. Rumours about his death continued to abound, especially after Marlowe's play about the king. G. P. Cuttino and Thomas W. Lyman, 'Where is Edward II?', *Speculum*, LIII/3 (July 1978), pp. 522–44.

10 Hergemöller, 'The Middle Ages', pp. 66, 70.

11 Michael Rocke, *Forbidden Friendships: Homosexuality and Male Culture in Renaissance Florence* (Oxford, 1996), p. 24.

12 Hergemöller, 'The Middle Ages', p. 74

13 Helmutt Puff, 'Early Modern Europe, 1400–1700', p. 87.

14 Titus Oates was a renegade Anglican priest who accused the Catholic Church of a plot to assassinate Charles II, assisted by Thomas Osborne, the Earl of Danby. Oates had been expelled from a couple of colleges, probably for sodomy – the case would have been known to readers. Rictor Norton, ed., 'The He-Strumpets, 1707–10', in *Homosexuality in Eighteenth-century England: A Sourcebook* (1 December 1999, updated 15 June 2008), at www. rictornorton.co.uk; also Rictor Norton, *Mother Clap's Molly House: The Gay Subculture in England, 1700–1830* (Stroud, 2006), p. 19.

15 A. D. Harvey, 'Prosecutions for Sodomy in England at the Beginning of the Nineteenth Century', *Historical Journal*, XXI (1978), pp. 939–48; Netta Murray Goldsmith, *The Worst of Crimes: Homosexuality and the Law in Eighteenth-century London* (Aldershot, 1998).

16 Samuel Pepys, diary entry for 1 July 1663.

17 Alan Bray, *Homosexuality in Renaissance England* (New York, 1982), p. 48.

18 John Dunton, *The He-Strumpets: A Satyr on the Sodomite Club* (1707). No edition survives, but it is included in Dunton, *Athenianism* (1710). He refers on p. 96 to 'Jermain, late Clerk of St Dunstan's in the East, who being charg'd with S—d—y, cut his Throat with a Razor.' Dunton is actually talking about a mass arrest of sodomites in 1707, but it seems he made a mistake, and is misremembering an event from 1701 in his reference to Jermain. Jermain and Germain are of course synonymous. There is no trial record because the man never went to trial. My thanks to Rictor Norton, who kindly supplied this information.

19 Tim Hitchcock, Robert Shoemaker, Clive Emsley, Sharon Howard and Jamie McLaughlin et al., *The Old Bailey Proceedings Online, 1674–1913*, www.oldbaileyonline.org, ref. t17211206–20 and t17220228-18, accessed 20 February 2009.

20 Norton, 'He-Strumpets', p. 107; see *Old Bailey Proceedings Online*, ref. t17350522–38; Henry Wolf, Sexual Offences, assault with sodomitical intent, 22 May 1735.

21 Norton, 'He-Strumpets', p. 107.

22 Trumbach argues that before 1700, most sexual relations which took place between men were in relationships where the passive partners were boys or permanent transvestites; by 1700, the situation had changed and adult men were meeting together in parks, in latrines and in taverns throughout the major cities in Europe. They recognized each other with slight indications of the head, or through verbal codes and signals; Randolph Trumbach, 'Prostitution', in *A Cultural History of Sexuality*, vol. IV: *In the Enlightenment*, ed. Julie Peakman (London, 2011), pp. 183–202.

23 Michel Rey, 'Parisian Homosexuals Create a Lifestyle, 1700–1750: The Police Archives', *Eighteenth-century Life*, IX (1985), pp. 179–91. For further insight into homosexuality in France, see the collection of essays in Jeffrey Merrick and Michael Sibalis, eds, *Homosexuality in French History and Culture* (London and Oxford, 2001).

24 Michel Rey, 'Police and Sodomy in Eighteenth-century Paris: From Sin to Disorder', in *Male Homosexuality in Renaissance and Enlightenment Europe*, ed. Kent Gerard and Gert Hekma (London, 1989), pp. 129–46.

25 Quoted ibid.

26 Theo van der Meer, 'The Persecution of Sodomites in Eighteenth-century Amsterdam', in *Male Homosexuality*, ed. Gerard and Hekma, pp. 263–307. 'Between 1730 and 1811, at least two hundred and twenty-eight men and women, suspected of sodomy, sodomitical acts or of compliancy, stood trial in 236 cases' (p. 264).

27 The event has been meticulously documented by Norton in *Mother Clap's Molly House*, pp. 54–7.

28 Polly Morris, 'Sodomy and Male Honor; The Case of Somerset, 1740–1850', in *Male Homosexuality*, ed. Gerard and Hekma, pp. 383–406.

29 H. G. Cocks, *Nameless Offences: Homosexual Desire in the Nineteenth Century* (London, 2003), p. 7.

30 Jonathan Katz, *Love Stories* (Chicago, IL, 2001), p. 194.

31 This quote is attributed to Dr Charles E. Nammack, police surgeon of New York, speaking about perverts, homosexuals and child

molesters (he did not appear to differentiate between them).
E. B. Foote MD, *HomeCyclopedia: Popular Medical, Social and Sexual Science* [1901] (London, 1912), p. 652.

32 William James, *Principles of Psychology*, II, p. 439.

33 Ellis quoting Albert Moll's *The Sexual Life of a Child* (New York 1919), chap. 4 in Havelock Ellis, *Studies in the Psychology of Sex* (New York, 1942), vol. I, Book IV, 'Sexual Inversion in Men', p. 80.

34 Ibid., p. 77.

35 Matt Houlbrook, *Queer London: Perils and Pleasures in the Sexual Metropolis, 1918–1957* (Chicago, IL, 2005), p. 60.

36 Ibid., p. 97.

37 Ibid., p. 1.

38 Ibid., p. 185

4 From Female Friendships to Lipstick Lesbians

1 See Alison Oram and Annmarie Turnbull, *The Lesbian History Sourcebook: Love and Sex Between Women in Britain from 1780 to 1970* (London, 2001); Judith Bennett has argued for a search for 'lesbian-like' behaviour as a way to try and understand poorly documented female same-sex desire in medieval history, since there is often no outright proof. Judith Bennett, '"Lesbian-Like" and the Social History of Lesbians', *Journal of the History of Sexuality*, IX/1–2 (January–April 2000), pp. 1–24.

2 Fragment no. 82. For female homosexuality in the Greek world, see Bernadette Brooten, *Love Between Women: Early Christian Responses to Female Eroticism* (Chicago, IL, 1996), pp. 29–186; N. S. Rabinowitz and L. Auanger, eds, *Among Women: From the Homosocial to the Homoerotic* (Austin, TX, 2002); Martin E. Kilmer, *Greek Erotica on Attic Red-figure Vases* (London, 1993), pp. 26–30. See also Daniel Ogden 'Homosexuality', in *A Cultural History of Sexuality*, vol. I: *In the Classical World*, ed. Mark Golden and Peter Toohey (London, 2011), pp. 37–54.

3 Plutarch, *Lycurgus*, 18.4; Sarah Pomeroy, *Spartan Women* (Oxford, 2002), pp. 29, 136, 165.

4 Lucian, *Dialogues of the Courtesans: Meret:* 5; Kate Gilhuly, 'The Phallic Lesbian: Philosophy, Comedy and Social Inversion in Lucian's *Dialogue of the Courtesans*', in *Prostitutes and Courtesans in the Ancient World*, ed. Christopher A. Faraone and Laura K. McClure (Madison, WI, 2006), pp. 274–91; see also Seneca, *Epistles*, 95.21.

5 Sister Wilfrid Parsons, trans., *Fathers of the Church: Saint Augustine: Letters* (Washington, DC, 1956), Letter 211, p. 50; see

Bernadette Brooten, *Love Between Women: Early Christian Responses to Female Eroticism* (Chicago, IL, 1996), pp. 350–51.

6 John Boswell, *Marriage of Likeness: Same-sex Unions in Pre-modern Europe* (London, 1994), p. 244.

7 Burchard of Worms, cols. 924, 967–8. See Robert Mills, 'Homosexuality: Specters of Sodom', in *A Cultural History of Sexuality*, vol. II: *In the Middle Ages* ed. Ruth Evans (London, 2011), pp. 56–79.

8 Helmut Puff, 'Female Sodomy: The Trial of Katherina Hertzdorfer (1477)', *Journal of Medieval and Early Modern Studies*, XXX/1 (2000), pp. 41–61.

9 Julie Peakman, *Lascivious Bodies: A Sexual History of the Eighteenth Century* (London, 2004), pp. 181–4; the full case is described in Judith Brown, 'Lesbian Sexuality in Renaissance Italy: The Case of Sister Benedetta Carlini', *Signs* (Summer 1984), pp. 751–8.

10 Helmut Puff, 'Homosexuality: A Beast with Many Backs', in *A Cultural History of Sexuality*, vol. III: *In the Renaissance*, ed. Bette Talvacchia (London, 2011), p. 70.

11 William Henry Whitmore, *The Colonial Laws of Massachusetts: Reprinted from the Edition of 1660, With the Supplements to 1672: Containing Also, the Body of Liberties of Fred B. Rothman & Co.* (Boston, MA, 1889).

12 George Androutsos, 'Hermaphroditism in Greek and Roman Antiquity', *Hormones*, V/3 (2006), p. 214; James Diggle, *Characters by Theophrastus* (Cambridge, 2004), p. 366; George Androutsos, Aristidis Diamantis, Lazaros Vladimiros, Emmanouil Magiorkinis, 'Bisexuality in Ancient Greek-Roman Society', *International Journal of Medicine*, I/2 (April–June 2008), p. 67. For an excellent assessment of hermaphrodites in history, see Alice Domurat Dreger, *Hermaphrodites and the Medical Invention of Sex* (Cambridge, MA, 1998).

13 Vern L. Bullough and Bonnie Bullough, *Cross-dressing, Sex, and Gender* (Philadelphia, PA, 1993), p. 29.

14 Kathleen P. Long, *Hermaphrodites in Renaissance Europe* (Farnham, Surrey, 2006); Ruth Gilbert, *Early Modern Hermaphrodites* (Basingstoke, 2002); Ambroise Paré (1510–1590), *On Monsters and Marvels* (Chicago, IL, 1982); Casper Bauhin, *De hermaphroditorum monstrosorumque partuum naturae* (1614).

15 Jane Sharp, *The Midwives' Book; or, The Whole Art of Midwifery Discovered Directing Childbearing Women How to Behave Themselves in Their Conception, Breeding, Bearing and Children* (London, 1671), pp. 40–42.

16 Ibid., p. 40.

17 James Parsons, *A Mechanical and Critical Enquiry into the Nature of Hermaphrodites* (London, 1741), pp. 13–14, 21.

18 Alan Bray, *The Friend* (Chicago, IL, 2003), p. 220.

19 Henry Fielding, *The Female Husband: or the Surprising History of Mrs Mary, alias George Hamilton* (London, 1746). This was a 23-page pamphlet priced at sixpence.

20 These cases and others are described in Peakman, *Lascivious Bodies*, pp. 174–200; and Emma Donoghue, *Passions Between Women: British Lesbian Culture, 1668–1801* (London, 1993).

21 Ophelia Field, *Sarah, the Duchess of Marlborough: The Queen's Favourite* (London, 2002)

22 Helen Whitbread, ed., *I Know My Own Heart: The Diaries of Ann Lister, 1791–1840* (New York, 1992), p. 201.

23 Denis Diderot, *Memoirs of a Nun*, trans. Francis Birrell (London, 1992), p. 129.

24 These cases have been uncovered by Theo van der Meer, 'Tribades on Trial: Female Same-sex Offenders in Late Eighteenth-century Amsterdam', in *Forbidden History: The State, Society and the Regulation of Sexuality in Modern Europe*, ed. John C. Fout (Chicago, IL, 1992), pp. 189–210.

25 Edward Carpenter, *Love's Coming of Age* (London, 1915), pp. 114–34.

26 Nelljean McConeghey Rice, *A New Matrix for Modernism: A Study of the Lives and Poetry of Charlotte Mew and Anna Wikham* (London, 2003), p. 35.

27 Penelope Fitzgerald, *Charlotte Mew and Her Friends* (London, 1984), pp. 137, 108.

28 Leila J. Rupp, 'Loving Women in the Modern World', in *Gay Life and Culture: A World History*, ed. Robert Aldrich (London, 2006), pp. 223–47, 234.

29 *New York Times*, 26 January 1892.

30 Havelock Ellis, *Studies in the Psychology of Sex* [1897] (New York, 1942), Book IV, *Sexual Inversion*, p. 201.

31 Ali Coffignon, *Paris vivant: La Corruption à Paris* (Paris, 1889), p. 301.

32 Ellis, *Sexual Inversion*, pp. 250–51.

33 Ibid., p. 256.

34 Robert Latou Dickinson and Lura Beam, *The Single Woman: A Medical Study in Sex Education* (London, 1934), p. 212.

35 For more on the New Woman, see Angelique Richardson and Chris Willis, eds, *The New Woman in Fiction and in Fact: Fin-de-siècle Feminisms* (London, 2001); Sally Ledger, *The New Woman, Fiction and Feminism at the Fin-de-siècle* (Manchester, 1997).

36 Diana Southami, *Wild Girls: Paris, Sappho and Art: The Lives of Natalie Barney and Romaine Brookes* (London, 2004).

37 *Women's Life*, 10 January 1920.

38 Alison Oram, *Her Husband Was a Woman: Women's Gender-crossing in Modern British Popular Culture* (London, 2007).

39 Hansard Parliamentary Debates, House of Commons, 5th series, CXLV, 1804–5.

40 Nigel Nicholson, *Portrait of a Marriage* (London, 1974), pp. 106–7.

41 Lesbian Herstory Educations Foundation pamphlet from The Archives, 'Radclyffe Hall's 1934 Letter about *The Well of Loneliness*' (New York, 1994), p. 2.

42 *Sunday Express* (19 August 1928), p. 10.

43 Frank Caprio, *Variations in Sexual Behaviour* (London, 1957), pp. 160–61; Frank Caprio, *Female Homosexuality: A Psychodynamic Study of Lesbianism* (New York, 1954), p. viii. Others were in agreement; according to Dr William G. Niederland, many lesbians suffered from a masculinity complex that could lead to serious difficulties if left unchecked. He suggested psychoanalysis as the answer.

44 Caprio, *Variations*, p. 177.

45 Eric Oakley, *Sex and Sadism Throughout the Ages* (London, 1965), p. 43.

46 Margaret Otis, 'A Perversion Not Commonly Noted', *Journal of Abnormal Psychology*, VIII/2 (1913), pp. 113–16.

47 Bernard Hollander, *The Psychology of Misconduct, Vice and Crime* (London, 1922), pp. 141, 144; C. Esther Hodge, *A Woman-oriented Woman* (West Sussex, 1989), pp. 26–8.

48 Oram and Turnbull, *Lesbian History Sourcebook*, p. 212; Alkarim Jivani, *It's Not Unusual: A History of Lesbian and Gay Britain in the Twentieth Century* (London, 1997), pp. 71–2.

49 See 'One Million Moms Drops Protest Against Ellen Degeneres and JC Penney', 8 March 2012, www.gossipcop.com.

5 From Transvestites to Transsexuals

1 Herodotus, *Histories*, 5.10; John Younger, 'Sexual Variations: Sexual Peculiarities of the Ancient Greeks and Romans', in *A Cultural History of Sexuality*, vol. 1: *In the Classical World*, ed. Mark Golden and Peter Toohey (London, 2011), pp. 80–83.

2 Mary M. Innes, trans., *The Metamorphoses of Ovid* [1955] (Harmondsworth, 1961), p. 315.

3 Martijn Icks, *The Crimes of Elagabalus: The Life and Legacy of Rome's Decadent Boy Emperor* (London, 2011), p. 99.

4 Ibid.

5 Suetonius, *The Twelve Caesars*, Nero, 28.

6 Elaine Bradtke et al., *Truculent Rustics: Molly Dancing in East Anglia Before 1940* (London, 2000). For further discussions and examples of cross-dressing, see Vern and Bonnie Bullough, *Cross-dressing, Sex and Gender* (Philadelphia, PA, 1993); Marjorie Garber, *Vested Interests: Cross-dressing and Cultural Anxiety* (London, 1992).

7 Gregory of Tours, *History of the Franks* (Middlesex, 1974), p. 570; reported in Nancy F. Partner, 'No Sex, No Gender', *Speculum*, LXVIII (1993), pp. 419–43; see also 'The Revolt of the Nuns at Poitiers', in the History Collection at http://digicoll.library.wisc.edu, accessed 17 June 2012.

8 Ibid.

9 Barbara Sher Tinsley, 'Pope Joan Polemic in Early Modern France: The Use and Disabuse of Myth', *Sixteenth Century Journal*, XVIII/3 (Autumn 1987), pp. 381–98.

10 See 'Fifth Private Examination', www.stjoan-center.com, accessed 5 April 2013.

11 *Norwich Gazette* (8–15 August 1741).

12 See Julie Peakman, *Lascivious Bodies: A Sexual History of the Eighteenth Century* (London, 2004), pp. 174–200 and 219–35; and Emma Donoghue, *Passions Between Women: British Lesbian Culture, 1668–1801* (London, 1993).

13 Theo Van der Meer, 'The Persecutions of Sodomites in Eighteenth-century Amsterdam: Changing Perceptions of Sodomy', in *The Pursuit of Sodomy*, ed. Kent Gerard and Gert Hekma (New York, 1989), p. 281. On the persecution of tribades and other similar cases in the Netherlands, see Theo van der Meer, 'Tribades on Trial: Female Same-sex Offenders in Late Eighteenth-century Amsterdam', in *Forbidden History: The State, Society and the Regulation of Sexuality in Modern Europe*, ed. John C. Fout (Chicago, IL, 1992), pp. 189–210.

14 See Peakman on D'Eon and De Choisy in *Lascivious Bodies*, pp. 201–18.

15 Katherine M. Brown, '"Changed into the Fashion of a Man": The Politics of Sexual Difference in a Seventeenth-century Anglo-American Settlement', in *The Devil's Lane: Sex and Race in the Early South*, ed. Catherine Clinton and Michele Gillespie (London, 1997), pp. 39–56; see also Wendy Lucas Castro, 'Stripped: Clothing and Identity in Colonial Captivity Narratives', *Early American Studies: An Interdisciplinary Journal*, VI/1 (Spring 2008), pp. 104–36.

17 Jonas Liliequist, 'Peasants Against Nature: Crossing the Boundaries between Man and Animals in Seventeenth and Eighteenth-century Sweden', *Journal of the History of Sexuality*, 1/3 (1999), pp. 393–423.

18 Governor John Winthrop, *History of New England, 1630–1649* (Boston, MA, 1825), II, pp. 48–9. Winthrop was first governor of Massachusetts Bay.

19 *Whitehall Evening Post* (13–15 October 1789); *London Evening Post* (30 April 1772–2 May 1772).

20 *Courier and Evening Gazette* (23 July 1799); *True Briton* (27 July 1799) reports him as James Drewry (with a different spelling of his surname).

21 Liliequist, 'Peasants Against Nature'.

22 *Bury and Norwich Post: Or Suffolk, Essex, Cambridge, Ely, and Norfolk Telegraph* (26 February 1823).

23 *Bury and Norwich Post* (31 March 1824).

24 'Summary of Prisoners for Trial at the York Assizes', *Hull Packet and Original Weekly Commercial, Literary and General Advertiser* (14 March 1826).

25 *Morning Post* (31 August 1830); *Liverpool Mercury* (16 August 1833).

26 Jacob de Bondt, *Historiae naturalis et medicae Indiae orientalis* (1631).

27 Ambroise Paré, *On Monsters and Marvels* [c. 1510], trans. Janis L. Pallister (Chicago, IL, 1982), pp. 67–8.

28 Sir Richard Manningham, *An exact Diary of what was observ'd during a close attendance upon M Toft, the pretended Rabbet-Breeder of Godalming in Surrey, from Nov 28 to Dec 7 following Together with an account of her confession of the fraud* (London, 1726), pp. 16–17; *A philosophical enquiry into the wonderful Coney-Warren, lately discovered at Godalming near Guildford, being an account of the birth of seventeen rabbits born of a woman [Mary Toft] at several times, and who still continues in strong labour, at the Bagnio in Leicester Fields* (London, 1726); J. Shaw, 'Mary Toft, Religion and National Memory in Eighteenth-century England', *Journal for Eighteenth-century Studies*, XXXII/3 (2009), pp. 321–38.

29 G. S. Rousseau, 'Imagination, Pregnant Women and Monsters in Eighteenth-century England and France', in G. S. Rousseau and Roy Porter, *Sexual Underworlds in the Enlightenment* (Manchester, 1987), pp. 86–100.

30 Ronald Hyman, *Marquis de Sade: Genius of Passion* (London, 2003), p. 151.

31 Reported in *Alienist and Neurologist*, p. 204; see Havelock Ellis, *Studies in the Psychology of Sex* (New York, 1942), vol. I, Part 2, 'Love and Pain', p. 151.

32 Dekkers, *Dearest Pet*, p. 18.

33 'Masters on Zoo', www.animalzoofrance.net, accessed 16 April 2013; also see Major Steven Cullen, 'Prosecuting Indecent Conduct in the Military: Honey, Should We Get a Legal Review First?', *Military Law Review*, CLXXIX (2004), p. 142.

34 Havelock Ellis, *Studies in the Psychology of Sex* (New York, 1942), vol. II, Part 1, 'Erotic Symbolism', p. 84.

35 Jens Rydström, 'Sodomitical Sins are Threefold: Typologies of Bestiality, Masturbation and Homosexuality, in Sweden, 1880–1950', *Journal of the History of Sexuality*, IX/3 (2000), pp. 240–76; see also Jens Rydström, *Sinners and Citizens: Bestiality and Homosexuality in Sweden, 1880–1950* (Chicago, IL, 2003).

36 Masters, *Hidden World of Erotica*, pp. 40, 148–50.

37 Mark Matthews, *The Horseman: Obsessions of a Zoophile* (New York, 1994), pp. 110–11.

38 Liliequist, 'Peasants Against Nature'.

39 Alfred C. Wardell, B. Pomeroy and Clyde E. Martin, *Sexual Behaviour in the Human Male* (Philadelphia, PA, 1948), pp. 667–678; Alfred C. Kinsey et al., *Sexual Behavior in the Human Female* (Philadelphia, PA, 1953), pp. 502–9.

40 The exact figures are 4.9 per cent for males and 1.9 per cent for females; Morton M. Hunt, *Sexual Behavior in the 1970s* (New York, 1974).

41 See David J. Rust, 'The Sociology of Furry Fandom' (2001), www.visi.com/~phantos/furrysoc, accessed 27 April 2012.

42 See 'Sexual Offences Act 2003', www.legislation.gov.uk, accessed 27 April 2012.

43 *Sunday Times* (12 November 2008).

44 *Liverpool Echo* (15 February 2011); *The Sun* (22 February 2011).

7 The Ties That Bind: Sadomasochism

1 According to the *Oxford English Dictionary*'s definition, sadism is automatically connected to the sexual.

2 John Younger, 'Sexual Variations: Sexual Peculiarities of the Ancient Greeks and Romans', in *A Cultural History of Sexuality*, vol. I: *In the Classical World*, ed. Mark Golden and Peter Toohey (London, 2011), pp. 55–86.

3 Leslie Kurke, 'Inventing the "Hetaira": Sex, Politics, and Discursive Conflict in Archaic Greece', *Classical Antiquity*, XVI/1 (April 1997), pp. 106–50; Mark Golden, 'Slavery and Homosexuality at Athens', *Phoenix*, XXXVIII/4 (Winter 1984), pp. 308–24; Sarah B. Pomeroy, *Goddesses, Whores, Wives and Slaves* (New York, 1975), p. 82.

4 Otto Kiefer, *Sexual Life in Ancient Rome* (London, 2000); Judith P. Hallett, 'Roman Attitudes Towards Sex', in *Civilizations of the Ancient Mediterranean*, ed. M. Grant and R. Kitzinger (New York, 1988), pp. 1265–78.

5 Suetonius, *Gaius Caligula*, 10–11, 27.

6 Suetonius, *Nero*, 26–28.

7 Ovid, *Art of Love*, 1.673–80.

8 Jacco Hamman, 'The Rod of Discipline: Masochism, Sadism and the Judeo-Christian Religion', *Journal of Religion and Health*, XXXIX/4 (Winter 2000). See Donald Capps, *The Child's Song: The Religious Abuse of Children* (Louisville, KY, 1995).

9 Marquis de Sade, *Justine, Philosophy in the Bedroom, and Other Writings*, trans. Richard Seaver and Austryn Wainhouse (New York, 1965), p. 449.

10 Laurence L. Bongie, *De Sade: A Biographical Essay* (Chicago, IL, 1998), p. 109.

11 Francine du Plessix Gray, *At Home with the Marquis de Sade* (London, 2000); Neil Schaeffer, *The Marquis de Sade* (London, 1999); Maurice Lever, *Marquis de Sade: A Biography* (London, 1993).

12 Robert Eisler, *Man into Wolf: An Anthropological Interpretation of Sadism, Masochism and Lycanthropy* (London, 1948), p. 74.

13 James Cleugh, *The Marquis and the Chevalier* (New York, 1951), p. 183.

14 Wanda von Dunajew (pseud.), *Meine Lebensbeichte* (1906), published in translation as Wanda von Sacher-Masoch, *The Confessions of Wanda von Sacher-Masoch*, trans. Marian Phillips et al. (San Francisco, CA, 1990), p. 11.

15 Ibid., p. 30.

16 'Foreword', in Richard von Krafft-Ebing, *Psychopathia Sexualis*, reprint of 12th edn [1903] (Berkeley, CA, 1999), p. 79.

17 Schiebinger Londa, 'Skeletons in the Closet: The First Illustrations of the Female Skeleton in Eighteenth-century Anatomy', in *The Making of the Modern Body: Sexuality and Society in the Nineteenth Century*, ed. T. Laqueur (Berkeley, CA, 1987), p. 53; Ludmilla Jordanova, *Sexual Visions: Images of Gender in Science and Medicine between the Eighteenth and Twentieth Centuries* (New York, 1989).

18 Ivan Crozier, 'Philosophy in the English Boudoir, Havelock Ellis, "Love and Pain", and Sexological Discourse on Algophilia', *Journal of the History of Sexuality*, XIII/4 (2004), pp. 275–305.

19 All the quotes from Ellis here and in the previous paragraph come from Havelock Ellis, *Studies in the Psychology of Sex*, vol. I, Part 2, Section 2: 'Love and Pain' [1903] (New York, 1942), pp. 66–188.

20 Ibid.

21 Ibid.
22 Charles Féré, *The Evolution and Dissolution of the Sexual Instinct* (Paris, 1904), pp. 163–4.
23 Among them Krafft-Ebing, Ellis and the French physicians Féré and naval surgeon Dr R. L. Laserre.
24 Moll cited by Ellis, 'Love and Pain', p. 105.
25 Albert Eulenburg, *Algolagnia: The Psychology, Neurology and Physiology of Sadistic Love and Masochism* [1902] (New York, 1934), p. 25.
26 Ibid.
27 Eric Oakley, *Sex and Sadism Throughout the Ages* (London, 1965), p. 18.
28 Dr Magnus Hirschfeld, *Transvestites*, trans. Michael A. Lombard-Nash [1910] (New York, 1991), p. 172.
29 Reports of the further attacks came from Charlotte von Schiller to Knebel but appear not to have been true.
30 Eulenburg, *Algolagnia*, p. 112.
31 Frank S. Caprio, *Variations in Sexual Behaviour* (London, 1957), p. 34.
32 William Renwick Riddell, 'A Case of Supposed Sadism', *Journal of the American Institute of Criminal Law and Criminology*, xv/1 (May 1924), pp. 32–41.
33 Eulenburg, *Algolagnia*, p. 104.
34 Gilles Deleuze, *Masochism: Coldness and Cruelty* (New York, 1989), p. 33.
35 A. B. Heilbrun Jr and David T. Seif, 'Erotic Value of Female Distress in Sexually Explicit Photographs', *Journal of Sexual Health*, xxiv (1988), pp. 47–57.
36 BBC 1 News, 7 December 2001; more recently the University of Michigan has undertaken tests to find that the brain's 'pleasure' chemical dopamine is released during pain. David J. Scott, Mary M. Heitzeg, Robert A. Koeppe, Christian S. Stohler and Jon-Kar Zubieta, 'Variations in the Human Pain Stress Experience Mediated by Ventral and Dorsal Basal Ganglia Dopamine Activity', *Journal of Neuroscience*, xxvi/42 (18 October 2006), pp. 10789–95. For the article, see www.jneurosci.org, accessed 16 April 2013.
37 Edmund Burke, *On the Sublime and Beautiful* [1756], Part 1, Section II (London, 1909–14).

8 Loving the Dead

1 For the pupose of this book, I have taken necrophilia to specifically mean desiring or acting out sexual activity with the dead, although I also explore it in terms of attitudes towards death in broader society and culture. Other historians have made inroads into extending the exploration of necrophilia to a broader base, for example, literature, politics, theatre and art: see Lisa Downing, *Desiring the Dead: Necrophilia and Nineteenth-century French Literature* (London, 2002); Lisa Downing, 'Death and the Maidens: A Century of Necrophilia in Female-authored Textual Production', *French Cultural Studies*, XIV/2/41 (2003), pp. 157–68; Adam Wilson, 'Democratic Necrophilia: The Eighteenth-century's Anxious Disease', *Anamesa*, V/1, The Democracy Issue (Spring 2007), pp. 42–66; J. Roach, 'History, Memory, Necrophilia', in *The Ends of Performance*, ed. P. Phelan and J. Lane (New York, 1995), pp. 23–30; Carol Christ, 'Painting the Dead: Portraiture and Necrophilia in Victorian Art and Poetry', in *Death and Representation*, ed. Sarah Webster Goodwin and Elisabeth Bronfen (Baltimore, MD, 1993), pp. 133–51; A. Aggrawal, 'A New Classification of Necrophilia', *Journal of Forensic and Legal Medicine*, XVI/6 (2009), pp. 316–20; A. D. Murray, 'The Reclassification of Extreme Pornographic Images', *Modern Law Review*, LXXII/1 (2009), pp. 73–90.
2 Herodotus, *Histories*, Book II, 89.
3 John Younger, 'Sexual Variations: Sexual Peculiarities of the Ancient Greeks and Romans', in *A Cultural History of Sexuality*, vol. I: *In the Classical World*, ed. Mark Golden and Peter Toohey (London, 2011), p. 86.
4 Herodotus, *Histories*, Book V, 91–93.
5 Jean Benedetti, *The Real Bluebeard: The Life of Gilles de Rais* (Stroud, 2003), p. 113.
6 Ibid., p. 115.
7 James Penney, *The World of Perversion: Psychoanalysis and the Impossible Absolute of Desire* (New York, 2006), p. 55.
8 Marquis de Sade, *Juliette* [1797] (New York, 1968), p. 539.
9 Philippe Aries, *L'Homme devant la mort* (Paris, 1977), p. 373.
10 Julie Peakman, 'Introduction', *Sexual Perversions* (Basingstoke, 2009), p. 38.
11 Elizabeth Bronfen, *Over Her Dead Body: Death, Femininity and the Aesthetic* (Manchester, 1992). See also Camille Naish, *Death Comes to the Maiden: Sex and Execution, 1431–1933* (London, 1991); Janet Todd, *Gender, Art and Death* (New York, 1993).
12 Rebecca May, 'Morbid Parts: Gender, Seduction and the Necro-gaze', in Peakman, *Sexual Perversions*, pp. 167–201.

13 Ludmilla Jordanova, *Sexual Visions: Images of Gender in Science and Medicine Between the Eighteenth and Nineteenth Centuries* (London, 1989), p. 55.

14 See Christ, 'Painting the Dead'.

15 See May, 'Morbid Parts'.

16 Cited in R.E.L. Masters and Eduard Lea, *Sex Crimes in History* (New York, 1964), p. 120.

17 Dr Léon Henri Thoinot, *Attentats aux moeurs, et perversion du sens génital* (Paris, 1898), pp. 477–85.

18 Henri Marie Beyle [Stendhal], *The Life of Henry Brulard* (Paris, 1890).

19 William Stekel, *Sadism and Masochism* (London, 1953).

20 H. H. Remsen Whitehouse, *A Revolutionary Princess: Cristina Belgiojoso Trivulzio: Her Life and Times* [1906] (New York, 2009); Antonio Fabris, ed., *Cristina Belgiojoso Trivulzi: An Italian Princess in the Nineteenth-century Turkish Countryside* (Venice, 2010).

21 For quotes below see Ben Harrison, *Undying Love: The True Story of a Passion that Defied Death* (London, 2001), pp. 88, 105, 104, 233.

22 J. P. Rosman and P. J. Resnick, 'Sexual Attraction to Corpses: A Psychiatric Review of Necrophilia', *Bulletin of the American Academy of Psychiatry and the Law*, xvii/2 (1989), pp. 153–63.

9 Too Close for Comfort: Incest

1 In a letter to Maria Gisburne, quoted by Elizabeth Archibauld, *Incest and the Medieval Imagination* (Oxford, 2003), p. 8.

2 Sophocles, *The Theban Plays* [translator E.F. Watling] (Harmondsworth, 1974), p. 64.

3 Tatum, *Patrician Tribune*, pp. 41–2.

4 Suetonius, *Gaius Caligula*, 24.

5 Suetonius, *The Twelve Caesars*, Nero, 28.

6 Vern L. Bullough and James A. Brundage, *Handbook of Medieval Sexuality* (New York, 2000), p. 338.

7 Arthur Brandeis, ed., *Jacob's Well: An English Treatise on the Cleansing of Man's Conscience* (London, reprint, 2009), p. 48, at Internet Archive, www.archive.org, 15 April 2013.

8 T. F. Hoad, ed., *Oxford Concise Dictionary of Etymology* (Oxford, 1996), p. 232; Elizabeth Archibauld, 'Incest Between Children and Adults in the Medieval World', in *Children and Sexuality*, ed. George Rousseau (Basingstoke, 2007), p. xiv.

9 Irina Metzler, 'Sex, Religion and the Law', in *A Cultural History of Sexuality*, vol. ii: *In the Middle Ages*, ed. Ruth Evans (London, 2011), pp. 101–19.

10 Marion Turner, *Chaucerian Conflict: Languages of Antagonism in Late Fourteenth-century London* (Oxford, 2007), pp. 52ff, 61.

11 Tommy Bengtsson and Geraldine P. Mineau, *Kinship and Demographic Behavior in the Past* (New York, 2008), p. 206.

12 Quoted in Adam Kuper, *Incest and Influence: The Private Life of Bourgeois England* (Cambridge, MA, 2009), pp. 61–2.

13 Lawrence Stone, *The Family, Sex and Marriage, 1500–1800* (London, 1990), p. 96.

14 Transcript online at www.folger.edu, accessed 6 July 2012.

15 The 32 private letters are held at the Folger Shakespeare Library, Washington, DC. For a modern account of the DuGard cousins (Samuel and Lydia) as well as Samuel DuGard's (printed) defence of the marriage of cousins, see the following publication from the Arizona Centre for Medieval and Renaissance Studies: Nancy Taylor, ed., 'Cousins in Love: The Letters of Lydia DuGard, 1665–1672', *Renaissance English Text Society*, XXVIII (Arizona, 2003), p. 140, on incest; Adam Kuper, 'Incest Cousin Marriage', *Past and Present*, CLXXIV/1 (2002), pp. 158–83.

16 R. I., *A Most Straunge, and True Discourse, of the Wonderfull Judgement of God: Of a monstrous, deformed infant, begotten by incestuous copulation, betweene the brothers sonne and the sisters daughter, being both unmarried persons* (London, 1600); Robert Hole, 'Consanguinity and a Monstrous Birth in Rural England, January 1600', *Social History*, XXV/2 (2000), pp. 183–99.

17 *The Rambler*, CLXX (2 November 1751).

18 *The Rambler*, CLXXI (5 November 1751).

19 Adam Kuper, *Incest and Influence: The Private Life of Bourgeois England* (Cambridge, MA, 2009), p. 27; Leanore Davidoff, *Thicker than Water: Siblings and Their Relations, 1780–1920* (Oxford, 2012).

20 Edgar J. McManus, *Law and Liberty in Early New England, 1620–1692* (Amherst, MA, 2009), p. 25.

21 Polly Morris, 'Incest or Survival Strategy? Plebeian Marriage within the Prohibited Degrees in Somerset, 1730–1835', *Journal of the History of Sexuality*, II/2 (1991), pp. 235–65.

22 *Oracle Bell's New World*, L (28 July 1789).

23 *Oracle Bell's New World*, LXXXII (3 September 1789).

24 Kuper, *Incest and Influence*, p. 55.

25 Ibid., pp. 54–5.

26 *Histoire de Dom Bougre, portier des Chartreux*, trans. Howard Nelson as *The Lascivious Monk* (Wiltshire, 1993), p. 286.

27 Marquis de Sade, *Incest* [*Eugénie de Franval*, 1800], trans., Andrew Brown, London, 2003), p. 48.

28 Anon., *A New Description of Merryland* (London, 1741), p. 20.

29 Donald Thomas, 'Preface', in *The School of Venus* [*L'Ecole des filles*, 1655] (London, 1972), p. 20.

30 Bryan Strong, 'Toward a History of the Experiential Family: Sex and Incest in the Nineteenth Century', *Journal of Marriage and Family*, xxxv/3 (August 1973), pp. 457–66.

31 Anon., *The Romance of Lust* [1883–7] (London,reprint, 1995), p. 7; also at www.gutenberg.org.

32 Henry Mayhew, *London Labour and the London Poor* (London, 1864); William Acton, *The Functions and Disorders of the Reproductive Organs in Childhood, Youth, Adult Age, and Advanced Life: Considered in Their Physiological, Social, and Moral Relations* (London, 1862); Charles Booth, *Labour and Life of the People* (London, 1891–1903).

33 Andrew Mearns and W. C. Preston, *The Bitter Cry of Outcast London* (London, 1883), p. 12.

34 Lewis Henry Morgan, *Systems of Consanguinity and Affinity of the Human Family* (Washington, DC, 1871).

35 Edvard Westermarck, in *The History of Human Marriage* (London, 1891), p. 433.

36 Richard Freiherr von Krafft-Ebing, *Psychopathia Sexualis*, reprint of 12th edn [1903] (Berkeley, CA, 1999), p. 513.

37 Ibid., pp. 513–15.

38 Havelock Ellis, 'Eonism', in *Studies in the Psychology of Sex* (New York, 1942), p. 24.

39 Sigmund Freud, *The Interpretation of Dreams* (New York, 1913), p. 296.

40 James L. Peacock and A. Thomas Kirsch, *The Human Direction: An Evolutionary Approach to Social and Cultural Anthropology* (New York, 1970), p. 100.

41 Conrad P. Kottack, *Cultural Anthropology* (New York, 1994), p. 22.

42 As Davidson has pointed out, Maureen Quilligan has argued recently that 'the interdiction against incest is a constant in all human societies, pivotal at all periods and in all places.' Michel Foucault has also suggested that incest was not seen as a major problem before the nineteenth century, which is not the case, as we can see by the number of medieval laws on the subject. Foucault says that the assumption that its prohibition was universal in earlier times was no more than a reflection back on the past of modern preoccupations. See N. S. Davidson, 'Sex, Religion, and the Law: Disciplining Desire', in *A Cultural History of Sexuality*, vol. II: *In the Renaissance*, ed. Bette Talvacchia (London, 2011), p. 93.

43 Lloyd DeMause, 'The Universality of Incest', *Journal of Psychohistory*, XIX/2 (Autumn 1991).

44 *Old Bailey Proceedings Online, 1674–1913*, www.oldbaileyonline. org:
ref. t19091012–67; t19100718–44; t19130204–70, accessed
4 February 2013.

45 Frank S. Caprio, *Variations in Sexual Behaviour* (London, 1957),
pp. 189–218.

46 M. C. Canavan, W. J. Meyer and D. C. Higgs, 'The Female
Experience of Sibling Incest', *Journal of Marital and Family Therapy*,
XVIII/2 (1992), pp. 129–42; Vernon Wiehe, *Sibling Abuse: Hidden
Physical, Emotional, and Sexual Trauma* (Lexington, KY, 1997);
H. Smith and E. Israel, 'Sibling Incest: A Study of the Dynamics
of 25 Cases', *Child Abuse and Neglect*, XI (1987), pp. 101–8; E. Cole,
'Sibling Incest: The Myth of Benign Sibling Incest', *Women and
Therapy*, I/3 (1982), pp. 79–89. Sibling incest was roughly five times
as common as other forms of incest, according to P. Gebhard,
J. Gagnon, W. Pomeroy and C. Christenson, *Sex Offenders:
An Analysis of Types* (New York, 1965).

47 *Guardian* (15 April 2012).

48 Toni A. H. McNaron and Yarrow Morgan, *Voices in the Night:
Women Speaking About Incest* (Minneapolis, MN, 1982), p. 11.

49 Anna Meigs and Kathleen Barlow, 'Beyond the Taboo: Imagining
Incest', *American Anthropologist*, CIV/1, pp. 38–49.

50 Beryl Satter, 'The Sexual Abuse Paradigm in Historical Perspective:
Passivity and Emotion in Mid-Twentieth-Century America', *Journal
of the History of Sexuality*, XII/3 (July 2003), pp. 424–64.

51 See 'Sexual Offences Act 2003', www.legislation.gov.uk, accessed
27 April 2012.

52 See 'Incest: An Age-old Taboo', 12 March 2007,
www.bbc.co.uk/news.

10 Child Love or Paedophilia?

1 Xenophon, *Constitution of the Lacedaimonians*, ii.1; A. V.
Yannicopoulos, 'The Pedagogue In Antiquity', *British Journal
Of Educational Studies*, XXXIII/2 (June 1985), pp. 173–9.

2 Pseudo-Demosthesenes, *Against Neaera*, 59.18–19.

3 Sandra R Joshel, 'Nucturing the Master's Child: Slavery and the
Roman Child-nurse', *Signs*, XII/1 (1986), pp. 1–22; see also Amy
Richlin, 'Invective Against Women in Roman Satire', *Arethusa*,
XVII/1 (Spring 1984), pp. 67–80, esp. pp. 71–2; and Richlin, *The
Garden of Priapus* (New Haven, CT, 1983), pp. 113–14.

4 Suetonius, *Tiberius*, 44.

5 Phillipe Aries, *Centuries of Childhood* (Harmondsworth, 1962),
p. 98.

6 Barbara A. Hanawalt, *Growing Up in Medieval London* (Oxford, 1993), p. 5.

7 18 eliz. 1, C.7, cited in Sir W. Blackstone, *Commentaries on the Laws of England* (Oxford, 1769), p. 212.

8 *Old Bailey Proceedings Online, 1674–1913*, www.oldbaileyonline. org: ref. t16781211e–2, accessed 16 April 2012.

9 Anthony E. Simpson, 'Vulnerability and the Age of Female Consent', in *Sexual Underworld of the Enlightenment*, ed. G. S. Rousseau and Roy Porter (Manchester, 1987), pp. 181–206.

10 Quoted in Phillipe Aries, *Centuries of Childhood* (Harmondsworth, 1962), p. 237.

11 Ibid., pp. 234, 253.

12 Ibid., p. 114.

13 See Joseph William Howe, *Excessive Venery, Masturbation and Continence* (London, 1883), mentioned in chapter Two.

14 Although Ariès cited above had argued that children did not exist in the medieval period and were treated as mini-adults, this theory has essentially been questioned by other historians: for example, see Albrecht Classmen, ed., *Childhood in the Middle Ages and the Renaissance* (Berlin, 2005); Barbara A. Hanawalt, *Growing Up in Medieval London* (Oxford, 1993); Shulamith Shear, *Childhood in the Middle Ages* (London, 1990); Linda Pollock, *A Lasting Relationship: Parents and Their Children Over Three Centuries* (London, 1987); Linda Pollock, *Forgotten Children: Parent–Child Relations from 1500 to 1900* (Cambridge, 1983).

15 Sir John Fielding, *A Plan for a Preservatory and Reformatory, for the Benefit of Deserted Girls* (London, 1758), p. 5.

16 See bibliography for Louise Jackson, Rictor Norton, Randolph Trumbach and other cases mentioned elsewhere in this book.

17 *Old Bailey Proceedings Online*: ref. t17510523–35, accessed 28 July 2011.

18 *Old Bailey Proceedings Online*: ref. t16800421–5, accessed 28 July 2011.

19 *Weekly Journal or British Gazetteer* (5 August 1727); *Weekly Journal or Saturday's Post* (6 January 1722).

20 *Daily Courant* (13 April 1730).

21 *Weekly Journal or British Gazetteer* (16 January 1731).

22 *Daily Gazetteer* (12 February 1737).

23 See Jenny Skipp, 'The Hostile Gaze: Perverting the Female Form, 1688–1800'; and Jennie Mills, 'Rape in Early Eighteenth-century London: A Perversion "so very perplex'd"', in *Sexual Perversions*, ed. Julie Peakman (London, 2009), chaps 5 and 6; Julie Peakman, *Lascivious Bodies: A Sexual History of the Eighteenth Century* (London, 2004), chaps 5 and 6; Tassie Williams, 'Female Fraud: Counterfeit Maidenheads in the Eighteenth Century', *Journal of the*

History of Sexuality, VI/4 (April 1996), pp. 518–48; Anna Clark, 'The Politics of Seduction in English Popular Culture, 1748–1848', in *The Progress of Romance: The Politics of Popular Culture*, ed. Jean Radford (London, 1986), pp. 47–72.

24 *London Evening Post* (25–27 July 1738).

25 *Weekly Journal or British Gazetteer* (19 June 1736).

26 *Daily Gazetteer* (28 September 1736).

27 *Old Bailey Proceedings Online*: ref. t16781211e–2, accessed 28 July 2011; Alfred Swaine Taylor, *Elements of Medical Jurisprudence* (London, 1844), p. 575.

28 H. G. Cocks, *Nameless Offences: Homosexual Desire in the Nineteenth Century* (London, 2003), p. 32.

29 Louise Jackson, *Child Sexual Abuse in Victorian England* (London, 2000), pp. 20, 29.

30 *Old Bailey Proceedings Online*: see under headings 'Crime, Justice and Punishment/Sexual Offences/Rape', www.oldbaileyonline.org, accessed 16 April 2013.

31 Jackson, *Child Sexual Abuse in Victorian England* (London, 2000), pp. 71–89.

32 Auguste Ambroise Tardieu, *Etude médico-légale sur les attentats aux moeurs* [1857] (Paris, 1995), p. 173.

33 Fielding, *A Plan for a Preservatory and Reformatory*.

34 Leslie Mitchell, *Lord Melbourne, 1779–1848* (Oxford, 1997).

35 There are far too many 'scientific' studies on the subject to mention here but for some views from the late 1970s and '80s, see K. Howells, 'Some Meanings of Children for Pedophiles', in *Love and Attraction*, ed. M. Cook and G. Wilson (Oxford, 1979): K. Howells, 'Adult Sexual Interest in Children: Considerations Relevant to Theories of Aetiology', in *Adult Sexual Interest in Children*, ed. M. Cook and K. Howells (London, 1981); D. Finkelhor and S. Araji, 'Explanations of Pedophilia: A Four Factor Model', *Journal of Sex Research*, XXII/2 (1986), pp. 145–61; James Horley, 'Cognitions of Child Sexual Abusers', *Journal of Sex Research*, XXV/4 (November 1988), pp. 542–5.

36 Jad Adams, *Madder Music, Stronger Wine: The Life of Ernest Dowson* (London, 2000), p. 56.

37 Quoted ibid., p. 14.

38 Jackson, *Child Sexual Abuse in Victorian England* (London, 2000), pp. 39, 62, 84.

39 Ibid., pp. 4–5.

40 W. T. Stead, 'The Maiden Tribute of Modern Babylon 1: The Report of Our Secret Commission', *Pall Mall Gazette* (6 July 1885).

41 Letter in the *Shield* (May 1880).

42 Richard Freiherr von Krafft-Ebing, *Psychopathia Sexualis*, reprint of 12th edn [1903] (Berkeley, CA, 1999), p. 465.

43 Ibid., pp. 418–19.

44 Havelock Ellis, *Studies in the Psychology of Sex*, vol. II, 'Erotic Symbolism' (New York, 1942), p. 14.

45 Havelock Ellis, *Studies in the Psychology of Sex*, 'Sexual Inversion in Women', vol. I, p. 260.

46 Frank S. Caprio, *Variations in Sexual Behaviour* (London, 1957), p. 251.

47 This is from my own recollections of childhood, as well of those of my cohorts.

48 As a timeline guide, Okami points out that there were no such index categories as sexual abuse, sexual harassment, sex offences, rape, incest, paedophilia and sexual sadism in 'Psychological Abstracts', but they had emerged by 1989: P. Okami, 'Child Perpetrators of Sexual Abuse: The Emergence of a Problematic Deviant Category', *Journal of Sex Research*, XXIX/1 (1992), pp. 109–30, 117.

49 For studies, see particularly Calderone from 1979 and Levine from 2002, cited in Richard D. Laws and William T. O'Donohue, *Sexual Deviance: Theory, Assessment and Treatment* (New York, 2008).

50 This data relates to pre-adolescent orgasm in Alfred Kinsey et al., *Sexual Behavior in the Human Male* (Philadelphia, PA, 1948), pp. 175–81.

51 Paedophile Information Exchange, *Paedophilia: Some Questions and Answers* (London, 1978).

52 Rev. Thomas Doyle, 'A Very Short History of Clergy Sexual Abuse in the Catholic Church', at www.crusadeagainstclergyabuse.com, accessed 24 May 2013.

53 Andrew Osborn, 'Belgium Still Haunted by Paedophile Scandal', *Guardian* (25 January 2002), www.guardian.co.uk; and 'Dutrous Affair Haunts Belgium Police', 22 January 2002, www.bbc.co.uk/news.

54 Frank D. Fincham, Steven R. H. Beach, Thom Moore and Carol Diener, 'The Professional Response to Child Sexual Abuse: Whose Interests Are Served?', *Family Relations*, XLIII/3 (July 1994), pp. 244–54.

55 'Paper Defends Paedophile Campaign', www.bbc.co.uk/news, 27 July 2011.

56 Rebecca Allison, 'Doctor Driven out of Home by Vigilantes', *Guardian* (30 August 2000), www.guardian.co.uk.

57 Patrick A. Langan and Caroline Wolf Harlow, 'Child Rape Victims', Crime Data Brief, Department of U.S. Justice (June 1994), www.prisonpolicy.org.

58 'Incest', *National Center for Victims of Crime and Crime Victims Research and Treatment Center* (Washington, DC, 1992). See www.ncvc.org, accessed 24 May 2013.

59 Jane F. Gilgun, 'We Shared Something Special: The Moral Discourse of Incest Perpetrators', *Journal of Marriage and Family*, LVII/2 (1995), pp. 265–81.

60 Nancy L. Fischer, 'Oedipus Wrecked? The Moral Boundaries of Incest', *Gender and Society*, XVII/1 (2003), pp. 92–110; Diane D. Broadhurst, 'Executive Summary of the Third National Incidence Study of Child Abuse and Neglect' (1996), www.childwelfare.gov; David Finkelhor and Jennifer Dziuba-Leatherman, 'Children as Victims of Violence: A National Survey', *Pediatrics*, XCIV/4 (1994), pp. 413–20, www.unh.edu; E. Driver and A Droisen, *Child Sex Abuse: Feminist Perspectives* (Basingstoke, 1989); Catharine A. McKinnon, *Feminism Unmodified: Discourse of Life and Law* (Cambridge, MA, 1987).

61 Supporter Gayle Rubin stated, 'Youth Liberation has argued for some time that young people should have the right to have sex as well as not to have it, and with whom they choose. The statutory structure of the sex laws has been identified as oppressive and insulting to young people'; Gayle Rubin, 'Sexual Politics, the New Right, and the Sexual Fringe', *The Leaping Lesbian* (February 1978). On research, see Theo Sandfort, *Boys and Their Contact with Men* (Elmhurst, NY, 1987).

62 For a full age of consent table, see Stephen Robertson, 'Age of Consent Laws', in 'Children and Youth in History', Item #230, at www.chnm.gmu.edu, accessed 8 July 2012.

11 The Games People Play

1 Herodotus, *The Histories*, trans. Aubrey de Sélincourt (Harmondsworth, 1977), Book II, 63, p. 153.

2 Malcolm Jones, 'Sex, Popular Beliefs and Culture', in *A Cultural History of Sexuality*, vol. II: *In the Middle Ages*, ed. Ruth Evans (London, 2011), p. 163.

3 See E. E. Evans Pritchard, *Witchcraft, Oracles and Magic Among the Azande* (Oxford, 1976), p. 238.

4 T. B. Howell, *A Complete Collection of State Trial, 1726–43*, vol. XVII (London, 1816), p. 156.

5 *Observer* (7 July 1799).

6 The Vagrancy Act 1824, Cap. 83, p. 699, at www.legislation.gov.uk, accessed 24 May 2013.

7 *Old Bailey Proceedings Online, 1674–1913*, www.oldbaileyonline. org, refs t18430102–451; t18431023–3081; t18490702–1411; t18570105–183;

t18600227–287, accessed 24 July 2006.

8 Richard von Krafft-Ebing, *Psychopathia Sexualis*, reprint of 12th edn [1903] (Berkeley, CA, 1999), Case 210 (1886).

9 Ben Karpman, 'The Psychopathology of Exhibitionism', *Psychoanalytic Review*, XIII/1 (January 1926).

10 Sigmund Freud, *On Metapsychology* (Harmondsworth, 1984); the theme of the rise of individualism was taken up by Gordon Rattray Taylor, *Sex in History* (London, 1959, reprint 1965), chap. 13, pp. 248–61.

11 Michael Mason, *The Making of Victorian Sexual Attitudes* (Oxford, 1994), pp. 67, 132; Paul Langford, *A Polite and Commercial People England, 1727–1783* (Oxford, 1999).

12 Porter Davis [pseud.], *Sexual Perversion and the Law* (El Segundo, CA, 1950) p. 10.

13 See, for example, E. E. Evans Pritchard, *Witchcraft, Oracles and Magic Among the Azande* (Oxford, 1976).

14 Frank S. Caprio, *Variations in Sexual Behaviour* (London, 1957), pp. 221–8.

15 Ibid., p. 228

16 Anthony Storr, *Sexual Deviation* (Harmondsworth, 1964), p. 95.

17 Ibid., p. 92.

18 Davis, *Sexual Perversion and the Law*.

19 All the above studies are mentioned in Philip Firestone, Drew A. Kingston, Audrey Wexler, John M. Bradford, 'Long-Term Follow-up of Exhibitionists: Psychological, Phallometric, and Offense Characteristics', *Journal of the American Academy of Psychiatry and the Law*, XXXIV/3 (2006), pp. 349–59.

20 D. Richard Laws and William T. O'Donohue, eds, *Sexual Deviance: Theory, Assessment, and Treatment* (New York, 1997), p. 62.

21 Erin Hatton and Mary Nell Trautner, 'Equal Opportunity Objectification? The Sexualization of Men and Women on the Cover of Rolling Stone', *Sexuality and Culture*, XV/256–78 (2011), at www.thegeenadavisinstitute.org; also references therein.

22 Andrew Anthony, 'The Naked Rambler is Making Us Look Silly', *Guardian* (17 January 2010); Neil Forsyth, 'The Naked Rambler, The Man Prepared to Go to Prison For Nudity', *Guardian* (23 March 2012).

23 Quoted in John Younger, 'Sexual Variations: Sexual Peculiarities of the Ancient Greeks and Romans', in *A Cultural History of Sexuality*, vol. 1: *In the Classical World*, ed. Mark Golden and Peter Toohey (London, 2011), pp. 53–78.

24 Tim Hitchcock and Michèle Cohen, *English Masculinities* (London, 1999), p. 28; Lawrence Stone, 'Libertine Sexuality in Post-Restoration

England: Group Sex and Flagellation among the Middling Sort in Norwich in 1706–07', *Journal of the History of Sexuality*, II/4 (1992), pp. 525–51.

25 Caprio, *Variations*, p. 228.

26 Storr, *Sexual Deviation*, p. 96

27 First recorded by Roger of Wendover, who died in 1236, in his *Flores Historiarum*; *Brewer's Dictionary of Phrase and Fable* (London,1981), p. 489.

28 Marquis de Sade, *Justine, Philosophy in the Bedroom and Other Writings*, trans. Richard Seaver and Austryn Wainhouse (New York, 1965), p. 257.

29 Lucienne Frappier-Mazur, 'Sadean Libertinage and the Esthetics of Violence', *Yale French Studies*, XCIV, 'Libertinage and Modernity' (1998), pp. 184–98.

30 John O'Connor, 'Attitude Toward Women', *Notre Dame English Journal*, II/2 (Spring 1967), pp. 13–22.

31 Louis S. London and Frank S. Caprio, *Sexual Deviations* (Washington, DC, 1950), pp. 557–75, on coprophilia.

32 N. Kenneth Sandnabba, Pekka Santtila and Niklas Nordling, 'Sexual Behavior and Social Adaptation Among Sadomasochistically-oriented Males', *Journal of Sex Research*, XXXVI/3 (August 1999), pp. 273–82.

33 There have been arguments about whether this is a work of fiction or fact and who wrote it. According to John Patrick Pattinson, 'Walter' was the engineer who built the Holborn viaduct in his article 'The Man Who Was Walter', *Victorian Literature and Culture*, XXX (2002), pp. 19–40; Vern Bullough, 'Who Wrote My Secret Life', *Sexuality and Culture*, IV (2000), pp. 37–60; Ian Gibson, *The Erotomaniac: The Secret Life of Henry Spencer Ashbee* (London, 1988), pp. 163–234; Eberhard and Phyllis Kronhausen, *My Secret Life: Walter the English Casanova* (London, 1967).

34 Phyllis Grosskurth, *Havelock Ellis: A Biography* (New York, 1980), pp. 286–7.

35 Ellis, *Studies in the Psychology of Sex*, I/2, 'Analysis of the Sexual Impulse', p. 59.

36 Havelock Ellis, *Studies in the Psychology of Sex*, II/2, 'Undinism', pp. 376–476.

37 Havelock Ellis, *My Life* (London and Toronto, 1940), pp. 68–9; Havelock Ellis, *Fountain of Life: Being My Impressions and Comments*, series 3, 'A Revelation' (London, 1924), pp. 359–60.

38 Ellis, *Studies in the Psychology of Sex*, II/1, 'Erotic Symbolism', p. 1.

39 Ellis, *Studies in the Psychology of Sex*, II/1, 'Sexual Inversion in Women', p. 258.

40 Cynthia Payne, *An English Madam: The Life and Work of Cynthia Payne* (London, 1982).

41 John Younger, 'Sexual Variations: Sexual Peculiarities of the Ancient Greeks and Romans', in *A Cultural History of Sexuality*, vol. I: *In the Classical World*, ed. Mark Golden and Peter Toohey (London, 2011), pp. 70–71.

42 *Francis de Sales, Jane de Chantal: Letters of Spiritual Direction*, trans. Péronne Marie Thibert (New York, 1988), p. 134. On early modern flagellation see also Peakman, *Mighty Lewd Books: The Development of Pornography in Eighteenth-century England* (London, 2003), pp. 161–85 and *Lascivious Bodies: A Sexual History of the Eighteenth Century* (London, 2004), pp. 236–50. Also see Niklaus Largier, *In Praise of the Whip: A Cultural History of Arousal* (New York, 2007).

43 Countess Marie Catherine D'Aulnoy, *Realation du voyage d'Espagne* (n.p., 1692), vol. II, pp. 158–64.

44 Johann Heinrich Meibom, *A Treatise of the Use of Flogging in Venereal Affairs* (London, 1761), p. 36.

45 Theresa Berkeley, *Venus School-Mistress; or, Birchen Sports* (London, *c.* 1810).

46 Anon., *The Romance of Lust* (Paris [?], 1895, reprinted Ware, 1995), p. 18.

47 Diane Atkinson, *The Marriage of Arthur Munby and Hannah Culwick* (London, 2003); Barry Reay, *Watching Hannah; Sexuality, Horror and Bodily De-formation in Victorian England* (London, 2002).

12 On Body Parts: Fellatio, Fetishism, Infibulations and Fisting

1 John Younger, 'Sexual Variations: Sexual Peculiarities of the Ancient Greeks and Romans', in *A Cultural History of Sexuality*, vol. I: *In the Classical World*, ed. Mark Golden and Peter Toohey (London, 2011), p. 75.

2 A copy of the *The Lascivious Hypocrite* ('1790') is in the Dawes Bequest at the British Library, London; Ashbee cites the book entitled *La Tartufe* [*sic*] *Libertin ou Le Triomphe du Vice (Par Le Marquis DE SADE) En Holland Chez Les Libraires Associés 1789*; see Henry Spencer Ashbee ['Pisanus Fraxi'], Bibliography of Prohibited Books, vol. II, *Centuria Librorum Assconditorum* (London, 1877; New York, 1962), p. 268. Translations announcing themselves as 'true and accurate' were frequently freely altered, if not completely spurious.

3 *The Quintessence of Birch Discipline* (London, privately printed, '1870' [real date of publication February 1883]; see Henry Spencer

Ashbee ['Pisanus Fraxi'], Bibliography of Prohibited Books, vol. III, *Cantena Librorum Tacendorum*, p. 258), p. 21; Anon., *The Romance of Lust* (Paris [?], 1873–6); Ashbee, vol. III, p. 183.

4 'Walter' [pseud.], *My Secret Life*, vol. V, chap. 6 (reprint Ware, 1996), p. 1820.

5 Richard Freiherr von Krafft-Ebing, *Psychopathia Sexualis*, reprint of 12th edn [1903] (Berkeley, CA, 1999), p. 322.

6 Havelock Ellis, *Studies in the Psychology of Sex* [1897] (New York, 1942), vol. I, 'Sexual Inversion in Women', pp. 206, 258; 'Sexual Selection in Men', p. 21.

7 Caprio, *Variations*, p. 237.

8 Krafft-Ebing, *Psychopathia Sexualis*, p. 187.

9 Ibid., Case 99 and Case 102, pp. 205–8.

10 Ibid., p. 189.

11 Chrétien De Troyes, *Arthurian Romances*, ed. and trans. W. W. Comfort (London, 1968), pp. 288–9; quoted by Cory James Rushton 'Sexual Variations', in *A Cultural History of Sexuality*, vol. II: *In the Middle Ages*, ed. Ruth Evans (London, 2011), pp. 84–5.

12 Louis S. London and Frank S. Caprio, *Sexual Deviations* (Washington, DC, 1950), p. 463.

13 Theresa Berkeley, *Venus School-mistress; or, Birchen Sports* (London, c. 1810), pp. 45–6. See also Julie Peakman, *Mighty Lewd Books: The Development of Pornography in Eighteenth-century England* (London, 2003), pp. 183–5; Julie Peakman, *Lascivious Bodies: A Sexual History of the Eighteenth Century* (London, 2004), pp. 250–54.

14 Quoted in Jonathan Katz, *The Invention of Heterosexuality* (Chicago, IL, 2007), p. 23.

15 Krafft-Ebing, *Psychopathia Sexualis*, Case 110, p. 216.

16 Suetonius, *Vitellius*, 2.

17 Translation of *Le roman de la rose* at http://margot.uwaterloo.ca, accessed 24 November 2011.

18 Restif de la Bretonne, *Le Pied de Fanchette* (Le Haye, 1769); see Havelock Ellis, *Studies in the Psychology of Sex*, II/1, 'Erotic Symbolism' (New York, 1942), pp. 19–20.

19 Krafft-Ebing, *Psychopathia Sexualis*, Case 91, pp. 196–8.

20 Ellis, 'Erotic Symbolism', p. 33.

21 Martin S. Weinberg, Colin J. Williams and Cassandra Calhan, '"If the Shoe Fits . . .": Exploring Male Homosexual Foot Fetishism', *Journal of Sexual Research*, XXXI/1 (1995), pp. 17–27.

22 A. J. Giannini, G. Colapietro, A. E. Slaby, S. M. Melemis and R. K. Bowman, 'Sexualization of the Female Foot as a Response to Sexually Transmitted Epidemics: A Preliminary Study', *Psychological Reports*, LXXXIII/2 (1998), pp. 491–2.

23 As seen in Chevaliers de Choisy and D'Eon; see Peakman, *Lascivious Bodies*, pp. 201–18.

24 Dr Magnus Hirschfeld, *Transvestites* [1910], trans. Michael A. Lombard-Nash (New York, 1991), p. 159.

25 Ronald M. Holmes, 'Sequential Predation: Elements of Serial Fatal Victimization', *Sexual Addiction and Compulsivity*, IV/1 (January 1997), pp. 33–42.

26 Marquis de Sade, *Justine, Philosophy in the Bedroom and Other Writings*, trans. Richard Seaver and Austryn Wainhouse (New York, 1965), pp. 686–7.

27 Both tales are told in depth in Peakman, *Lascivious Bodies*, pp. 266–9.

28 R. Haywood, P. E. Diete and A. W. Burgess, *Autoerotic Fatalities* (Toronto, 1983).

29 R. Milner, 'Orgasm of Death', *Hustler*, VIII (August 1981), pp. 33–4.

30 Murray J. White, 'The Statue Syndrome, Perversion, Fantasy, Anecdote?', *Journal of Sex Research*, XIV/4 (1978), pp. 246–9.

31 The original is in French, part of the Dawes Bequest at the British Library, London. It is said to be 'par Madame B*** (Avocat)', *La Femme Endormie* (Melbourne, 1899), pp. 10–11. Despite the imprint, nothing suggests an Australian origin; it looks like a perfectly produced French book.

32 Iwan Bloch, *The Sexual Life of Our Time* (London, 1908), p. 660.

33 All of these documentaries are posted on YouTube, accessed 25 May 2013.

34 My sincere thanks to Erika La Tour Eiffel for sharing her thoughts and opinions on OS.

35 See chapter Three.

36 G.P.S. Bianchi, *An Historical and Physical Dissertation on the Case of Catherine Vizzani, containing the adventures of a young woman who for eight years poised in the habit of a man . . . with some curious and anatomical remarks on the nature and existence of the hymen . . . On which are added certain needful remarks by the English editor* (London, 1751); G.P.S. Bianchi, *The True History and Adventures of Catherine Vizzani* (London, 1755).

37 Eva C. Keuls, *The Reign of the Phallus* (Berkeley, CA, 1985), pp. 68–9.

38 John Younger, Sexual Variations: Sexual Peculiarities of the Ancient Greeks and Romans', in *A Cultural History of Sexuality*, vol. I: *In the Classical World*, ed. Mark Golden and Peter Toohey (London, 2011), pp. 63–5.

39 John Money, Russell Jobaris and Gregg Furth, 'Apotemnophilia: Two Cases of Self-demand Amputation as a Paraphilia', *Journal of Sex Research*, XIII/2 (1977), pp. 115–25.

40 F. Tomasini, 'Exploring Ethical Justification for Self-demand Amputation', *Ethics Med*, XXII/2 (Summer 2006), pp. 99–115; see also Nikki Sullivan, 'Integrity, Mayhem, and the Question of Self-demand Amputation', *Continuum: Journal of Media and Cultural Studies*, XIX/3 (2005), pp. 325–33. The discussion is too broad to go into further here but there are many articles on the subject online, found under the search heading 'self-demand amputation'.

41 Tim Bayne and Neil Levy, 'Amputees by Choice: Body Integrity, Identity Disorder and the Ethics of Amputation', *Journal of Applied Philosophy*, XXII (2005), pp. 75–86.

42 For translation, see Marguerite Johnson and Terry Ryan, *Sexuality in Greek and Roman Society and Literature: A Sourcebook* (London, 2005), pp. 150–51.

43 Sade, *Justine, Philosophy in the Bedroom and Other Writings*, p. 257.

44 Barry Reay, *New York Hustlers: Masculinity in Modern America* (Manchester, 2010).

45 Jack Fritscher, 'The Catacombs: Fistfucking in a Handball Palace', *Drummer*, XXIII (July 1978), http://jackfritscher.com. This feature article is based on an interview of 7 December 1977 by Jack Fritscher, of his friends Steve McEachern and Michael Shapley, partners at the original Catacombs.

46 Gayle Rubin, 'The Catacombs: A Temple of the Butthole', in *Leatherfolk*, ed. Mark Thompson (Dublin, 2005), pp. 119–41; Linnea Due, 'Blackbeards Lost', in *Opposite Sex*, ed. Eric Rofes and Sara Miles (New York, 1998), p. 8.

47 *Huffington Post: Gay Voices*, www.huffingtonpost.com, 20 October 2011.

48 Helen Navin, 'Medical and Surgical Risks in Handballing', *Journal of Homosexuality*, VI/3 (1982), pp. 67–76.

49 Quoted in Thomas S. Weinberg, 'Sadomasochism and the Social Sciences: A Review of the Sociological and Social Psychological Literature', in *Sadomasochism: Powerful Pleasures*, ed. Peggy J. Kleinplatz and Charles Moser (London, 2006), p. 21.

BIBLIOGRAPHY

Classical Works

Aeschylus, *Myrmidons*
Apuleius, *Metamorphoses* (*The Golden Ass*)
Aristotle, *Generation of Animals*
—, *Physiognomonics*
Herodotus, *Histories*
Hippocrates, *On the Diseases of Women*
Homer, *Iliad*
Lucian, *Dialogues of the Courtesans*
Ovid, *The Art of Love*
—, *Metamorphoses*
Pliny the Elder, *Natural History*
Plutarch, 'Discourse on the Reason of Beasts', in *Morals*
—, 'Lycurgus', in *Parallel Lives*
Pseudo-Demosthenes, *Against Naerea*
Seneca, *Epistles*
Sophocles, *The Theban Plays*
Suetonius, *The Twelve Caesars*
Xenophon, *Hellenica*

Primary Texts

Acton, William, *The Functions and Disorders of the Reproductive Organs in Childhood, Youth, Adult Age, and Advanced Life: Considered in Their Physiological, Social, and Moral Relations* (London, 1862)
Barker, Priscilla, *The Secret Book: Containing Private Information and Instruction for Women and Young Girls* (Brighton, 1889)
Bayle, Pierre, *Letters of Abelard and Heloise*, trans. John Hughes (Project Gutenberg EBook #35977), www.gutenberg.org
Becker, Wilhelm Adolf, *Charicles; or, Illustrations of the Private Life of the Greeks* (London, 1866)

Bell, Ralcy H., *Self-Amusement and Its Spectres* (New York, 1929)

Berkeley, Theresa, *Venus School-Mistress* [1788] (London, 1810)

Bianchi, G.P.S., *An Historical and Physical Dissertation on the Case of Catherine Vizzani, Containing the Adventures of a Young Woman Who for Eight Years Poised in the Habit of a Man . . .* (London, 1751)

—, *The True History and Adventures of Catherine Vizzani* (London, 1755)

Bienville, M.D.T., *Nymphomania; or, A Dissertation Concerning the Furor Uterinus* (London, 1775)

Bloch, Iwan, *The Sexual Life of Our Time in its Relations to Modern Civilization* (London, 1908)

Bontius, Jacobus, *Historiae naturalis et medicae Indiae orientalis* (London, 1631)

Booth, Charles, *Labour and Life of the People* (London, 1891–1903)

Brandeis, Arthur, ed., *Jacob's Well: An English Treatise on the Cleansing of Man's Conscience* (London, 1900)

Brodie, R. J., and Co., *The Secret Companion: A Medical Work on Onanism* (London, 1845)

Burke, Edmund, *A Philosophical Enquiry into the Origin of Our Ideas of the Sublime and Beautiful* (London, 1756)

Burton, Robert, *The Anatomy of Melancholy* (1621; reprint 1855)

Carpenter, Edward, *Love's Coming of Age* (London, 1915)

'A Clergyman', *Onania; or, The Heinous Sin of Self-pollution, and All Its Frightful Consequences in Both Sexes* (London, 1710)

—, *Onania; or, The Heinous Sin of Self-pollution, and All Its Frightful Consequences in Both Sexes, Considered with Spiritual and Physical Advice to Those Who Have Already Injured Themselves by this Abominable Practice and Seasonable Admonition to the Youth of the Nation of Both sexes*, 8th edn (London, 1723)

Cleugh, James, *The Marquis and the Chevalier* (New York, 1951)

Coffignon, Ali, *Paris vivant: La Corruption à Paris* (Paris, 1889)

Crook, Helkiah, *Microcosmographia* (London, 1615)

D'Aulnoy, Countess Marie Catherine, *Relation du voyage d'espagne* (1692)

Davenport, John, *Aphrodisiacs and Anti-aphrodisiacs* (London, privately printed, 1869)

Dunton, John, *The He-Strumpets: A Satyr on the Sodomite Club* (London, 1707)

Ellis, Havelock, *My Life* (London and Toronto, 1940)

—, *Studies in the Psychology of Sex* [1897–1927] (New York, 1903, 1943)

Eulenburg, Albert, *Algolagnia: The Psychology, Neurology and Physiology of Sadistic Love and Masochism* [1902] (New York, 1934)

Evans Pritchard, E. E., *Witchcraft, Oracles and Magic Among the Azande* [1937] (Oxford, 1976)

Fielding, Henry, *The Female Husband; or, The Surprising History of Mrs Mary, alias George Hamilton* (1746)

Fielding, Sir John, *A Plan for a Preservatory and Reformatory, for the Benefit of Deserted Girls* (London, 1758)

Fonssagrives, J. B., *L'Education physique des garcons* (Paris, 1890)

Gervaise de Latouche, Jean-Charles, (attrib.), *Dom B., The Lascivious Monk* [1741], trans. Howard Nelson (Wiltshire, 1993)

Hall, Radclyffe, *The Well of Loneliness* (Paris, 1928)

Howe, Joseph William, *Excessive Venery, Masturbation and Continence* (London, 1883)

Howell, T. B., *A Complete Collection of State Trials, 1726–43*, vol. XVII (London, 1816)

Hunter, John, *A Treatise on Venereal Disease* (London, 1786)

Kellogg, J. H., *Plain Facts for Old and Young: Embracing the Natural History and Hygiene of Organic Life* [1877] (Burlington, IA, 1892)

Kinsey, Alfred C., Wardell B. Pomeroy and Clyde E. Martin, *Sexual Behavior in the Human Male* (Philadelphia, PA, 1948)

—, Wardell B. Pomeroy, Clyde E. Martin and Paul H. Gebhard, *Sexual Behavior in the Human Female* (Philadelphia, PA, 1953)

Kirk, Edward, *Talk With Boys About Themselves* (London, 1905)

Krafft-Ebing, Richard von, *Psychopathia Sexualis* [1866–] (Burbank, CA, 1999, reprint of 1903 12th edition)

Lallemand, C., *A Practical Treatise on the Causes, Symptoms, and Treatment of Spermatorrhoea*, trans. and ed. H. J McDougall (London, 1851, 2nd edn)

Luther, Martin, *The Estate of Marriage* [1522], trans. Walther I. Brandt (1962)

'Madame B*** (Avocat)', *La Femme endormie* (Melbourne, 1899)

Manningham, Sir Richard, *An Exact Diary of what was Observ'd during a Close Attendance upon Mary Toft, the Pretended Rabbet-Breeder of Godalming in Surrey, from Nov 28 to Dec 7 following Together with an Account of Her Confession of the Fraud* (London, 1726)

'Mrs Martinet' (pseud.), *The Quintessence Of Birch Discipline* (London, privately printed, '1870', 1883)

Mayhew, Henry, *London Labour and the London Poor* (London, 1851, 1864)

Mearns, Andrew, and W. C. Preston, *The Bitter Cry of Outcast London* (London, 1883)

Meibom, Johann Heinrich, *A Treatise of the Use of Flogging in Venereal Affairs* (London, 1761)

Millot, Michel, *L'Ecole des filles; ou, La Philosophie des dames* ['1668'] (1972)

Morgan, Lewis Henry, *Systems of Consanguinity and Affinity of the Human Family* (Washington, DC, 1871)

Osterwald, Jen Frederick, *The Nature of Uncleanliness* (London, 1707)

Paedophile Information Exchange, London, *Paedophilia: Some Questions and Answers* (London, 1978)

Paget, Sir James, 'Sexual Hypochondriasis', in *Clinical Lectures and Essays* (London, 1879)

Paré, Ambroise, *On Monsters and Marvels*, trans. Janis L. Pallister [1575] (Chicago, IL, 1982)

Parsons, James, *A Mechanical and Critical Enquiry into the Nature of Hermaphrodites* (London, 1741)

Pepys, Samuel, *The Diary of Samuel Pepys*, ed. Robert Latham and William Matthews, 9 vols (London and Berkeley, CA, 1970–83)

Peter Damian (Saint), *Book of Gomorrah* [1048] (Waterloo, ON, 1982)

Philosophical Enquiry into the Wonderful Coney-Warren, Lately Discovered at Godalming near Guildford . . . (London, 1726)

R. I., *A Most Straunge, and True Discourse, of the Wonderfull Judgement of God, Of a Monstrous, Deformed Infant, Begotten by Incestuous Copulation, betweene the Brothers Sonne and the Sisters Daughter, being both Unmarried Persons* (London, 1600)

Rétif de la Bretonne, *Le Pied de Fanchette* (La Haye, 1769)

The Romance of Lust [anon., pub. William Lazenby, 1873–6] (1995)

Rousseau, Jean-Jacques, *The Confessions* (London, 1782–89)

Rush, Benjamin, *Medical Inquiries and Observations Upon the Diseases of the Mind* (Philadelphia, PA, 1812)

Sade, Marquis de, *Incest* [*Eugénie de Franval*, 1800], trans. Andrew Brown (London, 2004)

—, *Juliette* [1797–1801], trans. Austryn Wainhouse and Richard Seaver (New York, 1968)

—, *Justine, Philosophy in the Bedroom, and Other Writings*, trans. Richard Seaver and Austryn Wainhouse, with introductions by Jean Paulhan and Maurice Blanchot (New York, 1965)

Sharp, Jane, *The Midwives Book; or, The Whole Art of Midwifery Discovered, Directing Childbearing Women How to Behave Themselves in Their Conception, Breeding, Bearing and Children* (London, 1671)

Stekel, Wilhelm, *Sadism and Masochism: The Psychology of Hatred and Cruelty* [1929] (London, 1935)

Stretzer, Thomas, *A New Description of Merryland* (London, 1741)

Le Tartufe libertin; ou, Le Triomphe du vice (par le Marquis de Sade), en Hollande, chez les libraires associés, 1789

Tatum, W. Jeffrey, *Patrician Tribune: Publius Clodius Pulcher* (Chapel Hill, NC, 1999)

Thoinot, Léon Henri, *Attentats aux moeurs et perversion du sens génital* (Paris, 1898)

Tissot, S.A.D., *Onanism* (London, 1766)

Venette, Nicolas, *Tableau de l'amour* [1686] (London, 1818)

'Walter', *My Secret Life* [*c.* 1888] (London, 1996)

Westermarck, Edward, *The History of Human Marriage* (London, 1891)

Whitbread, Helen, ed., *I Know My Own Heart: The Diaries of Anne Lister, 1791–1840* (New York, 1992)

Whitmore, William Henry, *The Colonial Laws of Massachusetts: Reprinted from the Edition of 1660* (Boston, MA, 1889)

Winthrop, Governor John, *History of New England, 1630–1649* (Boston, MA, 1825)

Secondary Texts

Adams, Jad, *Madder Music, Stronger Wine: The Life of Ernest Dowson* (London, 2000)

Aldrich, Robert, ed., *Gay Life and Culture: A World History* (London, 2006)

Allen, Peter Lewis, *The Wages of Sin: Sex and Disease* (Chicago, IL, 2002)

Archibald, Elizabeth, *Incest and the Medieval Imagination* (Oxford, 2003)

Ariès, Philippe, *Centuries of Childhood: A Social History of Family Life*, trans. Robert Baldick (Harmondsworth, 1962)

—, *L'Homme devant la mort* (Paris, 1977)

Atkinson, Diane, *The Marriage of Arthur Munby and Hannah Cullwick* (London, 2003)

Benedetti, Jean, *The Real Bluebeard: The Life of Gilles de Rais* (Stroud, 2003)

Bengtsson, Tommy, and Geraldine P. Mineau, *Kinship and Demographic Behavior in the Past* (New York, 2008)

Bongie, Laurence L., De Sade: A Biographical Essay (Chicago, IL, 1998)

Boswell, John, *The Marriage of Likeness: Same-Sex Unions in Pre-modern Europe* (London, 1994)

Boucé, P. G., *Sexuality in Eighteenth-century Britain* (Manchester, 1992)

Bradtke, Elaine, *Truculent Rustics: Molly Dancing in East Anglia Before 1940* (London, 2000)

Bray, Alan, *Homosexuality in Renaissance England* (New York, 1982)

—, *The Friend* (Chicago, IL, 2003)

Bronfen, Elisabeth, *Over Her Dead Body: Death, Femininity and the Aesthetic* (Manchester, 1992)

Brooten, Bernadette, *Love Between Women: Early Christian Responses to Female Eroticism* (Chicago, IL, 1996)

Bullough, Vern L., and James A. Brundage, *Handbook of Medieval Sexuality* (New York and London, 1996)

—, and Bonnie Bullough, *Cross Dressing, Sex and Gender* (Philadelphia, PA, 1993)

Burrus, Virginia, *The Sex Lives of Saints: An Erotics of Ancient Hagiography* (Philadelphia, PA, 2004)

Capps, Donald, *The Child's Song: The Religious Abuse of Children* (Louisville, KY, 1995)

Caprio, Frank S., *Female Homosexuality: A Modern Study of Lesbianism* (New York, 1954)

—, *Variations in Sexual Behaviour* (London, 1957)

Christ, C., S. W. Goodwin and E. Bronfen, *Painting the Dead: Portraiture and Necrophilia in Victorian Art and Poetry* (Baltimore, MD, 1988)

Clark, Anna, *Desire: A History of European Sexuality* (London, 2008)

Classmen, Albrecht, ed., *Childhood in the Middle Ages and the Renaissance* (Berlin, 2005)

Clinton, Catherine, and Michele Gillespie, eds, *The Devil's Lane: Sex and Race in the Early South* (New York and London, 1997)

Cocks, H. G., *Nameless Offences: Homosexual Desire in the Nineteenth Century* (London, 2003)

Dabhoiwala, Faramerz, *The Origins of Sex: A History of the First Sexual Revolution* (London, 2012)

Davidoff, Leanore, *Thicker than Water: Siblings and their Relations, 1780–1920* (Oxford, 2012)

Davidson, James, *The Greeks and Greek Love* (London, 2007)

Davis, Porter, *Sexual Perversion and the Law* (El Segundo, CA, 1950)

Dekkers, Midas, *Dearest Pet: On Bestiality* (London, 1994)

Deleuze, Gilles, *Masochism: Coldness and Cruelty*, trans. Jean McNeil and Aude Willm (New York, 1989)

Dickinson, Robert Latou, and Lura Beam, *The Single Woman: A Medical Study in Sex Education* (London, 1934)

Diderot, Denis, *Memoirs of a Nun* [c. 1760], trans. Francis Birrell (London, 1992)

Diggle, James, *Characters by Theophrastus* (Cambridge, 2004)

Dixon, Suzanne, *Reading Women* (London 2003)

Donoghue, Emma, *Passions between Women: British Lesbian Culture, 1668–1801* (London, 1993)

Downing, Lisa, *Desiring the Dead: Necrophilia and Nineteenth-century French Literature* (Oxford, 2002)

Dreger, Alice Domurat, *Hermaphrodites and the Medical Invention of Sex* (Cambridge, MA, 1998)

Duberman, M., M. Vicinus, and G. Chauncey, eds, *Hidden from History* (London, 1989)

DuGard, Lydia, *Cousins in Love: The Letters of Lydia DuGard, 1665–1672*, ed. Nancy Taylor (Tempe, AZ, 2003)

Eisler, Robert, *Man into Wolf: An Anthropological Interpretation of Sadism, Masochism and Lycanthropy* (London, 1948)

Ellis, Havelock, *Fountain of Life: Being My Impressions and Comments* (London, 1924)

Fabris, Antonio, ed., *Cristina Belgiojoso Trivulzio: An Italian Princess in the Nineteenth-century Turkish Countryside* (Venice, 2010)

Faraone, Christopher A., and Laura K. McClure, eds, *Prostitutes and Courtesans in the Ancient World* (Madison, WI, 2006)

Féré, Charles Samson, *The Evolution and Dissolution of the Sexual Instinct* (Paris, 1904)

—, *The Pathology of Emotions* (London, 1899)

Field, Ophelia, *Sarah, The Duchess of Marlborough* (London, 2002)

Fitzgerald, Penelope, *Charlotte Mew and Her Friends* (London, 1984)

Foote, E. B., *Home Cyclopedia of Popular Medical, Social and Sexual Science* [1901] (London, 1912)

Fout, John C., ed., *Forbidden History* (Chicago, IL, 1992)

Freud, Sigmund, *The Interpretation of Dreams* (New York, 1951)

—, *On Metapsychology* (Harmondsworth, 1984)

Garber, Marjorie, *Vested Interests: Cross-dressing and Cultural Anxiety* (London, 1992)

Gebhard, P., J. Gagnon, W. Pomeroy and C. Christenson, *Sex Offenders: An Analysis of Types* (New York, 1965)

Gerard, Kent, and Gert Hekma, *The Pursuit of Sodomy: Male Homo-sexuality in Renaissance and Enlightenment Europe* (London, 1989)

Gibson, Ian, *The Erotomaniac: The Secret Life of Henry Spencer Ashbee* (London, 1988)

Gilbert, Ruth, *Early Modern Hermaphrodites* (Basingstoke, 2002)

Goldsmith, Netta Murray, *The Worst of Crimes: Homosexuality and the Law in Eighteenth-century London* (Aldershot, 1998)

Goodwin, Sarah Webster, and E. Bronfen, *Death and Representation* (Baltimore, MD, 1993)

Grant M., and R. Kitzinger, *Civilizations of the Ancient Mediterranean* (New York, 1988)

Gray, Francine du Plessix, *At Home with the Marquis de Sade* (London, 2000)

Gregory of Tours, *History of the Franks* (Middlesex, 1974)

Grosskurth, Phyllis, *Havelock Ellis: A Biography* (New York, 1985)

Hallett, Judith P., and Marilyn B. Skinner, eds, *Roman Sexualities* (Princeton, NJ, 1997)

Hanawalt, Barbara A., *Growing Up in Medieval London* (Oxford, 1993)

Harrison, Ben, *Undying Love: The True Story of a Passion that Defied Death* (London, 2001)

Haywood, R., P. E. Diete and A. W. Burgess, *Autoerotic Fatalities* (Toronto, 1983).

Hirschfeld, Magnus, *Transvestites* [1910], trans. Michael A. Lombard-
Nash (New York, 1991)
Hitchcock, Tim, and Michèle Cohen, *English Masculinities* (London, 1999)
Hodge, C. Ester, *A Woman-Oriented Woman* [1920s] (East Wittering,
West Sussex, 1989)
Hollander, Bernard, *The Psychology of Misconduct, Vice and Crime*
(London, 1922)
Houlbrook, Matt, *Queer London: Perils and Pleasures in the Sexual
Metropolis, 1918–1957* (Chicago, IL, 2005)
Hunt, Morton, *Sexual Behavior in the 1970s* (Chicago, IL, 1975)
Hyman, Ronald, *Marquis de Sade: Genius of Passion* (London, 2003)
Icks, Martijn, *The Crimes of Elagabalus: The Life and Legacy of Rome's
Decadent Boy Emperor* (London, 2011)
Ingraham, Chrys, *Thinking Straight: The Power, Promise and Paradox of
Heterosexuality* (London, 2005)
Jackson, Louise, *Child Sexual Abuse in Victorian England* (London, 2000)
Jivani, Alkarim, *It's Not Unusual: A History of Lesbian and Gay Britain
in the Twentieth Century* (London, 1997)
Johnson, Marguerite, and Terry Ryan, *Sexuality in Greek and Roman
Society and Literature: A Sourcebook* (London, 2005)
Jordanova, Ludmilla, *Sexual Visions: Images of Gender in Science and
Medicine between the Eighteenth and Nineteenth Centuries*
(London, 1989)
Jorgensen, Christine, *A Personal Biography* (New York, 1967)
Katz, Jonathan, *Love Stories* (Chicago, IL, 2001)
—, *The Invention of Heterosexuality* (Chicago, IL, 2007)
Keuls, Eva C., *The Reign of the Phallus* (Berkeley, CA, 1985)
Kiefer, Otto, *Sexual Life in Ancient Rome* (London, 2000)
Kilmer, Martin E., *Greek Erotica on Attic Red-figure Vases* (London, 1993)
King, Helen, *Hippocrates' Women, Reading the Female Body in Ancient
Greece* (London, 1998)
Kleinplatz, Peggy J., and Charles Moser, *Sadomasochism: Powerful
Pleasures* (London, 2006)
Kottack, Conrad P., *Cultural Anthropology* (New York, 1994)
Kronhausen, Eberhard, and Phyllis Kronhausen, *My Secret Life: Walter
the English Casanova* (London, 1967)
Kuper, Adam, *Incest and Influence: The Private Life of Bourgeois
England* (Cambridge, MA, 2009)
Langan, Patrick A., and Caroline Wolf Harlow, *Child Rape Victims, 1992*
(U.S. Dept of Justice, Office of Justice Programs, Bureau of Justice
Statistics, 1994)
Langford, Paul, *A Polite and Commercial People: England, 1727–1783*
(Oxford, 1999)

Laqueur, T., *The Making of the Modern Body* (Berkeley, CA, 1987)

—, *Solitary Sex: A Cultural History of Masturbation* (New York, 2003)

Largier, Niklaus, *In Praise of the Whip: A Cultural History of Arousal* (New York, 2007)

Laws, D. Richard, and William T. O'Donohue, eds, *Sexual Deviance: Theory, Assessment, and Treatment* (London, 1997)

Ledger, Sally, *The New Woman: Fiction and Feminism at the Fin-de-siècle* (Manchester, 1997)

LeVay, Simon, *Queer Science: The Use and Abuse of Research into Homosexuality* (Cambridge, MA, 1996)

Lever, Maurice, *Marquis de Sade: A Biography* (London, 1993)

London, Louis S., and Frank S. Caprio, *Sexual Deviations* (Washington, DC, 1950)

Long, Kathleen P., *Hermaphrodites in Renaissance Europe* (Aldershot, 2006)

McManus, Edgar J., *Law and Liberty in Early New England, 1620–1692* (Amherst, MA, 2009)

McNaron, Toni A. H., and Yarrow Morgan, *Voices in the Night: Women Speaking About Incest* (Minneapolis, MN, 1982)

Mason, Michael, *The Making of Victorian Sexual Attitudes* (Oxford, 1994)

Masters, R.E.L., *The Hidden World of Erotica* (London, 1973)

—, and E. Lea, *Sex Crimes in History* (New York, 1963)

Matthews, Mark, *The Horseman: Obsessions of a Zoophile* (New York, 1994)

Merrick, Jeffrey, and Michael Sibalis, eds, *Homosexuality in French History and Culture* (London, 2001)

Miller, James, *The Passion of Michel Foucault* (New York, 1992)

Mitchell, Leslie, *Lord Melbourne, 1779–1848* (Oxford, 1997)

Mountfield, David, *Greek and Roman Erotica* (Fribourg, 1982)

Naish, Camille, *Death Comes to the Maiden: Sex and Execution, 1431–1933* (London, 1991)

Nicholson, Nigel, *Portrait of a Marriage* (London, 1974)

Norton, Rictor, ed., *Mother Clap's Molly House: The Gay Subculture in England, 1700–1830* (London, 1982)

Oakley, Eric, *Sex and Sadism throughout the Ages* (London, 1965)

Oram, Alison, *Her Husband Was a Woman: Women's Gender-crossing in Modern British Popular Culture* (London, 2007)

—, and Annmarie Turnbull, *The Lesbian History Sourcebook: Love and Sex Between Women in Britain from 1780–1970* (London, 2001)

Payne, Cynthia, *An English Madam: Life and Work of Cynthia Payne* (London, 1982)

Peacock, James L., and A. Thomas Kirsch, *The Human Direction: An Evolutionary Approach to Social and Cultural Anthropology* (New York, 1970)

Peakman, Julie, ed., *A Cultural History of Sexuality* (Oxford, 2011), 6 vols
—, *Lascivious Bodies* (London, 2004)
—, *Mighty Lewd Books: The Development of Pornography in Eighteenth-century England* (London, 2003)
—, ed., *Sexual Perversions* (Basingstoke, 2009)
—, ed., *Whore Biographies, 1700–1825* (London, 2008)
Penney, James, *The World of Perversion: Psychoanalysis and the Impossible Absolute of Absolute of Desire* (Albany, NY, 2006)
Philips, Kim M., and Barry Reay, eds, *Sexualities in History* (London, 2002)
Pollock, Linda, *A Lasting Relationship: Parents and Children over Three Centuries* (London, 1987)
—, *Forgotten Children: Parent-Child Relations from 1500 to 1900* (Cambridge, 1983)
Pomeroy, Sarah B., *Goddesses, Whores, Wives and Slaves* (New York, 1975)
—, *Spartan Women* (Oxford, 2002)
Porter, Roy, and Lesley Hall, *Facts of Life: The Creation of Sexual Knowledge in Britain, 1650–1950* (New Haven, CT, and London, 1995)
Rabinowitz, N. S., and L. Auanger, eds, *Among Women: From the Homosocial to the Homoerotic in the Ancient World* (Austin, TX, 2002)
Radford, Jean, ed., *The Progress of Romance: The Politics of Popular Culture* (London, 1986)
Reay, Barry, *New York Hustlers: Masculinity in Modern America* (Manchester, 2010)
—, *Watching Hannah: Sexuality, Horror and Bodily De-formation in Victorian England* (London, 2002)
Rice, Nelljean McConeghey, *A New Matrix for Modernism: A Study of the Lives and Poetry of Charlotte Mew and Anna Wickham* (London, 2003)
Richardson, Angelique, and Chris Willis, eds, *The New Woman in Fiction and Fact: Fin-de-siècle Feminisms* (London, 2001)
Richlin, Amy, *The Garden of Priapus: Sexuality and Agression in Roman Humor* (New Haven, CT, 1983)
Roach, J., 'History, Memory, Necrophilia', in *The Ends of Performance*, ed. P. Phelan and J. Lane (New York, 1995)
Rocke, Michael, *Forbidden Friendships: Homosexuality and Male Culture in Renaissance Florence* (Oxford, 1996)
Rofes, Eric, and Sara Miles, eds, *Opposite Sex: Gay Men on Lesbians, Lesbians on Gay Men* (New York, 1998)
Rousseau, George S., ed., *Children and Sexuality: The Greeks to the Great War* (Basingstoke, 2007)
—, and Roy Porter, eds, *Sexual Underworlds in the Enlightenment* (Manchester, 1987)
Rubin, Gayle S., *Deviations: A Gayle Rubin Reader* (Durham, NC, 2011)
Rydström, Jens, *Sinners and Citizens: Bestiality and Homosexuality in*

Sweden, 1880–1950 (Chicago, IL, 2003)

Sacher-Masoch, Wanda von, *The Confessions of Wanda von Sacher-Masoch*, trans. Marian Phillips et al. (San Francisco, 1990). Originally published as Wanda von Dunajew (pseud.), *Meine Lebensbeichte* (1906)

Salisbury, Joyce, *Church Fathers, Independent Virgins* (London, 1991)

Sandfort, Theo, *Boys on Their Contacts with Men: A Study of Sexually Expressed Friendships* (Elmhurst, NY, 1987)

Schaeffer, Neil, *The Marquis de Sade* (London, 1999)

Shahar, Shulamith, *Childhood in the Middle Ages* (London, 1990)

Southami, Diana, *Wild Girls: Paris, Sappho and Art: The Lives of Natalie Barney and Romaine Brookes* (London, 2004)

Stanley, Liz, *Sex Surveyed, 1949–1994* (London, 1995)

Stein, Edward, ed., *Forms of Desire: Sexual Orientation and the Social Construction Controversy* (London, 1990)

Stendhal (Marie-Henri Beyle), *The Life of Henry Brulard*, trans. John Sturrock (New York, 2002)

Stengers, Jean, and Anne Van Neck, *Masturbation: The History of a Great Terror*, trans. Kathryn Hoffmann (Basingstoke, 2001)

Stone, L., *The Family, Sex and Marriage in England, 1500–1800* (London, 1977)

Storr, Anthony, *Sexual Deviation* (Harmondsworth, 1964)

Sylvester, Louise M., *Medieval Romance and the Construction of Heterosexuality* (Basingstoke, 2008)

Tardieu, Auguste Ambroise, *Etude médico-légale sur les attentats aux moeurs* [1857] (Paris, 1995)

Taylor, Gordon Rattray, *Sex in History* (London, 1959)

Taylor, Alfred Swaine, *Medical Jurisprudence* (London, 1844)

Thomas, Keith, *Man and the Natural World* (London, 1983)

Thompson, E. P., *Customs in Common* (London, 1991)

Thompson, Mark, ed., *Leatherfolk: Radical Sex, People, Politics and Practice* (Los Angeles, 2005)

Todd, Janet, *Gender, Art and Death* (New York, 1993)

Troyes, Chrétien de, *Arthurian Romances*, trans. and ed. W. W. Comfort (London, 1968)

Trumbach, Randolph, *Sex and the Gender Revolution* (Chicago IL,, 1998)

Turner, Marion, *Chaucerian Conflict: Languages of Antagonism in Late Fourteenth-century London* (Oxford, 2007)

Wagner, Peter, *Eros Revived: Erotica and the Enlightenment in England and America* (London, 1998)

White, Chris, ed., *Nineteenth-century Writings on Homosexuality* (London, 1999)

Whitehouse, H. H. Remsen, *A Revolutionary Princess: Christina Belgiojoso-Trivulzio, Her Life and Times* [1906] (New York, 2009)
Wiehe, Vernon R., *Sibling Abuse: Hidden Physical, Emotional, and Sexual Trauma* (London, 1997)

Articles

Aggrawal, A., 'A New Classification of Necrophilia', *Journal of Forensic and Legal medicine*, XVI/6 (2009), pp. 316–20
Androutsos, George, 'Hermaphroditism in Greek and Roman Antiquity', *Hormones*, V/3 (2006), pp. 214–17
—, Aristidis Diamantis, Lazaros Vladimiros and Emmanouil Magiorkinis, 'Bisexuality in Ancient Greek-Roman Society', *The International Journal of Medicine*, 1/2 (April–June 2008), p. 67
Bayne, Tim, and Neil Levy, 'Amputees By Choice: Body Integrity Identity Disorder and the Ethics of Amputation', *Journal of Applied Philosophy*, 22 (2005), pp. 75–86
Bennett, Judith M., '"Lesbian-Like" and the Social History of Lesbians', *Journal of the History of Sexuality*, IX/1–2 (January–April 2000), pp. 1–24
—, 'Writing Fornication: Medieval Leyrwite and its Historians', *Transaction of the Royal Historical Society*, XIII (2003), pp. 131–62
Bockting, Walter O., and Eli Coleman, 'Masturbation as a Means of Achieving Sexual Health, *Journal of Psychology and Human Sexuality*, XIV/2–3 (2002), pp. 5–16
Brown, Judith C., 'Lesbian Sexuality in Renaissance Italy: The Case of Sister Benedetta Carlini, *Signs* (Summer 1984), pp. 751–8
Bullough, Vern L., 'Who Wrote My Secret Life?', *Sexuality and Culture*, IV/1 (2000), pp. 37–60
Canavan, M. C., W. J. Meyer and D. C. Higgs, 'The Female Experience of Sibling Incest', *Journal of Marital and Family Therapy*, XVIII/2 (1992), pp. 129–42
Crozier, Ivan, 'Philosophy in the English Boudoir: Havelock Ellis, *Love and Pain*, and Sexological Discourses on Algophilia', *Journal of the History of Sexuality*, XIII/4 (July 2004), pp. 275–305.
Cuttino, G. P., and Thomas W. Lyman, 'Where is Edward II?', *Speculum*, LIII/3 (July 1978), pp. 522–44
DeMause, Lloyd, 'The Universality of Incest', *Journal of Psychohistory*, XIX/2 (Fall 1991), pp. 123–64
Downing, Lisa, 'Death and the Maidens: A Century of Necrophilia in Female-authored Textual Production', *French Cultural Studies*, XIV/2 (2003), pp. 157–68

Fincham, Frank D., Steven R. H. Beach, Thom Moore and Carol Diener, 'The Professional Response to Child Sexual Abuse: Whose Interests Are Served?', *Family Relations*, XLIII/3 (July 1994), pp. 244–54

Firestone, Philip, Drew A. Kingston, Audrey Wexler and John M. Bradford, 'Long-Term Follow-up of Exhibitionists: Psychological, Phallometric, and Offense Characteristics', *Journal of the American Academy of Psychiatry and the Law*, XXXIV/3 (September 2006), pp. 349–59

Fischer, Nancy L., 'Oedipus Wrecked? The Moral Boundaries of Incest', *Gender and Society*, XVII/1 (2003), pp. 92–110

Frappier-Mazur, Lucienne, 'Sadean Libertinage and the Esthetics of Violence', *Yale French Studies*, 94: Libertinage and Modernity (1998), pp. 184–98

Gerressu, M., C. H. Mercer, C. A. Graham, K. Wellings and A. M. Johnson, 'Prevalence of Masturbation and Associated Factors in a British National Probability Survey', *Archives of Sexual Behavior*, XXXVII/2 (2007), pp. 266–78

Giannini, A. J., G. Colapietro, A. E. Slaby, S. M. Melemis and R. K. Bowman, 'Sexualization of the Female Foot as a Response to Sexually Transmitted Epidemics: A Preliminary Study', *Psychological Reports*, LXXXIII/2 (1998), pp. 491–8

Gilgun, Jane F., 'We Shared Something Special: The Moral Discourse of Incest Perpetrators', *Journal of Marriage and the Family*, LVII/2 (May 1995), pp. 265–81

Golden, Mark, 'Slavery and Homosexuality at Athens', *Phoenix*, XXXVII/4 (Winter 1984), pp. 308–24

Hall, Lesley A., 'Forbidden by God, Despised by Men: Masturbation, Medical Warnings, Moral Panic, and Manhood in Great Britain, 1850–1950', *Journal of the History of Sexuality*, II/3, Special Issue, Part 2: The State, Society, and the Regulation of Sexuality in Modern Europe (January 1992), pp. 365–87

Hamman, Jaco, 'The Rod of Discipline: Masochism, Sadism and the Judeo-Christian Religion', *Journal of Religion and Health*, XXXIX/4 (Winter 2000), pp. 319–28

Harvey, A. D., 'Prosecutions for Sodomy in England at the Beginning of the Nineteenth Century', *The Historical Journal*, XXI/4 (December 1978), pp. 939–48

Hatton, Erin, and Mary Nell Trautner, 'Equal Opportunity Objectification? The Sexualization of Men and Women on the Cover of *Rolling Stone*', *Sexuality and Culture*, XV (2011), pp. 256–78

Heilbrun Jr, A. B., and David T. Seif, 'Erotic Value of Female Distress in Sexually Explicit Photographs', *Journal of Sexual Health*, XXIV (1988), pp. 47–57

Hole, Robert, 'Consanguinity and a Monstrous Birth in Rural England, January 1600', *Social History*, xxv/2 (2000), pp. 183–99

Holmes, Ronald M., 'Sequential Predation: Elements of Serial Fatal Victimization', *Sexual Addiction and Compulsivity*, iv/1 (January 1997), pp. 33–42

Hunt, Alan, 'The Great Masturbation Panic and the Discourse of Moral Regulation in Nineteenth- and Early Twentieth-Century Britain', *Journal of the History of Sexuality*, viii/4 (1998), pp. 575–615

Hurteau, Pierre, 'Catholic Moral Discourse on Male Sodomy and Masturbation in the Seventeenth and Eighteenth Centuries', *Journal of the History of Sexuality*, iv/1 (July 1993), pp. 1–26

Joshel, Sandra R., 'Nurturing the Master's Child: Slavery and the Roman Child-Nurse', *Signs*, xii/1 (1986), pp. 3–22

Karpman, Ben, 'The Psychopathy of Exhibitionism', *The Psychoanalytic Review*, xiii/1 (January 1926)

King, Helen, 'Galen and the Widow: Towards a History of Therapeutic Masturbation in Ancient Gynaecology', *EuGeStA: Journal on Gender Studies in Antiquity*, 1 (2011), pp. 205–35

Kuper, Adam, 'Incest, Cousin Marriage, and the Origin of the Human Sciences in Nineteenth-century England', *Past and Present*, clxxiv/1 (2002), pp. 158–83

Kurke, Leslie, 'Inventing the *Hetaira*: Sex, Politics, and Discursive Conflict in Archaic Greece', *Classical Antiquity*, xvi/1 (April 1997), pp. 106–50

Liliequest, Jonas, 'Peasants Against Nature: Crossing the Boundaries between Man and Animals in Seventeenth- and Eighteenth-century Sweden', *Journal of the History of Sexuality*, i/3 (1999), pp. 393–423

Lytle, Ephraim, 'Apuleius' *Metamorphoses* and the *Spurcum Additamentum* (10.21)', *Classical Philology*, xcviii/4 (October 2003), pp. 349–65

MacDonald, Robert H., 'The Frightful Consequences of Onanism: Notes on the "History of a Delusion"', *Journal of the History of Ideas*, xxviii/3 (July–September 1967), pp. 423–43

Meigs, Anna, and Kathleen Barlow, 'Beyond the Taboo: Imagining Incest', *American Anthropologist*, civ/1 (March 2002), pp. 38–49

Money, John, Russell Jobaris and Gregg Furth, 'Apotemnophilia: Two Cases of Self-demand Amputation as a Paraphilia', *Journal of Sex Research*, xiii/2 (May 1977), pp. 115–25

Morris, Polly, 'Incest or Survival Strategy? Plebeian Marriage within the Prohibited Degrees in Somerset, 1730–1835', *Journal of the History of Sexuality*, ii/2 (October 1991), pp. 235–65

Murray, A. D., 'The Reclassification of Extreme Pornographic Images', *The Modern Law Review*, lxxii/1 (2009), pp. 73–90

National Center for Victims of Crime, and Crime Victims Research and Treatment Center, 'Incest' (1992)

Navin, Helen, 'Medical and Surgical Risks in Handballing', *Journal of Homosexuality*, VI/3 (1982), pp. 67–76

Neuman, P. R., 'Masturbation and Madness, and the Modern Concept of Childhood and Adolescence', *Journal of Social History*, VIII/3 (Spring 1975), pp. 1–27

Otis, Margaret, 'A Perversion Not Commonly Noted', *Journal of Abnormal Psychology*, VIII/2 (1913), pp. 113–16

Partner, Nancy F., 'No Sex, No Gender', *Speculum*, 68 (1993), pp. 419–43

Pattinson, John Patrick, 'The Man Who Was Walter', *Victorian Literature and Culture* (2002), vol. 30, pp. 19–40

Patton, Michael S., 'Masturbation from Judaism to Victorianism', *Journal of Religion and Health*, XXIV/2 (Summer 1985), pp. 133–46

—, 'Twentieth-century Attitudes toward Masturbation', *Journal of Religion and Health*, XXV/4 (Winter 1986), pp. 291–302

Puff, Helmut, 'Female Sodomy: The Trial of Katherina Hetzeldorfer (1477)', *Journal of Medieval and Early Modern Studies*, XXX/1 (2000), pp. 41–61

Rey, Michel, 'Parisian Homosexuals Create a Lifestyle, 1700–1750: The Police Archives', *Eighteenth-century Life*, 9 (1985), pp. 179–91

Richlin, Amy, 'Invective against Women in Roman Satire', *Arethusa*, XIVI/1 (Spring 1984), pp. 67–80

Riddell, William Renwick, 'A Case of Supposed Sadism', *Journal of the American Institute of Criminal Law and Criminology*, XV/1 (May 1924), pp. 32–41

Rosman, J. P., and P. J. Resnick, 'Sexual Attraction to Corpses: A Psychiatric Review of Necrophilia', *Bulletin of the American Academy of Psychiatry and the Law*, XVII/2 (1989), pp. 153–63.

Satter, Beryl, 'The Sexual Abuse Paradigm in Historical Perspective: Passivity and Emotion in Mid-Twentieth-Century America', *Journal of the History of Sexuality*, XII/3 (July 2003), pp. 424–64

Shaw, J., 'Mary Toft, Religion and National Memory in Eighteenth-century England', *Journal for Eighteenth-Century Studies*, XXXII/3 (2009), pp. 321–38

Stead, W. T., 'The Maiden Tribute of Modern Babylon, I: The Report of Our Secret Commission', *The Pall Mall Gazette* (6 July 1885)

Stevenson, David, 'Recording the Unspeakable: Masturbation in the Diary of William Drummond, 1657–1659', *Journal of the History of Sexuality*, IX/3–4 (July 2000), pp. 234–9

Stolberg, Michael, 'Self-Pollution, Moral Reform, and the Venereal Trade: Notes on the Sources and Historical Content of *Onania* (1716)', *Journal of the History of Sexuality*, IX/1–2 (January/April 2000), pp. 37–61

Stone, Lawrence, 'Libertine Sexuality in Post-Restoration England: Group Sex and Flagellation among the Middling Sort in Norwich in 1706–07', *Journal of the History of Sexuality*, II/4 (April 1992), pp. 511–26

Strong, Bryan, 'Toward a History of the Experiential Family: Sex and Incest in the Nineteenth-century Family', *Journal of Marriage and the Family*, XXXV/3 (August 1973), pp. 457–66

Sullivan, Nikki, 'Integrity, Mayhem, and the Question of Self-demand Amputation, *Continuum: Journal of Media and Cultural Studies*, XIX/3 (2005), pp. 325–33

Tomasini, F., 'Exploring Ethical Justification for Self-demand Amputation', *Ethics and Medicine*, XX/2 (Summer 2006), pp. 99–115

Wagner, Peter, 'The Veil of Medicine and Morality: Some Pornographic Aspects of the *Onania*', *Eighteenth-Century Studies*, VI/2 (September 1983), pp. 179–84

Weinberg, Martin S., Colin J. Williams and Cassandra Calhan, '"If the Shoe Fits . . .": Exploring Male Homosexual Foot Fetishism', *Journal of Sex Research*, XXXI/1 (1995), pp. 17–27

White, Murray J., 'The Statue Syndrome: Perversion, Fantasy, Anecdote?', *Journal of Sex Research*, XIV/4 (November 1978), pp. 246–9

Williams, Tassie, 'Female Fraud: Counterfeit Maidenheads in the Eighteenth Century', *Journal of the History of Sexuality*, VI/4 (April 1996), pp. 518–48

Wilson, Adam, 'Democratic Necrophilia: Eighteenth Century's Anxious Disease': *Anamesa*, V/1, The Democracy Issue (Spring 2007), pp. 42–66

Woodward, Samuel Bayard, 'Remarks on Masturbation: Insanity Produced by Masturbation; Effections of Masturbation with Cases', *Boston Medical and Surgical Journal*, XII (1835)

Yannicopoulos, A. V., 'The Pedagogue in Antiquity', *British Journal of Educational Studies*, XXXIII/2 (June 1985), pp. 173–9

Reference Books and Archives

The Concise Oxford Dictionary of Etymology, ed. T. F. Hoad (Oxford, 1996)

Criminal Registers for England and Wales, The National Archives, Kew, Surrey

Edythe Ferguson Collection, The Kinsey Institute, Indiana University

Harry Benjamin Collection, The Kinsey Institute, Indiana University

House of Commons Debates, Hansard Archive, Parliament of the United Kingdom, at www.parliament.uk/business/publications

Mass Observation Archive, University of Sussex, Brighton

New Larousse Encyclopaedia of Mythology, ed. Félix Gurand, trans. Richard Aldington and Delano Ames (London, 1985)

Oxford English Dictionary, at www.oed.com

ACKNOWLEDGEMENTS

My thanks must go to all the scholars who have worked in all the separate areas of the history of sexuality – from bestiality to sado-masochism. Without them, I would have been unable to build on my original research here and make a broader picture of sexual perversion in the West. I have tried to mention all who have had an impact on this book in the References, but there are many more who have influenced my work in the history of sexuality over the years, particularly all the contributors to the *Cultural History of Sexuality* project.

My thanks go to the librarians at the Harry Ransom Center, Texas; to those at the Kinsey Institute, Indiana, for their assistance; and to those at Sussex University Library, for their help on the Mass Observation Surveys. As usual, the librarians in the British Library have continued to be invaluable, particularly on the eighteenth-, nineteenth- and twentieth-century primary sources.

I thank the members of the H-Histsex@H-Net forum who assisted in many a query, and the continued support from friends and colleagues at Birkbeck, University of London. Among other friends and colleagues who helped were barrister Rosie Burns and Rictor Norton. Thanks also to Professor Mark Golden, Professor Helen King and Dr Anna Katharina Schaffner for reading parts of the book on the classical work and the sexologists respectively.

Without a great team at Reaktion Books, especially Aimee Selby, my editor, this book would not have been as good. My thanks go to them and to Michael Leaman for spotting a good title when he sees one and for letting me keep so many images in the book.

Most of the images come from my own collection of books, postcards and photographs and are my personal choice. While I enjoyed undertaking the picture research, I know I gave Harry Gilonis some trouble and less fun trying to obtain some of the more hard-to-find alternatives I requested. I thank him very much for all his hard work and assistance in attempts to retrieve the images I wanted. I also thank the Wellcome Library for the use of their images.

Most of all, as usual, my ultimate gratitude must go to my friend and partner Jad Adams, who cooked me many dinners, travelled with me on various research trips and helped me with the exploration on home turf. To him, I owe most happiness in life.

PHOTO
ACKNOWLEDGEMENTS

The author and publishers wish to express their thanks to the below sources of illustrative material and/or permission to reproduce it. (Some locations uncredited in the captions for reasons of brevity are also given below.)

Afrodisias Müzesi, Afrodisyas, Turkey: p. 270; from Ulisse Aldrovandi, *Monstrum Historia* (Bononia, 1642): pp. 193 (left), 195; Amon Carter Museum, Fort Worth, Texas: p. 100 (foot); from Anon, *Histoire de Dom Bougre, portier des Chartreux* (France, 1741): p. 283; from *Aristotle's Compleat Master Piece in Three Parts: Displaying the Secrets of Nature in the Generation of Man . . .* (n.p., 1753): p. 21; Ashmolean Museum, Oxford: p. 298; author's collection: p. 70; author's photographs: pp. 200, 258, 259, 389; Bargello Museum, Florence: p. 85; Berlin Sex Museum: p. 389; from Giovanni Boccaccio, *Opus de Claris Mulieribus* (Berne, 1539): p. 150; The Black Room, Las Vegas (www.theblackroomlasvegas.com): p. 382 (top); from Jean-Baptiste de Boyer (attrib.), *Thérèse Philosophe* (n.p., 1785): pp. 59, 126; British Library, London: pp. 29, 83; from *British Medical Journal*, 1/1484 (8 June 1889): p. 278; British Museum, London: pp. 77, 112, 240, 303, 316; photos © The Trustees of the British Museum: pp. 112, 150, 160, 196, 198, 217 (foot), 231, 250, 254, 303, 316; from R. J. Brodie, *The Secret Companion* (London, 1845): p. 62; from Nicolas Chorier, *L'Académie des dames* (n.p., 1680): pp. 44, 115, 116; from Mary Cowden Clarke, *World-Noted Women* (New York, 1883): p. 111; from F. J. Cole, *Early Theories of Sexual Generation* (Oxford, 1930): p. 55; from The Rev. Wm. M. Cooper, B. A. [James G. Bertram], *A History of the Rod . . .* (London, n.d.): pp. 81, 302; from Donatien-Alphonse-François de Sade, *Justine, ou les Malheurs du Virtu* (published 'en Hollande', 1791): p. 217 (top); from Donatien-Alphonse-François de Sade, *Justine, ou les Malheurs du Virtu* (published 'en Hollande', 1797): p. 218; from Donatien-Alphonse-François de Sade, *Histoire de Juliette, ou les Prosperités du Vice* (published 'en Hollande',

1797): pp. 220, 330, 352, 359, 369; from *The 'De Ss. Martyrum cruciatibus'
of the Rev. Father [Antonio] Gallonio* . . . (London, Paris: printed for the
subscribers, 1903): p. 215 (right); from Achille Devéria, *Diabolico Foutro
Manie* (Paris, 1835): p. 347; from John B. Ellis, *Free Love and its Votaries*
(New York, n.d.): p. 38; Galleria Borghese, Rome: p. 87; Gemäldegalerie,
Berlin: p. 86; from Conrad Gesner, *Historiae Animalium* (Zürich, 1551–8):
p. 193 (right); from Kenneth Grahame, *The Golden Age* (London, 1895):
p. 314; from *Le Grand Kalendrier et Compost des Bergiers* . . . (Troyes, 1529):
p. 215 (left); Herbert Art Gallery and Museum, Coventry: p. 349; from
Magnus Hirschfeld, *Sexualpathologie* (Bonn, 1921): p. 167; Hunterian
Museum, London: p. 251; from *The Illustrated London News*, 21 July 1877:
p. 157; from *Invocation a l'amour Chant philosophique* (London, c. 1825):
p. 54; Josef Mensing Gallery, Hamm-Rhynern: p. 328; The Josephinium,
Vienna: p. 258; Richard Von Krafft-Ebing Collection: p. 166; Kunst-
historisches Museum, Vienna: pp. 144, 272 (foot); Kunstmuseum, Basel:
p. 257; from Jean-Charles Gervaise de Latouche (attrib.), *Dom Bougre où
Le Portier de Chartreux* (Frankfurt, 1741): p. 92; 'Choisy Le Conin' (Franz
von Bayros), *Erzahlungen am Toilettentische* (privately published, 1908):
p. 178; Library of Congress, Washington, DC: p. 304; Library of the Royal
College of Physicians, Edinburgh: p. 251; from the *London Illustrated
News* (1843): p. 161; reproduced by courtesy of the Master and Fellows of
Trinity College, Cambridge: p. 362 left); from John Laws Milton, *On the
Pathology and Treatment of Spermatorrhoea* (London, 1887): p. 64; from
Albert Moll, *Handbuch der Sexualwissenschaften* (Leipzig, 1921): p. 67;
Musée du Louvre, Paris: pp. 74, 119 (left), 213, 281, 366; Musée d'Orsay,
Paris: p. 185; Museo Nazionale Archeologico, Tarquinia: p. 108; from
Alfred de Musset, *Gamiani, ou deux nuits d'excès* (Brussels, 1833): pp. 65,
370 (foot); Naples Archaeological Museum, Italy: pp. 16, 17, 182, 367, 368;
National Archaeological Museum, Madrid: p. 210; National Museum
Stockholm: p. 119 (right); New York Historical Society: p. 159; NY Carlsberg
Glyptotek, Copenhagen: p. 390; Palazzo Farnese, Rome: p. 272 (top);
from James Parsons, *A Mechanical and Critical Enquiry into the Nature of
Hermaphrodites* (London, 1741): p. 120; private collections: pp. 181 (foot),
241, 295, 311; Rijsmuseum, Amsterdam: p. 273; Shibden Hall, Yorks: p. 124;
La Specula, Florence: p. 259; Staatliche Antikensammlungen, Munich: pp.
78, 212, 242; Staatliches Museen, Berlin: p. 23; State Pushkin Museum, St.
Petersburg: p. 18; Tate, London: pp. 260, 312; from Léo Taxil, *Les Prostitutes
Contemporarie* (Paris, 1884): p. 133; from S.A.D. Tissot, *L'Onanisme; ou
dissertation physique sur les maladies produites par la masturbation* (Paris,
1836): p. 61; from S.A.D. Tissot, *L'Onanismo ovvero Dissertazioni sopra le
malattie cagionate dalle Polluzioni voluntarie* (Venice, 1785): p. 60; from
The Unexplained, vol. 12 (London, 1980): p. 153; Universitätsbibliothek
Heidelberg Cod. Pal. germ. 848 (Codex Manesse): p. 147; from Antonio

INDEX

Page numbers in *italics* refer to illustrations

Abélard, Pierre 26–8,
    404, 439
Aboriginal Australians
    193, 288
abstinence 22, 64, 179,
    348–9
Academie des dames, L'
    (Nicolas Chorier, erot-
    ica) 44, 52, 115–16
Achilles 78–9, 145, 239,
    242, 410
Acton, William 64, 66,
    286, 427
    *The Functions and
    Disorders of the
    Reproductive Organs*
    64–5
adultery 24–5, 41, 54–5,
    224, 275, 281
Agamemnon 145
age of consent 295,
    299–301, 317, 327, 398,
    400, 432
Agrippina 270, 274
Akhenaten 272
alcohol, alcoholism 202,
    210, 233–4, 287, 355,
    375
Aldrovandi, Ulisse,
    Monstrorum historia
    193, 195
algolagnia 225–9, 237
    see also pain
Allen, James 306
Allen, Thomas 112
Al-Razi 21
Altdorfer, Albert, *Lot*

and His Daughters 272
Amenhotep III 271
American Psychiatric
    Association 10–11, 106,
    237, 268
amputation, amputee
    sex 84, 210, 392–3,
    399–400
Anacreon 390
anal intercourse 15, 25,
    76, 80, 94, 96, 168,
    373–4
    see also sodomy
*Analysis of the Sexual
    Impulse* (Havelock
    Ellis) 351
anatomy, anatomists 54,
    61, 249–59
Anatomy Act of 1832 254
*Anatomy of Melancholy,
    The* (Robert Burton) 54
Anderson, Sir Robert 69
animal rights 206
animal sex farms 206
animals *see* bestiality
Anne, Queen of England
    122–3, 159
anodyne necklaces 57
anus 16, 22, 25, 207,
    231–2, 332, 348–9, 350,
    394
    see also anal inter-
    course; sodomy
anxiety 65, 70, 72, 138,
    290, 379
Aphrodite, Aphroditus
    110, 118

Apollodorus 13
apotemnophilia 392–3
    see also amputation
apprentices 53, 84,
    90–93, 186, 201–2,
    245–6, 297–8
Apuleius, Lucius, *The
    Golden Ass* 179, *181*
Aquinas, Thomas 25,
    49–50, 81
Ardisson, Victor 263–4
aristocracy, aristocrats
    84, 95, 152, 216, 223,
    248, 277, 358
Aristophanes 393
Aristotle 19, 79
    Generation of Animals
    19
Aristotle's Masterpiece
    (erotica) 21, 53
Arrowsmith, Stephen
    300
Atkinson, George 307
Aurelius, Marcus 146
auto-asphyxiation 237–8,
    383–4
Autopsy (television
    series) 265
Avicenna 21
avisodomy 199–202
Azande 331–2

baby play, adult 329,
    355–6
Balzac, Honoré de *A
    Passion in the Desert*
    197

Barends, Trijntje 157
Barker, Priscilla 68
Barney, Natalie Clifford
    132–4,
barracks 102, 111, 141–2,
    156, 262
Barrie, J. M. 312–13
bachelors 50, 64
Bayros, Franz von 178
Beam, Lura Ella, *One
    Thousand Marriages* 38
Beard, George M. 69
Beardsley, Aubrey 127, *129*
beatings 21, 139, 161,
    186–7, 210–11, 213–16,
    222, 224, 228, 235–6,
    301, 305, 309, 356,
    362–3
Beaufort, Lady Margaret
    299
Bedborough, Thomas 36
Beggar's Benison 52
Benjamin, Dr Harry 145,
    170–72, 174
Bennet, Charles 290
Bernard of Gordon 21
    Lily of Medicine 21
Bernis, François-Joachim
    de Pierre, Cardinal de
    301
Besant, Annie 38
bestiality 7, 11, 17–18, 25,
    33, 51, 179–208, 240,
    268, 276, 344, 397–8,
    401
    with birds *see* avi-
    sodomy
    with bulls 17, 180, 182
    with cows 17, 185,
    189–90, 192, 202–3
    with dogs 178, 185,
    187–9, 194–5, 202–4,
    207, 319
    with donkeys (asses),
    jennies 179, 186
    with horses, mares,
    ponies 175, 180–2,
    186–8, 197, 204
*Bête, La (The Beast, film,
    dir. Walerian
    Borowczyk) 197
Bible 22, 80, 113, 147, 161,
    243, 274, 314

Deuteronomy 22
    Genesis 49, 161, 274
    Leviticus 22, 80, 113,
    117–18, 179–80, 184, 243,
    274, 276
    Numbers 243
Bienville, M.D.T.,
    Nymphomania 60
Binet, Alfred 8, 36, 371–2
birth control *see* contra-
    ception
bisexuality 40, 76, 102,
    134, 138, 146, 165, 168,
    206, 379, 393, 401
Black Death 29, 243
Blandy, Mary 256
Bloch, Iwan 8, 34, 102, 336
Boccaccio, Giovanni 28,
    150
Body Integrity Identity
    Disorder (BIID) 392–3
Bondt, Jacob de 192–3
Bonny, Anne 156
*Book of Gomorrah (Liber
    Gomorrhianus,* Peter
    Damien) 80
Booth, Charles 286
Bora, Katherine von 30
Borel, Antoine, illustra-
    tions to *Thérèse
    philosophe 59, 126*
Boswell James 31–2, 52
Boucher, François,
    *Hercules and Omphale
    18*
bourgeoisie 55, 68, 285
Boulton, Ernest 95–7
Bradlaugh, Charles 38
Brandon, Lady Elizabeth
    309
Brady, Ian 320
Brandes, Bernd Jürgens
    399
breasts 68, 70, 124, 130–31,
    164, 171, 176, 256, 263–5,
    282, 318–19, 335, 337,
    372, 374, 385, 392, 399
breeches roles 156
Bretonne, Restif de la 377
Bride of Frankenstein
    (film, dir. James
    Whale) 255–6
Briqueville, Robert de 245

British Sex Survey 40
Brooks, Rebekah 324
Brooks, Romaine 132–5
Browning, Robert 260
Brudos, Jerome Henry
    380–81
Brygos Painter 298
buggery *see* anal inter-
    course, sodomy
Burke, Edmund, *On the
    Sublime and Beautiful*
    238
Burke, William 251–255
    see also Hare, William
Burney, Fanny 280
Burrell, Jonathan 191
Burton, Robert, *The
    Anatomy of Melancholy*
    54–5
Butler, Eleanor 123, 125
Butler, Josephine 315–16
buttocks, bottoms 230–31,
    332, 334, 338–9, 340,
    350, 356, 361, 372, 385
Byron, Lord George
    Gordon 281, 363

Cage aux Folles, La 164
Caligula 211, 274
Cameron, Julia Margaret
    317
Cannon, John 344
Capel, Richard 55
capital punishment
    49–50, 115, 188, 276,
    306
    burning 75, 82, 84,
    86–8, 94, 155, 184–7,
    247–8, 274, 276, 398
    hanging 75, 93, 96, 256,
    265, 383–4, 398
    public executions 243,
    256
Caprio, Frank 137–8,
    231–2, 320, 338–9,
    349–50
Caravaggio 88
    Amor Vincit Omnia 86
    *Boy with a Basket of
    Fruit 87*
Carlini, Bernadetta 114
Carpenter, Edward 36,
    98, 131

Carpoz, Benedict 50–51
Carracci, Annibale, *Zeus and Hera* 272
Carroll, Lewis (Charles Dodgson) 310–11
Carry On (films) 164
Cassius Dio 146
castration 28, 64, 84, 146, 152, 324
Cathars 81–2
Catte of Ingoldmells, Matilda 28
Charcot, Jean-Martin 69
chastity 8, 22, 29–30, 57, 155, 286, 297, 300
see also virgins
Chaucer, Geoffrey, *The Canterbury Tales* 28, 332
child abuse 213, 275, 291–2, 305–10, 314–15, 319–25
Child, Elizabeth 307
childbirth 43
childhood 99, 101, 134, 138, 167, 222, 228–9, 236, 248, 261, 288, 291–2, 295–8, 301–5, 310–18
children 11, 13–14, 24–5, 28, 38, 57, 63–6, 68–9, 76, 78, 82, 99, 126, 197, 213, 215, 221, 228, 233–4, 236, 244–8, 275, 285, 288–93, 295–327, 335, 341, 390, 400–02
Christianity, Christians 22, 29, 80, 179, 189, 192, 211, 215, 243, 274–5
see also Church
Christina, Queen of Sweden 109
Church
and bestiality 184–5
and children 301, 322, 401
cross-dressing (Joan of Arc) 153–5
and the dead 249
and incest 275–6
and lesbians 113–17
and marriage 28–30, 141

and masturbation 48–50
and sex 22–5, 299, 373
and sodomy 80–82, 87
see also Christianity
Church of Jesus Christ of Latter-day Saints, The 401
Churchill, Sarah, Duchess of Marlborough 122–3
Cicero 273
circumcision
male 400, 146
female 399
Clap, 'Mother' 94–5
Clary, Julian 164–5
Cleland, John 122, 344
Cleopatra VII 271
clergy (incl. priests) 25, 28, 30, 40, 56, 82, 85, 148, 152, 219, 243, 280, 283, 337
Cleveland Street raid 95
clitoris 58, 118, 120–22, 156, 170, 319, 365, 389
clitorodectomy 64
clubs 52, 88, 103, 105, 134, 163–5, 237, 306, 341, 379, 394, 396
coitus interruptus 49
Coke, Sir Edward 300
Collier, John, *Lady Godiva* 349
Comerre, Léon-Françoise, *Leda and the Swan* 181
Comfort, Alex, *Joy of Sex* 384
Committee for Research on Problems of Sex (U.S. National Research Council) 39
companionate marriage 30
Comstock Laws (Anti-Obscenity Act 1873) 37
conception 19–20, 25, 310, 373, 401
see also generation; procreation
concubine see mistress
Condorçet, Nicolas de 93
confessional 25, 30, 224, 291

congenital or hereditary defects and disease 36, 62, 98–9, 101–2, 130–31, 137–8, 226, 227–8, 236, 339, 372, 375, 379
see also degeneration; tainted families
Contagious Diseases Act 67, 315
contraception 37–8, 41–2, 64, 165, 295
Cooper, Stephen 307
coprophilia 348–50, 352, 355–6, 364
Corinthians 22
Cornbury, Edward Hyde, Lord 158–9
Coroners and Justice Act 2009 322
corsets, corseting 67, 167, 173, 229, 373, 380
Cosel, Carl von 265–7
Cotton, John (Puritan) 117
Courbet, Gustave, *Nude Woman with a Dog* 185
courts, trials 275, 279–80, 295, 297, 303–7, 320, 322, 334, 340, 343, 399
courtesans see prostitutes
courtly love 374, 376–7
cousins 271, 275–9, 281, 293
Couston, Thomas Smith 69
Cranach, Lucas the Elder 22, 198
Criminal Justice and Immigration Act 2008 268, 401
Criminal Law Amendment Act 1885 317
Crivelli, Bartolomea 114
Crocker, William Henry 334
Cromwell, Oliver 281
cross-dressing see transvestism
Crusades 82
Cruikshank, George 302
Cruikshank, Isaac Robert, *The London Monster* 231

Culam, Claudine de 187
Cullwick, Hannah 362–3
cult of girl child 310–11
cunnilingus 205–6, 264, 285, 320, 355, 365–9, 371, 375
  see also fellatio; oral sex
cutting see stabbing and cutting

D'Arcy, Ella 127
D'Aulnoy, Countess Marie Catherine 358
Damian, Peter 49, 80, 357–8
Daniel, John 290
Daniels, John 334
Darwin, Charles 35, 196, 279
David, Rape of the Sabine Women 213
Davis, Dr Katherine 70
Davis, Porter 337
Davy, Meredith 90
Debreyne, P.J.C. 63
Decameron (Giovanni Boccacio) 28
Deceased Brother's Widow's Marriage Act 1921 282
Deceased Wife's Sister's Marriage Act 1907 282
defecation 349, 352–3
defloration, cult of 306
degeneration 63, 101
Dekker, Albert 383
Delacroix, Eugène, The Bride of Abydos 281
Delamarre, Marguerite 123
Deleuze, Gilles, Masochism: Coldness and Cruelty 236
Demetrius of Apamea, On the Signs of Diseases 47
Denning, Abraham 189
depression see melancholia
Devéria, Achille 65, 347, 370
Dewey, Joseph 191
Diagnostic and Statistical Manual of Mental Disorders (DSMD) 10–12, 106, 381
Dick Cavett Show, The (television series) 173
Dickenson, Latou Robert, One Thousand Marriages 38
Diderot, Denis 123–4
Dietrich, Marlene 134, 136
dildo, penis substitutes, 48, 114–15, 248, 388–9, 402
Dioclese 79
Diogenes the Cynic 47
Dionysus 145, 181
divorce 30–31, 290, 339
dogging 346–7
domestic servants 68, 93, 297, 301, 344
dominatrix 329, 361
Donatello, David 85, 88
Donnisthorpe, Revd George 91
Dorland's Medical Dictionary 33
Douglas, Lord Alfred 96–7
Douglas, James 137
Dover, Kenneth 77
Dowson, Ernest 310–11
drag 103, 134, 162–4
  see also transvestism
Drucilla 274
drugs
  hormone 169
  for paedophiles 321, 324
  for pain 210
  for recreation 105, 237
Drummond, William 51–2
Drysdale, Sir George, Elements of Social Science 64
Duffus, George 90–91
DuGard, Samuel and Lydia 277
Dunton, John, He-Strumpets: A Satyr on the Sodomite-Club 88–9
Dürer, Albrecht, Martyrdom of St Catherine 213
Dutroux, Marc 322–3
dwarfs, midgets 390
Dyke, Antony van, George Villiers and His Brother 294
dysmorphia
  bodily 392–3, 400
  sexual 169–70

Eakins, Thomas, Swimming 99
East India Company 197
Ecole des filles, L' (erotica) 52
Edward II, King of England 82–3
Egbert, King of Wessex 184
ego-dystonic homosexuality 12
ejaculation, ejaculate 31–2, 49–50, 57, 63, 199, 202, 246, 308, 337, 350. 355, 371, 373, 383, 385, 389
  see also orgasm
Elagabalus 145–6
Electra complex 288
Ellis, Havelock 8, 36–8, 69, 101–2, 130–2, 174, 199, 202, 226–7, 288, 318–9, 351, 354–5, 371–3, 378–9
  Analysis of the Sexual Impulse 351
  Fountain of Life 351
  Sexual Inversion in Men 36
  Sexual inversion in Women 130–31
  Studies in the Psychology of Sex 36, 351
Ellis, John B., Free Love and Its Votaries 38
Emile (novel, Jean-Jacques Rousseau) 53, 301–2
Endore, Guy, The Werewolf of Paris 197
Entertainments National Service Association (ENSA) 164

epilepsy 61, 264, 336
erastes 76–80
Eriksson, King of Norway
 and Sweden 83
erōmenos 76–80
Eronania (book) 45, 57–8
erotica (in text) 9, 52–4,
 56–7, 124, 282–6, 285,
 309, 358–61
Esquire (magazine) 170
eugenics 35, 62
Eulenburg, Albert 228,
 234, 237
Eustathius of
 Thessalonica 239
Evans-Pritchard, Edward
 331–2
*Everything You Always
 Wanted to Know About
 Sex . . .* (film, dir.
 Woody Allen) 197
evolutionary theory 34–5,
 197, 227–8, 288–9
exhibitionism 33–4,
 329–44, 346–7, 364, 374
Exner, Max 70

*Factors in the Sex Life of
 2,200 Women* (survey)
 71
fairy tales 197
false memory syndrome
 292
*Fanny Hill see Memoirs of
 a Woman of Pleasure*
fantasies 98, 168–9, 209,
 216, 222–4, 228–9, 248,
 261, 263, 286, 319, 325,
 355, 356, 358, 360, 362,
 375, 380, 385, 393, 399
 see also sexual fantasies
Favorinus 296
fellatio, fellators, fellating
 356, 365–71, 373, 396
 see also cunnilingus;
 oral sex
female friendships 109,
 122–3
 see also lesbians
female husbands 110,
 121–2
feminism, feminists 126,
 264, 325

Femme endormie, La
 (erotica) 385
Fendi, Peter, 354, 370
Féré, Charlesm *The
 Evolution and
 Dissolution of the
 Sexual Instinct* 227
Ferguson, Edythe 173–5
Féron, E. F., *Gilles de Rais*
 245
fertility 356–7
 see also infertility
fetishism 11, 33–4, 237,
 350, 365, 371–84, 396
Fèvre, Thomas Le 186
Fielding, Henry 122
Fielding, John 303
First World War 134, 141,
 163
fisting 394–6
flagellation, flagellants,
 flogging, whipping 22,
 33, 80–81, 213, 238, 338,
 356–64, 376
flashers *see* exhibitionism
Fliess, Wilhelm 349
Formby, George 164
Fountain of Life
 (Havelock Ellis) 351
Frankenstein (Mary
 Shelley), 255
free love 37–8, 127
Freud, Sigmund 8, 36, 69,
 99–101, 198–9, 228–9,
 288, 319–20, 336,
 348–9, 373
 *Three Essays on the
 Theory of Sexuality*
 198–99, 229
 Totem and Taboo 288
Freundin, Die (magazine)
 134
Freyer, Hans 337
frigidity 15, 138
frotterism (rubbing) 121,
 339–40
Fulbert, Canon 26–8
furor uterinus 58
 see also nymphomania
furries *see* plushophilia

Galba, Roman emperor
 80

Galen 19, 47–8, 54
Galvani, Luigi 254–5
Ganymede 74–5, 88
gas masks 381
Gauthe, Father Gilbert
 322
Gavarni, Paul, *The Places
 of Pleasure* 345
Gay Pride 105, 107
Gazette Médicale
 (magazine) 199
generation, 19, 35, 57
 see also conception,
 procreation
genitalia 121
 see also labia; penis;
 vagina
Gentleman's Magazine
 250
gerontophilia 11, 221
Gesner, Conrad,
 Historiae animalium
 193
Giese, Karl 165
Gillray, James 31–2
gladiatorial games 210–11
Gladstone, William 361
Glazemark, Richard 280
Gloeden, Wilhelm von
 99, 326
Godiva, Lady 346, *349*
golden showers 237–8,
 329, 356
 see also urolagnia
Goltzius, Hendrik, *Lot
 and His Daughters 273*
Gordon, Mary 361
Gough, Stephen 342–3
Grahame, Kenneth 312,
 314
Green, Richard 172
Gregory of Tours 148
Grenfell, Joyce 164
Grien, Hans Baldung
 Death and the Maiden
 (Hans Baldung Grien)
 255, 257
 Three Witches, The
 Grien, Hans Baldung
 (art) 117
Gueulette, Simon 186
Guinevere 374

Hall, Radclyffe 137, 138–9, 142
The Well of Loneliness 137, 138–9, 173
Hall, Thomas 158–60
Hamill, Katharine Forrest 312
Hammond, Charles 95
Harding, William 305
Hare, William 251–5
see also Burke, William
Haworth, John 192
Hawtrey, Charles 164
Hello Dolly (play) 164
Héloïse d'Argenteuil 26–8
Herbert, Henry 306
herbs 18, 209
Herculaneum 10, 182
hereditary disease 62, 339, 372, 375, 379, 399
see also tainted families
hermaphroditism, hermaphrodites 110, 118–22, 171
Hermes 47
Herodotus 182–3, 239, 242, 330
Herridge, George 333
Hertner, Elisabeth 114–17
Hertzeldorfer, Katherina 114, 388
He-Strumpets . . ., The (poem, John Dunton) 88–9
hetairai 211, 296
see also prostitutes
heterosexuality 7, 13–43, 76, 102
Hickey, William 31–2
Hiller, Kurt 165
Hindley, Myra 320
Hippocrates, *On Diseases of Women*, 19, 48
Hirschfeld, Magnus 165–70, 229, 380
Sexualpathologie 167
Histoire de Dom Bougre, portier de Chartreux (erotica, attrib. J.-C. G de Latouche) 282, 283
Hoare, William 303
Hogarth, William 249–50
Hudibras Encounters

the Skimmington 160
Cunicularii . . . 196
The Four Stages of Cruelty 250
Hogg, Thomas 190
Holloway, John 91
Homer 78–9
homosexuality (general) 11–12, 165, 16, 175, 227, 290, 350, 394–5, 402
homosexuality (male) 7, 12, 33–4, 36, 75–107, 109, 131, 134, 139, 164, 168, 234–5, 268, 290, 350, 375, 384, 394–6
see also anal intercourse; sodomy
homosexuality (female) 137–8
see also lesbianism
homunculi 55–6
Hopkins, Elizabeth 300
hormones 170–72, 176, 392
hospitals 62, 380
Hot Lunch 350
Howe, Joseph 68
Hudson, Rock 103
Hue, Felix 334
Hunt, Arabella 121
Hunt, Morton 205
Hunter, John 71
Hunter, William 249
Hustler (magazine) 384, 394
Huxley, Thomas Henry, *Man's Place in Nature* 197
hybrids 192–9
Hygienic Methods of Family Limitations (Sanger and Haire) 38
hypersexual disorder 12
hysteria 70, 319–20

idiocy 286, 335
see also insanity
illegitimacy 41
imagination 58, 60, 122, 150, 196, 247, 248
immorality 25, 35, 38, 162, 180, 315
Morgan, Lewis Henry 287

impotence 17–18, 22, 37, 61, 71, 121, 149, 150, 152, 318, 358, 368
incest 7, 10–11, 33, 262–3, 270–93
infibulations 388–93
infertility 57, 273
see also fertility
insanity 21, 54, 56, 58, 60–62, 66, 70, 72, 128, 134, 224, 372
Institute for Sex Research 165
intercrural sex 16, 77, 79, 101, 246
International Statistical Classification of Diseases and Related Health Problems (ICD) 10–11, 268–9, 325
Internet 402
inversion
female *see* lesbianism
male *see* homosexuality
Isherwood, Christopher 103
Izzard, Eddie 165

James, Robert, *Medical Dictionary* 58
James, William 98–9
Jepson, Edgar 310
Johnson, William 307
Joiner, William 334
Jorgenson, Christine 172–3
Jung, Carl 288

Kaprovitsh, Ivan 230
Karolewski, Susan 291
Keller, Rosa 219
Kellogg, John Harvey 70
Kertbeny, Karl Maria 33, 75
Kierman, James G. 33
kinaidoi 79
Kinsey, Alfred C. 13, 39–40, 71–2, 170, 175, 204–5, 321
Kinsey Scale 40
Kirk, Edward 68–9
Knights Templar 81–3

Knowlton, Charles, *The Fruits of Philosophy* 38
Knox, Dr Robert 251–5
Kottak, Conrad P., 289
Kotzwara, Frantisek 383
Kraepelin, Emile 72
Krafft-Ebing, Richard von 8, 33–5, 69, 101, 109, 139, 141, 199, 200–02, 225–6, 263, 287–8, 317–19, 335, 339, 351, 362, 368–75, 384
Psychopathia Sexualis 109, 263, 335
Kronfeld, Arthur 165
kynodesme 390

La Rue, Danny 164
La Tour Eiffel, Erika 387–8
labia 319, 342, 365, 392
Ladder (magazine) 142
'Lady's Dressing Room, The' (Jonathan Swift) 348
Ladyboys 176
Laffite-Cyon, Françoise 37
Lamb, Ralph 29
Lancelot 374
Lars and the Real Girl (film, dir. Craig Gillespie) 387
Lascivious Hypocrite, The (erotica) 367
Lasègue, Charles 335
Lateran Council 25–6, 81, 275
Le Sueur, Eustache, *The Abduction of Ganymede* 74
Leader, Nicholas 90
Lees, Edith 37
Leeuwenhoek, Anton van 55
Leno, Dan 162
Lenoir, Police Lieutenant 93
lesbianism, lesbians 7, 9, 33, 37, 58, 98, 105, 109–43, 165, 176, 268, 285, 319, 344, 355, 371, 375, 388, 395, 397, 402

Levi, Michael 303
Lévi-Strauss, Claude 289
libertines 31–2, 51–3, 88, 286, 306, 332, 344, 358
Liddell, Alice 310, 313
Liébault, Jean 54
Lister, Anne 123–4
London Committee for the Suppression of the Traffic in British Girls . . . 315
London Monster 230–31
London Society for Prevention of Cruelty to Children (NSPCC) 314
Los Angeles, Municipal Code of 175
Lot 272, 273, 274
Love and Pain (Havelock Ellis) 226–7
love sickness 20–21
Lucian 111–13, 183
lunatic asylum 62, 72, 139, 339
lust-murders 34, 233–4, 261
see also rape
Luther, Martin 29–30
Lycomedes 145
Lysistrata Haranguing the Athenian Women (Aubrey Beardsley) 127, *129*

Mackenzie, Sir George 51, 188
madness *see* insanity
Mäele, Martin van, *La Grande danse macabre des vifs* (The Great Danse Macabre of the Quick Prick) *201, 203, 284, 307, 331*
Mahew, Henry 286
Mailly, Jean de 150
Malthusian League 38
Manningham, Sir Richard 196
Marie Antoinette, Queen of France 109
Mark Matthews, *The Horseman* (book) 179, 204

marriage 15, 29, 110, 121, 126, 128, 135, 138, 146, 204, 224, 263, 265, 295, 297, 299–300, 348, 361, 387
incestuous 271–82, 287, 289–90, 292
medieval period 25–30
Enlightenment 30–32
Marriage Act of 1835 282
Marriage Act of 1949 290
Married Love (Marie Stopes) 38
Marsham, Abigail 123
Marten, John 56
Martial 183, 344
martyrdom, martyrs 22, *214, 215*, 222, 224
masochism 24, 34, 209, 216, 221–9, 234–7, 372–3, 375, 393
Mass Observation 40, 455
Masters and Johnson (William H. Masters and Virginia E. Johnson) 42
masturbation 25, 33, 45–73, 94, 101, 118, 170, 184, 205, 262–3, 372–3, 378, 398
Matrimonial Causes Act 30
Maudsley, Henry 66
Max, Mon Amour (film, dir. Nagisa Oshima) 197
Mearns, Andrew, *Bitter Cry of Outcast London* (pamphlet) 286
Mechanical and Critical Enquiry into the Nature of Hermaphrodites, A (James Parsons) *119, 120, 120*
Megilla 112–13
Meibom, Johann Heinrich 358
Meiwes, Armin 399
melancholia (and depression) 17, 19–20, 54, 60, 138–9, 171, 229, 372
Melbourne, Lord 309

Memoirs of a Woman of Pleasure (*Fanny Hill*, John Cleland) 344
menstruation 19, 114, 300, 365
mental asylum *see* lunatic asylum
mental deficiency *see* idiocy, insanity
mental disorders
Merzbach, George 336
Mew, Charlotte 127–8
Michelangelo, *Last Judgement* 395
midwifery, midwives 48, 118–19, 121, 158,
Milagro de Hoyos, Maria Elena 265–7
Millais, John Everett 259, 310
  Ophelia 259, 260
  Cherry Ripe 310, *311*
Milligan, Stephen 384
microscope 55
mistresses 13, 24, 137, 146, 222–4, 282, 309, 344, 363, 385
Mitchell, Alice 130–31
Molay, Jacques de 82
Moll, Albert 99, 227, 264, 349, 355, 376
mollies 94–5
Money, John 172, 392–3
monks, monasteries 28, 30, 80–81, 92, 213
monogamy 22
Montorgueil, Bernard, illustration of bondage *226*
mooning 334
  see also exhibitionism
Morley, William 290
Most Straunge and true discourse . . . of incestuous copulation (pamphlet) 277
Munby, Arthur 362–3
Murder Act of 1752 251
Murphy, John Enoch 31
music halls 163
Muybridge, Eadweard, *Animal Locomotion* *319*

My Secret Life ('Walter', erotica) 350–51
Myrmidons (Aeschylus) 78
mythology 17, 180–83, 193, 239, 272–3

Napoleonic Code 53, 94, 301
Nast, Thomas, *Free Love* *39*
Nazis 35, 165
necking 42
necrolagnia *see* necrophilia
necrophilia 7, 33–4, 221, 234, 239–69, 373, 397–8, 401
Neaira 296
Nefertiti 272
Nero 80, 146, 181, 211, 270, 274
Nesbitt, J. M. 312
neurology 228, 230
neurosis 69, 378
New Description of Merryland, A (erotica) 282, 426
New Woman 126–31
newspapers 9–10, 109, 135, 137, 156, 191–2, 280, 315, 322, 332
Nikarete 296
nipples 183, 337
nocturnal emissions 49–50
  see also ejaculation
North American Man/Boy Love Association (NAMBLA) 326
nosegays 91, 375–6
nudism, nakedness, naturalists 334, 338–9, 341–3, *338*
nuns, nunneries 8, 26–8, 30, 113–14, 116, 123–4, 139, 148–50, 152, 213
Nymphomania; or, Treatise on Uterine Fury (M.D.T. Bienville) 60
nymphomania 58–60, 118, 127, 297

O'Grady, Paul 164
objectum sexuality (OS) 384–8
obscenity 36–8, 69–70, 204, 230, 333, 388
Oedipus 273
Oedipus complex 228–9
Of the Crime of Onan (book) 57
Offences Against the Person Act 1828 308
Offences Against the Person act 1861 96, 191
Ogle, Sir Thomas 332
Old Bailey 187–9, 289–90, 308
older men *see* gerontophilia
Onan (biblical story) 48–9
Onania; or, The Heinous Sin of Self-pollution (book) 56
onanism *see* masturbation
Onanism; or, a Treatise upon the Disorders . . . (Samuel Tissot) 60, *60, 61*
Onanism Display'd (pamphlet) 57
Onanism Examined and Detected (pamphlet) 57
oral sex 365–71
  see also cunnilingus; fellatio
orgasm 20, 47–8, 50, 72, 199, 209, 225, 227, 232, 261–2, 318, 321, 381, 384
Oschophoria 145
Oshima, Nagisa 197
Otis, Margaret 139
Ovid 52, 145
  The Art of Love 52, 211–12
  Metamorphoses 145

Paedophile Information Exchange (PIE) 321
paedophilia, paedophiles 7, 11, 33, 107, 221, 233, 244, 293, 295–327, 373, 397

Paget, Sir James 71
pain 64, 209–15, 224–9,
  232, 235–8, 361
  see also algolagnia
Painter of Berlin 77
Pall Mall Gazette 315
pamphlets 10, 37, 57, 109,
  156, 254–5, 277
Pan 47
papacy 81, 151, 152
  see also popes
paranoia 66, 392
paraphilia 11, 267–8, 325,
  339, 372, 380, 388, 392–3
Paré, Ambroise 118, 193
Park, Frederick 95–7
Parsons, James 119–20
passivity 259, 261, 325
Patroclus 78–9
patronage 277, 297
Paul of Aegina 19
Payne, Cynthia 356
pederasty 7, 77, 233, 298
peep-holes 344, 351
Peeping Toms 346
Peloponnesian War 296
penance 25, 49, 113–14,
  184, 276, 356–7, 361
penetration 16, 25, 114,
  207, 229, 243, 268, 308,
  392–3, 401–2
penis 17, 22, 48, 64, 112–4,
  118–9, 121, 156, 158,
  169–70, 172, 175,
  199–203, 207, 231, 337,
  339–42, 358, 365, 368,
  379, 389–92, 394, 399
penitentials 10, 24–5, 49,
  184, 275
Pepys, Samuel 9, 31, 52,
  90, 332
Percival, Thomas,
  Medical Ethics 308
Perkins, Ellen E., 68–9
Pettigrew, Rose 310, 312
petting 42, 45
Philip the Arab 79
Philolaus 79
Philosophical
  Transactions (Royal
  Society) 196
Picart, Bernard, The
  Perfumer 353

Pied de Fanchette, Le
  (Restif de la Bretonne)
  377
pilgrimage 30
pillory 90–91, 95, 306, 398
pirates 156
plague 63, 243, 273
Plato 79, 110, 318
Platter, Thomas 301
Pliny 390
plushophilia, plushies,
  furries 204–8
Plutarch 111, 183
Polari 103
Poltavchenko, Georgy 106
Pompeii 10, 16–17, 365–6,
  368
Ponsonby, Sarah 123, 125
Poor Law 162
popes 151, 152, 195
  Gregory III 275
  Gregory IX 84
  Innocent III 82
  Joan 150–52
  Leo IX 49
  Pascal II
Porn of the Dead (film,
  dir. Rob Rotten) 255
pornai 211
pornography see erotica
Poulter, Amy 121
Practical Treatise on the
  Causes . . . of
  Spermatorrhoea, A
  (Claude François
  Lallemand) 63
pregnancy 18–19, 41, 43,
  196, 236, 401
pre-marital sex 25, 28–9,
  41, 65
prepubescent, pre-
  puberty, 310, 325
Pre-Raphaelites 310, 259
  see also Millais, John
  Everett; Rossetti,
  Dante Gabriel; Siddal,
  Elizabeth
Present for a Papist; or,
  The Life and Death of
  Pope Joan, A (book) 151
priapism 47, 54, 57
Price, Mary 188
priests see clergy

Prince Albert (piercing)
  391
Principles of Psychology
  (William James) 98
prisons 139, 186–7,
  190–92, 196, 207,
  215–16, 219, 233–4, 262,
  267, 291–2, 300, 306,
  319, 323, 327, 332, 337,
  343, 347, 356, 381, 383,
  401
procreation 19, 24, 38,
  49–50, 55, 271, 276, 401
  see also conception;
  generation
prostitution, prostitutes
  13, 15, 24, 32, 41, 48, 53,
  67, 77, 79, 85, 88, 93–5,
  105, 111, 125, 131, 133, 138,
  162, 176, 199, 210–11,
  216, 219, 223, 251–3, 273,
  278–9, 296, 303, 315–16,
  335, 356, 361–2, 366, 375
psychosis 69, 219, 268
psychiatry, psychiatrists
  33, 61, 66, 98, 106, 170,
  198, 219, 227, 229, 231,
  237, 241, 261, 267–8,
  287, 320, 345, 349, 371,
  373, 376, 380–81, 398
psychoanalysis, psycho-
  analysts 33, 36, 99, 101,
  229, 288, 320, 338, 392
Psychopathia Sexualis
  (Richard von Krafft-
  Ebing) 109, 263, 335
Ptolemy XIII 271
puberty 41, 64–5, 99,
  297–8, 300–01
  see also prepubescent,
  pre-puberty
Pugno, Giuseppe 334
Pulcher, Clodius 365
Punishment of Incest Act
  1908 289
punishment see capital
  punishment
Puritans 55
Pygmalion 384

quacks 56, 58
Queensberry, Marquess
  of 97

Quintessence of Birch Discipline (erotica) 367–8

Rais, Gilles de 244–8, 300–01
Rambler, The (magazine) 278
Rampling, Charlotte 197
rape, rapists 25, 80, 91, 145–6, 151, 179–80, 211–13, 216, 228, 233, 247, 290, 300, 303, 305–8, 314, 318–19, 322–5, 340
Read, Mary 156
Rebecca Riots 161
Reformation 29–30, 94, 118, 151, 300, 336
Reformation of Manners 94
reproduction *see* conception; generation; procreation
Restoration 156, 281
Riddle of Male-Male Love (Karl Heinrich Ulrichs) 98
Riddell, William Renwick 233–4
Roe, Erica 335
Rolandina 85
role-play 206, 209, 237, 268, 329, 355–7, 362–3, 381, 396
Roman de la rose 27, 376
Romance of Lust (erotica) 285, 360, 368
romantic love 25–6, 191, 277, 374, 376
see also courtly love
Rose, Robert 191
Rossetti, Dante Gabriel 259–60
Roufon, George 306
Rouge, Nicolas le, *Christian Idea of the Torture Wheel* 215
rough music 160
Rousseau, Jean-Jacques 53, 301
Rowbottom, Joseph 192
Rowlandson, Thomas 31, 249–54, 333

Royal College of Surgeons 249, 253
Royal Society 120–21, 196, 249
rubber dolls 385–6, 287
Rue, Antoine de La 186
Rush, Benjamin, *Medical Inquiries and Observations* 61
Ryan, Michael, *Handbook of Medical Jurisprudence* 308
Rychard, Philip 297
Rydström, Jens 202

sadomasochism (S&M) 7, 11, 33, 139–40, 209–38, 268, 356, 362–3, 377, 381, 391, 394, 398, 394, 400, 402
Sacher-Masoch, Leopold von 221–5, 236
Angelika Aurore (Wanda) Rümelin 224
Anna von Kottowitz 221–2
Fanny von Pistor 222–3
The Heritage of Cain 224
The Separated Wife 222
Venus in Furs 221, 224
Sackville-West, Vita 136–7
Sade, Marquis de 75, 199, 209, 215–21, 248, 282, 329–30, 352, 359–60, 369
Aline et Valcour 216
Juliette 216, 220, 221, 248, 330, 348, 352, 359, 360, 369
Justine 216, 217, 218, 348, 361, 383
Les 120 journées de Sodome (*The 120 Days of Sodom*) 216, 221, 248, 329, 348
La Philosophie dans le boudoir (*Philosophy in the Bedroom*) 75, 216, 394
Eugénie de Franval (*Incest*) 282

sadism 11, 34, 138, 199, 209–11, 215–16, 219, 221, 225–37, 248, 268, 285, 319, 336, 348, 360, 363, 378
Sadism and Masochism (Albert Eulenburg) 228
sadomasochism 7, 11, 33, 209–38, 268, 329, 350, 356, 361–3, 397–8
safe sex 72
saints 22, 24, 213
St Antonius 50
St Augustine 24, 48, 113, 275
St Ambrose 275
St Catherine *214*
St Columbanus, the penitential of 49
St Francis of Sales 358
St Jerome 24, 184
St Joan (of Arc) 152–3, 244, 248
St John 195
St Juliana of Nicomedia 22
St Paul 24
St Radegund 149
Saltpêtrière hospital 62
Sanchez, Ricardo 200
Sanger, Margaret 37–8
Sapphist 109–10, 118
see also lesbianism
Sappho 110–11, 142
satyriasis 54
satyrs 47, 184
Saunders, Christopher 189–90
Scalbert, Jules, *The Bathers* 328
Scared Silent (television documentary) 232
School of Venus 285
schoolgirls 346
schoolmistresses 141, 318
schools 68, 139, 254, 301, 356,
boarding 68, 110, 139, 301, 356, 367
Schreiner, Olive, *The Story of an African Farm* 37
Schrenck-Notzing, Albert von 225, 227, 236–7

Schreuder, Anna 124
Scientific Humanitarian
    Committee 165
Scofield, Paul 164
scrofula 62
Scouting for Boys (Robert
    Baden-Powell) 68
Second World War 35,
    42, 141, 164, 203, 381
*Secret Book: Containing
    . . . Instruction for
    Young Women and
    Girls, The* 68
sede stercoraria 151–2
Sedley, Sir Charles 332
seed *see* seminal fluid;
    sperm
self-control 14, 24, 77, 79
self-harm, cutting 232
self-pollution *see*
    masturbation
seminal fluid, seed 20,
    47–9, 53, 55, 57, 94,
    190, 194, 274
servants *see* domestic
    servants
Seven Books of Medicine
    (book) 19
sex education 41–2, 165,
    325
sex games 329–64
Sex Offender's Act 1997
    323
sex manuals 19, 53
sex surveys 39–43
sex toys 45, 237
sexology, sexologists
    8, 33–6, 98, 101–2,
    131–2, 137, 168, 225–9,
    231–6, 264, 287, 289,
    318–19, 335–9, 341, 344,
    350–51, 362, 371–4,
    378–9
sexual assault 139, 186,
    212, 230, 235, 246, 248,
    290, 297, 300, 304, 308,
    314, 340–41, 384
*Sexual Behavior in the
    Human Female* (Alfred
    Kinsey et al.) 39
*Sexual Behavior in the
    Human Male* (Alfred
    Kinsey et al) 13, 39

sexual fantasies 168, 209,
    224, 380
    see also fantasies
sexual frustration 47
sexual inversion *see*
    homosexuality; les-
    bianism
Sexual Inversion in Men
    (Havelock Ellis) 36
*Sexual inversion in
    Women* (Havelock
    Ellis) 130–31
Sexual Offences Act 2003
    207, 268, 292, 401
Sexualpathologie (Magnus
    Hirschfeld) 167
sexual perversion 8–12,
    18, 33, 35, 73, 199, 225,
    228–9, 233, 247, 281,
    285, 318, 335, 337, 340,
    350, 397, 402
sexual positions 14–16
missionary position 13, 24
Shakespeare, William 155,
    157
Sharpe, Jane, *Midwives
    Handbook* 118–19
Shelley, Mary 255
Shelley, Percy Bysshe 271
shit, shitting *see*
    coprophilia
Shuvalov Painter *15*
siblings 128, 292–3, 397
Siddall, Elizabeth 259–60
Sillé, Gilles de 245
sin 25, 29–30, 45, 48–51,
    55, 69, 73, 80, 87, 114,
    147, 179–80, 188, 192,
    213, 273–4, 280, 285,
    301, 356–7, 366, 398
skimmington rides 160
slaves 78, 210–11, 296, 315
Sleeman, William Henry
    197
Smiles, Samuel 66
Smit, Maria 124
Smith, Bessie 134
social purity movements
    66–7, 315, 317
*Sodom; or, The
    Quintessence of
    Debauchery* (erotica,
    John Wilmot) 88

sodomitical subcultures
    93–107
sodomy 10, 25, 50–51, 55,
    76, 80–84, 87–96, 109,
    114, 117, 122, 179, 187,
    199, 206, 226, 268, 276,
    285, 300, 303, 307–8,
    367, 388, 398, 402
    see also anal inter-
    course
Soille, Jean de la 186
soldiers 78, 94, 103, 145–6,
    152–3, 156, 197, 199–200,
    203, 244
Somerset, Lord Arthur 95
Sophocles, *Oedipus Rex*
    273
Southy, Sarah 305
Spanner case 234–5, 400
sperm 20, 48–9, 55, 63–5,
    246, 267, 290–91, 350
spermatorrhoea 63–4
Spitzka, Edward Charles
    66
Sporus 146
Spranger, Bartolomeus,
    Hercules and Omphale
    144
Springer, Jerry 204
stabbing, cutting 230–32
Stafford, Margaret 334
Stead, W. T. 315–17
Steer, Philip Wilson
    310–12
Stein, Gertrude 134
Stekel, William 72, 263
Stendhal (Henri-Marie
    Beyle) 262–3
Stephenson, Robert
    Louis, *Strange Case of
    Dr Jekyll and Mr Hyde*
    197
sterility 53, 70
Stretton, Samuel 191
Stocker, Johannes 87
Stoker, Bram, *Dracula* 197
Stonewall 105
Stopes, Marie 38
Strabo 15
straight sex *see* hetero-
    sexuality
streaking 334
    see also exhibitionism

Studies in the Psychology of Sex (Havelock Ellis) 36, 351
Stübing, Patrick 291
submission 58, 212, 216, 225–6, 259, 278
Suetonius 80, 146, 181, 274, 296–7
surgery (and operation) 146, 149, 169–73, 173–6, 206, 391–3, 399
Susini, Clemente (wax model maker) 258–9
Swedish Animal Welfare Agency 207
Swift, Jonathan, 348–9, 383
Swinburne, Algernon Charles 361
Swinscow, Charles 95
Sybian Saddle 389
Symonds, John Addington 36

Tableau de l'amour conjugal (*Mysteries of Conjugal Love Reveal'd*, erotica, Nicolas Venette) 53
taboo 146, 180, 241–4, 267, 271, 275, 288–92, 342, 365, 398
tainted families 127, 286–7, 302, 318, 337, 339
Talk with Boys about Themselves (Edward Kirk) 68
Tardieu, Auguste Ambroise 261, 308–9
Taxil, Léo, *La Prostitution contemporaine* 133
Taylor, Benjamin 303–4
Taylor, Alfred Swaine, *Medical Jurisprudence* 308
Testard, Jeanne 216
thanatophilia *see* necrophilia
Thérèse philosophe (erotica) 59, 126, 383
Three Essays on the Theory of Sexuality

(Sigmund Freud) 198–99, 229
Tiberius 296
Tilley, Vesta 163
Tischbein, J.H.W, *Death of Penthesilea 241*
Tissot, S.A.D. 60
Onanism; or, a Treatise upon the Disorders . . . (Samuel Tissot) 60, 60, 61
Toft, Mary 195–6
toilets, bathhouses 94, 103, 105–6, 133, 103
Toklas, Alice B. 132–4
Torah 22, 179
torture 24, 84, 114, 117, 209, 211, 215, 220, 236, 244, 247–8, 261, 291, 391, 394
Totem and Taboo (Sigmund Freud) 288
Toulmouche, Adolphe 308
Tournier, Jean-Marc 189
transsexuality, transsexuals 145–6, 167–77, 393, 397, 399
transvestism, transvestites 11, 33, 89, 95–6, 103, 109–10, 121–2, 127, 144–77 , 229, 274, 380–81, 384, 397
Transsexuals and Sex Reassignment (Richard Green and John Money) 172
Treatise of the Use of Flogging in Venereal Affairs, A (J. H. Meibom) 358
Trenender, Robert 297
trials 9, 36, 38, 87, 90, 93–4, 97, 103, 107, 114, 121, 125, 154, 185–90, 203–4, 233, 247, 253, 256, 300, 306, 344, 367, 388
tribades *see* lesbians; Sapphists
Triptolemos Painter *14*
Trivulzio di Belgiojoso, Princess Cristina 264

Trosse, George 52
Troyes, Chrètien de 374
tumescence 351
Turnpike Trust 161

Ulrichs, Karl Heinrich 36, 98, 165
unnatural acts 8, 18, 83
uranism 34, 36
urolagnia, urination 237, 348, 350–55
urning 98, 168
uterus 53

vagina 13, 16, 20, 25, 31, 73, 146, 158, 169, 171–2, 175, 180, 183, 195, 202, 204, 206–7, 267, 332, 342, 355, 365, 373, 385, 389, 392, 394–5, 401–2
vaginal penetrative sex 13, 31, 73, 211, 355, 373, 401–2
Vagrancy Act 1824 333
'vanilla' sex 13
see also heterosexuality
vapours 60
venereal disease 56, 57, 64, 67–8, 137, 211, 222, 233–4, 305
Venette, Nicolas 53
Tableau de l'amour conjugal 53
Venus in the Cloister (erotica) 124
Vere Street case 95
Verschuur, Hendrikje 156–7
Vicary, John 90
Victoria, Queen of England 309
Video Voyeurism Prevention Act 2004 347
violence 93, 161, 211–21, 215–16, 227–8, 233–4, 236–7, 307, 363
virginity, virgins 15, 24, 28, 137, 158, 211, 297, 306, 315, 317, 368, 394
virility 22, 45, 52
Vizzani, Catherine 122, 389